**Fault-Tolerance Techniques
for Spacecraft Control
Computers**

Fault-Tolerance Techniques
for Spacecraft Control Computers

Mengfei Yang,
Gengxin Hua,
Yanjun Feng,
Jian Gong

National Defense Industry Press

Library of Congress Cataloging-in-Publication Data

Names: Yang, Mengfei, author. | Hua, Gengxin, 1965– author. | Feng, Yanjun, 1969– author. | Gong, Jian, 1975– author.
Title: Fault-tolerance techniques for spacecraft control computers / Mengfei Yang, Gengxin Hua, Yanjun Feng, Jian Gong.
Other titles: Hang tian qi kong zhi ji suan ji rong cuop ji shu. English
Description: Singapore : John Wiley & Sons, Inc., 2017. | Translation of: Hang tian qi kong zhi ji suan ji rong cuop ji shu. | Includes bibliographical references and index.
Identifiers: LCCN 2016038233 (print) | LCCN 2016051493 (ebook) | ISBN 9781119107279 (cloth) | ISBN 9781119107408 (pdf) | ISBN 9781119107415 (epub)
Subjects: LCSH: Space vehicles–Control systems. | Fault-tolerant computing.
Classification: LCC TL3250 .Y36513 2017 (print) | LCC TL3250 (ebook) | DDC 629.47/42–dc23
LC record available at https://lccn.loc.gov/2016038233

Cover design by Wiley
Cover image: pixelparticle/Gettyimages

Set in 10/12pt Warnock by SPi Global, Pondicherry, India

Printed in Singapore by C.O.S. Printers Pte Ltd

10 9 8 7 6 5 4 3 2 1

Contents

Brief Introduction

In this book, fault tolerance techniques are systematically presented for space-craft control computers.

The contents of this book are as follows:

- space environment where spacecraft control computers operate, and fault models of control computers;
- fault-tolerance architecture and clock synchronization techniques;
- fault detection techniques;
- space bus fault-tolerance techniques;
- software fault-tolerance techniques, including single version and N-version programming;
- SRAM-based FPGA fault-tolerance techniques with redundancy and reconfiguration;
- fault-injection techniques;
- intelligent fault-tolerance techniques, such as evolvable hardware fault-tolerance and artificial immune hardware fault-tolerance.

This book can function as a reference for persons engaged in the research and design of high-reliability computers, especially spacecraft computers and electronics, and also as a textbook for graduates engaged in research work in this field.

Preface

The control computer is one of the key equipment in a spacecraft control system. Advances in space technology have resulted in the functionality of the control computer becoming increasingly more complex. In addition, the control computer used in space is affected by the harsh elements of the space environment, especially radiation, necessitating the satisfaction of stringent requirements to ensure the control computer's reliability. Consequently, multiple fault-tolerance techniques are used in spacecraft design to improve the reliability of the control computer.

NASA (in the United States) has been using fault-tolerant computer systems in its spacecraft – for example, the self-testing and repairing (STAR) fault-tolerant computer – since the 1960s. China began to develop fault-tolerant computers for spacecraft in the 1970s. We utilized a fault-tolerant control computer in a satellite for the first time at the Beijing Institute of Control Engineering in the 1980s, and realized a successful on-orbit flight. Fault-tolerance techniques have subsequently been predominantly incorporated into control computers, and have contributed significantly to the success of spacecraft projects and missions.

The significance of fault-tolerance techniques in space technology has prompted us to publish this book, introducing the techniques that we use in spacecraft control computer research and design in China. The content of this book covers not only the fundamental principles, but also methods and case studies in practical engineering.

There are a total of eight chapters. Chapter 1 summarizes fundamental concepts and principles of fault-tolerance techniques, analyzes the characteristics of a spacecraft control computer and the influences of the space environment, and reviews the course of development of fault-tolerance techniques and development perspectives expected in the future. Chapter 2 introduces the typical architecture of a fault-tolerant computer and its key techniques, based on China's spacecraft projects and engineering practices. Chapter 3 presents frequently used fault models, based upon which, fault detection techniques of computer key components are discussed. Chapter 4 introduces the fault-tolerance techniques of several frequently used spacecraft control computer buses, with special focus on buses such as 1553B bus, CAN bus, and SpaceWire bus.

Chapter 5 outlines the fundamental concepts and principles underlying software fault-tolerance and emphatically discusses several concrete software fault-tolerance techniques, including single-version fault tolerance, N-version fault tolerance, and data diversity-based fault tolerance. Chapter 6 discusses the effect that space radiation has on field programmable gate arrays (FPGAs), and the fault models and dynamic fault-tolerance methods used in static random access memory (SRAM)-based FPGAs. Chapter 7 presents fault-injection relevant techniques based on practical engineering, primarily involving fault-injection methods, evaluation methods, and tools. Chapter 8 discusses the fundamental concepts, principles, and concrete implementation methods of state-of-the-art intelligence fault-tolerance techniques, and introduces two representative intelligence fault-tolerance techniques – specifically, evolvable hardware fault tolerance and artificial immune hardware fault tolerance.

All the authors listed in this book – Yang Mengfei, Hua Gengxin, Feng Yanjun, and Gong Jian – helped to plan it. Yang Mengfei, Gong Jian, and Feng Yanjun wrote Chapter 1; Yang Mengfei, Feng Yanjun, and Gong Jian wrote Chapter 2; Yang Mengfei and Gong Jian wrote Chapter 3; Hua Gengxin, Yang Mengfei, Feng Yanjun, and Gong Jian wrote Chapter 4; Feng Yanjun and Yang Mengfei wrote Chapter 5; Liu Hongjin, Yang Mengfei, and Gong Jian wrote Chapter 6; Hua Gengxin and Gong Jinggang wrote Chapter 7; and Gong Jian, Yang Mengfei, and Dong Yangyang wrote Chapter 8. Gong Jian and Feng Yanjun were responsible for formatting, while Yang Mengfei approved, proofread, and finalized the book.

Throughout the process of writing this book, we received significant support and assistance from leaders, experts, and colleagues at the Beijing Institute of Control Engineering, to whom we express our sincere thanks. We also wish to express sincere thanks to Wu Hongxin, academician at the China Academy of Science, for his encouragement and support. We also wish to express our sincere thanks to leaders and colleagues Zhang Duzhou, Yuan Li, Wang Dayi, Ding Cheng, Gu Bin, Wu Yifan, Yang Hua, Liu Bo, Chen Zhaohui, Liu Shufen, Lu Xiaoye, Wang Lei, Zhao Weihua, Wang Rong, Yuan Yi, Zhang Shaolin, and Wu Jun for their support. Publication of this book was made possible by financial aid from the National Science and Technology Book Publication Fund, to whom we express our sincerest thanks.

This book contains not only a summary of our practical work, but also our research experience, fully reflecting the present status and level of China's spacecraft control computer fault-tolerance techniques. This book combines theory with practice, and is highly specialized. As a result, it can function as a reference for persons engaged in the research and design of high-reliability computers, especially of spacecraft computer and electronics, and also as a textbook for graduates engaged in research work in this field.

We are fully aware that our expertise is limited, and that inconsistencies and errors may be present in this book. If any such instances are found, please do not hesitate to point them out.

1

Introduction

A control computer is one of the key equipment in a spacecraft control system. Its reliability is critical to the operations of the spacecraft. Furthermore, the success of a space mission hinges on failure-free operation of the control computer. In a mission flight, a spacecraft's long-term operation in a hostile space environment without maintenance requires a highly reliable control computer, which usually employs multiple fault-tolerance techniques in the design phase. With focus on the spacecraft control computer's characteristics and reliability requirements, this chapter provides an overview of fundamental fault-tolerance concepts and principles, analyzes the space environment, emphasizes the importance of fault-tolerance techniques in the spacecraft control computer, and summarizes the current status and future development direction of fault-tolerance technology.

1.1 Fundamental Concepts and Principles of Fault-tolerance Techniques

Fault-tolerance technology is an important approach to guarantee the dependability of a spacecraft control computer. It improves system reliability through implementation of multiple redundancies. This section briefly introduces its fundamental concepts and principles.

1.1.1 Fundamental Concepts

"Fault-tolerance" refers to "a system's ability to function properly in the event of one or more component faults," which means the failure of a component or a subsystem should *not* result in failure of the system. The essential idea is to achieve a highly reliable system using components that may have only standard reliability [1]. A fault-tolerant computer system is defined as a system that is designed to continue fulfilling assigned tasks even in the event of hardware

Fault-Tolerance Techniques for Spacecraft Control Computers, First Edition.
Mengfei Yang, Gengxin Hua, Yanjun Feng and Jian Gong.
© 2017 National Defense Industry Press. All rights reserved.
Published 2017 by John Wiley & Sons Singapore Pte. Ltd.

Figure 1.1 Fault categorization.

faults and/or software errors. The techniques used to design and analyze fault-tolerant computer systems are called fault-tolerance techniques. The combination of theories and research related to fault-tolerant computer techniques is termed fault-tolerant computing [2–4].

System reliability assurance depends on the implementation of fault-tolerance technology. Before the discussion of fault-tolerance, it is necessary to clarify the following concepts [4,5]:

1) Fault: a physical defect in hardware, imperfection in design and manufacturing, or bugs in software.
2) Error: information inaccuracy or incorrect status resulting from a fault.
3) Failure: a system's inability to provide the target service.

A fault can either be explicit or implicit. An error is a consequence and manifestation of a fault. A failure is defined as a system's inability to function. A system error may or may *not* result in system failure – that is, a system with a fault or error may still be able to complete its inherent function, which serves as the foundation of fault-tolerance theory. Because there are no clearly defined boundaries, concepts **1**, **2**, and **3** above are usually collectively known as "fault" (failure).

Faults can be divided into five categories on the basis of their pattern of manifestation, as shown in Figure 1.1.

"Permanent fault" can be interpreted as permanent component failure. "Transient fault" refers to the component's failure at a certain time. "Intermittent fault" refers to recurring component failure – sometimes a failure occurs, sometimes it does *not*. When there is no fault, the system operates properly; when there is a fault, the component fails. A "benign fault" only results in the failure of a component, which is relatively easy to handle. A "malicious fault" causes the failed component to appear normal, or transmit inaccurate values to different receivers as a result of malfunction – hence, it is more hostile.

Currently, the following three fault-tolerant strategies are utilized [4–6]:

1) Fault masking. This strategy prevents faults from entering the system through redundancy design, so that faults are transparent to the system, having no influence. It is mainly applied in systems that require high reliability and real-time performance. The major methods include memory

correction code and majority voting. This type of method is also called static redundancy.

2) Reconfiguration. This strategy recovers system operation through fault removal. It includes the following steps:
   - Fault detection – fault determination, which is a necessary condition for system recovery;
   - Fault location – used to determine the position of the fault;
   - Fault isolation – used to isolate the fault to prevent its propagation to other parts of the system;
   - Fault recovery – used to recover system operation through reconfiguration. This method is also defined as dynamic redundancy.

3) Integration of fault masking and reconfiguration. This integration realizes system fault-tolerance through the combination of static redundancy and dynamic redundancy, also called hybrid redundancy.

In addition to strategies **1**, **2**, and **3** above, analysis shows that, in certain scenarios, it is possible to achieve fault-tolerance through degraded redundancy. Since degraded redundancy reduces or incompletely implements system function, this book will not provide further discussion on it.

The key to fault tolerance is redundancy – no redundancy, no fault-tolerance. Computer system fault-tolerance consists of two types of redundancies: time redundancy and space redundancy. In time redundancy, the computation and transmission of data are repeated, and the result is compared to a stored copy of the previous result. In space redundancy, additional resources, such as components, functions or data items, are provided for a fault-free operation.

Redundancy necessitates additional resources for fault-tolerance. The redundancies in the above two categories can be further divided into four types of redundancies: hardware redundancy, software redundancy, information redundancy, and time redundancy. In general, hardware failure is solved with hardware redundancy, information redundancy, and time redundancy, while software failure is solved with software redundancy and time redundancy.

1) Hardware redundancy: In this type of redundancy, the effect of a fault is obviated through extra hardware resources (e.g., using two CPUs to achieve the same function). In this scenario, the failure of one CPU can be detected through comparison of the two results. If there are triple CPUs, masking of one CPU's failure is achieved through majority voting – a typical static redundancy strategy. It is possible to set up a dynamic fault-tolerant system through multiple hardware redundancies, such that backup components replace the ones that fail. Hybrid redundancy incorporates static and dynamic redundancy. Hardware redundancy, which ranges from simple backup to complex fault tolerance structures, is the most widely used and basic redundancy method, and is related to the other three because they all need extra resources.

2) Software redundancy: In this type of redundancy, faults are detected and fault tolerance achieved by using extra software. Using the rationale that different people will *not* make the same mistake, fault tolerance is achieved by developing different versions of the same software using different teams, to avoid the same errors being induced by certain inputs.

3) Information redundancy: This type of redundancy achieves fault-tolerance through extra information (e.g., error correcting code is a typical information redundancy method). Information redundancy needs the support of hardware redundancy to complete error detection and correction.

4) Time redundancy: In this type of redundancy, fault detection and fault-tolerance are achieved over time – for example, a user may repetitively execute certain program on certain hardware, or adopt a two-out-of-three strategy with the result for an important program.

Because of the extra resources involved, redundancy inevitably affects system performance, size, weight, function, and reliability. In the design phase of a computer system with high-reliability requirement, it is necessary to balance all application requirements to select the appropriate redundancy method and fault tolerance structure. In order to reflect all aspects of a fault-tolerant computer system's implementation and research, this book covers system architecture, fault detection, bus, software, FPGA, and fault injection, and introduces intelligence fault tolerance technology.

1.1.2 Reliability Principles

1.1.2.1 Reliability Metrics

Qualitative and quantitative analysis and estimation are essential in the design of fault-tolerant computer systems. The major features involved are reliability, availability, maintainability, safety, performability, and testability, with each feature having its own qualitative and quantitative specifications [4,5,7].

1) **Reliability and its measurement ($R(t)$)**

   Reliability is the ability of a system to function under stated time and conditions. Assume that the system is operating normally at t_0. The conditional probability that the system is operating normally at $[t_0, t]$ is defined as the system's reliability degree at time t, denoted as $R(t)$. Further, the conditional probability of the system operating abnormally at $[t_0, t]$ is defined as the system's unreliability degree at time t, denoted as $F(t)$. Reliability and unreliability have the following relationship:

   $$R(t) + F(t) = 1$$

   The failure probability density function can be calculated according to the system's unreliability, i.e., $f(t) = \dfrac{dF(t)}{dt}$.

2) **Availability and its measurement ($A(t)$)**

   Availability is the proportion of time a system is in a functioning condition. The normal operation of the system at time t is defined as the system's availability degree at t, denoted as $A(t)$. This is also termed transient availability, with mathematical expectation called steady-state availability.

3) **Maintainability and its measurement ($M(t)$)**

   Maintainability is the ability of a system to recover its required function when the system operates under specified conditions, and is repaired following specified procedures and methods. Assume that the system failed at t_0; the probability of the system being successfully repaired within $[t_0, t]$ is defined as its maintainability degree, denoted $M(t)$.

4) **Safety and its measurement ($S(t)$)**

   Safety is the nature of a system *not* to endanger personnel and equipment. Assume that the system is operating normally at t_0. The probability $R(t)$ that the system is operating normally at $[t_0, t]$, plus the conditional probability of the system being in failsafe mode, is defined as the safety degree of the system at $[t_0, t]$, denoted $S(t)$. Failsafe mode is a mode in which the system stops functioning without jeopardizing human life. Therefore, high reliability results in high safety, but high safety does *not* necessarily result in high reliability.

5) **Performability and its measurement ($P(L, t)$)**

   Performability is the ability of a system to maintain part of its function and gracefully degrade when failure occurs. The probability of the system operating at performance of level L or above is defined as the system performability degree at time t, denoted $P(L, t)$. Reliability requires that all functions be properly operational, whereas performability requires only that a portion of the functions be properly operational.

6) **Testability and its measurement**

   Testability is the extent of how difficult a system can be tested, detected, and fault-located – that is, how difficult and complex the test can be. There is currently no universal definition of testability degree; consequently, it is usually measured with test cost.

In summary, fault tolerance is a system's ability to complete its targeted function in the presence of a fault. Fault tolerance techniques are the major methods employed to achieve system reliability. Of the six features described above, reliability and availability are the most important. Therefore, we focus on these two features in the ensuing discussion.

Because $R(t)$ is the probability of the system being in continuous operation within $[t_0, t]$, system mean time to failure (MTTF) and mean time between failure (MTBF) are closely related. MTTF is the time that has elapsed before system failure. MTTF is the mathematical expectation of unrepairable system operating time before failure, i.e.,

$$MTTF = \int_0^\infty t \cdot f(t)dt = -\int_0^\infty t \cdot dR(t) = -[tR(t)]_0^\infty + \int_0^\infty R(t)dt = \int_0^\infty R(t)dt$$

When the system lifetime follows an exponential distribution, that is, $f(t)$ is a constant λ, i.e. $R(t) = e^{-\lambda t}$, then:

$$MTTF = \int_0^\infty e^{-\lambda t} dt = \frac{1}{\lambda}$$

For a repairable product, MTBF is the mean time between two consecutive failures. Let MTTR represent system recovery time, the difference between MTTF and MTBF is specified by the following equation:

$$MTBF = MTTF + MTTR$$

Availability $A(t)$ is the proportion of time during which the system is available within $[t_0, t]$ (proportion of normal operation time vs. total operation time). It can be calculated using MTBF, MTTF, and MTTR – that is:

$$A(t) = MTTF/MTBF = MTTF/(MTTF + MTTR)$$

The definition of MTTF and MTBF verifies that reliability and availability are *not* positively correlated – that is, high availability does *not* necessarily result in high reliability. For example, given a system that fails once per hour, its recovery time is 1 second and its MTBF is 1 hour, which is quite low, but its availability is $A = 3599/3600 = 0.99972$, which is very high.

1.1.2.2 Reliability Model

A reliability model is widely used at the design phase of a computer system to calculate, analyze, and compare its reliability. As described in the following section, the reliability model includes serial connection, parallel connection, and multiple modular redundancy.

1) **Serial connection model**

A serial connected system is a system in which the failure of one unit will cause the failure of the entire system. Its reliability model is a serial model, shown in Figure 1.2, which is the most widely used model:

In a serial connected system, if every unit follows the exponential distribution, then the mathematical model of the serial model is:

$$R(t) = \prod_{i=1}^{n} R_i(t) = \prod_{i=1}^{n} e^{-\int_0^t \lambda_i(t) dt} \tag{1-1}$$

where:
$R(t)$ is the reliability of the system;
$R_i(t)$ is the reliability of each unit;
$\lambda_i(t)$ is each unit's probability of failure;
n is the total number of units.

Figure 1.2 Serial connection model.

The lifetime of the system follows an exponential distribution if the lifetime of each unit follows exponential distribution. The failure probability of the system λ is the summation of the failure probability of each unit λ_i, as shown in the following equation:

$$\lambda = -\frac{\ln(R(t))}{t} = -\sum_{i=1}^{n}\frac{\ln(R_i(t))}{t} = \sum_{i=1}^{n}\lambda_i$$

The MTBF is:

$$MTBF = \frac{1}{\lambda} = \frac{1}{\sum_{i=1}^{n}\lambda_i}$$

Equation (1-1) shows that the reliability of a system is the product of each of its unit's reliability. The more units there are, the lower the system reliability. From a design point of view, in order to improve the reliability of a serial connected system, the following measures may be taken:

- minimize the number of units in the serial connection;
- improve the reliability of each unit, reduce its probability of failure $\lambda_i(t)$;
- reduce operation time t.

2) **Parallel connection model**
A parallel connected system is a system in which only the failure of all units will cause the failure of the system. Its reliability model is a parallel model, shown in Figure 1.3, which is the simplest and most widely used model with backup:
The mathematical model of the parallel model is:

$$R(t) = 1 - \prod_{i=l}^{n}(1 - R_i(t)) \tag{1-2}$$

where:
$R(t)$ is the reliability of the system;
$R_i(t)$ is the reliability of each unit; and
n is the total number of units.

Figure 1.3 Parallel connection model.

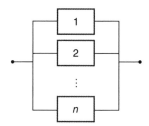

For the usual two-unit parallel system, if the lifetime of each unit follows an exponential distribution, then:

$$R(t) = e^{-\lambda_1 t} + e^{-\lambda_2 t} + e^{-(\lambda_1 + \lambda_2)t}$$

$$\lambda(t) = \frac{\lambda_1 e^{-\lambda_1 t} + \lambda_2 e^{\lambda_2 t} - (\lambda_1 + \lambda_2) e^{-(\lambda_1 + \lambda_2)t}}{e^{-\lambda_1 t} + e^{\lambda_2 t} - e^{-(\lambda_1 + \lambda_2)t}}$$

Equation (1-2) shows that although the unit probability of failure $\lambda_1 \lambda_2$ is a constant, the parallel system probability of failure λ is *not*. For a system with n parallel connected identical units, if the lifetime of each unit follows an exponential distribution, the system reliability is given by:

$$R_i(t) = 1 - \left(1 - e^{-\lambda t}\right)^n$$

Compared to units with no backup, the reliability of the system is significantly improved. However, the amount of improvement decreases as more parallel units are incorporated into the system.

3) **Multiple Modular redundancy ($r/n(G)$) model**

Consisting of n units and a voting machine, a system that operates normally when the voting machine operates normally and the number of normal units is no less than $r(1 \leq r \leq n)$ is defined as an $r/n(G)$ voting system. Its reliability model is defined as the $r/n(G)$ model, shown in Figure 1.4, which is a type of backup model.

The mathematical form of the $r/n(G)$ model is:

$$R(t) = R_m \sum_{i=r}^{n} C_n^i R(t)^i (1 - R(t))^{n-i}$$

where:

$R(t)$ is the reliability of the system;

$R(t)^i$ is the reliability of each of the system's units (identical for each unit); and

R_m is the reliability of the voting machine.

If the reliability of each unit is a function of time and its lifetime failure probability λ follows an exponential distribution, then the reliability of the $r/n(G)$ system is:

$$R(t) = R_m \sum_{i=r}^{n} C_n^i e^{-i\lambda t} \left(1 - e^{-\lambda t}\right)^{n-1}$$

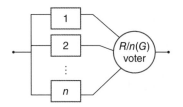

Figure 1.4 The $r/n(G)$ model.

Assuming n is an odd number, an $r/n(G)$ system that operates normally when the number of normal units is no less than $k+1$ is defined as a majority voting system. A majority voting system is a special case of an $r/n(G)$ system. A two-out-of-three system is the most common majority voting system.

When the reliability of the voting machine is one, and the failure probability of each unit is a constant λ, the mathematical form of the majority voting model is:

$$R(t) = 3\,e^{-2\lambda t} - 2\,e^{-3\lambda t}$$

If $r=1$, $r/n(G)$ is a parallel connected system, and the system reliability is:

$$R(t) = 1 - (1 - R(t))^n.$$

If $r=n$, $r/n(G)$ is a serial connected system, and the system reliability is:

$$R(t) = R(t)^n.$$

1.2 The Space Environment and Its Hazards for the Spacecraft Control Computer

A spacecraft control computer is constantly exposed to a complex environment that features factors such as zero gravity, vacuum, extreme temperature, and space radiation, in addition to maintenance difficulties. The complexity of the operating environment challenges the computer and often results in system faults during orbit missions [8]. It is particularly important to implement fault tolerance techniques in a spacecraft control computer.

1.2.1 Introduction to Space Environment

1.2.1.1 Solar Radiation
Solar radiation is the most active and important aspect of space radiation. Long-term observation shows that solar activity can be categorized into two types, based on the energy levels of the particles and magnetic flux released: slow type and eruptive type. Each type has its own radiation effect on a spacecraft.

In slow type activity, the corona ejects solar winds comprising electrons and protons as major components, accounting for more than 95% of the total ejected mass, with speeds of up to 900 km/s. Helium ions account for 4.8%, and other particles account for an even smaller percentage [9]. In a solar wind, the flux of a low-energy particle is high, and that of a high-energy particle is low. In the quiet period of solar minima, particles at 1 AU (150 000 000 km) consist of low-energy solar wind and a few galactic cosmic rays (GCRs).

Eruptive solar activity includes coronal mass ejection (CME) and solar flares, which can also be called a solar particle event (SPE), a solar proton event, or a relativity proton event. During an eruptive solar activity, streams of charged particles and high-energy radiation are released into space. The speed of the high-energy particles exceeds 2000 km/s. In the most severe five minutes of the eruption, most particles at 1 AU are high-energy particles, with a flux level higher than that of the solar quiet period by several orders of magnitude.

In the 11-year solar cycle, the probability of CME and flare is low during solar minima and high during solar maxima. Compared with the static slow activity, eruptive solar activity is a low probability event with a very short duration and very low energy, but very high power. As the flux level of eruptive solar activity is higher than that of slow solar activity by several orders of magnitude, it has a severely destructive effect on space electronics and astronauts and, hence, is the focus of space radiation research.

With ion emission, the above two types of solar activities emit interplanetary magnetic fields as well. The magnetic field intensity of eruptive solar activity is extremely high and interacts with the magnetic field of the earth, thereby negatively affecting low orbit satellites and the earth environment.

1.2.1.2 Galactic Cosmic Rays (GCRs)

GCRs are from the outer solar system and feature very low ion densities, extremely high-energy levels, and isotropic emissions. They comprise 83% protons, 13% ammonium ions, 3% electrons, and 1% other high-energy level particles. The total energy and flux of a GCR are extremely low. During solar maxima, the GCR flux increases slightly. Conversely, during solar minima, the GCR flux decreases slightly.

1.2.1.3 Van Allen Radiation Belt

The interplanetary magnetic field emitted from solar activity interacts with the magnetic field of the earth, and deforms the earth's magnetic sphere in such a manner that the sun side is compressed and the other side is extended. This effect redirects the charged ions emitted towards the earth to leave the earth along a magnetotail direction, so that nature of the earth may evolve. The shape of the earth's magnetic layer resembles that of a comet's tail, as shown in Figure 1.5.

Those ions that cross the magnetopause and arrive in the vicinity around the earth are captured by the earth's magnetic field. These captured ions form an inner/outer belt around the earth, with the south and north poles as its axis. The capture zone was first discovered by Van Allen and, hence, can also be called the Van Allen radiation belt. The inner belt is situated in a shell space above the meridian plane within latitude range $\pm 40°$ (the shell space is above the equator at an altitude in the range 1.2 L to 2.5 L, where L is the radius

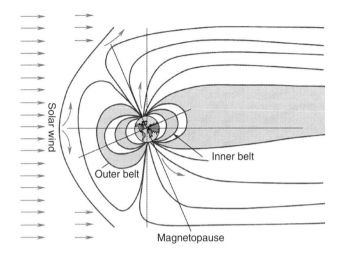

Figure 1.5 Magnetic layer of the earth and radiation.

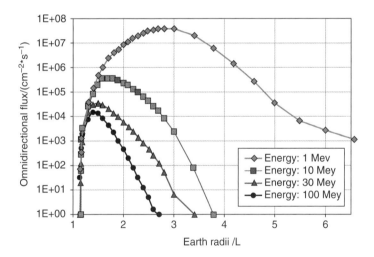

Figure 1.6 Energy spectrum of protons.

of the earth, $L \approx 6361\,km$, $L = 1$ means on the surface of the earth). Protons and electrons constitute most of the inner belt. The outer belt is situated in a shell space above the meridian plane within the latitude range $\pm 55°$ to $\pm 70°$ (the shell space is above the equator at an altitude in the range $2.8\,L$ to $12\,L$). The relationship of flux and the position of the protons and electrons inside the Van Allen radiation belt are shown in Figures 1.6 and 1.7.

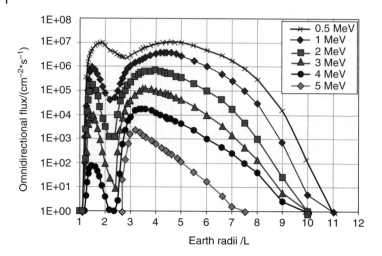

Figure 1.7 Electron distribution above the equator.

Because of the inhomogeneity of the earth's magnetic field, there are high-energy level protons at an altitude of 200 km above the South Atlantic negative abnormal zone. In addition, the accumulation of magnetic force lines at the polar zone leads to an increase in the high-energy level particle flux in those areas [10].

The components and distribution of high-energy level particles within the Van Allen radiation belt are stable when there is no eruptive solar activity. However, when there is eruptive solar activity, or the planetary magnetic field disturbs the earth's magnetic field, the high-energy level particles' flux and spectrum increase significantly, and the Van Allen radiation belt moves closer to the earth. As a result, geo-satellite electrical facilities (even ground facilities) will fail.

1.2.1.4 Secondary Radiation
When original high-energy level particles penetrate a spacecraft's material, a nuclear reaction is produced, which in turn excites secondary particles and rays, including the strong penetrative types, such as bremsstrahlung and neutrons.

1.2.1.5 Space Surface Charging and Internal Charging
Surface charging results from plasma and the photoelectric effect. Because the mass of electrons in plasma is significantly lower than that of other particles, the speed of the electrons is correspondingly significantly higher than that of other particles. When a satellite is immersed in the uncharged plasma, first a large number of electrons and a small number of other particles are deposited

onto the surface of the satellite, to form electron collection current I_e and ion collection current I_i; the surface of the material produces secondary electronic radiation and ions, which form surface-deposited ion radiation current I_{si}, leaving electronic radiation current I_{se}; and the impact of incident electrons on the surface of the material produces reflected electrons to form reflected electron current I_b. If the material is situated in a lit region, the surface emits photons, which forms photon photoelectric current I_p. Hence, the total current on the surface of the material is given by $I_t = I_e - (I_i + I_{si} + I_{se} + I_b + I_p)$.

At the beginning of charging, as a result of the high speed of the electrons, electron collection current constitutes most of the total current and creates a negative potential that is continuously reduced, until the summation of the repulsive force to electrons and the attractive force to ions result in the total current being zero. The effect is a negative potential with respect to plasma – that is, absolute surface charging. Surface potential is related to the energy level and density of plasma. Research shows that when immersed in 100 eV and 300 eV plasma, the respective potentials of the satellite surface are −270 V and −830 V. Because of the thermal plasma environment in high orbit, the large number of deposited electrons in polar orbit and the cold plasma environment in non-polar-orbit, the negative surface potential of satellite in high orbit and polar orbit is more severe than that of those in non-polar low-earth orbit.

At the lighted surface, the continuous light irradiation results in departure of electrons from the satellite surface, owing to the photoelectric effect. The lighted surface gradually takes on a positive potential of around several volts to dozens of volts, while the unlighted surface maintains a relatively high negative potential. The potential difference between the two surfaces is defined as relative surface charging, which is the major factor contributing to damage to a satellite when it enters or leaves the earth's shadow.

Internal charging is induced by electrons with energy levels higher than 50 keV residing within poor or isolated conductors after penetration of the spacecraft's skin. Because the flux of high-energy level electrons in high orbit and polar orbit is relatively large, satellites in these orbits experience more severe internal charging problems than in others. In addition, during CME and solar flare periods, the flux of high-energy level electrons surges and lasts a long time. This also leads to serious internal charging problems.

1.2.1.6 Summary of Radiation Environment

The natural space radiation environment is composed of multiple particles with continuous energy levels and flux. These particles contribute to stable factors such as solar winds, the Van Allen radiation belt and GCRs, and eruptive factors such as solar flares and CME. Wilson *et al.* provided a rough illustration of the space environment particles and their energy spectra, as depicted in Figure 1.8 [11].

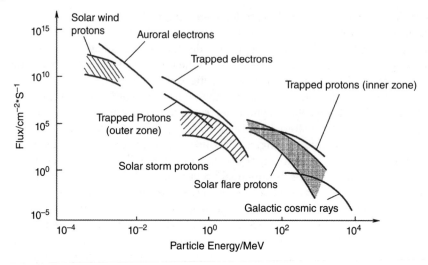

Figure 1.8 Space radiation environment.

1.2.1.7 Other Space Environments

In addition to space radiation, a spacecraft is subjected to other special space environments and their corresponding negative effects. These include the following:

1) Vacuum environment: when a satellite is in orbit, its electrical equipment is in a very low pressure environment, namely a "vacuum" environment. During launch and the return phase, the electrical equipment is in a gradually changing pressure environment.
2) Thermal environment: the vacuum environment a satellite is in and the huge temperature difference between the satellite's lighted and unlighted sides invalidate the normal convection thermal control method. This is a new challenge to thermal control. The current practice is to perform thermal control with thermal conduction and radiation.
3) Atomic oxygen, space debris, and so on.

1.2.2 Analysis of Damage Caused by the Space Environment

The above space environment will cause permanent, transient, and intermittent electrical equipment and computer failures. The damage caused can be categorized into total ionizing dose (TID), single event effect (SEE), internal/surface charging damage, displacement damage (DD), etc.

1.2.2.1 Total Ionization Dose (TID)

When high-energy level particles penetrate into metal oxide semiconductor (MOS) or bipolar devices and ionize oxides (SiO_2), electron and hole pairs that possess composite and drifting types of movements are produced. Without an external electric field, composite movement is dominant; with an external electric field, electrons and holes move in opposite directions along the direction of the field. The high mobility of electrons results in them quickly leaving the oxides, and holes start to accumulate. This process is defined as gate-oxide hole capture. The higher the electric field and electron mobility, the higher the capture ratio. This explains why TID damage is more severe than damage for uncharged components.

An electric field also forms from surface capture at the Si-SiO$_2$ interface. For a negative MOS (NMOS) with an N channel, when $V_g > 0$ V, surface capture results in negative charge accumulation; for a positive MOS (PMOS), when $V_g < 0$ V, surface capture results in positive charge accumulation.

The extra electric field produced by gate-oxide and surface capture parasitizes the function area of the components, and leads to drifting of the threshold voltage V_{th} and transmission delay T_{pd}, increase in the static current I_{cc}, and attenuation of the transistor's amplification coefficient. Components will fail after these damages exceed a certain limit.

At the outset, the major effect of environmental radiation is gate-oxide capture. However, over time, surface capture becomes more dominant. Therefore, the V_{th} of PMOS is monotone drifting, while the V_{th} of NMOS shows a "rebound phenomenon," which negatively drifts at the beginning, then changes to positive drifting.

Gate-oxide capture anneals at normal temperature (approximately 20–23.5 °C) and achieves accelerated annealing at high temperatures (e.g., 100 °C). Further, it is recoverable damage. Surface capture accumulates charge slowly and steadily. It anneals at normal temperature, but does *not* anneal at high temperatures. Under extreme conditions, high temperatures will even intensify the effect of surface capture and TID, which is difficult to recover from, or is unrecoverable [12].

1.2.2.2 Single Event Effect (SEE)

The causal chain of SEE damage is as follows:

Plasma track resulting from high-energy level particle ⇒ charge's movement within the track ⇒ activation of parasitized components or weak components ⇒ all kinds of damage. Based on the effect of SEE, it can be categorized into single event latch-up (SEL), single event upset (SEU), single event burnout (SEB), and so on.

1.2.2.2.1 Single Event Latch-up (SEL)

SEL is caused externally by current resulting from the potential difference within the "transient plasma needle" before its disappearance. The track of transient plasma is produced by the transient ionization of high-energy level particles entering the Si and SiO$_2$ areas [13].

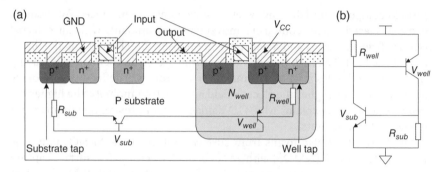

Figure 1.9 PNPN component: (a) NOT gate. (b) Equivalent circuit.

SEL is caused internally by the parasitic PNPN structure [14]. The PNPN component parasitizes the circuit of the complementary MOS (CMOS), as the NOT gate shown in Figure 1.9(a). The n^+ of the NMOS on the P substrate, p^- of the P substrate, and n^+ of the N well contact pad form a parallel parasitic NPN transistor, V_{sub}. The p^+ of the PMOS on the N well, the n^- of the N well, and the p^+ of the P substrate contact pad form a vertical parasitic PNP transistor, V_{well}. Figure 1.9(b) is the equivalent parasitic PNPN circuit, in which R_{well} and R_{sub} are the parasitic resistances of the well and substrate contacts, respectively.

Under normal conditions, the collector junction of V_{sub} and V_{well} are zero offset, the emitter junction is positively biased, and the PNPN component is in the cut-off state. The impedance between V_{cc} and GND is high. When high-energy level particles enter between the well and substrate, current is produced in this area because of the potential difference. Consequently, the well and substrate are turned on transiently. The result is a voltage drop on R_{well} and R_{sub} which, in turn, makes the emitter junction of V_{sub} positively biased. If the positive bias value is sufficiently large, it turns on V_{sub}, and V_{sub} turns on V_{well}. Consequently, the PNPN component is in a positive feedback state and V_{cc} and GND are in a low impedance state, with a large current that will fuse metal wire and permanently damage the component if no current limiting measures are taken.

The parasitic PNPN structure is a unique damage mode of a CMOS circuit. There are three requirements for the occurrence of latchup:

1) The loop gain β must be greater than one.
2) In order to start the latchup positive feedback, there must be proper excitation to provide necessary bias and starting current.
3) The electrical power supply must provide enough current to maintain latchup positive feedback.

In a CMOS chip, there are many parasitic resistors and bipolar transistors that may become involved in latchup positive feedback. The consequence is a parasitic circuit that is more complex than that shown in Figure 1.9. Latchup current differs as the number of parasitic circuits varies.

Single event snapback (SES) damage may occur in the OFF state of an NMOS transistor. The equivalent circuit is the horizontal parasitic NPN bipolar transistor, and its parasitic resistor on the base junction [15]. When heavy ions hit the source, as a result of the potential difference between the source and the substrate: current flows and a potential difference exists across the parasitic resistor to meet the requirements for amplification of the excitation of the parasitic bipolar junction transistor (BJT); the emitter junction is positively biased; and the bias of the collector junction is the reverse. Furthermore, the potential difference between the source and the substrate provides the necessary BJT turn-on current and turn-on state maintaining current through the parasitic resistor. Long-term BJT turn-on current results in permanent thermal damage to the NMOS transistor.

1.2.2.2.2 Single Event Upset, Turbulence, and Failure Interruption (SEU, SET, Single Event Functional Interrupt (SEFI))

The rationale for SEU can be described as follows: If the movement of the charge resulting from the potential difference within the vicinity of the plasma track is sufficiently large, the relevant unit's logic state will change (i.e., logic state upset will occur). When only a single digit is upset in a byte, the event is termed SEU, and the upset of multiple digits is termed multiple bits upset (MBU). As illustrated in the SRAM shown in Figure 1.10, when heavy ions turn on the NMOS transistor in the lower left corner through bombardment, the

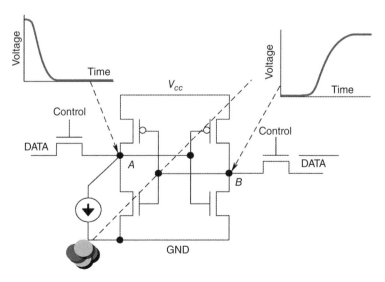

Figure 1.10 Physical essence of SEU damage.

logic state of point A will change from one to zero because it is grounded. This, in turn, will lead to a change in point B's logic state from zero to one. In addition to the SRAM, time sequential components, such as flip-flops and latches, will also experience SEU failure. In fact, because of the complexity of the component's structure, the actual fault mechanism is more complex than that depicted in Figure 1.10.

When SEU occurs in a control or configuration unit (e.g., the working mode selector of a network protocol chip, address register of a CPU, or configuration unit of an FPGA), component failure can result (i.e., SEFI) [16].

When heavy ions bombard the sensors of analog devices, the analog signal will experience transient turbulence, which can lead to incorrect circuit action if the turbulence amplitude exceeds a certain level, namely, a single event transient effect (SET). It is obvious that SET and SEU share the same intrinsic physical mechanism [17].

1.2.2.2.3 Damage to Power Component

The common technique used to increase the current capacity of the power type metal oxide semiconductor field-effect transistor (MOSFET) is to connect thousands of MOS transistors or strip shaped transistors in parallel, with a large contact area between the source and the drain. Figure 1.11 shows the topology of a MOS transistor. There is a vertical parasitic NPN BJT between

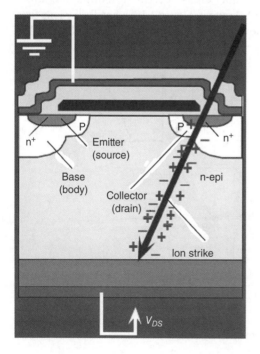

Figure 1.11 MOSFET parasitic BJT structure that leads to SEB.

the source and the substrate below it. The emitter is an n^+ source, the base is a *p* well, and the collector is an extended *n* substrate.

When a MOSFET is turned off, the source has a high voltage. The penetration of high-energy level particles through this high voltage source zone (emitter of the parasitic BJT) results in the activation of a vertical parasitic BJT. The high voltage of the MOSFET produces a high current between the parasitic BJT's emitter and collector that breaks down and melts the high voltage n^+ – that is, SEB occurs [18]. SEB will NOT occur when the power MOSFET is turned on and there is a discharge path between the source and the drain. The structure of the power BJT is the same as that of the parasitic BJT; consequently, the risk of SEB in power type high voltage BJTs is high [19]. The damage mechanism shows that high voltage is a necessary condition for SEB. Power MOSFETs, BJTs, and logic MOS transistors operating at low voltages will *not* experience SEB failure. This is an effective measure to protect against SEB.

In addition, when a power MOS transistor is turned off, a single event gate rupture (SEGR) may occur [20]. As shown in Figure 1.12(a), bombardment by heavy ions to the lower part of the gate will produce high density plasma in the vicinity of the ion's track within the substrate. The electric field results in the electron-hole pair drifting in the opposite direction to accumulate charge, as shown in Figure 1.12(b). The gate-oxide functions as a capacitor with a large amount of charge. When the voltage between the two ends of the capacitor is sufficiently high, it will break down the gate-oxide structure and result in unrecoverable damage.

(a)   (b)

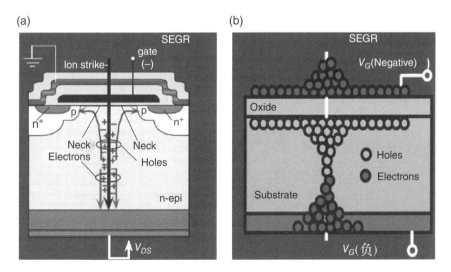

Figure 1.12 Physical mechanism of SEGR damage.

1.2.2.2.4 Micro-dose Effects

With advances in the manufacturing process, the feature size of a single transistor is comparable to the ionization track of a single high-energy level heavy particle. The dose deposited by a single high-energy level particle's impact on an IC is large enough to cause a single MOS transistor to fail in a fixed state, which results in it *not* responding to offset changes (i.e., stuck bit failure) [21].

1.2.2.3 Internal/surface Charging Damage Effect

The casual chain of charged damage is as follows: radiation environment ⇒ internal/surface charged ⇒ ESD ⇒ all kinds of damage. Absolute surface charging does *not* cause damage, whereas relative surface charging produces ESD to form intense current and electromagnetic interference (EMI). This can result in analog components producing false signals, digital signal state upsets, and eventually latchup in CMOS component.

1.2.2.4 Displacement Damage Effect

When incoming high-energy level particles hit electrical components and materials, their arrival at the nucleus of the crystal lattice will result in Kulun elastic collisions. The nucleus of the lattice acquires mechanical energy during the collision, and leaves its normal position to form lattice defects in the component's functional area. If the energy of the incoming particle is sufficiently large, it will displace the atoms within the lattice to form a defect cluster. Lattice defect degrades component feature specifications (transistor amplification coefficient, conversion efficiency of solar cells, CCDs, and other photoelectric devices), and results in defects accumulating until the component loses its functionality. Therefore, displacement damage is the result of accumulative effect [22].

The manifestation of displacement damage is similar to that of TID damage, but the nature of the two differ:

1) Different damage mechanisms; TID leads to component damage through loss of energy induced by ionization, whereas displacement damage leads to component damage through loss of energy induced by the transfer of mechanical energy.
2) The target of displacement damage includes bipolar components, solar cells, and photoelectric devices (e.g. CCDs), whereas the target of TID damage is more extensive.
3) TID is relevant to the charging state of the component, whereas displacement damage is irrelevant to the charging state of the component.

1.2.2.5 Other Damage Effect

Vacuum and vacuum discharge: Vacuum discharge occurs in the 10^3–10^{-1} Pa low vacuum range. Low vacuum discharge mainly affects electrical instruments operating in the ascending or return phase, such as the guidance, navigation, and control (GNC) computer. When the vacuum level reaches 1×10^{-2} Pa or higher, it produces micro-discharge, corona discharge, which produces a damage effect that is significant to a satellite's power supply system.

A space computer system will have to contend with the space environment described above. Thus, in order to mitigate the effects of the space environment effect, improve system reliability, and ensure mission success, the implementation of fault tolerance techniques in the spacecraft control computer is essential.

1.3   Development Status and Prospects of Fault Tolerance Techniques

Advancements in computer technology have resulted in expansions in a variety of fields in which it is applied. Computer technology is used extensively in fields such as aeronautics, astronautics, defense, finance, and industrial control. People are relying ever more increasingly on computers (e.g., in space applications). Owing to the catastrophic losses that would result from computer failure and the irreparable nature of most systems, computer systems are now expected to possess the ability to perform major functions with high reliability when component failure occurs or, at least, not to result in serious consequences. This demand underlies the emergence and advancement of computer fault tolerance techniques.

Computer fault tolerance techniques began with Von Neumann's proposal that high reliability could be achieved through the use of redundant low reliability components. First generation computers (1946–1957) were composed of electron tubes, relays, and delay line memory, whose high failure ratio and susceptibility to transient faults resulted in limited MTTF (several minutes to 2–3 hours). It was necessary to adopt fault detection and recovery techniques; for example, at that time, IBM 650 and UNIVAC all implemented parity checks to improve reliability.

Implementation of fault tolerance techniques in the space industry began in the 1960s [23–25]. In the late 1960s, the Jet Propulsion Laboratory (JPL) in America put the fault-tolerant computer STAR, designed for the Apollo program, into operation, and employed a fault detection module to identify faults. Transient fault was masked through result comparison and rollback. Tolerance to permanent fault was achieved through replacement of permanently failed units. STAR proved to be a milestone in the development of fault-tolerant computer techniques [26].

Another typical fault-tolerant computer was placed in the JPL "Voyager" deep space explorer. This adopted a dual hot backup dynamic fault tolerance strategy through mutual monitoring with information exchange between the two computers. If one failed, the other one would take over automatically or be remotely controlled. "Voyager" operated in space for 35 years. The dynamic redundancy fault-tolerant computer architecture was extensively used in subsequent models.

A fault-tolerant computer was also employed on space shuttles in the 1980s [27]. This computer consisted of four homogeneous machines and a heterogeneous machine. Each homogeneous machine consisted of a CPU for mission calculation and an IOP for input and output. During critical mission phases, all four homogeneous machines operated simultaneously, to mask any isolated fault that may occur in one machine by employing the voting mechanism. Only the astronaut could downgrade the quadri-modular redundancy to triple modular redundancy (TMR). Furthermore, if a determinate fault occurred in the TMR, the astronaut could downgrade from TMR to dual hot backup. Finally, if there was a fault in the dual hot backup, it could be identified if it was a common software bug, and the astronaut could switch to the heterogeneous machine. The fault-tolerant computer successfully fulfilled its flight mission during the 20 years of space shuttle operation time.

In China, research on space fault tolerance techniques began in the 1970s. The fault tolerance architectures used for the control computer can be categorized into fault masking type, fault detection type, and system reconfiguration type [28,29]. In a spacecraft computer system, the most commonly used is the fault masking type, which is defined as static redundancy. It applies redundant resources (e.g., hardware, software, time, and information) to mask the effect of a fault, so that system operation is ensured.

In the 1980s, the Beijing Institute of Control Engineering (BICE) applied dual machine fault tolerance architecture to the onboard computer in a spacecraft control system for the first time. Satellite programming and attitude control was achieved using an Intel 3000I2L CPU and small-scale CMOS devices. The satellite was launched in 1987, and China's first onboard computer successfully fulfilled its satellite control mission. Since then, the computer system applied in the control system has varied in accordance with the mission of the spacecraft.

The recoverable spacecraft control computer, designed in the mid-1980s, with maiden flight launch in 1992, is a typical fault masking, detection, and system reconfiguration fault tolerance model. The computer's adoption of a triple redundancy/single redundancy (TMR/S) structure to perform real-time fault detection and disposition significantly improved system reliability. Its implementation of a feedback test method improved the self-diagnostic capability of the system. The structure was a special case of N-modular redundancy, which applied three identical machines running identical software. The three outputs resulting from the same input was transmitted to a voting machine, whose output was based on the mechanism of majority voting. If one of the machines failed, the correct output of the other two could be used to mask the failure. If a machine failed permanently, it would be cut off to avoid additional machine failure induced false vote or incapability to vote. A post-cut-off system could be reconfigured as a single-machine system; hence, it was defined as a triple/single module fault-tolerant system.

The advantage of the system lay in the fact that its excellent masking effect could eliminate the effect of transient fault on the system and maintain continuous control when a single machine failed permanently, plus its strong self-diagnosis and self-switching ability. The TMR/S structure was applicable to both short period control and real-time control. In addition, this structure was also applied in the GNC system of the Shenzhou manned spacecraft to perform guidance, navigation, and control functions; it fulfilled the mission.

As the demand for spacecraft and satellites with a lifetime greater than two years increased after the 1980s, onboard control computers began to adopt a cold backup, cold-hot backup module reconfiguration type of fault tolerance structure, which integrates fault detection and diagnosis, static redundancy design, system reconfiguration, and operation recovery techniques. This structure is also defined as a dynamic redundancy structure, with major features such as fault detection, fault location, failed module cut off, redundant resource start up, and system operation maintenance. The core technology is control process continuity maintenance during the computer system reconfiguration period. This is necessary to apply measures to the overall system to minimize the effect of "interruption" to the system.

A typical fault tolerance structure includes multiple machine cold backups, module-level cold backups, and cold-hot backups. These technologies have been applied in resource satellites, communication satellites, remote sensing satellites, and navigation satellites; for example, a resource satellite's control computer has multiple cold backups, plus emergency modules to solve system lifespan and reliability problems. The satellite itself also has a reconfigurable module, hardware monitored and switched control computer, which consists of two identical machines – one in operation and the other standing by without being powered on. If the CPU board, I/O board, or memory board of the operating computer fails, or part of those fails, the microcontroller-centered hardware would replace the failed one by starting another cold-backup identical module to ensure system operation. A single machine in cold-backup state could improve overall system reliability and simultaneously reduce the TID effect on computers.

Another example is a communication satellite's integration of static and dynamic redundancy, dual comparison backup, and multiple working modes, including full single machine, reconfigurable single machine, and single machine cold backup. Dual hot backup mode is applicable to SEE, because the comparison between the two outputs can eliminate transient disturbance effects. Cold backup can minimize the effect of TID on computers; hence, it is applicable to long-term operation requirements. Module-level reconfiguration can improve the reliability of the overall system. With the development of IC technology, multiple machine cold backup, combined with the emergency module method, is used extensively in spacecraft control computers, such as computers on resource, communication, remote sensing, and navigation satellites.

Throughout the development of fault tolerance techniques over the past several decades, spacecraft fault-tolerant computers have succeeded prominently in space applications. The development of fault-tolerant computers is greatly promoted by the leading of space applications and driving of techniques' improvements. As higher requirements resulted from the growth of China's space industry, the research on fault-tolerant control computers has become more focused on the following areas [30]:

1) Highly dependable spacecraft fault-tolerant computer architecture. With higher requirements for computer systems in space missions, newer and higher fault-tolerant computer and architecture techniques should be studied.
   - Because performance improvements require a parallel structure, it is necessary to study how to utilize resources in a parallel structure to meet the performance requirements while attaining reliable fault-tolerance, especially in the aspects of task scheduling and reconfiguration techniques.
   - The increased complexity of system functionality requires a distributed system architecture, a centralized system architecture, or a combination of these two, which makes it necessary to study new fault tolerance interconnection techniques, including wireless connection.
   - The extension of adaptability to failure mode resulting from dependability improvements makes it necessary to study a computer fault tolerance structure that can tolerate malicious faults (Byzantine failure mode).
2) Fault tolerance technique for system on chip (SoC). SoC (including SoC implemented with SRAM-based FPGA) is now being used extensively in spacecraft control computers, resulting from the spacecraft's requirement for more powerful functions, low power consumption, small size, and light weight. In these applications, the new challenges from space environment make it necessary to study the following:
   - Failure mode, fault detection, fault identification, recovery, and reconfiguration technology of SoC.
   - Radiation hardening techniques.
   - A reliable system design technique based on intellectual property (IP).
3) Intelligence fault tolerance technique. Further development of space exploration requires that the onboard computer possesses self-failure processing and recovery abilities. As a result, it is necessary to study intelligent techniques:
   - Hardware evolutionary techniques that are able to solve problems in practical applications.
   - Realization of artificial immunity techniques in fault-tolerant computers.

4) Construction and verification techniques for highly dependable software. Because the guarantee of high dependable software is an important aspect of spacecraft fault tolerance techniques, it is necessary to study the following:
   - How to improve the reliability of current software fault tolerance techniques in applications.
   - Software dependability assurance systems.
   - Space software formal verification methods.
   - Integrated environments for dependable software verification.
5) Fault tolerance verification technique. Aiming at new fault models and new fault tolerance structures, new fault tolerance verification techniques are necessary, including the following:
   - Simulation techniques for fault-tolerant computer verification environments.
   - New fault injection techniques (including no-probes techniques and no-stubs techniques).
   - Automatic test-case generation techniques and fault tolerance performance estimation techniques.

References

1 Von Neumann J (1956). Probalilistic logics and the synthesis of reliable organisms from unreliable components. In: Shannon C E and McCarthy J (eds). *Automata Studies*. Princeton: Princeton University Press.

2 Avizienis A (1997). Toward systematic design of fault-tolerant systems [J]. *IEEE Computer Magazine* **41**(4), 51–58.

3 White R V, Miles F M (1996). *Principles of fault-tolerance* [C]. IEEE proceedings of the eleventh annual applied power electronics conference and exposition, March 3–7 1996, 1, 18–25.

4 Hu Mou. (1995). *Computer fault-tolerance technology* [M]. Beijing: China Railway Publishing House.

5 Yuan Youguang, Chen Yinong. (1992). *Fault-tolerance and fault avoidance techniques and their applications* [M]. Beijing: Science Press.

6 Yang Shiyuan. (1989). *Fault diagnosis and reliability design of digital system* [M]. Beijing: Tsinghua University Press.

7 Zeng Shengkui, Zhao Yandi, Zhang Jianguo, Kang Rui, Shi Junyou. (2001). *System reliability design and analysis* [M]. Beijing: Beihang University Press.

8 Leach K R Bedingfield, Alexander M. (1996). *Spacecraft system failures and anomalies attributed to the natural space environment* [R]. NASA-RP-1390, NASA.

9 Russell C. (2000). The solar wind interaction with the earth's magnetosphere: a Tutorial [J]. *IEEE Transactions on Plasma Sciences* **28**(6), 1818–1830.

10 Mullen E, Ginet G, Gussenhoven M, *et al.* (1998). SEE relative probability maps for space operations [J]. *IEEE Transactions on Nuclear Science* **45**(6), 2954–2963.

11 Wilson J, Townsend L, Schimmerling W, *et al.* (1991). *Transport methods and interactions for space radiations*. Reference Publication-1257, Dec. 1991.

12 Shaneyfelt M, Schwank J, Fleetwood D, *et al.* (2004). Annealing behavior of linear bipolar devices with enhanced low-dose-rate sensitivity [J]. *IEEE Transactions on Nuclear Science* **51**(6), 3172–3177.

13 Dussault H, Howard J, Block R, *et al.* (1995). High-energy heavy-ion-induced charge transport across multiple junctions [J]. *IEEE Transactions on Nuclear Science* **42**(6), 1780–1788.

14 Troutman R R. (1986). *Latch-up in CMOS technology* [M]. Boston: Kluwer Academic Publishers.

15 Koga R, Kolasinski W. (1989). Heavy-Ion-Induced Snapback in CMOS Devices [J]. *IEEE Transactions on Nuclear Science* **36**(6), 2367–2374.

16 Koga R, Penzin S, Crawford K, *et al.* (1997). *Single event functional interrupt (SEFI) sensitivity in microcircuits* [A]. In: Proc. 4th Radiation and Effects Components and Systems (RADECS), Cannes, France, Sep. 1997, pp. 311–318.

17 Adell P, Schrimpf R, Barnaby H, *et al.* (2000). Analysis of single-event transients in analog circuits [J]. *IEEE Transactions on Nuclear Science* **47**(6), 2616–2623.

18 Adolphsen J, Barth J, Gee G. (1996). First observation of proton induced power MOSFET burnout in space: the CRUX experiment on APEX [J]. *IEEE Transactions on Nuclear Science* **43**(4), 2921–2926.

19 Titus J, Johnson G, Schrimpf R, *et al.* (1991). Single event burnout of power bipolar junction transistors [J]. *IEEE Transactions on Nuclear Science* **38**(6), 1315–1322.

20 Allenspach M, Brews J, Mouret I, *et al.* (1994). Evaluation of SEGR threshold in power MOSFETs [J]. *IEEE Transactions on Nuclear Science* **41**(6), 2160–2166.

21 Oldham T, Bennett K, Beaucour J, *et al.* (1993). Total dose failures in advanced electronics from single Ions [J]. *IEEE Transactions on Nuclear Science* **40**(6), 1820–1830.

22 Srour J, Marshall C, Marshall P. (2003). Review of displacement damage effects in silicon devices [J]. *IEEE Transactions on Nuclear Science* **50**(3), 653–670.

23 Wensley J H, *et al.* (1978). SIFT: Design and analysis of a fault tolerant computer for aircraft control [C]. *Proceedings of the IEEE* **66**, 1240–1254.

24 Jenkins D R (1996). *Space Shuttle, the history of developing the national space transportation system* [M]. Walsworth Publishing Company.

25 Urban G *et al.* (1998). A survivable avionics system for space application. *FTCS-28* 372–381.

26 Avizienis A, Gilley G C, Mathur F P, Rennels D A, Rohr J A, Rubin D K. (1971). The STAR (self-testing and repairing) computer: an investigation of the theory and practice of fault-tolerant computer design. *IEEE Transactions on Computers* **20**(11), 1312–1321.

27 Hanaway J F, Moorehead R W (1989). *Space shuttle avionics system*. NASA.

28 Yang Mengfei, Guo Shuling, Sun Zengqi. (2005). On-board computer technology for spacecraft control applications. *Aerospace Control* **23**(2), 69–73.

29 Feng Yanjun, Hua Gengxin, Liu Shufen. (2007). Review of research on anti-radiation of aerospace electronics [J]. *Journal of Astronauticas* **28**(5),1071–1080.

30 Yang Mengfei, Hua Gengxin. (2005). *Current status and future development trends of aerospace computer technology* [C]. The First Annual Conference of Chinese Society of Astronautics.

2

Fault-Tolerance Architectures and Key Techniques

2.1 Fault-tolerance Architecture

In current missions, multiple fault-tolerance architectures are generally adopted in the design of spacecraft control computers [1]. Fault-tolerance architectures are essential in the implementation of systematic fault-tolerance, which can be divided into module-level redundancy and system-level redundancy. Various implementation approaches have been proposed from a variety of design viewpoints. The hardware fault-tolerance implementation approaches are categorized into: hot backup and cold backup from the backup manner point of view; dual-computer backup and multi-computer backup from the redundant computer number point of view; and static redundancy and dynamic redundancy from the fault recovery manner point of view. The corresponding approaches are determined by the design requirement of the system.

In the design process of spacecraft computer systems, factors such as reliability, autonomy, lifetime, weight, power, and volume determine the fault-tolerance design approaches applied. For real-time systems that demand high reliability and security requirements, static approaches can be applied. In such cases, the typical method used is "two-out-of-three", which has been applied in the design of the control computers of recoverable satellites. For systems with high-lifetime requirements, such as high-orbit communication satellites, cold-backup approaches can be applied. For systems with special high-reliability requirements, such as the GNC computers of the Shenzhou Manned Spacecraft, a hybrid redundancy approach, which combines the dynamic and static approaches, has been applied. The typical fault-tolerance approaches outlined above are discussed in this section.

Fault-Tolerance Techniques for Spacecraft Control Computers, First Edition.
Mengfei Yang, Gengxin Hua, Yanjun Feng and Jian Gong.
© 2017 National Defense Industry Press. All rights reserved.
Published 2017 by John Wiley & Sons Singapore Pte. Ltd.

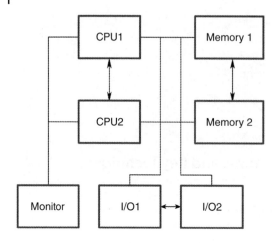

Figure 2.1 Structure of module-level redundancy.

2.1.1 Module-level Redundancy Structures

The module-level redundancy structure is the premier approach applied in the design of fault-tolerance systems. In the 1960s, after the low integration degree of the integrated circuit of that time, STAR, the first spacecraft fault-tolerant computer in the world was designed using module-level redundancy structures, and this was subsequently utilized in the Apollo spacecraft [2]. Based on the structure, most module-level computers utilize redundancy to improve the level of system reliability.

A computer is typically composed of modules such as CPU, random access memory (RAM), and I/O, so failure can be detected and processed by module-level redundancy [3]. The module-level redundancy approach can be divided into dual-backup and multi-backup. The mechanism of the FT approach mainly involves detection of faults in the system and subsequently reconfiguring the system. Thus, fault detection and processing are important functions in a module-level redundancy system. The typical structure is such a system is shown Figure 2.1. The mechanism employs modular monitoring and processing to implement the failure processing function.

A structure of this kind can also adopt the hot-backup and cold-backup approaches, the difference between the two approaches being the method of fault detection and processing applied. Using the hot-backup approach, the respective results are compared to detect the failure, and the monitor is responsible for the judgment and the reconfiguration. Using the cold-backup approach, the monitor is employed to detect the failure and reconfigure the system, and sometimes analysis of the results and self-test can be employed to detect the failure and reconfigure system. Generally, the module-level redundancy structure adopts the dual-backup approach. The reliability of the dual-backup approach can be computed as follows:

$$Hot - backup\ R = R_{mon} \cdot \left(2R_{CPU} - R_{CPU}^2\right)\left(2R_{MEM} - R_{MEM}^2\right)\left(2R_{I/O} - R_{I/O}^2\right)$$

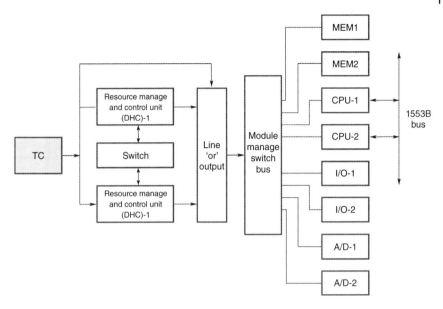

Figure 2.2 Organization of modules in the control computer.

where R_{mon} is the reliability of the monitor, R_{CPU} is the reliability of the CPU, R_{MEM} is the reliability of the memory, and $R_{I/O}$ is the reliability of the I/O.

A system based on the redundancy structure is more reliable than a system with the same system-level redundancy structure. However, it is too complex for the modules to reconfigure, and failure is difficult to process in this case. In addition, there are too many parts in the system that are used in common and, thus, there are many single-point failure (SPF) modes existing in the system. The extra redundancy modular method can be applied to solve the SPF modes, but this method can influence system performance. Therefore, throughout the engineering process, the practical requirement of the system determines how to balance the complexity and avoid SPFs.

This structure has been widely applied in the design of earth resource satellite series and communication satellite series. For example, in a sun-synchronous orbit long-lifetime resource satellite, reliability and security are very important requirements. As a result, the distributed and hierarchical system architecture is employed to guarantee the high reliability of the attitude and orbit control computer (AOCC). The system utilizes the FT structure method of module-level cold backup and dynamic reconfiguration. The system (Figure 2.2) is composed of a CPU board, RAM, I/O board, A/D&D/A board, and a dual hard core (DHC) board, which comprises the main and backup computers. The DHC is the core of the FT design and is employed to detect the status of all boards and power the boards on and off. The DHC has the ability to switch autonomously, and to switch the modules and reconfigure the system according to the FT management schedule.

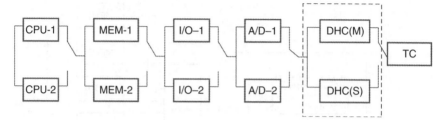

Figure 2.3 Reliability model of the control computer.

In addition, this AOCC provides two fault-tolerance management methods: the autonomous method and the tele-control method. The excellent characteristics of the system include highly efficient hardware, flexibility of modules reconfiguration, high reliability, and meeting the requirements of high-lifetime satellite projects. A reliability model with this structure is shown in Figure 2.3.

With the development of IC technology, the ratio of module redundancy has decreased, and the design method is implemented by module-level function design inside the chip. The method is also applied in high lifetime and high-reliability system projects.

2.1.2 Backup Fault-tolerance Structures

Backup fault-tolerance structure is one of the most common fault-tolerance methods [3]. Compared to module-level redundancy structure, the main difference is that the backup fault-tolerance structure employs an independent computer as the backup unit. Typically, backup fault-tolerance structure can be divided into cold-backup, hot-backup, and warm-backup methods. The warm-backup method can be regarded as a type of hot-backup, so it is not discussed in this section.

2.1.2.1 Cold-backup Fault-tolerance Structures

In cold-backup fault-tolerance structures (Figure 2.4), only one computer is powered on; the others are all powered off. When the computer on duty develops a fault, the system switches to the backup computer to take over the work. In this system, three main factors should be emphasized: (1) fault detection; (2) switching of backup computer and main computer; and (3) restoration of system status. The fault detection is the base of cold-backup FT system implementation and, in this system, the main fault detection methods include the system self-test, program resumption, "two-out-of-three" in the data segment, and watchdog timer (WDT). The system self-test can detect most faults in the system, but the self-test function should be guaranteed to work normally. On the other hand, assignment of self-test time is very important, as a time span that is too long or too short can negatively

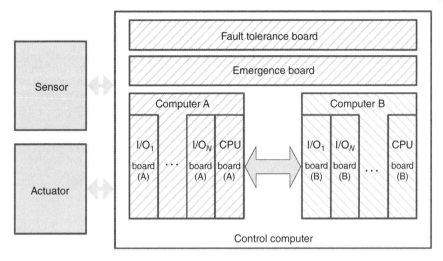

Figure 2.4 Dual-computer cold-backup fault-tolerance structure.

affect the detection efficiency and its effect. The time span of the self-test should be determined by the practical requirements of the system.

Regardless of length of the self-test time, there are cases where self-testing does not work. As a result, the following three problems are encountered:

- The first is that the self-test cannot detect the transient faults that occur outside of the time span.
- The second is that the self-test cannot detect permanent faults outside of the time span.
- The third is that the self-test may itself be in error.

To solve these problems, other FT methods should be added to the system, such as the error detection and correction (EDAC) code technique.

For transient faults, the common solution is to compare the results obtained when the program is running repeatedly. The other solution is to adopt "two-out-of-three" for the key data.

The WDT technique is primarily adopted for permanent faults. WDT is a fault detection technique that monitors the system's running status using monitor, normal set, and reset function modules. The monitor function module can be complex or simple. If the monitor module is complex, the self-reliability of FT needs be considered. The time span of clear-dog and computer switching also needs to be considered.

The failure rates of the two computers are defined as λ_1 and λ_2, and should be exponential distributions. Thus, the reliability of cold-backup FT structures is:

$$R(t) = e^{-\lambda_1 t} + e^{-\lambda_2 t} - e^{-(\lambda_1 + \lambda_2)t}$$

The structure can be applied in high-lifetime satellite systems, and is applied widely in the design of spacecraft control computers. Many practical projects are designed with this structure. A typical project is outlined below.

This satellite has two processor boards and I/O boards with the same functions to construct the dual-computer FT structures. An FT board manages the dual-computer switching function and, when a fault occurs in the main computer, the backup computer is switched into operation by the FT board. If a fault occurs in the backup computer, an emergency board with elementary functions is switched into operation by the FT board. The computer in the dual-computer structure is usually structured as a minimum system added by the I/O circuit boards. The FT structure above is shown in Figure 2.4.

2.1.2.2 Hot-backup Fault-tolerance Structures

Hot-backup FT structures can improve real-time fault detection by comparing the two computers. In contrast to cold-backup structures, the backup computer in hot-backup FT structures is powered on, and the two computers share a channel to exchange and compare important data with each other, in order to guarantee the fault detection of the control system and the real-time ability. In this structure, dual computers with the same hardware structure work in parallel and run the same program. The input ports of dual computers are connected in parallel, and the gating of the output ports are controlled by the switching circuit, which permits only one output signal to be sent out.

Figure 2.5 shows the structure of the dual-computer hot-backup. The hardware circuit used for dual-computer switching is implemented using a timer monitor in cooperation with a corresponding logic control circuit. Each computer has a corresponding normal flip-flop that can be reset by a normal signal

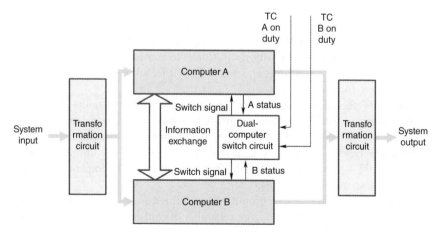

Figure 2.5 Dual-computer hot-backup FT system structure.

and also by a timer signal. If the flip-flop does not receive a normal signal from a certain computer before the timer signal, which means that the corresponding flip-flop has not been reset, the timer signal will generate the switching signal that gets the other normal computer to take on the work. If both computers work normally and no switching signal is generated, the output signal of either computer can be the output of the satellite computer system, and the gating status does not change. If both computers are operating abnormally (both computers cannot send out the normal signal), then computer B is appointed to be the main computer and computer A to be the backup computer, which guarantees that one computer is on duty in the worst case status, and continual switching of computers is avoided.

To avoid a breakdown of the whole system occurring from a transient fault, the I/O data exchange interfaces are joined to the single computer, and the two single computers employ the interfaces to exchange and compare key data. The physical interface is implemented in hardware, and the practical comparison function is implemented in software. If the results of data calculation from both computers are not equal, then the system stops computing and outputting data, and the system switches to self-test status. If the results of the self-test are favorable, the data obtained during this period are assumed to be the result of a transient fault and can be ignored. Thus, the data for the next cycle are then computed and outputted continually. If the results of the self-test are not favorable, the computer is deemed to have a fault, in which case the monitor and switch circuit will switch in the other computer autonomously.

To guarantee the reliability of the switching function, a parallel tele-control command switching circuit is provided in addition to the autonomous switching function. When the tele-control command system is on duty, autonomous switching system is disabled, and the output data from dual computers are determined by tele-control commands.

In addition, software is also used in the implementation of the fault-tolerance system. The software includes dual-computer information exchange and comparison programs, and dual-computer switching management programs.

1) Through the data exchange interface fixed between the two computers, the data from each computer can be exchanged with the other computer in the response mode. A software function for dual computers data comparison is provided, which is called after the output data from the single computer are ready. The result of data comparison can show if the data are valid or not. The data exchange function is implemented by the query mode, which can induce the overtime of data receiving. When the time has expired, the result of data comparison is defined to be invalid.

2) The dual-computer switching management program performs a self-test on the single computer functions during the idle time of the single computer, and the decision strategy operates on the result of comparison of the dual

computers data and the result of self-test. The judgment strategy is defined as follows. If both self-test result and the comparison result of the dual computers data are valid, the management program outputs the valid result, and the dual computers keep their current status. If the self-test result is invalid, the management program outputs the invalid result, and the switching circuit switches the computer that produced the valid self-test result into operation. If the comparison results of the dual computers data are both invalid, the management program stops the dual-computer data comparison function.

The reliability of dual-computer hot-backup is defined as follows. The reliability of each computer is given by R_0; thus, the theoretical reliability of dual computers is $2R_0 - R_0^2$. Because of the influence of the switching circuit (with reliability R_c), the actual reliability of the dual-computer system is $(2R_0 - R_0^2)R_c$.

The first spacecraft computer in China was constructed using this kind of structure. It successfully completed its first flight in 1987.

2.1.3 Triple-modular Redundancy (TMR) Fault-tolerance Structures

Both the module redundant and multi-computer redundant structures discussed above are dynamic FT structures. The process of implementing the FT functions is comprises three sub-processes: (1) fault detection; (2) fault positioning; and (3) recovery. A system of this kind has the virtue of long lifetime, but the sub-processes consume much of the system time. Therefore, for high-lifetime real-time systems, static FT structures should be employed. The typical method used in static FT structures is the TMR structure [4], a structure composed of no less than three computers. The TMR structure employs the "two-out-of-three" principle to implement FT. This principle obeys the majority rule, so the system is valid as long as two computers are valid. Figure 2.6 illustrates the structure.

Assuming that the reliabilities of all modules are equal, the reliability is represented by R_M and the reliability of the voter is represented by R_V, then the reliability of the system is:

$$R = (3R_M^2 - R_M^3)R_V$$

The emphasis of the structures is to implement the two-out-of-three function – that is, to implement the design of the voter. Two methods are employed to implement the voter: hardware voter and software voter. The truth table for the hardware voter is shown in Figure 2.7.

The features of the hardware voter are that it works clearly and fast, but it has a single functional point that will cause the system output to be invalid if its output is invalid. Furthermore, as the number of hardware voter output

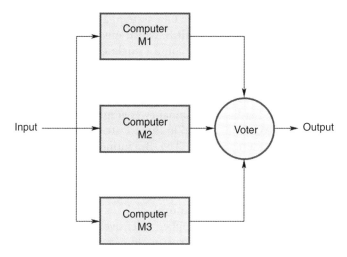

Figure 2.6 TMT fault-tolerance structure.

channels increases, the voter system becomes more complex, which reduces the reliability of the system and has a negative impact on the performance of computers. The high execution speed of the system requires critical synchronization ability, which is difficult to implement. Consequently, a software voting and hardware output selection method has been proposed to solve the problem. In this method, the capacity of the data communication among the modules is augmented to exchange the voting data, and the judgment strategy of status voting is employed for the output selection circuit. The software voter method can overcome the problem mentioned above, but also increases the system time, and the synchronization problem of system also needs to be solved.

Ma	Mb	Mc	V
0	0	0	0
0	0	1	0
0	1	0	0
0	1	1	1
1	0	0	0
1	0	1	1
1	1	0	1
1	1	1	1

Figure 2.7 Truth table for the hardware voter.

The practical requirements determine the voters selected. In the design and implementation of the system, the synchronization problem should be considered and solved. This is discussed in the following sections.

TMR is the basic mode of the majority systems. To increase the reliability, four, five, and even more computer redundant structures can be adopted. However, as the redundancy increases, the increase in the reliability of the system ceases to be linear, so the system efficiency also decreases gradually. Consequently, the tri-computer structure is generally applied in practical systems, whereas four-computer and five-computer structures are seldom applied.

To increase the reliability and the efficiency of a system, a variety of TMR structures is presented to implement the TMR/S, which means that, when a fault occurs, the system can be degraded to become a single-computer system by the tri-computer voter, in order to increase the system operation lifetime. Furthermore, to tolerate more complex faults, an FT structure composed of four or more computers should be employed. For example, to tolerate the Byzantine fault model, enough hardware redundancy is employed to tolerate arbitrary fault modes, with the computer used in this FT structure called the Byzantine recovery fault-tolerant computer. The Byzantine fault-tolerance computer structure can tolerate any possible fault-tolerance modes without the prediction of system fault mode, and the implementation of the system only requires the minimum of fault-tolerance content zone, connectivity, synchronization, and simple data exchange protocol.

The tolerance of the TMR FT structure is applied extensively in control systems. A typical application is the TMR/S FT structure of recoverable satellites. TMR/S is an FT structure that increases the reliability and real-time ability of the system. The main property of this structure is its adoption of the tri-computer redundancy method to implement its FT function. More specifically, tri-computer faults are detected and judged by arbitration and data exchange, with the normal single computer eventually taking on the output work of the whole onboard computer system. The onboard computer of the Shenzhou spacecraft also has a TMR/S structure, which provides high reliability and real-time ability to finish the project successfully.

In the TMR/S structure system, three computers with the same hardware structure run the same program at the same time. The input points of the three computers are one to three structures, and the output is decided by the arbitration management control unit, composed of hardware and software, with only one computer being permitted to send data out every time. Figure 2.8 shows the FT structure. In addition to including three redundant computers with the same hardware, the structure is composed of several components and key technologies, as described below.

1) The structure supports bilateral communication among three computers in full-duplex serial communication mode.
2) The structure supports synchronization of the system. The synchronization can be divided into two levels: periodic synchronization in the macro and synchronization in the micro. By the periodic property of the control system, synchronization in the macro is implemented by the unified clock timer circuit system. This circuit is independent of all three computers, so the reliability of the structure is not dependent on any of the three computers. The clock timer circuit system also employs redundancy design to guarantee its reliability. Synchronization in the micro is synchronization within the period, which guarantees that the local computer is not

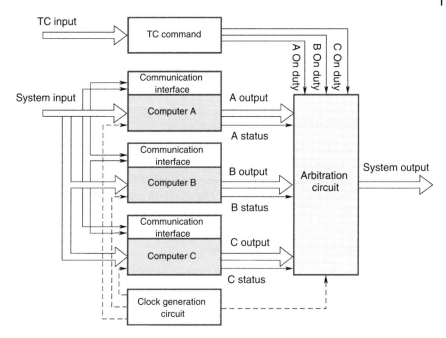

Figure 2.8 TMR/S Tri-computer FT structure.

influenced by the other two computers. In the data exchange process among three computers, the data may be received incompletely or over a period of time. In this situation, the micro synchronization method employs the timer interrupt mode to overcome problems.

3) Supporting status-output function. The computer itself can send status data to the arbitration management unit. Depending on the status data, the arbitration management unit then determines which computer is on duty.

4) Output of the arbitration management unit circuit. Depending on the computer status data and the tele-control command, the arbitration management unit circuit generates the on-duty signal to determine which computer's output data should be sent as the output data of the system.

The arbitration management unit identifies one computer of the three as the output data source, according to the work status of every computer or the tele-control command. More specifically, after two-out-of-three voting, the three computers send out respective signals representing their normal status. Then, using the signals sent, the output data of one computer is determined to be the output of the system, and the outputs of other two computers are masked. In addition, the tele-control command can also select the output data source and shield the other two computers.

The FT structure is implemented using the software voting and hardware implementation method. The outstanding properties of the structure include strong anti-instantaneous fault ability and good synchronization. If one fault occurs, the system can operate normally and maintain its reliability and real-time ability.

2.1.4 Other Fault-tolerance Structures

In addition to the FT structures discussed above, there are also cold-backup and hot-backup hybrid FT structures and FT structures that are implemented in software. Examples include software-implemented fault-tolerance (SIFT), and the TMR + SCD FT structure applied in a certain satellite project.

2.2 Synchronization Techniques

As a precondition for a system to operate correctly, synchronization is a key problem that has to be solved for a real-time FT control computer system. The synchronization technology is introduced in this section. First, the basic concept and fault modes of the synchronization clock system are presented. Then, the synchronization clock algorithms, including the hardware, software, and hybrid synchronization methods, are described. Next, multi-computer synchronization methods are presented and the data exchange synchronization problem in the synchronization clock system is discussed. Finally, a real-time system synchronization problem caused by interruption is described.

2.2.1 Clock Synchronization System

2.2.1.1 Basic Concepts and Fault Modes of the Clock Synchronization System

2.2.1.1.1 Basic Concepts
The clock system provides the key time-based signal for the computer, and is the foundation of correct operation of the computer and the control system. With the extensive development of VLSI technology, large-scale processing systems can be designed and implemented with a powerful CPU, memory, and controller having special functions. By replicating the CPU and memory, a real-time control computer system can be constructed as a redundancy FT system. For example, in the tri-module redundancy system, three modules produce three copies of data for one common object, and the final available result is decided by the majority voter. In the distributed computer system, a global clock as the foundation of the system can simplify design function points such as the set of checkpoints, communication between the interactive processes, resource distribution, and transactions.

The simplest solution is to offer the same clock signal to every process module or computer as a common clock. This solution can solve the clock synchronization problem among the modules and, consequently, was applied widely in the past. However, the common clock is a single-point function, and it therefore threatens the reliability of the system. As a result, it is necessary for the system to employ FT methods to construct a reliable synchronization method. This section focuses on this issue.

A clock can be defined as a device that changes between two statuses of high and low periodically. Thus, the synchronization clock can be defined as a group of clocks in which each clock is synchronous only if any two non-faulty clocks are synchronous within a certain time limit δ – or, in other words, the error between the rising edge and the descending edge of every synchronization clock is within time limit δ [5–9].

2.2.1.1.2 Fault Modes

The establishment of a fault model is a key problem for FT clock systems, and that is the restriction of the clock signals of fault modules. The following are some of the most common fault models [10–13] :

1) Stuck-at 0/1 fault model. In this model, a fault module keeps sending the same binary clock signal to the other clock modules.
2) Fully connected fault model. In this model, all the fault modules send a consistent clock signal to the other models.
3) Byzantine fault model. In this model, a fault module can take actions such as sending any incorrect clock data to other modules. In other words, the fault modules can send different clock signals to different modules at different times.
4) Other fault models. Other models include the frequency drift, phase shifting and jitters, duty cycle variation, and amplitude error models.

2.2.1.2 Clock Synchronization Algorithm

2.2.1.2.1 Hardware Clock Synchronization Algorithms [5–7]

Hardware clock synchronization algorithms are mainly designed using continuous correction based on the voltage controlled oscillator, or discrete correction based on an autonomous oscillator. In these two design methods, some clock modules with the same structures are connected to each other. Then, if any fault occurs in any module, the remaining modules can continue sending the synchronization clock signals.

The design of continuous correction is based on the phase-locked loop principle. In this design, every hardware clock synchronization module has a clock signal receiver. The receiver is employed to monitor the clock pulse signals from other modules, compare the signals with the local signals, generate reference signals, and then correct the local output frequency of the local clock oscillator after

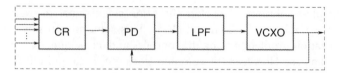

Figure 2.9 Schematic diagram of the phase-locked loop (PLL) clock circuit.

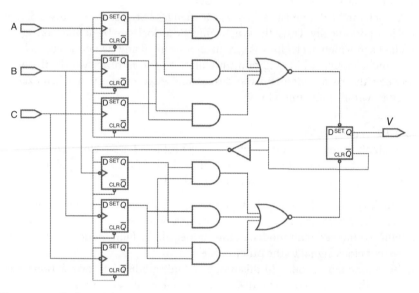

Figure 2.10 Clock module receiver circuit.

appropriate filtering. By controlling every clock frequency, the clock phase in the overall network is locked, resulting in synchronization. The synchronization is on the precondition that the initial phase difference of every clock has an upper bound. A schematic diagram for this design is shown in Figure 2.9.

Smith presented the first synchronization algorithm for a fault-tolerant multi-processor that could tolerate one Byzantine fault with a maximum of four clocks. In this algorithm, every clock module receiver circuit (shown in Figure 2.10) that is sensitive to transformation of status receives their clock signals from the other three modules, then sorts the rising edge and the descending edge of the signals of the three clocks, and selects the second status transformation signal as the signal of the reference clock. The synchronization between the local clock and the reference signal is implemented using a phase-locked loop. The results of experiments conducted show that the maximum error in this clock system is about 50 ns. However, the algorithm cannot be extended to the common situation, because it cannot tolerate more than one Byzantine fault.

A clock system comprising seven clocks can tolerate two Byzantine faults. The five non-faulty clock nodes are labeled a, b, c, d, and e, and the fault clock nodes are labeled x and y. Assuming the clock's data transmission delay can be ignored, then the orders of all the non-faulty clock nodes are the same in the clock sequences of all nodes. If the fault clocks behave unpredictably, their position observed in the clock sequences will be different for the two sets of clocks. For example, a group of sequences could be as follows:

- The sequence observed by a: x y a b c d e
- The sequence observed by b: x y a b c d e
- The sequence observed by c: a b c d e x y
- The sequence observed by d: a b c d e x y
- The sequence observed by e: a b c d e x y

According to the algorithm presented by Smith, every node selects the reference clock signal using the midpoint method. For the example above, every node will select the third clock signal as the reference clock signal except for itself. Therefore, nodes of a, b, c, d, and e are synchronized with nodes b, a, d, and c. Thus, two synchronization groups, {a, b} and {c, d, e}, are produced. Hence, non-synchronization clock groups are produced, and the clocks in the same group can maintain synchronization with each other, although clocks in different groups cannot.

Krishna, Shin, and Butler presented a solution in which every node p takes the $f_p(N, m)$th clock of its own clock sequence as the reference signal, and:

$$f_p(N,m) = \begin{cases} 2m & \text{if} \quad A_p < N - m \\ m + 1 & \text{if} \quad A_p \geq N - m \end{cases} \tag{2-1}$$

guarantees that all the non-faulty clocks are in one group. In the formula, N is the total number of clocks, m is the maximal number of faults tolerated by the system, and A_p is the position in the clock sequence that is apperceived by node p itself. If $N \geq 3m + 1$, regardless of what fault behaviors the fault node is, the clock reference signal selected by the equation can guarantee clock synchronization of all non-faulty nodes.

For the example outlined above, if $N = 7$ and $m = 2$, then:

$$f_p(7,2) = \begin{cases} 4 A_p < 5 \\ 3 A_p \geq 5 \end{cases} \tag{2-2}$$

Thus, a is synchronized with b, b is synchronized with c, c is synchronized with d, d is synchronized with e, and e is synchronized with c. Hence, the synchronization sequence can guarantee that all the non-faulty nodes are in one set.

In the method presented by Shin and Butler, the selection of the reference signals is based on the position in the clock signal sequence sensed by the local clock, which results in more hardware complexity of every node. This is because the clock signals received by the hardware should be sorted first, then the reference clock signals selected dynamically by the validation of the local clock position in the clock sequence.

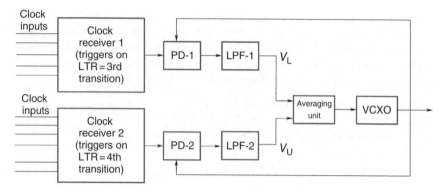

Figure 2.11 A clock module in the average algorithm.

For this problem, Vasanthavada and Marinos proposed a method that is slightly different from the method above. As shown in Figure 2.11, the method employs two reference clock signals instead of one. In their proposed method, all the clock signals received need not be sorted completely, and only the $m + 1$th and $N - m - 1$th signals need to be determined temporarily. The method only needs to set a counter to identify the $m + 1$th and $N - m - 1$th clock signals, respectively, which is implemented easily in hardware. The local clock can compute the phase differences between the two reference signals, respectively, and calculate the average of the two differences to adjust the local clock signal.

The most distinct advantage of the clock synchronization algorithms above is the fact that the maximal value of the clock difference between them is orders of magnitude less than the value of the software algorithms. However, hardware algorithms have two main drawbacks:

1) All hardware algorithms require that the network be connected completely. In the network, the reliability of clock synchronization relies on the failure rate of the connections more than the clock itself. An excessive number of connections can result in problems of fan-out and fan-in.
2) All the algorithms above are presented on the precondition that the transmission delay can be ignored. However, in high-speed operation systems, the time delay caused by the physical connections through the modules cannot be ignored.

Although the related solutions are presented for the two problems, they still have not been completely solved. Thus, in the practical design of the systems, the practical situation should be considered and a determination made as to whether hardware clock synchronization methods should be applied or not.

2.2.1.2.2 *Software Clock Synchronization Algorithms [8,9,14–18]*

To overcome the complex problems occurring in hardware synchronization methods, software clock synchronization algorithms are presented for various applications.

1. The Convergence-averaging Algorithm The convergence-averaging algorithm is based on the following idea. Every node of a clock process broadcasts a "resync" message, and then waits for some time to collect the "resync" messages broadcast from other nodes. For every "resync" message, the clock process records the time signature of the message's arrival, according to the local clock. At the end of the waiting time, the clock process estimates the difference between the local clock and other nodes' clocks, then calculates the fault-tolerance average of the estimation differences. The local clock is then adjusted by the tolerance average before the next "resync" message arrives. The algorithm can be divided into two algorithms, according to the function employed to calculate the adjustment values:

1) CNV algorithm: The average of the estimation differences is regarded as the adjustment value by every node. To restrict the influence on the average from the wrong clocks, the differences estimated have a boundary and, if differences are larger than the boundary, then those differences are set to zero.

2) LL algorithm: To restrict the influence on the average from the wrong clocks, the m maximums and minimums are eliminated (here, m is the maximal number of faults tolerated by the system), and the median value of the remaining differences is regarded as the adjustment value.

The most significant limitation of the convergence-averaging algorithm is that it can only be applied in a network that is connected completely, which results in the algorithm unable to be updated easily. Moreover, the restrictions include errors in reading each other's clocks bounded by the upper value, and the initialization of the clocks should be synchronized. The errors guaranteed by the convergence-averaging algorithm in the worst case are always greater than the boundary of the reading errors; thus, consideration of the scope of the error in reading a clock is crucial. In addition to reading errors, the errors in the worst case come from the interval of resynchronization, clock drift, clock drift rate, the number of faults that can be tolerated, the sum of the clocks in the system, and the duration of the interval in reading each other's clocks in the clock process. Of all the factors above, the reading error has the greatest effect on the error in the worst case status.

2. The Convergence Non-averaging Algorithm As CNV and LL, the convergence non-averaging algorithm is the discontinuous updating algorithm. However, it does not employ the average principle to synchronize the non-faulty clocks.

Using the algorithm, every node sends the request periodically to be the system synchronizer, and all the non-faulty nodes are aware of the time span of the nodes attempting to be the system synchronizer. Even if all the nodes are non-faulty, only one node can be the system synchronizer. If the system synchronizer fails, the algorithm designed can enable the remaining non-faulty nodes to take the place of the faulty node to keep on synchronizing the system, despite the wrong action of the faulty node.

Like the convergence-averaging algorithm, the convergence non-averaging algorithm also requires the time span of the initial synchronization and maximum time delay of message transmission. However, it does not require the nodes in the network to be connected completely. Instead, the convergence non-averaging algorithm requires the judgment schema by which the node can decode the message for itself. Thus, the other nodes cannot produce the same message or modify the message without notifications. This can be implemented by the digital signature and a suitable broadcasting algorithm. As long as all the non-faulty nodes can communicate with each other, the synchronization can be guaranteed by the convergence non-averaging algorithm. However, with degradation of the system connectivity, the error in the worst case status guaranteed by the algorithm will increase.

In the convergence non-averaging algorithm, when the local clock of the node reaches the time for next "resync" or the node receives a signed message from other nodes, indicating that those nodes have synchronized their clocks, this node will resync the clock itself. To prevent the faulty node from producing a false resync, every node will validate any message before acknowledgment. The algorithms are divided into HSSD and ST algorithms, according to the validation method employed:

1) The HSSD algorithm. With this algorithm, the node acknowledges the validity of the resync messages, and resynchronizes even though its clock time is ahead of the time of the resync only under the following conditions:
   • All the signatures of the messages are valid, which indicates that the messages are credible.
   • The time signatures of the messages are consistent with the resync time.
   • The time of the message reception is approximately the resync time.
2) The ST algorithm. With this algorithm, the node doubts all the resync messages, such that when the node receives messages from $m + 1$ other nodes that declare they have resynchronized, the node will resynchronize before its clock reaches the next resync time. Thus, at least one non-faulty node clock can be guaranteed to reach the resync time. In contrast to the HSSD algorithm, this algorithm does not require sending the time of synchronization message, which can eliminate any possible invalid models observed in the same clock synchronization period.

The major limitation of the convergence non-averaging algorithm is that the error in the worst case status is greater than the greatest time delay of the message transmission between any two nodes. In a large distributed system connected partially, the error of these algorithms is at the tens of milliseconds level in the worst case status, which is not acceptable in some applications.

3) The sliding window algorithm (SWA). SWA is one of the more novel convergence algorithms. In this algorithm, the estimated values of all n clocks are processed by the SWA convergence function and, if no estimated value of a special clock can be available, (such as when the node does not receive any resync message), the estimated value can be substituted by the value nil alone. The n estimated values can be regarded as points in the timeline, and the convergence function presented by the SWA slides a suitable size window from left to right, causing it to be named the "sliding window" convergence function.

As long as a clock estimation value is located in the left boundary of the sliding window, SWA will record the position of the window and the amount and layout of the clock estimation value in the window. The record of this kind is called the window instance, and the nil value is ignored by the convergence function. Consequently, n window instances at most can be produced by the sliding process. First, the sliding process is executed. Then a window instance with the most clock-estimated values is selected. If two or more window instances with the most clock-estimated values exist, the window instance whose differences of estimated values are the lowest is selected. Once a window instance is selected, the SWA function returns the median value of all the clock-estimated values in the window instance, and then the median value is employed to adjust the local time.

4) The consistency algorithm. An entirely different theory from the convergence algorithm is employed by the consistency algorithm. This algorithm regards the clock values as data, and attempts to guarantee consistency via the interactive consistency algorithm. The consistency algorithm is a distributed algorithm, and can guarantee the consistency of the private value of a sending node appointed among the non-faulty nodes by a series of data exchanges. For consistency, two predefined conditions must be satisfied:

- All non-faulty nodes must be consistent with the private value of the sender.
- If the sender is non-faulty, the values consistent with the other non-faulty nodes should be equal to the private value of the sender.

Note: The non-faulty nodes must be consistent with the private value of the sender, whether the sender is faulty or not. However, if the sender is faulty, the value consistent with the other non-faulty nodes need not be equal to the private value of the sender.

In the consistency algorithm, at the end of every resync interval, every node regards its local time as a private value, and sends the value to other nodes via an interactive algorithm. Using the clock values from the other nodes, every node can compute the estimated error difference from the other nodes, and then the median value of the errors is employed to adjust the local clock at the beginning of the next resync interval.

Like the convergence algorithms, the consistency algorithm requires the range of the error in reading. Using the algorithms, the error in reading occurs because of the small difference in time between the two nodes, labeled p and q, and the two parameters determine the clock value of the other node, labeled r. Nodes p and q can be consistent with the clock value of r, the estimated values of the errors between p, q, and r are computed, respectively, and the values obtained will be marginally different. In addition to the boundary of the error in reading, the algorithms based on consistency require specific conditions to execute an interactive algorithm. These conditions include the fewest nodes, sufficient connectivity, and the boundary of the message transmission delay.

This clock synchronization scheme can be extended to tolerate more than one Byzantine fault, but it requires data exchange by at least $m+1$ rounds, where m is the maximum number of faults that can be tolerated, and more time is consumed. However, the error guaranteed by the consistency algorithms in the worst case status is always less than the error guaranteed by the convergence algorithms.

5) The probability algorithm. The greatest limitation of the algorithms discussed above is that they mainly depend on the maximum of the error in reading in the worst case status, which is a major problem for future distributed systems, because the error in reading can be augmented with enlargement of the system. To solve the problem, Cristian proposed a probability synchronization approach that reduces the error in the worst case scenario to the value expected by the approach. Invariably, the consumption added by the algorithm increases rapidly as the error values decrease. Otherwise, in contrast to the other algorithms discussed, the possibility of this algorithm losing synchronization is not nil, and this possibility increases as the error expected decreases.

Using the key idea presented by Cristian, on the assumption that the probability distribution of the delay of the message transmission is known, and every node is employed to read the clocks of the other nodes several times, and if the value read in this round is employed to decide the adjustment value after every reading, then the greatest error of the node can be computed. For sufficient reading times, a node can read the other clock values that can be close to the precision appointed by the expected probability. The approaches especially satisfy the master-slave structure, and a clock is appointed or selected as the main node, with the other clocks as slave nodes.

The time of reading is limited by the implementation of this approach, and is related to the cost of the system directly, which means that a node is always disabled to read the clock of the main node to the precision expected – an action that will result in loss of synchronization. The second limitation is that it is not fault-tolerant, and cannot easily detect the invalidation of the main node. Furthermore, it is very complex and time-wasting to appoint or select a new main node using the algorithm.

To compare the advantages and disadvantages of all kinds of software synchronization algorithms, some performance indexes are selected. The requirement for a complete connection network by the performance indexes determines whether the algorithm can be updated easily, and also determines the size of the network. If a complete connection is required, the size of the network should not be very large and the algorithm cannot be updated frequently, which is a limitation. Because of the existence of the error in reading, the decline sensed in the receiving process is different from the actual decline existing between the two clocks. This mistake comes from the unexpected change of the transmission delay between the two nodes.

Some algorithms require knowledge of the upper boundary of the error in reading, which definitely will increase the workload of the algorithms. The requirement for synchronization of clock initialization is not a vital problem, because it is guaranteed by some known algorithms, but much work is still required. The error in the worst case performance presents the precision of synchronization algorithms and, if the error is too large, the algorithms cannot be accepted in many applications. The size of the data exchange can influence the execution speed and time of the algorithms, and some algorithms with large size data exchanges can cause network blockages. An algorithm's complexity is based on the comprehensive comparison of the performance above – the more problems there are, the more complex the algorithms are and, generally, the functions implemented are more powerful. Finally, the applicable scope of the algorithms is a very important performance index that determines which algorithms are applied in what processes.

2.2.1.2.3 *Hybrid Clock Synchronization Algorithms*

1) *The CNV-improved method.* Ramanatha and Shin proposed a hybrid synchronization algorithm that improves the CNV algorithm. The CNV algorithm has a number of problems: (1) Transmission node fault. (2) Delay between the receiving and sending signals. (3) Delay between the receiving and processing signals.

During a specified time in the resynchronization interval, every node broadcasts the local clock signal, and every node receives different copies of signals from all other nodes, which may be transmitted through different relays. When a node receives a clock message sent by some other nodes, it records the time of arrival of every signal and then, in accordance with the broadcast algorithm, it relays the signal to the other nodes. Before relaying the signal, the time that has elapsed since receipt of the signal is appended to the clock signals. At the end of the resynchronization interval, it computes the skews between the local clock and the clock of the source node for each copy it has received. The clock process then selects the $(m+1)$ value as an estimate of the skew between the two clocks. The average of the estimated skews over all nodes is used as the correction to the local clock, to implement synchronization. The hardware circuit can be employed to finish recording the time and compute the error in the time.

The advantages of the algorithm are as follows. It does not require an independent clock network, and the sending of clocks can be executed at any time throughout the synchronization period, which avoids the blocking of the network that occurs when multiple nodes are sending messages simultaneously. The most important advantage is that the maximum clock error of the algorithm is less than that of other ordinary algorithms by two to three orders of magnitude, and the algorithm is not sensitive to delays in data transmission. The hybrid clock synchronization algorithm must be implemented in the topology structure supported by high reliability, and can be applied in large systems that are not connected completely and support the broadcast mechanism especially.

2) *Software clock synchronization with constraints.* Using the analysis above, to tolerate Byzantine faults, the number of computers in the system must satisfy the relation $3m+1$ (where m is the number of the faults), which will reduce the efficiency of the system resources further. In addition, the correction of the clock results from the error, which does not necessarily give the best result. For these problems, to increase the efficiency of the system resource, a clock synchronization method of $2m+1$ computers is presented.

Firstly, from the analysis, the implementation of software synchronization is based on the processors, and further analysis shows the strategy of two-grade diagnosis to solve the problems when Byzantine faults occur.

In the software clock system, the synchronization is implemented by the local clock data read by each processor and the data exchanged with each other. Thus the basic structure of any process can be simplified by dividing it into two parts – that is,

processor = processor's local clock + other parts of the processor

Thus, the clock faults (Pc) can be separated from the other faults (Po). Whatever type of fault Pc is, the data of Pc is unique at the time the clock data are read. While Po is faulty, other methods can be employed to process it. Consequently, the synchronization strategy of this method is to synchronize in time after the decision as to whether Po is faulty is made by the system diagnosis methods. Here, the synchronization methods when Pc is faulty are discussed, on the assumption that Po is not faulty.

As stated above, because the time is definite when Po is reading Pc at time t (even if Pc has any faults), the data are definite during the data exchange period also.

Supposing n computers are in the system, and the computers are presented as $P_1, P_2, ..., P_i, ..., P_n$.

Theorem 2.1 In a system of n computers, the condition for the synchronization is $n \geq 2m + 1$ when there are m faults occurring in the system.

Proof. Under the condition that $n = 2m + 1$, if there are m faults in the system, then $2m + 1 - m = m + 1$ means that there are no faults in the system. Then, according to the contrast with each other, m faulty clocks can be located by the majority. Consequently, the synchronization clock can be found by calculating $m + 1$ clocks. This completes the proof of Theorem 2.1.

The methods for determining the synchronization point of each clock are as follows. Suppose that P_i ($i = 1, 2, ..., n$) gets the clock time $S_t = \{t_{p1}, ..., t_{pi}, ..., t_{pn}\}$ in an exchange.

Step 1. For $\forall_i$, compute Δ_{ij} ($j = 1, 2, ..., n, j \neq i$)

Step 2. For $\forall_i$, according to $\Delta_{ij} \leq \delta$, for i, if the count of $\Delta_{ij} \leq \delta$ is m, then P_i is not faulty, else P_i is faulty, and so the sum of no faults is given by $S_n = \{P_i\}$ ($i = 1, 2, ... m + 1$).

Step 3. Compute the median of the time values of S_n, then get the unified clock t_b.

Step 4. Adjust clock p_i by the difference between t_b and t_{pi} to set the system in one synchronization point.

Step 5. End.

For example, in a system with $m = 2$, $n = 5$, assume that $\sigma = 1$, and the computers in the system are presented as P_1, P_2, P_3, P_4, P_5, and $S = \{4, 2, 5, 4, 2\}$.

Step 1. Compute $\Delta_{ij} \leq \delta$,

Step 2. For P_1, if $\Delta_{13} \leq \delta$, $\Delta_{14} \leq \delta$, then P_1 is not faulty.

For P_2, if $\Delta_{25} \leq \delta$ and only $1 < m$, then P_2 is faulty.

For P_3, if $\Delta_{13} \leq \delta$ and $\Delta_{34} \leq \delta$, then P_3 is not faulty.

For P_4, if $\Delta_{14} \leq \delta$ and $\Delta_{34} \leq \delta$, then P_4 is not faulty.

For P_5, if $\Delta_{25} \leq \delta$ and only $1 < m$, then P_5 is faulty.

$S_n = \{P_1, P_3, P_4\}$

Step 3. $S_n = \{P_1, P_3, P_4\}$, corresponding to t_{pi}, where $i = \{4, 5, 4\}$; sorting in ascending order, the result is $\{4, 4, 5\} \approx 4.33$.

Step 4. For P_1, $4.33 - 4 = 0.33$, set the clock 0.33 earlier.

For P_2, $4.33 - 2 = 2.33$, set the clock 2.33 earlier.

For P_3, $4.33 - 5 = -0.67$, set the clock 0.67 later.

For P_4, $4.33 - 4 = 0.33$, set the clock 0.33 earlier.

For P_5, $4.33 - 2 = 2.33$, set the clock 2.33 earlier.

Step 5. End.

Following the analysis of the P_i structure, this section presents the synchronization method based on the grade strategy to solve the $n = 2m + 1$ synchronization problem when a Byzantine fault occurs in the clock. The method is demonstrated by an example. The method in which the system tolerance structure is combined can conserve system resources and increase system efficiency, which is helpful in the implementation of the synchronization clock system.

2.2.2 System Synchronization Method

2.2.2.1 The Real-time Multi-computer System Synchronization Method

As discussed in the last section, because of the complexity of the hardware clock synchronization system and the delay of the circuit, the hardware clock synchronization method is seldom applied. The clock synchronization methods widely applied are the software clock synchronization method and the hybrid clock synchronization method – which is actually the software method supplemented by the hardware method. In addition to clock synchronization, the data exchange is required to guarantee normal operation in a multi-computer FT system. Thus, correct execution and synchronization of the exchange is a critical link in implementation of the synchronization system, which also means that synchronization of the clock only is not sufficient. This section presents synchronization of the implementation of data exchange. This is in the form of the waiting time limited method, which has been shown by experiments to be the preferred solution to the data exchange synchronization problem in the system.

In the fault-tolerance control computer system, in addition to the synchronization measures for the inputs and outputs, the typical method of data exchange implements control, diagnosis, and reconstruction of the software. The synchronization of dual-computer and multi-computer data exchange is very important for the operation of those systems [19–24]. Hence, the data exchange synchronization problems are discussed below.

Two modes are applied in the data exchange: the response mode and the non-response mode. The communication utilized in the non-response mode does not require that the data exchange between the two devices be acknowledged. In contrast, response mode communication requires a response of either "received" or "not received" after sending the data. In the non-response mode, the start time, the data volume, and the rate of the communication are the factors involved. The data exchange in the control system is periodic in general, so the interval is constant. If the period of the exchange is synchronous, the variety range is also known.

For example, if the period is T, the time for FT processing is T_1 (including the communication time), and the time for the system operation is in the time span P_{min} to P_{max}, where P_{min} is the minimum processing time and P_{max} is the maximum. The data exchange in the system is executed after the processing (the tolerance fault processing and the processing data result from the task). Thus, the start time of the exchange is between P_{min} and P_{max}. Obviously, in this case, $P_{max} + T_1 < T$ and, in the design of the control system, the available time of the system is restricted to be less than 80% in general, which is a rigorous requirement. In the non-response mode, the end time of the communication determines the system synchronization. Further, if the time is available, the synchronization is easily implemented, especially in a system that communicates once in one period. However, for a system that communicates several times in one period, the waiting time between communications needs to be considered carefully; this problem is discussed in detail below.

For the response communication mode, the synchronization requirement is more rigorous. From the analysis above, in the worst case status, if the operating time of one computer is P_{min}, and that of the other is P_{max}, then the waiting time must be set as $P_{max} - P_{min}$. However, P_{min} and P_{max} are, in fact, difficult to estimate precisely in a real-time system. Although many methods for estimating the program execution time have been proposed, such as estimation of WCET, the error remains large, and the errors in the estimation of P_{max} and P_{min} are even larger. For the system in which communication takes place only once, the adverse impact of the error is not very obvious; however, it is very vital in a multi-time communication system. If the waiting time is not set reasonably, the normal operation of the system will be strongly influenced. Thus, this mode is seldom applied in the system design.

In the FT design of the control computer system, the FT process is required to implement the FT function, so the control period can be divided into system operating time and FT processing time. Within the FT processing time, because the status and process results of all the devices need to be acquired, the data should be exchanged over a period of time. To guarantee system synchronization after data exchange, a synchronization method is required. A time limited method is thus presented here [25].

Assume that the multi-computer system is composed of three computers, P_1, P_2, and P_3. The data exchange among them is shown in Figure 2.12.

In the fault-tolerance process, the local computer sends data to the other two computers, receives data from them, and then executes the FT process. An example of the procedure utilized by P_1 is given in the flowchart shown in Figure 2.13.

In the procedure, there are two waiting statuses. If the timeout function is not provided, the system will keep waiting because of the faulty situation. Therefore, two waiting periods are inserted into the flow to guarantee normal system synchronization operation. The FT processing with the waiting time inserted is shown in Figure 2.14.

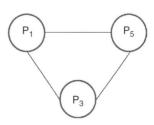

Figure 2.12 Tri-computer system data exchange.

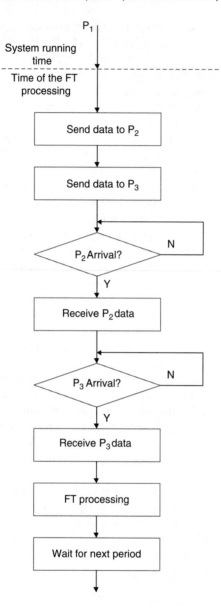

Figure 2.13 Fault-tolerance processing procedure.

The data exchange among the three computers begins when the system enters the FT process. Two modes are employed to receive data: query mode and interruption mode. The first mode is analyzed here. If the time at the beginning of the data exchange is between P_{max} and P_{min}, which is set as t_1, in order for the data to be received correctly, the maximum waiting time should be $\Delta t_w = P_{max} - P_{min}$.

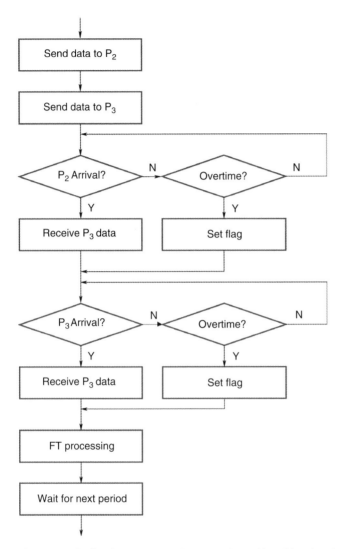

Figure 2.14 Fault-tolerance processing procedure with waiting time inserted.

The span of t_{11} is P_{max} to P_{min}, so the waiting time of Δt is at least $\Delta t = P_{max} - P_{min}$. Hence, the minimum waiting time for data exchange in a tricomputer system is $P_{max} - P_{min}$. In query mode, if the data is exchanged many times, the data exchange will be more complex. Therefore, in the system design, interruption mode is employed to receive data. The tri-computer data exchange system is implemented using the waiting time limited method, which means that the method is feasible and effective.

2.2.2.2 System Synchronization Method with Interruption

The problem of clock synchronization and system synchronization has been discussed above, but clock synchronization alone is not adequate in real-time systems with interruptions. In a real-time control system, real-time interruption must be set to respond for external tasks. Consequently, in such systems, clock synchronization should be guaranteed, and the interruption has an influence on the system synchronization, which should also be considered, because it is very important for system synchronization. The multi-computer system is discussed in this section.

A multi-computer system is one that has two (dual-computer) or more computers. The normal operation means that the results are acquired using certain rules (the unified data of the dual-computer system, the voter by majority of more than three computers in a system).

In the operation of a real-time system, interruption is applied widely for high real-time requirement. For event processing, synchronization of the system is easy to implement using the interruption mode, but it is different for a system that receives external input data. A realistic case is outlined as follows.

Assume that a system comprises three computers that operate simultaneously, and the result of the system is acquired by the three confirming two. Further, operation of the system requires external input, and the input data should be input after the commands are sent. Because of the transparency and realization for the output of the external data, the data fetching commands cannot be sent one by one, so the command of fetching the external data is decided by the three confirming two, and then sent by hardware gating. Thus, in one sample period, all the external data can be acquired, which satisfies transparency requirements. Figure 2.15 shows the implementation flow.

In the data exchange process between the computer system and external devices, the external devices send the interrupt signals and the data type, and the computer responds to the interrupts by parsing the data type and sending the data fetching command. The external devices then send the data to the computer system, which receives the data.

The above process shows that the data fetch command should be sent synchronously in order for the data to be received correctly. However, in reality, it is impossible to implement synchronization of the data fetching command of the tri-computer. In an actual system, it is very important for the system to receive data correctly. Thus, a method for reliably acquiring data needs be implemented.

For the convenience of analysis and without loss of generality, the clocks of the tri-computer are assumed to be the same, which means that the three clocks are synchronous. Obviously, in the simplest solution, the data fetch command is not required, and the data can be received byte by byte after the interrupt. However, although this solution can solve the synchronization problem, the response for the interrupt is time-consuming, and the solution

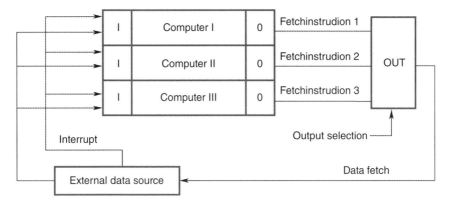

Figure 2.15 Data input structure of a multi-computer system.

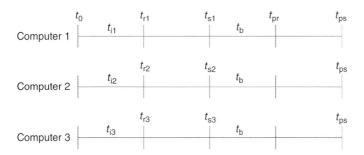

Figure 2.16 Sequence of the computers.

increases the system uncertainty and the software complexity. In addition, the solution decreases the system reliability. Consequently, this solution is inadvisable for high real-time and high-reliability systems.

The other solution similar to the DMA function is not applied in space systems, because it increases the complexity and decreases the reliability of the system.

The system shown in Figure 2.16 is discussed below.

Assume that the interrupt time is t_0, the times for sending the data fetching command are t_{s1} (computer 1), t_{s2} (computer 2), and t_{s3} (computer 3), and the three computer response times for the interrupt are t_{r1}, t_{r2}, t_{r3}. Because of the relativity between t_{s1}, t_{s2}, and t_{s3} and t_{r1}, t_{r2}, and t_{r3}, which means they have a fixed relation, it is reasonable to consider analysis of t_{r1}, t_{r2}, and t_{r3} only.

In this system, data acquisition by the system relates closely to the following times, which include the time of the interrupt signal of the external device (presented as t_0), t_{s1}, t_{r1}. The time of interrupt response of the computer also relates to the CPU interrupt mode. If the interrupt is the hardware interrupt, and the response mode relates to the response after the current command is finished, the response time also relates to the longest time (presented by t_i) of command execution. It also relates to the time (presented as t_b) of the data fetch command sent from the computer to the external devices, and the time (presented as t_{pb}) of the data sent from the external devices to the computer.

In general, t_b is equal to t_{pb}, so they can be represented by one value, t_b. Hence, the time of the system relates to the times t_0, t_{s1}, t_{s2}, t_{s3}, t_i, and t_b. The relations of these times are analyzed below, and the condition for receiving data correctly is subsequently proposed. The analysis below assumes that the differences in the time delay occurring along the transport path can be ignored. Assume that there are n computers receiving data.

In a multi-computer system, although the clocks are the same, the computers cannot synchronize absolutely after operating the system for a while, because of the influence of many factors. Consequently, the times when the commands are executed by the three computers may be different. The times are presented as t_{i1}, t_{i2}, and t_{i3}.

Theorem 2.2: The three computers can receive external data normally if and only if t_{ij} satisfies the condition $\max t_{ij} < t_b$.

Proof. Because only one computer can be selected to accept the external output without loss of generality, computer 1 is should be selected. Assuming that the response time of computer 1 is t_{r1}, the time required for the data from computer 1 to get to the external devices is $t_{r1} + t_b$. On receiving the command data, the external device sends data to the computer system, and the time from the external device to computer 1 is $t_{r1} + t_b + t_b$. Further, $t_{r1} + 2t_b$ is the time for the first set of data.

The arrival time of the first set of data is $t_{11} = t_{r1} + 2t_b$, and it is $t_{i1} + 2t_b$ starting at t_0.

The arrival time of the second set of data is $t_{11} + t_b$.

The arrival time of the nth set of data is $t_{11} + (n - 1)t_b$.

For computer 2, the arrival time of the first set of data is $t_{21} = t_{11} + 2t_b$.

If $t_{21} - t_{11} = 0$, the data can be received correctly. To guarantee that computer 2 receives the data correctly, the first set of data must be received completely before the second set of data arrives – that is:

$$t_{22} = t_{21} + t_b$$

$$t_{22} > t_{11} - \text{that is,} \, t_{21} + t_b > t_{i1} + 2t_b$$

$$t_{12} + 3t_b > t_{11} + 2t_b - \text{that is,} \, t_{i2} + t_b > t_{i1}$$

$$t_{11} - t_{i2} < t_b$$

Similarly,

$$t_{11} - t_{i3} < t_b$$

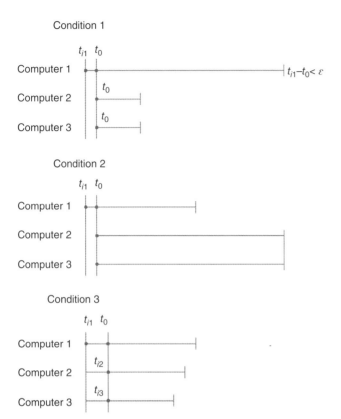

Figure 2.17 Tri-computer execution scenario.

In the worst case scenario, the operation of the three computers is as illustrated in Figure 2.17.

Consequently, for all the scenarios above, the system can receive the data correctly if it satisfies $\max_{ij} < t_b$.

Corollary 1.   From Theorem 2.2, the corollary is as follows:

For good synchronization of the system, larger t_b and smaller execution time t_i are best. In a practical system design, the instructions that consume too much time should be seldom used, such as the x86 string instructions. The decision of t_b should be considered to balance the practical requirement if the serial port is utilized. For abundant machine time, the frequency of the computer period should be slower and the baud rate should be lower.

More generally, Theorem 2.2 can be extended to a system composed of n computers:

Theorem 2.3:   In a system composed of n computers, any computer in the system can receive the external data only under the condition that $\max_{ij} < t_b$.

Two instances are ignored by the analysis above. First, the processing time of the computer. Second, if the interrupt can influence the execution process, the only requirement is that the execution process time is less than t_b. If the practical instance cannot satisfy the requirement, an extra delay should be inserted into the external device to solve the problem.

For the second instance, there are two solutions. The first solution is to use multiple interrupt instances. For these instances, once the interrupt is responded to, other interrupts must be shut off temporarily until the data for the interrupt responded to are received completely. This method is the one most commonly used in the computing function and practical satellite control systems. In the second solution, the new interrupt can be responded to in the interrupt process without shutting off the other interrupts. This solution relates to the interrupt processing time. The interrupt processing time, p_t, must satisfy $p_t + \max t_i < t_b$. In a practical system, this condition generally cannot be satisfied, so the second solution is not advisable.

2.3 Fault-tolerance Design with Hardware Redundancy

In an FT system, the redundancy used is the basic method. Therefore, the design of the redundancy is very important, and it is very important to design the system without a single point of failure [26]. Referring to practical engineering, the concept, the flow, and the basic properties of the FT redundancy design are presented.

2.3.1 Universal Logic Model and Flow in Redundancy Design

In general, the redundancy design can be depicted as shown in Figure 2.18.

1) The Basic Function Unit (BFU) is the minimal unit with complete functions and no redundancy.
2) The Isolation and Protection Unit (IPU) has a function that guarantees that a backup fault does not influence the normal operation of the other backups.
3) The Cross-Strapping and Switching Unit (CSSU) is the functional unit that provides the cross-strapping and signal flows switching.
4) The Fault Detecting and Managing Unit (FDMU) is the functional unit that monitors the health status of the BFU, IPU and CSSU, determines whether there is a fault, and sends out the redundancy management command after a fault has been determined to have occurred.

The FDMU, CSSU, and IPU are the three key elements that should be considered in the redundancy design. These units can be implemented using

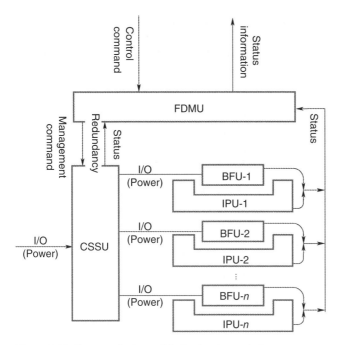

Figure 2.18 Common logic model of redundancy design.

different methods. The flow of the redundancy design is the iterative optimization in the processes of scheme argumentation, design and implementation, validation by analysis, and validation by testing. Redundancy design flow emphasizes reason and validation. The reasonability of a scheme is based on the quantitative computation and then, from the analysis, the reliability is improved. Subsequently, the reliability is validated and improved further by testing.

2.3.2 Scheme Argumentation of Redundancy

2.3.2.1 Determination of Redundancy Scheme

In general, qualitative judgment and quantitative analysis are applied to determine whether the redundancy is required and to establish the details of the redundancy scheme.

According to the total project requirement and failure mode and effects analysis (FMEA), the qualitative judgment determines which design should be applied by the redundancy design [27,28]. A design that cannot be determined by qualitative judgment should be determined by quantitative analysis.

Quantitative analysis detects the weakness of the design using reliability computation, determines whether redundancy is required, and optimizes the redundancy scheme. The common flow of the quantitative analysis is as follows.

1) *Structure backup scheme.* In detail, the simple design scheme should be structured first, then it can be designed from the components located in the base layer. From the bottom up, the module-level, component-level, and the subsystem-level redundancy scheme, respectively, can be structured. For the backup scheme, the serial or parallel structure, the cold or hot structure, and the quantity of the backup should be determined. According to QJ 2172A-2005 and QJ 3161-2002, the reliability distribution, the reliability model, the reliability computation, and other related technologies are applied to structure the backup scheme.

2) *Quantitative comparison.* The schemes can be compared primarily using the quantitative reliability computation and the other quantitative factors, including the reliability, weight, volume, power, and cost can be referenced. If possible, a simulation or structuring test prototype system can be applied in the comparisons.

3) *Iteration cycle.* The design of the quantitative scheme is a process optimized by multi-iteration cycles. For example, as the triode is used to drive the relay, according to the MIL-HDBK-217 F model, the failure rates of the triode and the relay in three years are 6.14624×10^{-5} and 0.002432, respectively. If the simple design cannot satisfy the reliability, the relay should be designed for redundancy first and, if reliability is still not satisfied, the triode should also be designed for redundancy.

2.3.2.2 Rules Obeyed in the Scheme Argumentation of Redundancy

1) *Global rules.* The redundancy scheme should be designed from the system level and should be optimized globally, not individually, to avoid the negative effects caused by the wooden buckets effect and having too complex a design for the redundancy scheme. Based on the quantitative prediction of the reliability, the weakness of the system should be designed as a redundancy to reflect the reasonability of the scheme.

2) *Individual rules.* The functions of the redundant modules should be individualized to avoid possible dependence or restriction resulting from an unreasonable design. The common causes of failure should be avoided also.

The backup scheme should be structured with the priority of the lowest layer, in which the lowest layer contains the elements, followed by modules, then the components, then the sub-systems in the highest layer.

2.3.3 Redundancy Design and Implementation

2.3.3.1 Basic Requirements

The reliability of the three key elements should be taken into account in the redundancy design, to avoid the potential failures caused by the reliability design itself. The power design, testability design, and other aspects should also be considered. Early in the design, according to the redundancy logic models, the elements and circuits should be divided to correspond to the three key elements. This not only contributes to the simplicity and modularity of the design scheme, but also contributes to the validation by analysis and the validation by testing.

2.3.3.2 FDMU Design

As one of the three key elements, FDMU is applied in most redundancy designs to implement the failure detection and management. In the implementation, the majority voting, comparison, self-test, watchdog, and other detection subsystems (current, position, temperature sensors) are adopted to detect failures. For the design of FDMU, the following should be guaranteed:

1) The failure of FDMU should not influence the normal operation of the system. For example, the electrical explosive device (EED) detection circuit of a certain project is shown in Figure 2.19. The 10 Ω resistor in the detection circuit will burn out because the FDMU is short-circuited to the ground. In the improved design, a 1 kΩ resistor is inserted in the test line to solve this problem.

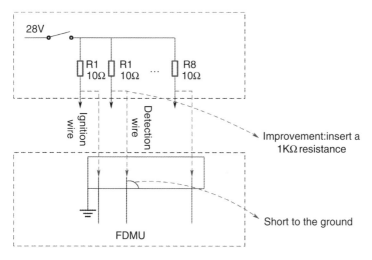

Figure 2.19 Example of system fault caused by FDMU.

2) When the detection unit fails, the FDMU should emit an alarm in time and manage the failure in order to avoid it extending to other units and producing fatal effects, or the failure turning into an unrecoverable failure itself. For example, the single event latch-up should be detected to power off on time, and the power supply to the bus bar should be guaranteed influence-free before the power-off of the latch-up. Hence, a permanent fault caused by the single-event latch-up can be avoided.

3) The integrity rule of detection information. BFU, CSSU, and IPU send the failure information as detailed as possible, so that the FDMU can implement the correct redundancy management according to the detailed failure information.

4) The direct detection rule. The object should be detected as directly as possible, not indirectly.

5) For the FT design of FDMU, the failure detection threshold should be set reasonably to guarantee that the FDMU can operate normally in all life cycles, and under all kinds of environmental conditions. This means that the FDMU should not take wrong action caused by the sensitivity, or take no action caused by the inertness.

6) If the tele-control management coexists with the autonomy management, the following should be guaranteed:
   - The tele-control management is always preferred.
   - The recycle switching mode of the main and the backup should be considered for the autonomy management design.
   - In general, the signal of the autonomy management is the single-pulse output.

2.3.3.3 CSSU Design

As one of the three key elements, CSSU is employed to implement the connection and switching of the power and the signal. The following should be guaranteed in the CSSU design:

1) That the CSSU itself has no SPF. A design reference by signal type is proposed in Table 2.1. If the CSSU is single-point, the serial connection, the parallel connection, the serial/parallel connection, or the parallel/serial connection can be applied, depending on the situation. For example, for the failure of the collector short-circuit to the emitter in the triode, the parallel connection redundancy design can be applied.

2) The alienation principle among the BFUs. Each BFU should have independent CSSU and IPU, to avoid SPF. For example, as shown in Figure 2.20(a), the CSSU1/IPU1 is a single-point for the backups A1 and A2, while no single-point is present in Figure 2.20(b).

Table 2.1 Design reference by signal type.

Switching signal	Digital switch	Analog switch	Relay	Transistor/ MOSFET	232, 422, 1553, I²C, CAN
Power	—	—	●	○	—
Low speed analog weak current	—	●	●	●	—
High-speed analog weak current	—	●	○	●	—
Low speed digital	●	●	●	●	●/○
High-speed digital	●	○	○	●	●/○

Note: ● optional; ○ concrete analysis; — not optional.

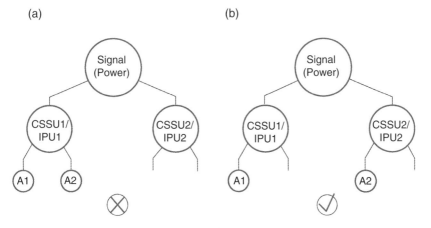

Figure 2.20 The alienation principle among the BFUs.

2.3.3.4 IPU Design

As one of the three key elements, IPU is employed to isolate failure. The complete derating design and FMEA should be employed in the IPU design:

1) The pressure endured by the IPU in the normal and abnormal status should be calculated, and the IPU should be designed using the complete derating. Then, the IPU is guaranteed not to be invalid because of overstressing, and will have the ability to recover the failure of the object that is being protected.
2) The isolation protection has no fixed modes, and the IPU is designed reasonably, according to the FMEA results of the IPU and the object being protected.

Table 2.2 IPU elements and application references.

Type of object protected					IPU elements			
	diode	resistor	capacitor	transformer	OA (operational amplifier)	OC (optical coupler)	fuse	Hall device
power	●	○	—	○	—	—	●	—
analog	●	○	○	○	●	○	—	●
level	●	●	—	—	○	●	—	○
pulse	○	●	●	○	○	●	—	○

Note 1: ● optional; ○ concrete analysis; — not optional.
Note 2: A combination of multiple protections can provide complete protection on some occasions.

In addition, the CSSU in Table 2.1 has an isolation protection function, and other specific isolation protection elements can be selected, and also the common IPU elements. The application references are summarized in Table 2.2.

1) Diode: using the one-way characteristic, the diode provides a constant zero or constant one fault protection. In the practical application, the concrete protection mode is determined by the results of the FMEA of the object being protected.

   a) The constant 0 fault protection: when the multiple outputs receive data in parallel, one output of the constant 0 fault is guaranteed not to influence the normal value received by the others.

   b) The constant 1 fault protection: when the multiple inputs send data in parallel, one input of the constant 1 fault is guaranteed not to influence the normal value sent by the others.

2) Resistor: the resistor connected in series to the redundancy digital input of the CMOS can guarantee that the single input fault not influence the other redundancy inputs.

3) Capacitance and transformer:

   a) Protects multi-to-one circuit outputs and guarantees that one specific output fault does not influence the normal output of others to send signals.

   b) Protects one-to-multi-circuit inputs, and guarantees that one specific input fault does not influence the normal input signals of others to receive signals.

   c) The transformer can protect the AC power and some analog signals (such as the 1553B coupling transformer). Its application should be carried out according to concrete analysis.

Table 2.3 Application scope and the advantages and disadvantages of a power supply isolation protection circuit.

Power supply isolation protection circuit	Application scope	Advantages	Disadvantages
Over-current protection circuit	All scale circuit protection	More fault modes, recoverable	More complex in the circuit or need to introduce new types of elements
Diode	Short-circuit fault of redundancy power	simple	Degrades voltage and one-way protection effect
Fuse	The redundancy design: the breaking of the fuse cannot result in invalidation of the whole satellite	simple	unrecoverable
Current-limiting resistor	Small-scale redundancy design	simple	Temporary solution

2.3.3.5 Power Supply Isolation Protection

The power itself is usually designed as with redundancy, so therefore the power supply isolation protection is separated from the IPU design. Power failure is mainly caused by loss of isolation protection design in the power, and the source of the failure is the lack of analysis of common-cause failures and ignorance of the latency factors. Complete isolation protection design should be employed for the power supply. Each backup BFU should be supplied with power that is as independent as possible; if not, power isolation protection among the backup BFUs should be employed, to avoid a single BFU becoming an SPF.

In general, a diode, a current-limiting resistor, a fuse, or an over-current protection circuit can be used in the power supply isolation protection circuit. The application scope and the advantages and disadvantages are shown in Table 2.3.

The following points need to be specially emphasized:

1) The over-current protection circuit is preferred.
2) If the fuse is chosen, the key function should not be degraded after the fuse breaks.
3) Caution should be exercised when using the current-limiting resistor. If this resistor is employed, it should be rated for use in the worst case scenario. The value of the resistance should be guaranteed not to decrease when a short-circuit occurs.

2.3.3.6 Testability Design

The testability of the redundancy function and the circuit can be improved using the following methods: improving the design scheme; increasing the test points; direct or indirect telemetry methods. The direct telemetry method should be employed to the key action and the key redundancy management module. The reliability of the untestable items in the redundancy design should be guaranteed by process control and other related methods. For example, in the parallel redundancy fuse circuit, the jumper set in a backup channel is open-loop at the initial stage to make every fuse testable. After finishing the test, the jumper is shortened. Thus, the "untestable" item can be testable.

2.3.3.7 Others

1) The redundancy structure and circuit should be simplified, as unexpected failure can occur as a result of unnecessary logic. For each detailed function, the implementation circuit should be as simple as possible. For each element, consideration should be given to whether it can be eliminated or merged with other elements.
2) Independent principle of the external interface: The redundant external interface should be as independent as possible, to eliminate SPF caused by the elements used in common. If it cannot be independent, isolation protection methods should be adopted.
3) Heterogeneous principle: If possible, the redundancy schemes should be different.
4) The topology structure should be "O" shapes, not "Q" shaped, if the dual-point-dual-line method is adopted. As shown in Figure 2.21(a), in the "O" shape topology, a broken circuit failure in any position of the circuit does not influence the communication of the signals. Conversely, as shown in Figure 2.21(b), in the "Q" shape topology, a broken circuit failure has occurred between computers C and B, so computer C cannot communicate with other computers.

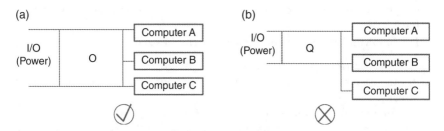

Figure 2.21 Dual-point-dual-line redundancy design.

2.3.4 Validation of Redundancy by Analysis

2.3.4.1 Hardware FMEA

With its bottom-up approach, hardware FMEA can identify any possible failure modes. From analysis of the failure effects, the weakness of the system can be found, and improvement measures can be employed to increase the reliability. As one of the elements of the redundancy reliability analysis and design, the hardware FMEA can be employed to analyze the FDMU, CSSU, and IPU systematically. All the failure modes of each element should be analyzed, to guarantee that no unacceptable failure exists in the system.

2.3.4.2 Redundancy Switching Analysis (RSA)

RAS technology is a specific application of FMEA in redundancy analysis, which analyzes whether SPF can affect the redundancy switching function. The general procedure of RSA is as follows:

1) The complete circuit diagram, with redundancy backup modules, is marked and drawn.
2) The interface part is refined into every element.
3) All the failure modes of every element are analyzed, to guarantee that the redundancy switching is not influenced by the failures.

In RSA, broadcast failure is prevented and the switching can work successfully when failure occurs. Based on the results of RSA, the test cases are designed in the debugging and test regulations. According to the regulations, the analysis result can be validated by the failure injection method. For example, as shown in Figure 2.22, loads L1 and L2 are driven by the cold backups A1 and A2, respectively. If the interface resistance on the condition of A1 power-off is lower than the output resistance on the condition of A2 power-on, the output resistance of A2 will be reduced by the resistance of A1 when VD1 has short-circuit failure. Then, A2 cannot drive L1 and L2 at the same time. Consequently, because of the VD1 short-circuit failure, backup A1 cannot be switched to backup A2, whereas backup A2 can be switched to backup A1. To avoid this switching failure, diodes VD1 to VD4 are implemented with redundancy via a serial connection. If the resistances of A1 and A2 are sufficiently large when A1 and A2 are powered off, the problem of invalid switching can be eliminated.

2.3.4.3 Analysis of the Common Cause of Failure

As a subset of FMEA, analysis of the common causes of failure involves investigation of whether a single failure occurring inside the redundancy system can cause two or more failures in the redundancy system or a related external object (or the failures occur within a short time in series). To increase the reliability of the system, it should be guaranteed that no common cause of

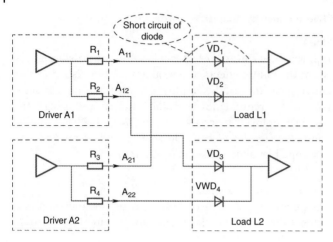

Figure 2.22 RAS demonstration.

failures exists among the redundancy backups and between the redundancy backups and the external objects. The relation and dependence among the redundancy backups are the innermost common cause of failure. Thus, independence is the best method to overcome the common cause of failure. More specifically:

1) Independence of the redundancy modules should be guaranteed and the number of electrical interfaces that depend on each other, and the operations that are restricted by each other, should be reduced.
2) If possible, the heterogeneous design is preferred.
3) The redundancy modules should be set in different areas to avoid all the redundancy modules failing when one area is damaged.

2.3.4.4 Reliability Analysis and Checking of the Redundancy Power

The power itself is usually designed with redundancy, and the redundancy scheme is applied in the power switching. Ability analysis of the power isolation and protection is one of the key points of redundancy reliability analysis. The power isolation protection mechanism should be employed among the redundancy powers and the redundancy modules. The items to check are as follows:

1) For the redundancy power, it should be guaranteed that no failure modes are broadcast among the backup powers. The hot-backup power is generally a balanced supply.
2) It should be guaranteed that a single short-circuit in the bus bar does not influence the supply of the system. All the redundancy backups and other loads supplied by the bus bar should be selected first, then the power

isolation protection design of all the redundancy backups and loads should be analyzed, to guarantee that a single short-circuit does not influence the supply by the bus bar.

3) Independent power supplies are preferred for the redundancy modules. If this is not possible, complete isolation protection should be provided.
4) For the power isolation protection design, the following should be guaranteed:
   a) The isolation protection circuit should be as close to the power source point as possible, to cover more failure modes.
   b) The protection threshold should be set reasonably to guarantee that short-circuit protection cannot be triggered by the peak value of the power consumption.
   c) When using the hierarchical protection mechanism, if the module in the bottom layer is over current, the protection device of the bottom layer can be started up first.
   d) When using a fuse, the key function should not be degraded after the fuse breaks.
   e) When using a self-recoverable power protection device, the delay time of self-recovery should satisfy the system's real-time requirement.
5) The reliability of the cables and connectors in the power channel cannot be ignored:
   a) The cables of the redundancy power should be an independent bundle, and the cables of the redundancy power should not be bound with other cables. A sufficiently safe distance should be maintained among the backup cables.
   b) The power cables and connectors should ensure sufficient voltage and have sufficient isolation ability. Further, the current in the cables should be derating. The power pin and its return pin in the connector should be at a sufficiently safe distance.

For example, a certain satellite temperature measurement redundancy circuit is shown in Figure 2.22. In the circuit, R_{ti} is the thermistor of the small resistance, and R_i is a precision resistor with a large resistance. The thermistor is fixed in every temperature measurement point, and the assembly environment of the thermistor is complicated. Consequently, it is easy for the thermistor to short-circuit to the structure ground. The precision resistor is fixed in the detection-box, and its assembly environment is better. Thus, it is not easy for the precision resistor to short-circuit to the ground. The unhealthy design is shown in Figure 2.23(a). In this circuit, if one thermistor R_{ti} is short-circuited to the ground, the power will be pulled down, resulting in all the redundancy detection channels becoming invalid. The correct design is shown in Figure 2.23(b). In this case, even if one thermistor R_{ti} is short-circuited to the ground, the only result is that this redundancy detection channel will be invalid, as opposed to all channels.

(a)

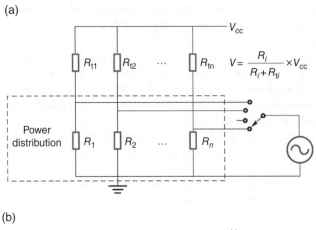

(b)

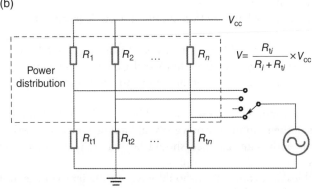

Figure 2.23 Satellite temperature measure redundancy circuits.

2.3.4.5 Analysis of the Sneak Circuit in the Redundancy Management Circuit

The purpose of analysis of the sneak circuit is to detect unexpected functions under the assembly condition of the different statuses and sequences. The redundancy management circuit is the key safety circuit and the emphasis on the analysis of the sneak circuit. Its safety should be guaranteed for unexpected functions in the redundancy management circuit not to be active in any case. For example, as shown in Figure 2.24, the two backups cannot operate at the same time, as a result of the redundancy circuit. If the switching is in the position to enable switching autonomously, the backup can be active manually or autonomously. If the switching is in the position to disable switching autonomously, the backup can only be active manually. The condition of the sneak circuit is that the switching is in the position to enable switching autonomously, while the signal for starting backup 2 autonomously is true. When backup 1 is started manually, it is on duty. However, a sneak circuit will be produced, as

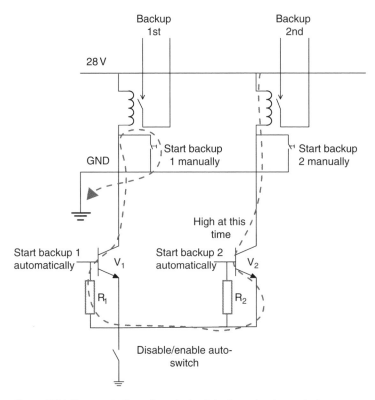

Figure 2.24 Demonstration of sneak circuit in the redundancy design.

shown by the dashed lines. The sneak circuit will start up backup 2 to be on duty, such that backup 1 and backup 2 will be on duty at the same time. The solution for the problem is to add a diode to the emitter of the triode to prevent the possible sneak circuit.

2.3.5 Validation of Redundancy by Testing

2.3.5.1 Testing by Failure Injection
Because validation only by analysis is somewhat limited, testing is employed for further validation. In redundancy testing, the regular functions are tested first to validate the correctness of the theoretical design. Then, according to the measurement of the specific performance of BFU, FDMU, CSSU, and IPU, the parameters can be adjusted to achieve a very robust redundancy circuit. In addition to the regular test, a failure injection test should be executed. Using the black-box method, every BFU should be tested by failure injection and, using the white-box method, every element of the FDMU, CSSU, and IPU should be tested by failure injection. The failure injection should satisfy the test coverage requirement.

2.3.5.2 Specific Test for the Power of the Redundancy Circuit

The power isolation protection between the redundant power itself and the backup power is a key link in the redundancy design. The instant of the power being on or off (especially when the power is on) is the peak period of the redundancy failure. Thus, the ability for power isolation protection and the instant of the power being on or off should be tested especially, to guarantee a reliable supply to the redundancy system. In the prototype design stage, the short-circuit failure of the redundancy power itself and the redundancy load should be simulated, to validate the effectiveness of the safe measurement of the redundancy power and the redundancy load. Note that, in the prototype design stage, a current regulator can be employed to simulate the load; by regulating the bearing current of the current regulator, the normal work current, the latch-up, and the abnormal current existing during a short-circuit can be simulated. The voltage bearing and isolation of the cables and connectors should be emphasized in the test.

The spacecraft power on/off performance (including the sequence requirement) should be simulated to validate the reliability of the power being on/off in the redundancy system. The slow release characteristic of the charge left in the object tested should be considered completely, to guarantee that failure does not occur in the instant when the power is being switched on or off.

2.3.5.3 Other Things to Note

The on-ground test should be executed according to the on-orbit operation manual, as closely as possible. The redundancy system should be operated according to the on-ground test process. Other things to note include the following:

1) Consistency in process: The on-ground test process should be kept consistent with the on-orbit operation manual.
2) Consistency in environment: The environment should be set according to the on-orbit vacuum, thermal, and electromagnetic conditions, in order to find the problems completely.
3) If the requirement cannot be met, equality between the on-ground test and on-orbit operation should be proven by analysis or simulation methods.

References

1 Yang Mengfei, Guo Shuling, Sun Zengqi (2005). On-board computer technology for spacecraft control applications. *Aerospace Control* **23**(2), 69–73.
2 Avizienis A, Gilley G C, Mathur F O, Rennels D A, Rohr J A, Rubin D K (1971). The STAR (self-testing and repairing) computer: an investigation of the theory and practice of fault-tolerant computer design. *IEEE Transactions on Computers* **C-20**(11), 1312–1321.

3 Yang Mengfei (1994). Essential issues and strategies of space applicable fault-tolerance computers. *Aerospace Control* **12**(2), 35–39.

4 Wang Guiying, Yang Mengfei, Chang Longxing (1990). Triple modular fault tolerant computer system for satellite control system. *Aerospace Control* **8**(4), 51–56.

5 Smith T B (1981). *Fault-tolerant clocking system* [C]. 11th IEEE International Symposium on Fault-Tolerant Computing (FTCS-11), Portland, ME, 1981.

6 Shin K G, Ramanathan P (1987). Clock synchronization of large multiprocessor system in the presence of malicious faults[J]. *IEEE Transactions on Computers* **36**(1), 2–12.

7 Davies D, Wakerly J F (1978). Synchronization and matching in redundant systems[J]. *IEEE Transactions on Computers* **27**(6), 531–539.

8 Olson A, Shin K G, Jambor B J (1995). *Fault-tolerant clock synchronization for distributed systems using continuous synchronization messages.* Twenty-Fifth International Symposium on Fault-Tolerant Computing, 1995 (FTCS-25), 154–163.

9 Cristian F, Fetzer C (1994). *Probabilistic internal clock synchronization* [C]. IEEE Proceedings of 13th Symposium on Reliable Distributed Systems, 22–31.

10 Yuan Yi, Yang Mengfei, Zhao Weihua (2006). Implementation of a software method in clock initial synchronization problem[J]. *Control Engineering* (**1**), 17–24.

11 Zhao Weihua, Yang Mengfei, Yuan Yi (2005). Survey of clock synchronization methods researches[J]. *Control Engineering* (**5**), 11–19.

12 Shin K G, Ramanathan P (1987). *Diagnosis of processors with byzantine faults in a distributed computing system* [C]. 17th International symposium on Fault-Tolerant Computing (FTCS-17), July 6-8, 1987, Pittsburgh, PA, 55–60.

13 Ramanathan P, Shin K G, Butler R W (1990). Fault-tolerant clock synchronization in distributed systems. *IEEE*, October, 33– 42.

14 Pfluegl M J, Blough D M (1995). A new and improved algorithm for fault-tolerant clock synchronization[J]. *Journal of Parallel and Distributed Computing* **27**, 1–14.

15 Olson A, Shin K G (1994). Probabilistic clock synchronization in large distributed systems[J]. *IEEE Transactions on Computers* **43**(9),1106–1112.

16 Pfluegl M J, Blough D M (1991). *Evaluation of a new algorithm for fault-tolerant clock synchronization* [C]. IEEE Proceedings of Pacific Rim International Symposium on Fault Tolerant Systems, 38–43.

17 Fetzer C, Cristian F (1995). *An optimal internal clock synchronization algorithm* [C]. IEEE Proceedings of the Tenth Annual Conference on Computer Assurance, COMPASS'95, Systems Integrity, Software Safety and Process Security. 187–196.

18 Pease M, Shostak R, Lamport L (1980). Reaching agreement in the presence of faults [J]. *Journal of the ACM* **27**(2), 228–234.

19 Preparata F P, G Metze, R T Chien (1967). On the connection assignment problem of diagnosable system[J]. *IEEE Transactions on Electronic Computers* **EC-16**, 848–854.

20 Simeu E, Abdelhay A (2001). *A robust fault detection scheme for concurrent testing of linear digital systems* [C]. Proceedings of Seventh International On-line Testing Workshop, 209–214.

21 Pomeranz I, Reddy S M (2002). Built-in test sequence generation for synchronous sequential circuits based on loading and expansion of input sequences using single and multiple fault detection times [J]. *IEEE Transactions on Computers* **51**(4), 409–419.

22 Shyue-Kung Lu, *et al.* (2003). *Combinational circuit fault diagnosis using logic emulation* [C]. Proceedings of the 2003 International Symposium on Circuits and Systems, 5, 549–552.

23 Fenton W G *et al.* (2001). Fault diagnosis of electronic systems using intelligent techniques: a review[J]. *IEEE Transactions on Systems, Man and Cybernetics, Part C: Applications and Reviews* 269–281.

24 Sanghun Park, *et al.* (2000). *Designing built-in self-test circuits for embedded memories test* [C]. Proceedings of the second IEEE Asia Pacific Conference on ASICs, 315–318.

25 Meyer J F (1981). *Closed-form solutions of performability* [C]. In: Proceedings of 11th IEEE International Symposium on Fault-Tolerant Computing (FTCS-11), Portland, ME, 1981, 66–71.

26 Li Haiquan, Li Gang (2003). *Analysis and design of system reliability* [M]. Beijing: Science Press.

27 Stamatis D H (2005). *Fault mode effective analysis (FMEA) – from theory to practice* (2nd edition) [M]. Beijing: National Defence Industry Press.

28 Kang Rui, Shi Rongde (2006). *FMECA technique and its application* [M]. Beijing: National Defence Industry Press.

3

Fault Detection Techniques

Fault detection is the major method used to enable a fault-tolerant system to acquire reliability and reconfigurability. This chapter discusses the fault detection techniques of computer system components (CPU, memory, and I/O) computer architecture, and implementation.

3.1 Fault Model

A fault model is the essence of a fault-tolerance technique, in which the first step is fault location and detailed fault determination, followed by fault analysis and categorization [1,2]. The correctness and rationality of the fault model directly affects fault detection, recovery algorithm selection, and fault-tolerant system design. The categorization of typical faults for the purpose of impact identification and fault location is defined as modelization [1]. The typical fault that represents a specific fault set is defined as a modelized fault.

There are two basic principles for the modelization of faults, and the first is to reflect the effect of a fault on an electric circuit or system correctly (i.e., other than representativeness and correctness, comprehensiveness should be included). The second is to simplify the fault modelization process, so that calculation and processing can be conveniently performed. It is obvious that these two principals are contradictory; hence, compromise is a must.

The variation of research focus and application problem results in variations in the fault model. Before selection of the fault model, the first step is to consider the research focus, electric circuit, components, system implementation technique, facilities, software, and other resources necessary for research and development. In summary, fault modelization significantly affects fault detection. An excellent modelization solution will develop and improve the fault detection principle and method.

Fault-Tolerance Techniques for Spacecraft Control Computers, First Edition.
Mengfei Yang, Gengxin Hua, Yanjun Feng and Jian Gong.
© 2017 National Defense Industry Press. All rights reserved.
Published 2017 by John Wiley & Sons Singapore Pte. Ltd.

Fault modelization could be categorized from temporal and spatial aspects [1,3]. The temporal aspect is the duration of a fault, whereas the spatial aspect is the location of the fault in a circuit or the physical size of the circuit layer. The spatial aspect of a fault model can also be defined as the physical layer fault model.

3.1.1 Fault Model Classified by Time

1) Permanent fault: a permanent fault is a hardware malfunction that always occurs until reparation or maintenance measures are taken. For hardware, a permanent fault is an irreversible physical change, such as a failed circuit, a broken wire, etc.
2) Transient fault: a transient fault is the opposite of a permanent fault. A transient fault consists of intermittent faults and instantaneous faults.
3) Intermittent fault: an intermittent fault occurs and disappears at intervals repetitively. Causes include performance fluctuation induced by component parameter changes, unreliable connectors or cold solder joint, temperature, moisture, and vibration.
4) Instantaneous fault: instantaneous faults occur and disappear momentarily and non-repetitively within a short duration. Causes include power and magnetic disturbance, or space radiation. This type of fault may occur only once within a long period, but might produce data error and even system paralysis.

Statistical data show that transient faults account for a large percentage of all faults. They are the major cause of system failure. An early report from the US Air Force indicates that transient faults account for 80% of all faults, and a subsequent report from IBM stated that 90% of faults are transient faults. Therefore, the question of how to correct failures induced by transient faults is a major problem for fault tolerance techniques and fault-tolerant computer systems.

3.1.2 Fault Model Classified by Space

A hardware hierarchy consists of transistor level, gate level, function level, and so on. Each level has its own fault model [1,4–7]. The lower the fault model in the hardware hierarchy, the lower the cost for fault processing, and the smaller the number of faults that the model can cover. Hence, more models are necessary to cover all faults. A higher level model can cover faults that need multiple lower level models.

1) *Transistor switch level fault model.* The transistor is the basic unit of digital circuits and is located at the lowest level. Hence, the transistor switch level fault model, which is at the lowest model level in the hierarchy, includes the following physical faults:
   - Open circuit and short circuit of connection wire.
   - Time delay of physical fault.

- Cross talk and coupling of junction point.
- Component degradation, among which the most common is the open or short transistor fault model.

2) *Gate-level fault model.* The gate-level fault model is also called a logic level fault model, and is the most extensively used model, owing to its convenience in establishment and implementation, its applicability to producing test code for complex systems with Boolean algebra, and its adaptivity to multiple circuits. Frequently used gate-level fault models include the following:

i) Stuck-at fault model: the stuck-at fault model reflects the status of the individual signal or wire (e.g., input and output pin of a gate, or connection wire) is permanently stuck at a fixed logic value during system operation. In a digital system, the signal that is stuck at logic high is defined as stuck-at-1 (denoted as s-a-1), while the signal that is stuck at logic low is defined as stuck-at-0 (denoted as s-a-0).

The stuck-at fault model specifies that each input or output signal may get stuck at one or zero permanently, and the stuck status will *not* modify the function of the gate. In particular, fault models s-a-1 and s-a-0 target the logic functions of a circuit and have no direct relationship on the specific physical fault. Therefore, s-a-1 and s-a-0 faults not only refer to node and power short-circuit failure or the short circuit between node and ground, but also collection of faults that make the logic level of a node stuck at high or low, which reflects the fact that each hardware level has its own fault model.

ii) Bridging fault model: a bridging fault is a type of short-circuit fault, the cause of which varies, and it might modify circuit's topological structure to change the circuit function fundamentally. Therefore, it is impossible to study all types of bridging faults. The common practice is to study the most frequently occurring ones – for example, there are two types of bridging faults. One is a short-circuit fault produced by signal wires, in which there is no feedback; another is a short-circuit fault that produces a feedback. In addition, signal short circuit produces "wired AND" and "wired OR" effects, which are equivalent to traditional AND and OR gates, respectively – in other words, a wired-AND/ wired-OR fault model. There is a dominant fault model; when a signal's driving capability is comparatively larger than another one, bridging of the two signals will make both outputs stronger.

iii) Breaks in lines fault model: the breaks in lines fault model is also called the open circuit fault model, which is the opposite of the short-circuit fault model, and is rarely used.

iv) Function fault model: a function fault is the malfunction of a digital circuit's basic component, which includes logic gates such as AND, OR, and NOT gates, and flip-flops. A basic component's function fault will affect the function of the overall system.

v) Delay fault model: Although this fault model is related to time, it does *not* refer to the persistence of fault in the time domain, but the fault induced by delay in the time domain and will affect sequential circuits or systems that require timing response.

3) *Function module-level fault model.* Complex digital circuits are composed of function modules, and each module is realized by a logic circuit. On many occasions, it is necessary to know whether a module is faulty; in such cases, function level fault models are helpful. A function module-level fault model covers the fault scope of the transistor switch level fault model and gate-level fault model. Its fault processing ability is higher than that of the other two models. Hence, a fault tolerance strategy is applied to the function module-level fault model in many industrial applications. However, with this type of model, high accuracy is difficult to achieve, because the higher level of abstraction results in a higher possibility of losing information. Examples of function module-level fault models include decoder fault models, multiplexer fault models, memory fault models, programmable logic array (PLA) fault models, and microprocessor fault models.

Further study on fault models focuses on the following aspects:

1) Modeling of redundancy design for integrated chips with respect to SoC/system on programmable chip (SoPC) techniques.
2) Fault models for design failure as a result of the development of computer system design techniques and tools.
3) Interaction of digital and analog circuit faults.
4) Fault model accuracy improvement, and further analysis of the effect of space environment on circuits.

3.2 Fault Detection Techniques

This section discusses the concept and scope of fault detection techniques. The focus is on single-machine scenarios, which include CPU, memory, and I/O fault detection techniques. This section also presents several commonly used methods.

3.2.1 Introduction

Fault detection is the detection of faults through single or multiple methods. The most commonly used technique is the dual redundancy technique, which adopts two identical backup modules to detect faults via output comparison. This technique is simple, affordable, and applicable to all computer design scopes and hierarchies, with little effect on performance. It can detect all faults, excepting that of the comparison circuit. One variation on dual module redundancy is integration with other techniques to improve coverage of certain types of faults. One method to improve coverage is the switch and comparison technique in C.mmp multiple processor CPUs. This technique was first applied in the data structure of the memory, and was later extended to other computer components. In addition to single faults and non-overlapping faults, the switch and comparison technique can also cover most identical faults that affect both backups. The major defect of dual redundancy is that the same fault tends to occur to both backups (common mode fault), especially when both backups share the same design defect or reside in the same IC. In addition, the reliability and fault detection of comparison circuit are major flaws of the dual redundancy backup technique.

Error detection code is another extensively used fault detection method. It is the implementation of information redundancy – for example, in the parity error detection code technique, an additional bit is inserted into every binary byte so that the final digit is composed of odd parity code or even parity code, according to the implementation method. Error detection code is applicable to real-time fault detection.

One of the most affordable fault detection methods in industrial applications is the cumulative sum method, which is carried out by adding s number of bytes to a block based on module number n, where n is arbitrary. Cumulative sum is applicable to scenarios in which there are large amounts of data. However, the larger the amount of data, the more time is required to calculate the sum. Hence, this forms a major challenge to real-time systems.

There are also methods that use arithmetic code, cyclic code, and WDT fault detection techniques.

Although dual redundancy and coding techniques are the commonly used fault detection methods, they are ineffective against faults in comparison circuits (dual redundancy module) or SPF of decoder/detector. In order to solve the above problem, self-check, fault-insurance, and safe-failure design techniques are applied in the design of general purpose logic, comparator circuits, and validators [8–10].

A single computer in a spacecraft is composed of CPU, memory, I/O, and so on. The following sections discuss the fault detection method used for each component.

3.2.2 Fault Detection Methods for CPUs

Because a CPU is the core of the system operation, it is important to detect CPU faults in a timely and accurate manner. Before the discussion on the fault detection method used for the CPU, the fault model used for the CPU is first outlined below.

The CPU is one of the most complex ICs. The cause and manifestation of CPU faults vary, but there are two major types of faults: permanent faults (hard faults), which result from permanent failure of the electric component; and transient faults (soft faults), which result from various kinds of radiation (space radiation), electromagnetic environment, and so forth. Transient faults can change the CPU state, but can be recovered from.

3.2.2.1 Fault Detection Methods Used for CPUs

3.2.2.1.1 Fault Detection Through Hardware Redundancy

This method detects CPU faults through the increase in the hardware circuit. It consists of the following:

1) *Error detection and correction code (EDAC)*: In this method, error detection and correction code circuit is placed in the CPU in the design phase to produce a self-checking CPU. EDAC is composed of error detecting code and error correcting code. The most commonly used error detecting codes are parity code, Berger code, and m of n code. The most commonly used EDAC is Hamming code [11–13].

   EDAC increases hardware costs, because of the fact that it is implemented through an increase in the hardware component. Hardware cost increase of the CPU, based on EDAC, is related to the code system. The increases are in the range 38–60%, according to typical experimental data.

   EDAC possesses a high fault-detection ratio. It can detect both permanent and transient faults with excellent real-time capability.

2) *Backup CPU*. In this scenario, a backup CPU is adopted at the system IC level (e.g., PAD microcomputer). This method also possesses a high fault detection ratio and can detect both permanent and transient faults with excellent real-time capability. However, because dual modules require a fault comparison circuit, the hardware cost increase is greater than 100% and it is difficult to achieve timing synchronization [14–17].

3.2.2.1.2 Software Method

Another method for CPU fault detection is time redundancy, of which two types exist. Type 1 detects faults by repeatedly running identical function codes and comparing the outputs.

Type 2 detects CPU faults using self-testing code.

1) *Dual mode software comparison*. A basic form of time redundancy is to run two codes with identical functions, which is also called dual mode software comparison. The codes can either be identical, or different versions of the same function (owing to the independence of the code, it might detect more faults – e.g., defects in design and common causes of

failures). The fault detection is achieved by comparing the output of the two codes. Because this method significantly increases time cost, and code size varies as the function varies, it is difficult to generate an application-free method. Hence, application of the dual mode software comparison method is limited.

2) *Self-testing code method.* Another form of time redundancy involves designing CPU self-testing code, through whose periodical running CPU faults are detected. The feature of this method is that the test method is independent of the CPU mission. It is related only to the CPU architecture. The time required for the test is fixed with the possibility to design code with different time spans for different system requirements. Self-testing code is extensively used in real-time control computer systems.

3.2.2.2 Example of CPU Fault Detection

The following discussion presents a self-testing method example for a certain type of CPU.

In general, the CPUs currently applied in industry consist of the following components: interface part, which is responsible for address output, data transmission and reception, and external interface of the control signal; and operative part, which includes command and control, arithmetic and logic execution unit, and register groups. With advancements in CPU development, CPUs that had internal memory emerged. Because the memory test is discussed in detail in Section 3.2.3, the CPU test here is focuses only on the interface and operative parts. Without loss of generality, the following section will discuss the 80C86 self-testing system widely used in the space industry, which can be extended to other CPUs.

The 80C86 is a 16-bit CPU IC that comprises an execution unit (EU) and a bus interface unit (BIU). The two internal bus interconnected units operate independently and asynchronously, as shown in Figure 3.1.

The 80C86 CPU comprises three parts: the register part; the arithmetic and logic execution part; and the operation control part. Hence, the instruction system consists of three parts: register related instruction; arithmetic operation related instruction; and operation control related instruction. Because the determination of 80C86 CPU faults depends on whether the CPU can execute instructions properly, CPU fault detection is transformed to the state of CPU execution of instructions. Therefore, CPU fault detection through state testing on CPU execution of instructions is proposed.

3.2.2.2.1 CPU Permanent Fault Detection Method

Because the manifestation of instruction faults differs as instructions differ, the categorization of CPU instruction systems is the essence of fault detection

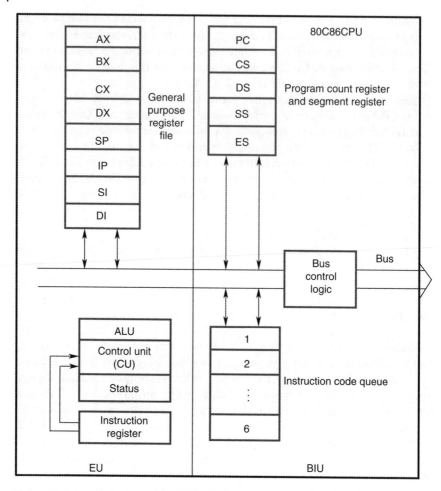

Figure 3.1 Internal structure of the 80C86 CPU.

based on instruction type. According to instruction operation and CPU architecture, instruction sets can be classified into three groups: the register related instruction set, the arithmetic operation instruction set, and the control related instruction set. CPU fault detection code can be programmed on the basis of the above analysis.

1) *Register instruction set.* The function of a register is to temporarily store data, status, or the value of critical parameters and variables. Fault detection is achieved through value comparison between data written into a register and data read out of the register. The code for AX register test is:

```
mov ax,0
cmp ax,0
jnz ax_fault
mov ax,5555 h
cmp ax,5555 h
jnz ax_fault
mov ax,0aaaah
cmp ax,0aaaah
jnz ax_fault
mov ax,0ffffh
cmp ax,0ffffh
jnz ax_fault
jmp ax_ok ;AX correct
ax_fault: ;AX fault
```

2) *Arithmetic operation instruction set.* The function of arithmetic operation is to process data and logic operation. Fault detection is achieved through determination of the operation of predefined data. The code is similar to that of the register instruction test code, so it is not listed here.

3) *Control operation instruction set.* The function of the control operation instruction set is to control program operation. Fault detection is achieved through analysis of the instruction execution and the test results obtained from the test program designed (details of the code are not listed here).

The above methods focus on permanent fault detection and the coverage for transient fault is low.

3.2.2.2.2 *CPU Transient Fault Detection*

In space environments, the major cause of computer transient faults is space radiation, the manifestation of which is SEU phenomena. The following discussion is primarily on transient fault detection induced by SEU.

1. Failure Behavior Analysis In order to find a solution for transient fault detection, it is necessary to discuss what will happen in the CPU parts after the SEU effect with respect to program operation.

1) *Bus control logic.* Bus control logic depends on the external sequential relation, including Max./Min. working mode control, operating address/access address, and access time function. When SEU occurs, the above working states change. The details are as follows:

- If the CPU is operating at its maximum mode when SEU occurs, the CPU will change to minimum working mode and the time sequence will be chaotic. As a result, either memory access will be faulty or program runs fly.

- If the CPU is operating at its minimum when SEU occurs, the CPU will change to maximum working mode and the time sequence will be chaotic. As a result, either memory access will be faulty or program runs fly.
- Operation address is incorrect or time sequence increases/decreases, which leads to program chaos or run fly.

It is obvious that these phenomena are observable via certain methods.

2) *Program counter and segment register.* This is a group of registers that are affected by state upset, but manifestation varies. The 16-bit PC is an offset pointer for program operation and, together with CS, this forms the final program operation address. If any bit of the PC is changed from 0 to 1, or 1 to 0, the program operation will change accordingly. Except in rare cases (e.g., in a group of NOP instructions, the low bit error of the PC will NOT affect program operation negatively), the operation change will result in an error which is observable. The 16-bit CS is a program segment register, whose bit change will result in significant program jump (the minimum is 16 bytes). It is possible to observe whether the CS state has upset through tracking identifier setup or program operation result. DS and ES are two 16-bit registers used for data segment and data extension segment address storage. They are configurable during program operation. Hence, the state of DS and ES can be determined through program reading/writing of these two registers, and the state upset of DS and ES are thus observable. They store the segment address in the stack SS, which remains constant during program operation. Hence, SS fault detection can be achieved via the predefined stack value.

3) *Instruction register and instruction code queue register.* This is a group of 16-bit registers used to improve the 80C86 operating speed. When a certain bit in the instruction register is toggled, the change in the execution of the instruction will result in error. It is worth noting that the variation of these register instructions leads to variation of the results, which may *not* manifest itself in certain scenarios (e.g., the instructions after program jump tend to have this type of problem). In order to detect SEU as much as possible, application of program jump should be limited.

4) *General register group.* The value of general registers can be predefined, according to program needs. The state change of these registers can be detected through test programs.

5) *State register.* The function of the state register is to store the state information of program operation (e.g., whether the result is zero, or whether there is overflow and carry bit). A typical side-effect after SEU includes program jumping over to other parts of the processing code, thus changing the operation result. Sometimes there is no change at all, owing to the reconfigurability of these states as the program operates, and the fault is recovered before negative effects occur. This scenario is time-dependent. The state of this register can be read by the program, hence it is observable.

6) *ALU.* This is a circuit composed of combinational logic (or its equivalent). The effect of SEU on the ALU is transient and not registered. The

detectability of ALU fault depends on the occurrence of SEU at the moment of particle penetration of the general register. When SEU occurs, the fault is detectable and stored. When it does *not* occur, the fault is *not* detectable and *not* stored with any side/negative effect, which might lead to error. Because, in the majority of industrial applications, there is no error produced, no further discussion will be presented on ALU faults.

7) *CU*. This register is responsible for instruction decoding and executive code generation. It is combinational logic without memorization ability. The SEU effect is not memorized on it, but can be manifested through the instruction execution result. Hence, CU faults are observable.

According to the above analysis, the effect of SEU on the internal circuit of the 80C86 is summarized as follows: (1) program execution sequence change, or program runs flying; (2) data operation result change; (3) data stored in the register change; (4) no side effect.

2. Fault Detection Method The following are the detection methods used according to the CPU faults described above:

1) Monitor program track and reset immediately, once it goes flying or unexpectedly steps into branches, and record as one SEU event. This method can detect most SEU effects in the instruction registers and related registers discussed above.
2) Monitor program track and compare program operating sequence with planned sequence to detect SEU, once the program unexpectedly steps into recoverable branches other than the predefined sequence.
3) Test periodically and determine SEU through the register group. At the beginning of the test, pre-set certain values to registers and check if the values change. Because the focus is on state upset induced by SEU, pattern sensitive fault is ignored here.
4) Arrange interruption and calling routine to detect whether stack segment and stack pointer are faulty as a result of SEU.
5) Perform full instruction set test to detect SEU phenomena in CU.

The prerequisite for the above methods is normal operation of the program, without which fault detection *cannot* be performed. In order to detect CPU failure that may result in program malfunction, other methods are necessary to ensure normal operation. One such method is the watchdog technique, which includes two types of methods: the WDT and the watchdog processor. The former is extensively used, owing to its simplicity and ease of application.

3.2.3 Fault Detection Methods for Memory

The most extensively used memory in real-time control computer systems is semiconductor memory, which can be classified as read only memory (ROM) and RAM [15,16].

3.2.3.1 Fault Detection Method for ROM

The function of the ROM is program storage, which is necessary for space applications. The following sections discuss fault types and detection methods, respectively.

3.2.3.1.1 Fault Model for ROM

ROM consists of an address decoding part and a data storage unit. The fault model for ROM is listed as follows:

1) Address decoding fault:
   i) One address corresponds to multiple storage units – that is, upon selection of one storage unit, multiple storage units are chosen. The output may or may *not* be correct. It is also defined as a one vs. many address fault.
   ii) Multiple addresses corresponding to one storage unit – that is., as a result of fault, multiple addresses correspond to the data in one storage unit. The data output of this storage unit is determined at this point. However, the storage units selected by the multiple addresses originally are not the same, so the output data are not the same with maximal probability. When this type of fault occurs, the output data cannot meet the requirement of the selected units. It is also called many vs. one address fault.
   iii) Cross address fault – that is, the predefined address is changed to a different value as a result of fault. For example, because of decoder failure, the chosen address is changed from X1 to X2 (X1 $\neq$ X2).
   iv) Out of address range – that is, as a result of decoder failure, no unit is selected.
2) Storage unit fault:
   i) Stuck 0 fault – that is, value of a bit is stuck at 0.
   ii) Stuck 1 fault – that is, value of a bit is stuck at 1.

In addition to the faults described above, there are coupling faults and data sensitive faults, whose probability of occurrence is lower than **1** and **2** above. Hence, the focus of discussion is on **1** and **2**.

3.2.3.1.2 Fault Detection Methods for ROM

Because of the real-time requirement in space control computer systems, the fault detection methods used for ROM are the encoding detection method and the cumulative sum method. The fault coverage and real-time performance of the two methods are discussed below.

1) Encoding detection method:
   i) Parity bit method, which detects single bit error in a byte through additional parity bit. Its capability is limited to single error detection in a storage unit. It is ineffective for the remaining types of faults.

ii) EDAC method. This is extensively used in RAM. On its application in ROM, the detection range is similar to that of the parity bit method. This method is designed to detect faults in storage units, and cannot detect faults in the address decoder. Hence, with additional hardware and improvement in real-time performance, the fault detection coverage is low. Consequently, EDAC is rarely used for ROM failure detection in industrial applications.

Conclusion: because of the encoding detection method's need for extra resources and inability to detect address decoding faults, application of it in industry is rare even though it possesses excellent real-time performance.

2) The cumulative sum method.

Another fault detection method used for ROM is the cumulative sum method, which achieves fault detection by periodically calculating the sum of the data stored in ROM and comparing the result to a pre-calculated value.

Assume that the number of bits in a ROM is m, the storage space of the system is $S = |P_0, P_1, ..., P_i...,P_{n-1}|$, and the size of the storage space is n:

The cumulative sum with the carried bit method consists of two types:

Assume that the cumulative sum is s; then the sum of all storage units is given by:

$$s = \sum_{i=1}^{n-1} p_i = c \cdot 2^m + s_i \tag{3-1}$$

The cumulative sum can be denoted in two sections, one for the carried bit c and the other for the mantissa of the sum s_1.

Because the number of bits for each storage unit is m, and the maximum value stored is $2^m - 1$, the number of units is given by:

$$s = \sum_{i=0}^{n-1} p_i = \sum_{i=0}^{n-1} (2^m - 1) = n \cdot (2^m - 1) = n \cdot 2^m - n < n \cdot 2^m \tag{3-2}$$

The number of carried bits is thus determined. In equation 3-2, the number of carried bits is n. As m and n are now known, the number of storage units needed for the carried bit is also known. For example, if $m = 16$ and $n = 64$ kB, then $y = 216 = 64$ kB (i.e., only one byte is necessary).

The following are the conclusions drawn for the cumulative sum fault detection method:

- Single bit error in a single storage unit is detectable.
- Multiple-bit errors in a single storage unit are detectable.
- Multiple-bit errors in multiple storage units may or may not be detectable.

The following are conclusions drawn for the decoder fault detection method:

- One-to-many type faults are detectable.
- Many-to-one type faults, i.e., multiple addresses corresponding to one address, are detectable.
- Cross address failure is not detectable.
- Address out of range type faults are detectable.

3) The blocked cumulative sum method

In the case of massive storage space and high real-time, the carried bit cumulative sum method is inapplicable. In order to meet the above requirements, and to improve fault detection ratio in the address decoder, a blocked storage space and interval storage space cumulative sum method is presented for ROM detection. This method divides the storage space into l blocks and selects one byte from each block to calculate the cumulative sum. This method can greatly improve the cross-faults detection ratios, and can consequently improve the detection ratio of ROM faults

In this method, the storage space is divided into l blocks; with the size of each block as n/l, the blocks are represented as b_1-b_l, as shown in Figure 3.2.

Each block contains n/l number of bytes, hence n/l cumulative sums are formed. That is:

$$s_0 = p_{b1,0} + p_{b2,0} + \cdots + p_{bl,0}$$

$$s_{l-1} = p_{bl,l-1} + p_{b2,l-1} + \cdots + p_{l,l-1}$$

in which $p_{i,j(i=1,2\ldots l; j=0,2,\ldots,l-1)}$ is the jth byte in the ith block.

The above analysis shows that the cumulative sum method is more applicable, as a result of its advantage on fault coverage and detection time. The blocked

Figure 3.2 Blocked storage space structure.

cumulative sum method is more advantageous than the other methods. Further, its detection timing can be configured to accord with industrial application requirements. Thus, it is the recommended method.

3.2.3.2 Fault Detection Methods for RAM

Decades of research on memory test methods have produced a variety of feasible methods, such as the ping-pong test method and the mode sensitive test method [18]. The following sections discuss the fault model and test methods for RAM, respectively.

3.2.3.2.1 Fault Model for RAM

The current fault model for RAM includes the following:

1) Stuck 0/stuck1 fault – that is, a bit of the memory is either permanently 0 or 1.
2) Decoding fault – that is, decoding circuit failure. The decoding circuit is a necessary part of the storage system. A decoding fault will result in the following:
   - Inefficient address selection and data acquisition.
   - Multiple unit operation when targeting single unit operation in one-to-many address access.
   - Single unit operation when targeting multiple unit operation in many-to-one address access.
3) Fault coupling – that is, the fault of one unit couples to the nearby unit and results in fault in the nearby unit.
4) Data pattern mode sensitive fault. RAM fault depends on the content stored in the data pattern (sensitive) – that is, some content produces error, some do not.

Because **1** and **2** above are the most common types of faults, resulting in many test methods being proposed, this section's test method discussion focuses on these.

3.2.3.2.2 Test Method

Depending on the application of the buffer, the test methods are classified into two types: tests with buffer and tests without buffer.

1. **Test Methods with Buffer**   The process utilized by a test method with a buffer is shown in Figure 3.3. This type of method's primary focus is resource efficiency and detection coverage, as it applies a real-time control computer. Resources include spatial resource and temporal resource. Larger buffers require many spatial resources, whereas smaller buffers reduce detection probability. Temporal resource depends on the size of the blocks and is related to real-time performance, which will be negatively affected if too much time is

consumed in the test. In order to adapt to the real-time requirement, the test is performed either periodically, or during the computer's idle mode. The size of the storage space and the test period depend on the system. The test block is typically 1–4 kB, and the test period is equal to the control system's control period.

The test methods commonly used with buffer are the gallop method and the ping-pong method. These two methods belong to the N2 type of test algorithm, in which the ping-pong method is a simplified version of the gallop method. It possesses similar features to the gallop method, and ensures the realization of information change and address translation when reading data. Test results on storage matrix, decoder, address access time, storage unit writing, and matrix information retention are excellent.

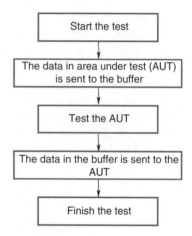

Figure 3.3 Typical memory test process.

The gallop method is also called the roaming method. The following is the test process utilized by this method:

1) Write 0(1) to all units.
2) Write 1(0) to A_0, read 0(1) from A_1. Read 1(0) from A_0, read 0(1) from A_1, then read 0(1) from A_2. Read 1(0) from A_0, read 0(1) from A_2, read 0(1) from A_3, Read 1(0) from A_0,....., until all units are completed.
3) Change the written value of A_0 to 0(1), read 1(0) from A_1, repeat the above steps.

The process used by the Gallop algorithm performs 1 roaming, then 0 roaming. The following is the solution (for convenience of discussion, A_0, A_1, A_2, A_3,...A_{n-1} are addressed in increasing order from the starting position):

1) From the starting position, write "0" to all units addressed in increasing order.
2) From the starting position, write "1" to the first unit A_0, read the value "0" of the second unit A_1.
3) Read the value "1" of A_0, read the value "0" of A_1, then read the value "0" of A_2.
4) Read the value "1" of A_0, read the value "0" of A_2, then read the value "0" of A_3.
5) Read the value "1" of A_0, read the value "0" of A_3, then read the value "0" of A_4.
....
(n) Read the value "1" of A_0, read the value "0" of A_{n-2}, then read the value "0" of A_{n-1}.

That concludes the operation of A_0. Consequently, the operation of A_1 begins:

(n + 1) Write "1" to the second unit A_1, read the value "0" from the third unit A_2.
(n + 2) Read the value "1" of A_1, read the value "0" of A_2, then read the value "0" of A_3.
(n + 3) Read the value "1" of A_1, read the value "0" of A_3, then read the value "0" of A_4.
(n + (n–2)) Read the value "1" of A_1, read the value "0" of A_{n-2}, then read the value "0" of A_{n-1}.

That completes the operation for A_1. Consequently, the operation for A_2 begins. Repeat the above process until the operation for A_{n-2} is completed, i.e., roaming of one is finished.

Then roaming of zero starts. Change the written value of A_0 to 0, read the value "1" of A_1,.... repeat the above steps.

The process utilized by the gallop method is similar to roaming in the 1(0) matrix. Its time complexity is $O(n^2)$, and the time consumed for the test is relatively long. The gallop test method is able to detect fixed faults, transition faults, and coupling faults. Because of the high time complexity, it is rarely used in industrial applications.

The test process for the ping-pong method is as follows:

1) Write zero into all units.
2) Change the value of the first unit A_0 to "1", then read out to verify.
3) Read the value "0" from the second unit A_1, read value "1" from the first unit A_0.
4) Read value "0" from the third unit A_2, read value "1" from the first unit A_0.
5) Read value "0" from the third unit A_3, read value "1" from the first unit A_0.
   ………
   (n + 1) Read value "0" from the highest unit A_{n-1}, read value "1" from the first unit A_0.

That completes the operation for A_0. Consequently, the operation for A_1 begins.
Reset the first unit A_0 to "0", then perform the following test:

(n + 2) Change the value of the second unit A_1 to "1", then read out to verify.
(n + 3) Read value "0" from the third unit A_2, read value "1" from the second unit A_1.
…...
((n + 1) + (n–1)) Read value "0" from the highest unit A_{n-1}, read value "1" from the second unit A_1.

That completes the operation for A_1. Consequently, the operation for A_2 begins.
Reset the second unit A_1 to "0", follow the above steps until the operation of A_{n-1} is completed, i.e., roaming of one is finished.

The ping-pong method shares similar features to the gallop method, but the test time is only two-thirds that of the gallop method's. Hence, the ping-pong method is extensively used in large capacity semiconductor function tests. In order to improve the test efficiency, in real applications, the value written into the storage unit is 55AA or AA55, instead of 0 or 1.

2. Test methods without buffer There are two types of problems in test methods with a buffer. The first is the necessity for storage buffer, and the prerequisite for conducting a buffer passing test before testing the RAM; this not only increases expense on resources (more storage space is used), but also disables follow-up tests if the buffer fails. The second is the limitation on system resources. Test coverage of RAM depends on the size of the buffer. Theoretically, its size should be equal to that of the RAM to be tested, but in reality this is difficult to achieve. This section introduces a test method without buffer, which tests stuck 0/stuck 1 type of the fault and address decoding fault, as described previously.

Assume that the storage unit is a t16 bit byte, then the size of the RAM is n, the storage unit address is denoted as $A_0 \ldots A_{n-1}$, the content of each storage unit is denoted as $[A_i]$ ($i = 0, \ldots, n-1$), the registers available for the test are AX, BX, CX, DX, SI, and DI. The test process for stuck 0/stuck 1 type of faults is as follows:

```
1)  CX ← n, i ← 0, flag for fault clearance.
2)  Read AX ← [Aᵢ].
3)  ĀX → [Aᵢ] (ĀX is the negation of AX).
4)  BX ← [Aᵢ].
5)  If ĀX ≠ BX, then jump to (9).
6)  ĀX → [Aᵢ].
7)  CX ← CX – 1, i ← i + 1.
8)  If CX = 0, then jump to (10), else jump to (1).
9)  Set flag of fault.
10) Return.
```

Test process for the address decoding type of fault is as follows:

```
1)  CX ← n, i ← 0, flag for fault clearance.
2)  j ← i, SI ← 0.
3)  AX ← [Aᵢ].
4)  BX ← [Aⱼ₊₁].
5)  If ĀX = BX, then SI ← SI + 1.
6)  j ← j + 1, if j ≠ n, then jump to (4).
7)  ĀX → [Aᵢ], j ← i.
8)  BX ← [Aⱼ₊₁].
```

9) If $\overline{AX}$ = BX, then SI ← SI – 1.
10) $j \leftarrow j + 1$, if $j = n$, then jump to (8).
11) If SI ≠ 0, then jump to (14).
12) If $\overline{AX}$ ≠ [A_j], then jump to (14).
13) AX → [A_j], $i \leftarrow i + 1$, if $i \neq n$, then jump to (2), else jump to (15).
14) Set flag of fault.
15) Return.

3.2.4 Fault Detection Methods for I/Os

Input/output (I/O) is a major part of any system. As the degree of integration and function of I/O becomes higher and stronger, the probability of I/O failure becomes accordingly higher. Therefore, it is necessary to study I/O fault detection methods. Because the I/O system is a passive component, whose fault can be detected through a feedback method, fault detection in an I/O system is relatively convenient. The structure of test is shown in Figure 3.4.

At the input part, a control gate method can be applied for the test – that is, the system provides an additional test signal. By the same token, the test of output part is through the output of the feedback input. Whether an I/O system is faulty depends on the comparison between input and output.

In tests conducted of real-time systems, special attention should be given to the following items:

1) Elimination of test hardware influence on the system – that is, additional hardware for input and output fault detection should *not* become a faulty component of the system and affect system operation negatively. Special measures should be taken at the design phase.
2) Avoidance of negative effects on system operation due to additional test programs. Special measures on time sequence should be taken at the design phase.
3) Avoidance of negative effect on normal system input and output when designing a program for I/O testing.

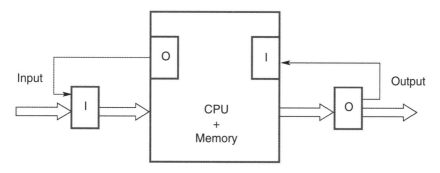

Figure 3.4 I/O test structure.

References

1 Hu Mou (1995). *Computer fault tolerance technology* [M]. Beijing: China Railway Publishing House.

2 Yea-Ling Horng, *et al.* (2000). *A realistic fault model for flash memories* [C]. Proceedings of 9th Asian Test Symposium 274–281.

3 Gong Jian, Yang Mengfei, Wen Liang (2009). Study on FPGA fault models in evolutionary fault tolerance [J]. *Chinese Space Science and Technology* **29**(3), 57–62.

4 Zachriah S T, Chakravarty S (1999). *A comparative study of pseudo stuck-at and leakage fault model* [C]. Proceedings of 20th International Conference on VLSI Design, 91–94.

5 Abraham J A *et al* (2002). *A comprehensive fault model for deep submicron digital circuits* [C]. Proceedings of the First IEEE International Workshop on Electronic Design, Test and Applications 360–364.

6 Zhuo Li, *et al* (2003). *A circuit level fault model for resistive opens and bridges* [C]. Proceedings of 21st VLSI Test Symposium 379–384.

7 Emmert J M, Stroud C E, Bailey J R (2000). A new bridging fault model for more accurate fault behavior. IEEE Proceedings of Autotestcon, Sept 18–21. 481–485.

8 Marouf M A, Friedman A D (1978). *Design of self-checking checkers for berger codes* [C]. In: Digest Eighth International Fault-Tolerant Computing Symposium. IEEE Computer Society, 179–184.

9 Kaneda S, E Fujiwara (1980). *Single byte error correcting – double byte error detecting codes for memory systems* [C]. Tenth International Symposium on Fault-tolerant Computing (FTCS-10), 1–3 October, 1980, Kyoto, 41–46.

10 Hyde P D, Russell G (2004). A comparative study of the design of synchronous and asynchronous self-checking RISC processors [C]. Proceedings of 10th IEEE International On-line Testing Symposium 89–94.

11 Rao T R N, Fujiwara E (1989). *Error-control coding for computer systems* [M]. Englewood Cliffs, NJ: Prentice-Hall.

12 Crouzet Y, Landrault C (1980). Design of self-checking MOS-LSI circuits: Application to a four-bit microprocessor [J]. *IEEE Transactions on Computers* **29**(6),532–537.

13 Halbert M P, Bose S M (1984). *Design approach for a VLSI self-checking MIL-STD-1750A microprocessor* [C]. Fourteenth International Conference on Fault-Tolerant Computing (FTCS-14), Kissimmee, Florida.

14 Chavade J, Crouzet Y (1982). *The PAD: A self-checking LSI circuit for fault detection in microcomputers* [C]. Twelfth. International Symposium on Fault Tolerant Computing (FTCS-12), Santa Monica, CA.

15 Lala P K (1985). *Fault tolerant and fault testable hardware design* [M]. Englewood Cliffs, NJ: Prentice-Hall.

16 Johnson B W (1989). *Design and analysis of fault tolerant digital systems* [M]. Englewood Cliffs, MA: Addison-Wesley.

17 Caldwell D W, Rennels D A (1988). *Minimalist fault masking, detection and recovery techniques for mitigating single event effects in space borne microcontrollers.* UCLA Computer Science Department Technical Report TR-98005.

18 Yang Mengfei, Sun Zengqi, Gong Jian (2005). A new memory fault detection method applying for real time systems [J]. *Chinese Space Science and Technology* **25**(6), 26–29.

4

Bus Techniques

This chapter introduces basic bus technique concepts. The focus is on the fault-tolerance features of typical buses that are widely used in spacecraft, with practical applications as examples.

4.1 Introduction to Space-borne Bus

4.1.1 Fundamental Concepts

A bus is a set of signal wires that connects computer devices (or electronic components) and acts as a common channel for data transmission. The implementation of buses in a spacecraft has the following advantages:

1) Simplified system architecture, which results in decreased system complexity and increased system reliability.
2) Reduced volume and weight, which results in convenient cable arrangement, due to a reduced amount of wire.
3) Convenient system expansion, which results in more novel and flexible configurations, and convenience of system modularization.
4) Convenient interface design – that is, any equipment that connects to the bus adopts a similar interface.
5) Convenient equipment software design, which promotes access to different interfaces in order to operate on different addresses of the corresponding interface.
6) Convenient fault diagnosis and maintenance at reduced cost.

Consequently, bus techniques are widely used in spacecraft.

4.1.2 Fundamental Terminologies

1) Protocol: a protocol is a defined set of rules that controls data transmission between entities. The major elements of a protocol are data interchange format,

Fault-Tolerance Techniques for Spacecraft Control Computers, First Edition.
Mengfei Yang, Gengxin Hua, Yanjun Feng and Jian Gong.
© 2017 National Defense Industry Press. All rights reserved.
Published 2017 by John Wiley & Sons Singapore Pte. Ltd.

signal level, coordinated action, error processing, sequential matching, and signal sequence control information. The computer communication model is based on the open system interconnection (OSI) model of the international organization of standardization. The OSI model defines a hierarchical structure for communication protocols, which includes physical layer, data link layer, network layer, transport layer, session layer, presentation layer, and application layer. Peer protocols are used for communication between the same layers, (i.e., for a given layer, the communication entities adopt the same protocol). Interface protocols are used for communication between different layers – that is,, i.e., each layer serves the upper layer through the interface, and conceals details of function realization. Based on the complexity of the buses, current space-borne buses are acquired through modification of the OSI model.

2) Data rate: the speed at which data is transmitted from one device to another. The unit used is bit/s. For serial transmission, the data signaling rate is defined as:

$$S = \frac{1}{T}\log_2 n$$

where T is the unit signal code-element duration, with unit s; and n is the number of states of the signal. For dual state information, 1 Baud = 1 bit/s. For example, for each code-element within a 20 ms duration, a 50 bit/s (50 Baud) data rate corresponds to two signal states: "0" and "1."

3) Channel working mode: this is a channel's time division feature, which includes full duplex, half duplex, and simplex. Full duplex means that both ends of the channel can send and receive data simultaneously; half duplex means that, at any given time, only one end can send or receive data; simplex means that only one end can send data, and the other end can only receive data.

4) Channel transmission mode: a method used to synchronize the sending and receiving ends. It includes asynchronous transmission and synchronous transmission. Asynchronous transmission divides data into character blocks, each of which synchronizes with other blocks through its starting bit and ending bit. Synchronous transmission means that the time each/bit signal appears corresponds to a fixed time frame – that is, the sending and receiving time of every/bit signal is predictable.

5) Signal pattern: a description of the signal voltage transmission method, which includes single end signal and differential signal. Single end signal is expressed with voltage compared with common system ground. Differential signal is expressed with voltage between two transmission lines.

4.2 The MIL-STD-1553B Bus

Drafted by United States, the 1553B bus is a time division multichannel military standard bus that defined the physical and data link layers. Its transmission method is half duplex, and the encoding method used is Manchester

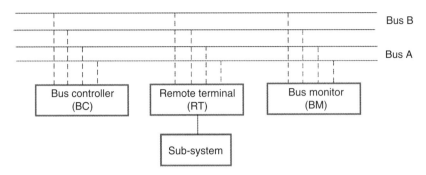

Figure 4.1 Structure of the 1553B Bus.

coding with a 1 Mb/s data rate. A bus controller, remote terminal, and bus monitor are all on the bus. As shown in Figure 4.1, all nodes share a common physical layer and, at any particular time, only one node is allowed to send data, although all nodes can receive. The receiving node is identified via its address. This is a command/response bus, in which the bus controller has absolute authority over data transmission on the bus [1–3]. As regards reliability, the 1553B specifies a set of fault-tolerant features, including fault detection, location, isolation, and recovery. The 1553B has a dual redundancy structure – that is, the system can switch to another channel to continue data transmission when one channel fails. Currently, 1553B is widely used in electrical systems on China's satellites.

The 1553B data bus uses a command/response type of protocol, and its hardware consists of a bus controller (BC), a remote terminal (RT), and a bus monitor (BM).

1) The bus controller: The bus controller is the only terminal that is responsible for initiating and setting up data transmission.
2) The remote terminal: The remote terminal is a terminal that does *not* function as the bus controller or bus monitor.
3) The bus monitor: The bus monitor is a terminal that is responsible for receiving bus communication assignments and extracting needed information afterwards. It records and analyzes data sources by "monitoring" information transmission, but does not participate in bus communication.

4.2.1 Fault Model of the Bus System

In a general application, the 1553B bus can be divided into three functional modules: Physical circuit, bus controller, and remote terminal, as shown in Figure 4.2. The physical circuit comprises all the shielded twisted pairs and the coupling/isolation transformers that connect every terminal. It is an information transmission channel [1].

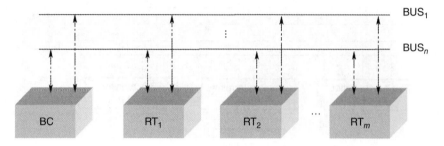

Figure 4.2 1553B Bus system function module.

In order to process faults better, it is necessary to perform analysis at a more abstract level. The hardware physical fault model can be classified as transistor switch level, gate level, and function module level, based on the level of abstraction.

The following conditions may cause failure of the 1553B bus:

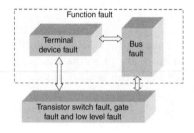

Figure 4.3 System level fault distribution structure of the 1553b bus.

1) Terminal abnormality (software abnormality, etc.).
2) Bus controller abnormality (software abnormality, etc.).
3) Bus controller control IC abnormality.
4) Terminal bus controller control IC abnormality.
5) Communication circuit physical suspension.
6) Communication circuit crossing over strong electromagnetic area.
7) Damage to isolation/coupling transformer.
8) Failed terminal or critical component abnormality on the bus control board.

From a manipulation point of view, the above faults can be divided into function level faults and underlying level faults, as shown in Figure 4.3. It is necessary to include all faults in order to analyze underlying faults. For instance, the cause of failure of a logic gate might mean failure of the component and, hence, it is categorized as an underlying fault, which must be considered in the system level fault-tolerance mechanism. Because of the large number of terminals in the bus, the complexity of similar analysis makes function level analysis and the fault-tolerance method more practical in industrial applications.

Although function level analysis shielding of transistor level and gate-level faults decreases the accuracy of fault description and ignores those faults that do *not* affect the function level, it does cover faults that affect bus system functions and result in system failure, so that fault manipulation, system life, and function are improved.

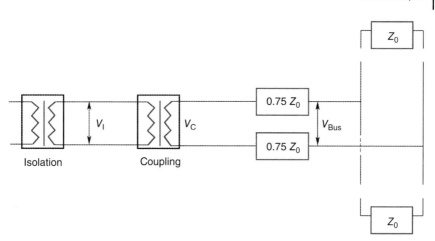

Figure 4.4 Bus-level structure.

For convenience of description, the function fault model is setup from both the 1553B bus level and the terminal level point of view [4].

4.2.1.1 Bus-level Faults

The bus level is the physical link of the bus system. It includes the physical bus, coupling transformer, and isolation transformer, whose function is to ensure proper data and protocol control information transmission, as shown in Figure 4.4 (single bus). Abnormality of the bus can result in bus-level faults, a broken physical bus will cause suspension of communication, and adhesion of wires or EMI between two buses will induce communication errors.

Abnormality of the bus-level transformer is more complex. It is necessary to keep the bus voltage within a certain range, so that communication is guaranteed. Suppose the peak-to-peak bus voltage is VBUS = 7 V (the 1553B protocol specifies 6 V–9 V), the peak-to-peak voltage of the right hand side of the coupling transformer is VC, the peak-to-peak voltage of right hand side of the isolation transformer is V1, Z0 is the 1553B characteristic impedance at a bus data rate of 1 Mbit/s (the 1553B protocol specifies 75 Ω), and the winding ratio of the coupling transformer is 1 : 1.414.

When the terminal is sending data,

$$V_C = (0.75\,Z_0 + 0.75\,Z_0 + 0.5\,Z_0) \times V_{BUS}/(0.5\,Z_0) = 28V$$

$$V_1 = V_C/1.414 = 20V$$

When the terminal is receiving data, from the bus perspective, the input impedance of the transformer is in the range 2000–3000 Ω (within the 75.0 kHz to 1.0 MHz frequency range), far greater than 75 Ω; hence, it can be considered as infinite.

$$V_C = V_{BUS} = 7V$$

$$V_1 = V_C/1.141 = 5V$$

The possible failure of a transformer includes coil short, broken coil, or winding ratio abnormality, among which the most influential on bus performance is the coupling transformer right hand side short circuit, as shown in Figure 4.4. Although the two serial connected 0.75 Ω Z_0 can protect the bus, the circuit's disability for data transmission makes it equivalent to a broken circuit. The broken transformer's internal winding results in bus access being broken. Winding ratio abnormality leads to voltages V_1 and V_C deviating from the protocol specified – hence, data transmission on the bus is abnormal.

In summary, the bus hierarchy fault model can be manifested as bus communication suspension and bus communication data abnormality. Physical failure of bus components leads to permanent fault, while external disturbances such as EMI can make transient data transmission abnormal. The failure modes can be categorized as permanent faults and transient faults.

4.2.1.2 Terminal Level Faults

The major task of the 1553B bus system is accomplished by terminal level software and hardware with complex structure. The terminal level consists of two types of terminals to accomplish its task – bus controller and remote terminal. A terminal is composed of a node and a bus interface unit. Technically, a real node has multiple functions. For example, a control subsystem's node needs to accomplish a set of complex tasks, such as control parameter sampling, control algorithm realization, and control bus communication, as the solid line block diagram in Figure 4.5 shows. This section focuses on bus subsystem reliability improvement, so the following concept of node is abstracted as possessing control bus communication function only – that is, observe BIU through simplification of node and interface unit as a single individual element, as the dotted line block diagram in Figure 4.5 shows.

The hardware core of the interface unit includes control logic and sending/receiving buffer RAM. The control logic consists of message data format protocol control logic, Manchester II data encoding/decoding logic, and RAM control logic. A message data format protocol control logic fault can result in illegal output or failed output of sync-word, word count, message bit count, and digital parity check code. Manchester II data encoding/decoding logic fault can lead to illegal Manchester encoding and abnormal data-induced terminal incompetency to identify data. RAM control logic fault can produce

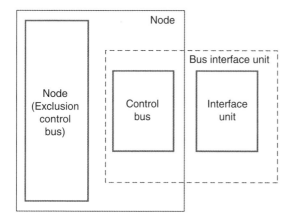

Figure 4.5 Terminal bus interface.

incorrect buffering, manifested as incapability to send and receive data. Stuck at "0" or ("1") error or multiple units coupling fault could result in terminal failure induced by data error in the bus.

In summary, considering the different functions and importance of the bus controller and remote terminal, the terminal level device function fault is categorized as follows:

- Fault of bus controller BIU due to disabled bus controller's communication with other terminals. This type of failure will not spread to other terminals.
- Fault of bus controller BIU due to faulty data or command. This type of failure will affect other terminals on the bus.
- Fault of remote terminal BIU due to inability to respond to bus controller command, so data and message status word cannot be sent.
- Fault of remote terminal BIU due to inability to respond to bus controller command and sending incorrect data or message status word. This type of failure will affect other terminals on the bus.

Based on the influence over other nodes, terminal device level fault model can be categorized as follows: silent fault, which means the external environment is *not* affected after induced system failure; and malicious fault, which means the external environment is affected after induced system failure.

The above fault model does not cover the scenario of mistakenly identifying received correct data as faulty data, as shown in Figure 4.6. The consequences are:

1) Sending faulty data because of affected BIU output;
2) Mistakenly identified received data is used by the terminal CPU, hence it does *not* affect the BIU bus output.

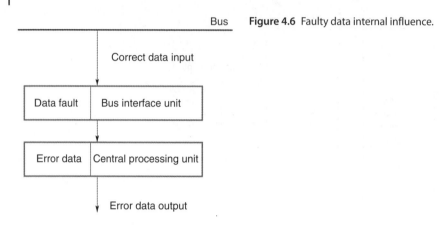

Figure 4.6 Faulty data internal influence.

This section discusses bus communication fault – that is, fault in data interchange between BIU and bus, and fault in data transmission over the bus. In order to tolerate this type of fault, it is possible to adopt a BIU redundancy structure to perform BIU comparison and a voting fault-tolerance mechanism, so that the accuracy of data transmission is guaranteed.

Bus level and terminal level faults are independent of each other, because the bus level and terminal level are independent modules of the bus system. Statistically, these two types of faults are unrelated, and need respective analysis and calculation so that system reliability analysis can be further simplified.

4.2.2 Redundancy Fault-tolerance Mechanism of the Bus System

On the basis of the function level fault model, the improvement of bus system reliability is achieved through implementation of resource redundancy, fault mask, and system reconfiguration at the bus layer and terminal layer, respectively. Resource redundancy includes spatial redundancy and temporal redundancy. Spatial redundancy includes static redundancy and dynamic redundancy. Temporal redundancy includes retry, rollback, and restart. Time and cost restrain system fault-tolerance strategies. Time is determined by the values of two critical parameters: system deadline and fault-tolerance latency, represented as T_{SD} and T_{FL}.

System time limit is the maximum time duration of the system remaining in its expected state space after the system function becomes invalid after failure. Fault-tolerance latency is all the time needed for error detection, fault location, and system reconfiguration. Cost comprises the factors that are necessary to complete the fault-tolerant function, such as price, weight, volume, and power consumption. The purpose of fault-tolerant system design is to achieve fault-tolerance latency within the range of system time limit at minimal cost. The cost of spatial redundancy is relatively high, but needs shorter time, so it is applicable to a system with rigorous time requirement. The cost of temporal redundancy is relatively low and needs longer time, so it is applicable to a system with little real-time requirement.

When the system fails, the 1553B fault-tolerance mechanism should complete fault detection, location, and system reconfiguration within minimum time without losing data, or with minimal data loss. In order to ensure the working continuity of the bus system, it is necessary to finish system reconfiguration within a period after fault identification. China's application includes the communication satellite platform and the ShenZhou spacecraft return cabin; both possess a period less than 100 ms, and are typical applications of short period. The French Ariane 5 fault-tolerance mechanism requires that fault identification and system recovery time do not exceed 300 ms. Considering the recovery time requirements of worldwide spacecraft systems, and necessary margin of control and communication period other than that occupied by the system recovery time, the order of magnitude of the system time limit, TSD, is set at 10 ms, which is also the range of the 1553B bus system redundancy mechanism's fault-tolerance latency, T_{FTL} [4,5].

4.2.2.1 The Bus-level Fault-tolerance Mechanism

Bus communication suspension means that there is unrecoverable fault within the bus physical layer, which includes broken twisted pairs in the communication link system, poor contact of connectors, or damaged bus transformers. Bus communication abnormality means that the abnormality due to the EMI or winding ratio of the transformer will cause faults in one or multiple digits or even all messages, illegal Manchester encoding, data synchronization header fault, and data discontinuity.

Fault location mechanism includes the following:

- Software, whose purpose is to setup the parity check bit to determine if there is odd digit error, determine if there is a lost data bit through receiving the command word, determine if the time interval between the data words is out of range (data discontinuity), and determine if there is loss of status word and bus switch fault, through the setup of status work response and timeout clock counting.
- Hardware, whose purpose is to determine if the synchronous header is legal when the protocol control logic is receiving data, and to determine if the Manchester encoding is legal through decoding logic.

The 1553B internal bus controller is responsible for coordinating all message transmissions. The remote terminal outputs state word after receiving the message. The method used by the fault location mechanism is to adopt a dual redundancy structure made up of two physical buses, working in active and standby mode, respectively. Normally, the message can be transmitted through only one working bus. The standby works as a backup for the operating bus.

Figure 4.7 Longest message on the 1553B bus.

The bus controller determines if there is any communication circuit fault through the fault location mechanism; if there is a fault, the message is re-sent on the working bus. If the fault remains after multiple retransmissions, it is sufficient to determine that the working bus has failed and, thus, a switch must be made to the backup bus. This type of fault-tolerance mechanism latency depends on the time needed in the message transmission on the bus.

The 1553B bus protocol specifies a data rate of 1 Mbit/s, i.e., it takes 1 μs to transmit 1 bit. The worst case scenario for the dual bus redundancy mechanism is that a fault appears when the 1553B bus is transmitting the most time-consuming message (information interchange between remote terminals). The full message first sends the "receive" command word to the target remote terminal, then sends the "send" command word to the source remote terminal, after which the source terminal responds with status word and sends out the maximum 32 data word. Finally, the target terminal responds with the receiving data state word, as shown in Figure 4.7. In a real application, the maximum message timeout waiting time is 130 μs (i.e., TTIMEOUT_MAX = 130 μs).

The longest message transmission time is T_{MSG} (T_{CMD} is the command word transmission time; $T_{LOOPBACK}$ is the loop test time),

$$T_{MSG} = 2 \times T_{CMD} + 2 \times T_{STATUS} + T_{LOOPBACK} + T_{DATA}$$
$$= 2 \times 20 \times 1 + 2 \times 20 \times 1 + 20 \times 1 + 32 \times 1 \times 20 = 740\,\mu s$$

On detecting the abnormity in the above bus communication, the bus controller first resends the same message N times (where N is 2 or 3); for the above worst scenario, N = 3. If the fault remains after resending of the message, it is necessary to switch buses, resulting in a time cost with a magnitude of milliseconds; thus, the contribution to the longest fault-tolerance latency T_{FTL} is small. The corresponding longest fault-tolerance latency (including the interval between messages, typically around 1 ms) is:

$$T_{FTL} = N_{MSG} + N_{TIMEOUT\_MAX} + N_{GAP} = 3 \times 720 + 3 \times 130 + 3000$$
$$= 5.420 \text{ ms} < T_{SD}$$

The above analysis shows that the fault-tolerance latency T_{FTL} meets the requirement of the system time limit.

4.2.2.2 The Bus Controller Fault-tolerance Mechanism

The bus controller terminal coordinates all communications on the bus. The essence of ensuring bus working reliability is to improve the reliability of the 1553B bus system's BC, which is the core of the 1553B. The importance of the bus controller demands fast system reconfiguration of the backup when the host fails.

Cold backup is *not* powered up in standby mode. A cold backup is only setup when the bus controller cannot meet the synchronization requirement between the host and the backup. Moreover, it cannot meet the real-time requirement because of host/backup switching (system reconfiguration), and powering up the backup takes a long time. Warm backup avoids the power-up process in system reconfiguration, but it is difficult to synchronize host and backup. Hot backup does not have the above difficulties, but traditional hot backup is still problematic. Because at any given time there is only one BC in operation, the host/backup BC should be connected to the bus through a special mechanism (called the arbitration mechanism).

Fault detection with this type of backup will occur if the host/backup controller's output is consistent through the comparator in the arbitration module. The hardware comparator conducts digit-to-digit comparison between the host and the backup – that is, the host/backup controller will have to start up simultaneously within a certain tolerance range, and the data output will be synchronized within the tolerance range. The data transmission rate of the 1553B bus is 1 M bit/s. It takes 1 µs to transmit one bit, which means that, in order to distinguish the output of the host/backup, the tolerance range should be at the nanosecond level. It is difficult to achieve this magnitude of synchronization.

Using feedback data output of the host/backup to perform comparison through software is another method that can be utilized. Because the internal 1553B control data output logic performs protocol-specific Manchester II encoding, hardware decoding logic is a must in order for the software to retrieve data, which results in a very complex design. Furthermore, even if the above fault identification problem is solved, the arbitration unit still needs an extra strobe circuit to enable the backup to receive data from the bus and stop the backup sending data to the bus during normal operation. However, the 1553B logic data transceiver line is multiplexed, which further increases the difficulty of strobe circuit design.

The bus controller cannot adopt the isomorphic hot backup method, because of its specific characteristics. To simplify the function and logic of the traditional hot backup, and avoid the above difficulty, one method that can be used is to transform one of the monitor terminals (MTs) of the 1553B bus into a BC monitor terminal, which is equivalent to BC backup. From the perspective of the 1553B, the BC backup works in MT/BC mode. From the perspective of backup type, the BC backup is a heterogeneous hot backup that executes dissimilar software on various hardware platforms. The function of bus controller is focused on control bus communication only, so implementing a redundancy structure is simple and convenient. Therefore,

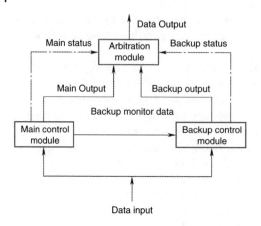

Figure 4.8 Bus controller dual modular redundancy.

a dynamic redundancy structure achieved through MT is simpler than a static redundancy structure, because of the 1553B bus system's limit on the BC fault-tolerance structure.

4.2.2.2.1 Dual Modular Redundancy of the Bus Controller

A normal dual modular redundancy solution can perform fault detection without fault-tolerance. However, with an additional fault location and switching technique, fault-tolerance can be achieved. The dual modular redundancy structure is shown in Figure 4.8. It consists of host control module, backup control module, and arbitration module. The fault detection and fault location depends on the following three conditions:

1) Periodically, a "status OK" signal is sent to the arbitration logic while monitoring the host through the monitor timer (watchdog logic). The BC consists of control logic and a sending/receiving RAM buffer. In order for the timer to monitor these logics, it is necessary to implement the 1553B protocol specified offline loop self-test, which connects the data sending and receiving ends to form an internal offline closed loop structure without using the bus. This facilitates digit-to-digit comparison of the sent data and the received data, to determine whether the sync-header of the data word, encoding, decoding, number of digits, and parity check of the data word are the same. The sending/receiving RAM buffer sets the parity bit to perform the parity check each time data are read. After the above logic detects a hardware fault, it does not reset the monitor timer, resulting in the timer reporting to the arbitration logic.

2) Periodically, a "status OK" signal is also sent to the arbitration logic while monitoring the backup through the monitor timer. The fault detection and determination mechanism utilized are the same as those above.

3) The backup operates at MT mode to maintain synchrony with the host message and also, meanwhile, compares the task of the host controller and the expected bus communication protocol task through the bus monitor, to determine if they are consistent.

Fault detection is achieved through dual machine comparison and fault location is achieved through the monitor timer. Inside the primary backup's sub-module, fault location is achieved through the monitor timer. The fault location result, and the tracking and comparison result of the backup controller, are sent to the arbitration module, to form an overview of the system malfunction status. This mechanism can detect host failure and backup failure, and also perform system reconfiguration.

The dynamic dual modular fault-tolerance mechanism successfully solves the silent-fault problem. For malicious fault (sending incorrect data to the bus), fault identification is performed with the host/backup comparison mechanism. The redundancy structure processes the malicious fault located by the monitor timer. Any fault that could not be located by the monitor timer is processed according to the mechanism in the condition of fault 1.

Although the dual modular redundancy structure reflects the fundamental principle of the bus controller fault-tolerance mechanism, its deficiency includes: its strict requirements on the self-detection capability of the function module and the function of the arbitration module; the complex state of fault and state transition; and the high reliability required for the fault location process performed by the monitor timer.

4.2.2.2.2 N-modular Redundancy of the Bus Controller

The N-modular redundancy of the bus controller is an alternate structure. Usually, the primary module performs system output, in which it adopts various fault detection and fault location techniques to determine the failed module, then reconfigures and recovers the system. The N-modular redundancy of the bus controller consists of BC group and an arbitration mechanism, as shown in Figure 4.9.

In the BC group, BC is the host that controls the bus with the arbitration module, and the backups are the hosts for MT. The total $N - 1$ backups can be divided into three subsets – specifically, $A\{1... i\}$, $B\{1 ... j\}$, $C\{1 ... k\}$ – among which $i + j + k = N - 1$. The controller of subset A is the hot backup, the controller of subset B is the cold backup, and the controller of subset C is the failure controller. In the system's initial state, in the BC group, the value of i and j are determined according to system reliability requirement and cost.

During system operation, the controllers of A monitor the host and send a judgment to the arbitration module at certain system message synchronization points. The arbitration module then votes according to the majority win mechanism, to determine the host's state.

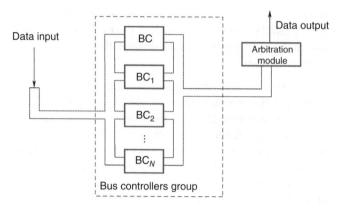

Figure 4.9 N-modular redundancy of the bus controller.

The host should continue working if the majority of backups in A consider that the host is normal and, meanwhile, the value of the opposition of the opponent increases by one. The opponent is considered to have malfunctioned if the value of the opposition exceeds a preset limit, in which case the opponent is grouped into subset C and its power shut down through the feedback control circuit. In the scenario where the value of the opposition does *not* exceed the limit, a warning notice is sent to the opponent.

The host is powered off through the feedback circuit if the majority of backups in A consider that the host is abnormal, and the backup with the least number of opposing votes is upgraded to host. Further, a cold-backup unit in subset B is initialized as a member of subset A to monitor the host. The powered-off host is grouped into subset C.

It is possible to form various redundancy topology structures through the definition of the number of bus controllers in subsets A and B. For example, $i = 2$, $j = 2$ signifies a triple hot backup and dual cold-backup structure; $i = 3$, $j = 0$ signifies that the three backups in subset A form a two-out-of-three system to determine the host BC status; and $i = 1$, $j = 0$ signifies that the system has evolved into a bus controller dual redundancy topology structure, of which the BC dual module redundancy structure is a special case. This method not only achieves fault-tolerant capability for silent and malicious faults, but also simplifies the fault status identification of the dual redundancy structure. It provides flexibility to fault-tolerance structure design by balancing the fault-tolerant feature, cost, and definition of subsets A and B based on reliability, volume, and weight requirements.

4.2.2.2.3 Distributed Redundancy Mode of the Bus Controller
Distributed redundancy of the bus controller terminal refers to the forming of a chain-shaped backup controller topology, via transformation of the backup controller module into RT's sub-function module and the combination of

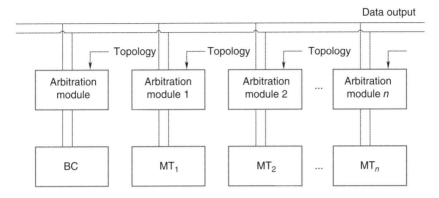

Figure 4.10 Distributed redundancy mode of the bus controller.

RT and the sub-function module. From the 1553B bus system perspective, RT operates in RT/MT mode and appears to possess RT/MT/BC capability. This method requires high self-detection performance from the bus control system and its backup system. In addition to detecting faults within the system, another very important function is to block output when the system has failed, in order to prevent fault diffusion.

Because BC possesses multiple backups on the bus, it is necessary to implement a replacement policy. Token delivery is a recommended method to elect a candidate backup controller – that is, a backup controller has the right to be a host only after it acquires the token and the right to acquire the token is removed if the backup fails after becoming the host. There are various token acquisition and delivery mechanisms, including token delivery follows ascending order of RT address code (i.e., at any time the token holder is the controller that has never been a host with minimum address code). This method conducts a maximum degree of redundancy backup to the core controller on the bus, physically separates the host bus controller and its backup, and eliminates fault diffusion of public resource failure (such as power failure) induced with simultaneous failure of host and backup.

4.2.2.3 Fault-tolerance Mechanism of Remote Terminals

Important remote terminals need redundancy to improve their fault-tolerant capability. The advantage of RT over BC is that the bus allows multiple RT to exist, and the hot backup of RT can also connect to the bus as a remote terminal. Because the host/backup of the RT can use various addresses, the bus controller can communicate with the host and backup, respectively, so that a consistent status between host and backup is achieved. These features make the fault-tolerance structure of the remote terminal easier to realize, and more diversified than that of the bus controller.

In the remote terminal fault-tolerance structure, there are two types of backup terminals: one that does not occupy a terminal address and has a working mode of cold backup or monitor hot backup; and one that occupies a terminal address and operates simultaneously with the host. The following is various fault-tolerance topology structures based on combination of the number of RT addresses occupied by the redundancy structure (denoted r) and various working modes:

- When $r = 1$, the subsystem of the remote terminal occupies a terminal address – that is, the backup terminal cannot operate simultaneously with the host on the bus as an RT. This is similar to the scenario with the bus controller, so it is possible to transplant the redundancy structure of the bus controller. With minor modifications, the dual module and N-modular redundancy structure of the bus controller can be implemented on the remote terminal.
- When $r = 2$, the subsystem of the remote terminal occupies two terminal addresses. This is an isomorphic hot backup, which combines with the monitor functioning as an RT to form a heterogeneous two-out-of-three fault-tolerance structure. Additional cold-backup reserve can maintain a long-term dual hot standby fault-tolerance structure. The host and backup machines simultaneously operate as two independent terminals on the bus. The bus controller communicates with the host and backup, respectively, while the monitor terminal monitors the host/backup dual machine and compares the sent data with the running result of the monitor itself. The output is determined through a two-out-of-three mechanism to detect faults within the RT subsystem. If the running result of the monitor is consistent with one terminal, but inconsistent with the other, the latter is deemed to be one that has failed. CPU terminates the failed terminal, based on the result of the comparison described, and will simultaneously power on, initialize, and reconfigure a terminal of the cold-backup group, based on its host/backup status, to reconstitute the redundancy structure. If the running result of the monitor is *not* consistent with both terminals, the monitor is deemed to be abnormal. In such a case, the CPU will terminate the monitor, based on the result of comparison, and will select a terminal from the cold-backup group to reconfigure into a monitor, so that integration of the fault-tolerance structure is ensured.
- When $r = 3$, the subsystem of the remote terminal occupies three terminal addresses. This is a TMR structure that will monitor and compare the three machines' bus data through a monitor that acts as a voter. The bus controller performs identical communication with the three machines, and the monitor compares the data of the triple redundancy and performs a vote to locate the failed terminal. In this case, the monitor is not operating as an RT, but only compares the output data of the triple machine. In order to maintain a long-term TMR structure, it is possible to replace the failed terminal in the triple machine with multiple cold backups.

With the aid of the bus controller, it is possible to compare the data response of the redundant RT to locate the failed terminal, after which the bus controller will notify the normal terminal to terminate the failed one. However, through transplantation of the function of the remote terminal subsystem into the bus controller, this method will negatively influence the BC function, by inducing unclear task assignments, and will sever the coupling between the bus controller and the remote terminal subsystem. Consequently, it runs counter to concurrent design of the bus system.

As with the bus controller, the above described redundancy mechanism can process silent and malicious faults in the terminal fault model with the monitoring function of the monitor. The larger the value of r is, the greater the number of structural combinations and addresses occupied, and repetition of the terminal messages input and output on the bus occupies bandwidth. This jeopardizes the normal bus communication and reduces performance. The value of r needs to be balanced between reliability and system specifications.

In a real system design, the redundancy structure selection depends on the mission hierarchy and resource constraints. The following is an example of a 1553B bus fault-tolerance structure on a spacecraft. As shown in Figure 4.11, a triple machine is adopted, and the control computer connects to the external system through the bus. The BIU adopts a dual machine hot backup structure with RT address. The BIU self-detection capability enables it to detect all kinds of faults (e.g., BIU processor fault and physical fault at the local RT address) and feedback BIU health information to units of the triple machine hot backup system and data management subsystem. One end of the BIU is connected to the data management subsystem through the 1553B bus network, and the other end is connected to the three machines through an asynchronous serial port.

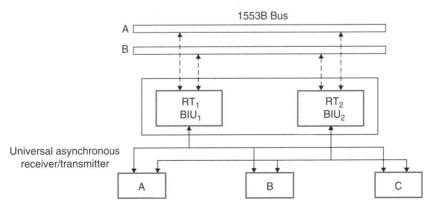

Figure 4.11 Structure of the control computer system of a spacecraft.

The following is the system's information flow and fault-tolerance strategy:

The control computer receives information from the data management subsystem: after the two BIUs (with different RT addresses) receive the program control instructions sent from the data management subsystem, the instructions are forwarded to the three hot backup machines through the 1-sending-3-receiving serial port. Considering the health status of the two BIUs, the three machines receive the two forwarded sets of instructions simultaneously, and compare the instructions so that only one of the instruction sets is implemented (if both BIUs are healthy, the data from BIU1 are selected).

The control computer sends data to the data management subsystem: after the three machines send data to the two BIUs through the 1-sending-2-receiving asynchronous serial port (the selection logic of the machine on duty will connect the asynchronous serial port to the output data while masking the output of the other two machines), each BIU forwards the data to the data management subsystem through the 1553B. Considering the health status of the two BIUs, the data management subsystem compares the received data, such that only one set of BIU forwarded healthy data is implemented (if both BIUs are healthy, the data from BIU1 are selected).

The above strategy avoids the control computer's incompetence of sending data to the data management subsystem and receiving program control instructions induced by a BIU failure with the dual redundancy fault-tolerant RT design.

4.3 The CAN Bus

Bosch, a company in Germany, developed the controller area network (CAN) bus – a serial data communication protocol for distributed real-time control applications – to perform data interchange between large numbers of controllers and test instruments in an automobile [6]. The CAN bus is a multi-master bus with twisted pair, coaxial cable and fiber optics as media. Its highest data rate is 1 Mb/s. The integration of the functions of the physical and data link layers in the CAN bus communication interface enables the CAN bus protocol to perform frame processing, which includes bit stuffing, block coding, cyclic redundancy check, and priority discrimination. The major feature of the CAN protocol is that it replaces traditional station coding with communication data block coding. Because the CAN protocol has no limit on the number of nodes (the limit of the ID range results in a maximum of 255 nodes), the variable number of nodes provides networking flexibility. In a multi-station structure, all nodes have equal right (i.e., any node can send data when the bus is free). On the basis of priority, a non-destructive bus arbitration is adopted. Priority is distinguished with message ID, which is unique in the network. Messages are broadcast so that all nodes can receive them. Each node will filter the messages depending on its individual needs.

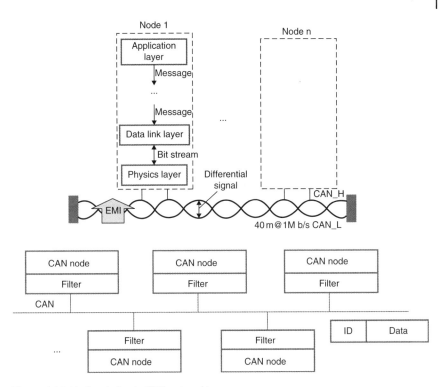

Figure 4.12 Node relation in CAN networking.

4.3.1 The Bus Protocol

Compared with the OSI 7 layer standard network model, the CAN protocol focuses on the physical and data link layers. The application layer is defined by the user. Layers 3 to 6 are NOT involved, as shown in Figure 4.13.

The physical and data link layers use the ISO 11898 protocol. Each application domain defines its application layer respectively. For example, the communication protocol file defined for the CAN bus of the spacecraft control system is an application layer protocol [7].

In the ISO 11898 protocol, CAN2.0 exists in two forms: BasicCAN, with an 11 digit identifier, and PeliCAN, with a 29 digit identifier, corresponding to the CAN2.0A and CAN2.0B protocols, respectively.

4.3.2 Physical Layer Protocol and Fault-tolerance

4.3.2.1 Node Structure

The logic structure of a node consists of computational element, bus controller, and bus transceiver, although manifestation varies as system varies, as shown in Figure 4.14.

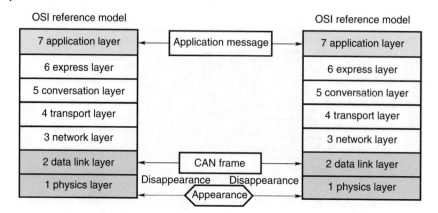

Figure 4.13 CAN Protocol Layer and OSI.

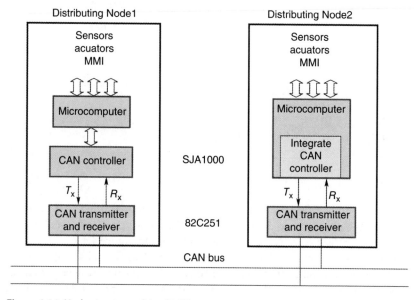

Figure 4.14 Node structure of the CAN bus.

4.3.2.2 Bus Voltage

The signal on a CAN bus is transmitted through differential voltage transfer, so that the CAN driver can avoid noise and fault-tolerance. The two signal wires are called CAN_H and CAN_L, with a static voltage of 2.5 V.

The dominant place is defined with logic 0 when the voltage of CAN_H is higher than that of CAN_L; the recessive place is defined with logic 1 when the voltage of CAN_L is higher than that of CAN_H.

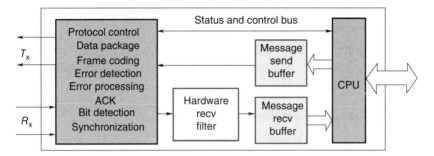

Figure 4.15 Structure of the CAN bus controller.

4.3.2.3 Transceiver and Controller

A CAN wire transceiver provides a cost-efficient interface that transforms 5 V logic level to symmetrical line level. The following are features of the transceiver:

1) Satisfies ISO 11898-2 requirement for 1 Mb/s data rate.
2) Has bus protection capability with anti-environment instant jamming.
3) Reduces RF interference (RFI) with gradient control.
4) Has thermal, power supply, and grounding short-circuit protection.
5) Experiences no influence from nodes that are NOT powered on.
6) Has a low current standby mode.

The structure of the CAN bus controller is shown in Figure 4.15.

4.3.2.4 Physical Fault-tolerant Features

Physically, there are nine possible fault scenarios [8,9] (Figure 4.16):

1) CAN_H open circuit.
2) CAN_L open circuit.
3) CAN_H short circuit to VBAT.
4) CAN_L short circuit to GND.
5) CAN_H short circuit to GND.
6) CAN_L short circuit to VBAT.
7) CAN_H short circuit to CAN_L.

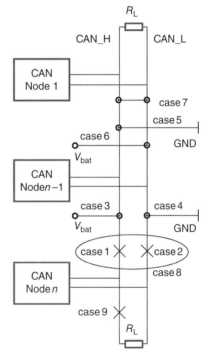

Figure 4.16 Nine fault scenarios in the CAN bus physical layer.

8) CAN_H open circuit to CAN_L.
9) Terminal resistance open circuit.

In reality, the bus will be paralyzed if the 2.5 V common mode voltage is affected by the fault. Only in scenario **9** is it possible for some local nodes to be able to carry out communication.

4.3.3 Data Link Layer Protocol and Fault-tolerance

4.3.3.1 Communication Process
The communication process of the CAN bus network is shown in Figure 4.17.

4.3.3.2 Message Sending
A node tests the bus status before sending a message. A node is able to send messages only when the bus is idle. The sending node needs to perform backward reading, to determine if the sent bit and the bit read back are identical.

A dominant digit may cover a recessive digit. When, and only when, all the nodes are sending the recessive bit, the bus is in "recessive" mode.

4.3.3.3 The President Mechanism of Bus Access
The president mechanism of bus access uses node ID to arbitrate. The smaller the ID number, the higher the priority. However, messages with higher priority should *not* interrupt messages with lower priority. This non-destructive arbitration mechanism implements the carrier sense multiple access/collision avoidance technique.

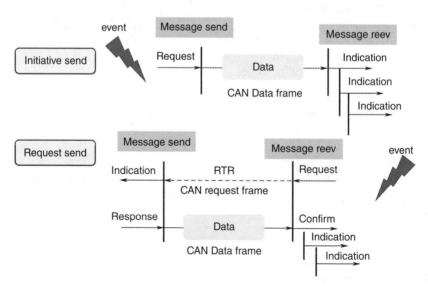

Figure 4.17 CAN bus communication process.

Carrier sense means that before sending a message each node has to check if there is data transmission on the bus. The node cannot send data until there is no ongoing data transmission on the bus. In addition, there is no physical carrier.

Multiple access means that all nodes on the network connect to the same line with the multiple point access method and broadcast data.

Collision avoidance means that the node keeps checking the sent data during the sending process, to ensure that no collision with data from other nodes has occurred. Messages with higher priority are re-sent first following a collision.

4.3.3.4 Coding

Because the non-return-to-zero (NRZ) coding method possesses more information for a given bandwidth, the message is more compact. However, NRZ cannot ensure that sufficient potential jumping edge is available for synchronization, which leads to accumulation of node timer error. Thus, the bit stuffing method is implemented, to ensure that sufficient potential jumping edge exists for synchronization.

Bit stuffing is the insertion of a bit with reversed polarity into a bit stream after the sending node has sent five consecutive identical bits. The receiving node checks the number of bits with identical polarity, and removes the stuffing bit to restore data, as shown in Figure 4.18.

4.3.3.5 Data Frame

The following are the CAN frames type:

1) *Data frame*: carries data from the transmitter to the receiver. It consists of standard and extended frames.
2) *Remote frame*: transmitted by a bus unit to request the transmission of the data frame with the same identifier.

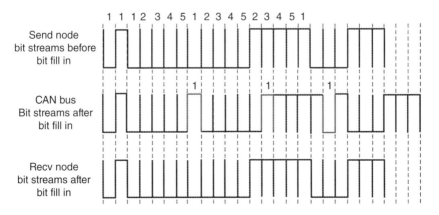

Figure 4.18 CAN bus coding.

3) *Error frame*: transmitted by any unit on detecting a bus error.
4) *Overload frame*: used to provide for an extra delay between the preceding and succeeding data or remote frames.
5) *Interframe space*: this is the bit field that separates the data frame from the other frames.

The standard frame and extended frame of the data frame correspond to the CAN2.0A and CAN2.0B protocols, respectively, as shown in Figure 4.19.

4.3.3.6 Error Detection
The following faults are detectable:

1) Bit error
2) Stuff error
3) ACK error
4) Form error
5) CRC error.

The sending node is typically responsible for detecting bit error, form error, and ACK error, whereas the receiving node is responsible for stuffing error, form error, and CRC error.

Following a bit error, stuff error, form error, or ACK error, an error frame is sent immediately after the current sending bit. Following a CRC error, the error frame is sent immediately after the bit following the ACK delimiter. After the error frame is sent, the bus will re-send the message when it is idle.

Every node has a Receive Error Counter (REC) and a Transmit Error Counter (TEC). When reception and transmission errors occur, REC and TEC increase; when the message is successfully received and transmitted, REC and TEC decrease. The value of REC and TEC may change the fault mode of the nodes. As illustrated in Figure 4.20, the following are the three fault modes of a node:

1) Error active: in this fault mode, the node's bus communication is normal. When a fault occurs, the node sends an active error frame.
2) Error passive: in this mode, the node can perform communication with constraint (sending two messages consecutively). When a fault occurs, the node sends a passive error frame.
3) Bus off: in this mode, the node can neither send nor receive messages.

If there is only one node on the bus that does *not* receive any response after sending a data frame, the node will enter error passive mode instead of bus off mode, because the maximum value of TEC counting is 128.

The CAN bus is widely used in spacecraft applications. For example, on certain space missions, the CAN bus constitutes a real-time, medium speed, information control network that connects the central computer and the IMU, solar sensor, motor control and driver module, navigation camera,

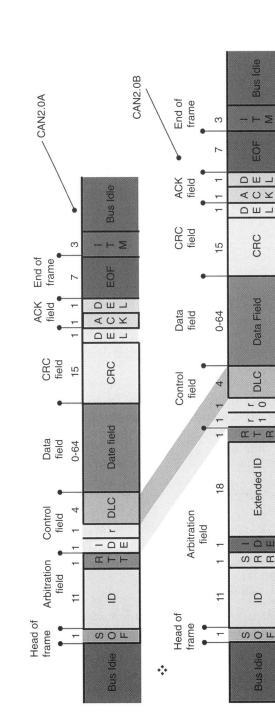

Figure 4.19 CAN bus frame formats.

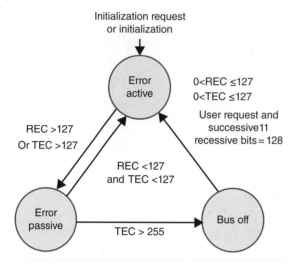

Figure 4.20 Relationship between the three fault modes.

obstacle avoidance camera, and payload to perform inter-communication. Each CAN network adopts a CAN-A or CAN-B dual bus structure, as shown in Figure 4.21 [6,9,10].

In the physical topology, the above system implements a dual bus backup design to ensure bus switching when physical failure occurs, as described in Section 4.3.2. A specific protocol that includes bus responding sequence and fault processing mechanism is designed for the application layer to ensure normal bus communication.

4.4   The SpaceWire Bus

SpaceWire is a simple and reliable bus technique for space applications. Based on IEEE1355 and low voltage differential signal (LVDS), it consists of multiple nodes and a bidirectional high-speed digital serial connection router with a data rate of 400 Mb/s [11].

SpaceWire has the following features:

1) Full duplex, point-to-point serial data transmission bus that achieves data coding and transmission with a pair of bidirectional differential signals.
2) Maximum cable length of 10 m. The mini nine-pin D connector is specifically designed for space applications.
3) A 350 mV high-speed transmission capability, achieved with the implementation of the LVDS technique.
4) Implementation of the IEEE 1355 DS coding method.

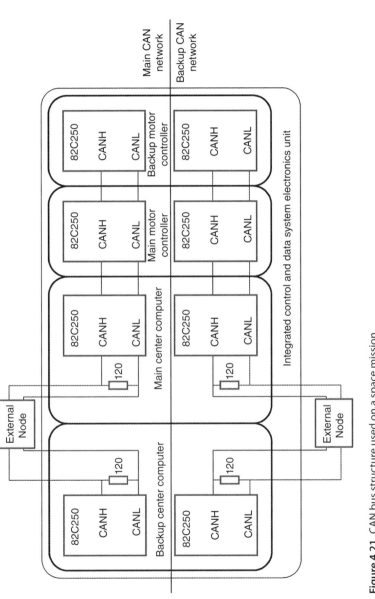

Figure 4.21 CAN bus structure used on a space mission.

5) The network consists of SpaceWire nodes connected by a SpaceWire router. The nodes can be interconnected with either SpaceWire cable for direct connection, or a SpaceWire router for indirect connection.

6) Six protocol layers: physical layer, signal layer, character layer, switching layer, network layer, and packet layer, corresponding to the physical layer and data link layer of the OSI model.

4.4.1 Physical Layer Protocol and Fault-tolerance

4.4.1.1 Connector

Connecting SpaceWire equipment together is achieved with the SpaceWire connector and SpaceWire cable. The nine-pin D type connector, based on ESA ESCC3401/701, is specifically designed for space applications. It consists of eight signal lines. In order to meet the requirement on EMC, the internal shielding of the connector should share a common signal ground with that of the SpaceWire cable.

4.4.1.2 Cable

A typical SpaceWire cable consists of four twisted pairs, with each transmitting a balanced differential signal. There is a shielding layer outside each twisted pair and its respective cable. In order to achieve high-speed data rate, the maximum cable length recommended for the SpaceWire protocol is 10 m. The cable is based on ESA ESCC3902/003.

4.4.1.3 Low Voltage Differential Signal

The SpaceWire protocol specifies that the LVDS technique should be applied for signal transmission. LVDS is a differential signal technique with low oscillation amplitude that can perform tens of megabit/s data communication with low noise and power consumption through low voltage amplitude and driving current. Focusing on SCI, IEEE P1596.3 (Published in March, 1996) defines the electrical features of LVDS and the package switching code of the SCI protocol. ANSI/EIA/EIA-644 (Published in November 1995) defines the electrical features of LVDS, specifies its maximum data rate as 655 Mb/s, and a theoretical data transmission speed of 1.823 Gb/s when implemented in no-distortion media. Because both standards specify that LVDS is irrelevant to the physical media, the interface is able to perform its normal functions as long as the signal is transmitted to the receiver through the media, with acceptable noise edge and skew tolerance [12].

It is well known that the differential data transmission method is more resistant to common mode input noise signal than single line transmission. Because the current and voltage amplitudes of the two differential signal lines are in opposite directions, and noise is coupled to both lines, the noise is neutralized when the receiving end calculates the difference between the two lines.

Voltage across 100Ω termination resistor

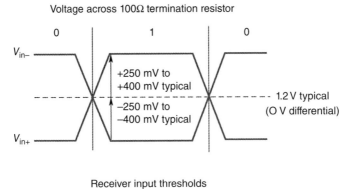

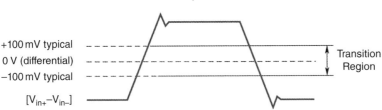

Figure 4.22 LVDS signal transmission voltage.

Noise is further reduced as a result of the constant current source's non-inclination to peak. The electromagnetic field is also smaller around the differential signal lines than around the single line, because the fields of the two lines neutralize each other. LVDS has three topology types: point-to-point (the typical topology), bidirectional communication over twisted pair, and point to multi-point. Point to multi-point is the topology most applicable to short transmission distance. LVDS is applicable both to inter-PCB connection within a unit and to inter-unit connection between units. Its typical output signal voltage is shown in Figure 4.22.

An LVDS driver adopts a logic based on the current. The driver output current provided by a 3.5 mA constant current source is transmitted to a 100 Ω terminal resistor and fed back to the driver along the media. The two pairs of transistors in the driver control the direction of the current that passes the resistor. When the transistor marked "+" is open, and the transistor marked "−" is off, the current with the direction shown in Figure 4.23 by the arrow sets up a positive voltage on the resistor, otherwise, the reverse current sets up a negative voltage. Hence, effective logic "0" and logic "1" are produced. The LVDS specification requires that the LVDS receiver possesses high input resistance, to ensure that most of the current passes through the terminal resistor. The 3.5 mA constant current source produces a 350 mV voltage.

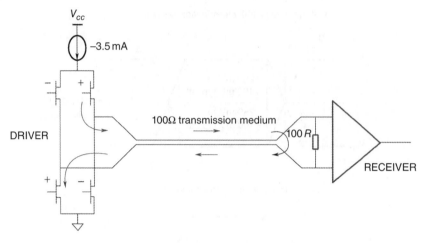

Figure 4.23 Operating principle of LVDS.

The following features of LVDS make it attractive for data transmission:

1) Its virtually constant driving current reduces current source noise swings.
2) Elimination of potential difference between the ground of the LVDS driver and receiver enables tolerance to ± 1 V grounding potential difference.
3) Noise immunity resulting from application of twisted pair.
4) Neutralization of weak electromagnetic field produced by small current signal with reversed direction.
5) No need for specific power supply to provide electricity.
6) The receiving end needs only a 100 Ω terminal resistance.
7) Safe operation with fault – that is, the receiver is high (*not* activated) in the following abnormal scenarios: the receiver is powered on, the driver is not powered on, input short circuit, input circuit broken, etc.
8) Power consumption of each driver/receiver pair is 50 mW, compared with 120 mW for ECL.

4.4.1.4 Data Filter (DS) Coding

In the SpaceWire protocol, data is transmitted with the NRZ coding. NRZ coding means that the voltage remains constant within a code-element interval – that is, instead of logic high or low, voltage level switching is used to distinguish "1" and "0." The data change as the voltage level switches; conversely, the data remain the same as that of the previous clock cycle when there is no voltage level switching [12].

The NRZ signal is transmitted through the D signal line of the SpaceWire node, and detected with the corresponding node's D signal receiver. Meanwhile, the node's S signal line transmits a filter signal that is received by the

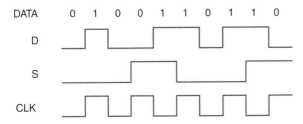

Figure 4.24 Data filter coding.

corresponding node's S signal receiver. The filter signal changes when there are two consecutive NRZ data bits. The exclusive OR (XOR) calculation between data signal and filter signal produces a signal that can be used as a synchronous clock for data transmission. As shown in Figure 4.24, the CLK signal can be produced with XOR calculation between the D and S signals, and the S signal can be produced via XOR calculation between the D and CLK signals.

The SpaceWire protocol adopts a data filter coding strategy in order to increase the tolerance to signal skew. Consequently, a maximum tolerance of 1 bit time can be achieved, compared with the normal data and clock coding strategy's 0.5 bit time. Both IEEE1355-1995 and IEEE1394-1995 employ this data filter coding strategy.

One SpaceWire communication link consists of two pairs of differential signals, which send data and filter signals in opposite directions – that is, a total of eight lines are needed to perform bidirectional full duplex communication.

As a high-speed serial bus, the maximum data transmission speed of SpaceWire is 400 Mb/s; hence, the influence of skew and jitter cannot be over-emphasized. Many factors can result in signal jitter and skew, such as cable connector, PCB wiring, and transmitter and receiver circuits. Therefore, the maximum data rate of different systems varies.

4.4.2 Data Link Layer Protocol and Fault-tolerance

4.4.2.1 Packet Character

A SpaceWire data packet consists of SpaceWire characters. The following is an introduction to the SpaceWire character definition and parity check strategy.

The SpaceWire protocol defines two types of characters: data character, and control character and code.

- *Data character*: With a length of 10 bits, a data character comprises eight bits of data, one bit for parity checking, and one bit that is used as the data control flag, as shown in Figure 4.25. When the data control flag is "0," the current packet being sent is a data character; otherwise, the packet being sent is a control character. The lowest data bit is transmitted first in the sending sequence.

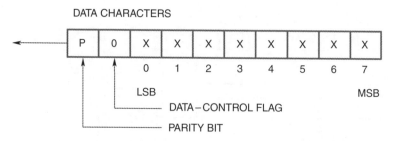

Figure 4.25 SpaceWire data character.

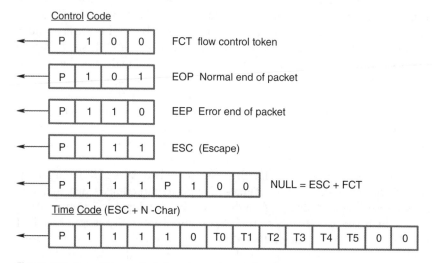

Figure 4.26 SpaceWire control character and control code.

- *Control character*: With a length of 4 bits, a control character comprises two control bits, one parity check bit, and one data control flag bit. When the data control flag is "1," the current packet being sent is a control character; otherwise, the packet being sent is a data character. The two control bits form four combined coding modes and four control characters – namely, ESC, EOP, EEP, and FCT.
- Control code: The SpaceWire protocol defines two types of control codes – NULL and TimeCode. The NULL control code, which consists of one ESC and one FCT, is used to initialize the communication link and maintain the activated link. TimeCode control code, which consists of one ESC and one data character, with six bits of time information stored in T0-T5, is used for time distribution of the SpaceWire network.

The SpaceWire control character and control code are shown in Figure 4.26.

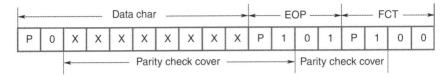

Figure 4.27 Coverage area of SpaceWire parity check.

4.4.2.2 Packet Parity Check Strategy

In every data or control character, there is a parity check bit to detect fault in the data or the control character. As shown in Figure 4.27, the parity check bit either covers the eight preceding bits of the data, plus the parity check bit and the data control flag immediately after, or it covers the two preceding control bits plus the parity check bit and the data control flag immediately after.

In addition to the scenarios described above, focus will be on the SpaceWire transmission mode after the communication link is reset and link failure, in which case the data and filter signal are set to zero. After the transmitter is activated, because the first character sent is NULL and an even parity check strategy is implemented, the first data bit on the D signal line is the parity check bit with value "0." Thus, the first step signal in the communication link occurs on the filter signal line.

4.4.2.3 Packet Structure

Following the definition in IEEE 1355-1955, a SpaceWire packet consists of three sections: packet header, data block, and packet ending marker. The header includes zero or several data characters in a table to provide the destination node's address or transmission route. The data block stores the data to be sent. The SpaceWire protocol defines two types of packet-ending markers:

1) EOP: Normal packet end marker.
2) EEP: Faulty packet end marker, i.e., it indicates that a fault occurred during packet transmission.

Because the SpaceWire protocol does not define a starting marker for packet transmission, the first data character immediately after the packet ending marker is the start of the next packet. Further, the SpaceWire protocol supports packet routing in the network.

4.4.2.4 Communication Link Control

The communication link control is defined at the SpaceWire exchange layer, which categorizes the above SpaceWire data character, control character, and control code into L_Char and N_Char. L_Char includes FCT and ESC of the control character, control code NULL, and TimeCode. The other control and data characters all belong to N_Char. For the purpose of initializing the

SpaceWire communication link and switching the encoder/decoder state, transmission of L_Char is limited at the exchange layer, and does *not* reach the packet layer. N_Char can be transmitted to the packet layer, as its function is to confirm the end of packet transmission and process fault. The SpaceWire communication link control employs a strategy that uses data stream control token. When the data stream control token is transmitted from node A to node B, node A is ready to receive data from node B. The stream control token is as follows:

1) A node sends a stream control token to signify that its receiving buffer has enough space for more than eight N_Chars.
2) There is an N_Char counter inside both the transmitter and receiver of a node, with 56 as the maximum value used for counting the number of N_Chars transmitted and received.

SpaceWire's exchange layer specifies the setup time for the communication link, of which the reset interval of the data and filter signals is 555 ns and the detection time for communication link disconnection fault is 727 ns (eight clock cycles) – 1000 ns (10 clock cycles).

The following is a detailed analysis of the SpaceWire encoder/decoder, which is the core of the protocol. According to the SpaceWire exchange layer protocol used, the encoder/decoder consists of state machine, transmitter, and receiver [12–15].

4.4.2.4.1 State Machine

The state machine of the SpaceWire encoder/decoder controls all the operations of the link interface, including initialization of the link, normal operation, and fault recovery service. The six states of SpaceWire and state switching are illustrated in Figure 4.28.

1) *Error-reset state.* In the error-reset state, the system switches when it reconfigures itself, current transmission is interrupted, and fault occurs in the communication link initialization process. In this state, the transmitter and receiver should be reconfigured. When the reset signal is invalid and delayed for more than 6.4 μs, the state machine switches to the error-wait state unconditionally.
2) *Error-wait state.* This state can only be reached from the error-reset state. In the error-wait state, the receiver is started and the transmitter is in the reset state. If a NULL is received, the condition for gotNULL is set up. During normal operation, the error-wait state will switch to the ready state unconditionally after a 12.8 μs delay. The state machine will switch to error-reset state if a communication link disconnection fault occurs in the error-wait state, or a parity check error occurs after the gotNULL condition has been setup, or an escape fault occurs, or a character other than NULL is received.

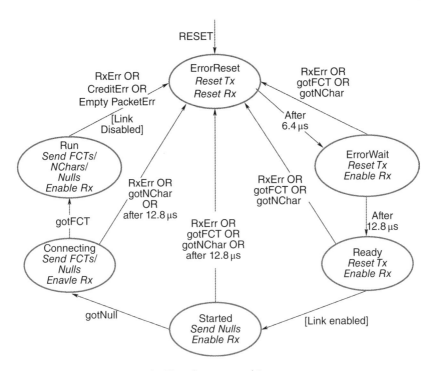

RESET

ErrorReset
Reset Tx
Reset Rx

RxErr OR
CreditErr OR
Empty PacketErr

RxErr OR
gotFCT OR
gotNChar

[Link
Disabled]

After
6.4 µs

Run
Send FCTs/
NChars/
Nulls
Enable Rx

ErrorWait
Reset Tx
Enable Rx

RxErr OR
gotNChar
OR
after 12.8 µs

RxErr OR
gotFCT OR
gotNChar

gotFCT

After
12.8 µs

Connecting
Send FCTs/
Nulls
Enavle Rx

RxErr OR
gotFCT OR
gotNChar OR
after 12.8 µs

Ready
Reset Tx
Enable Rx

gotNull

Started
Send Nulls
Enable Rx

[Link enabled]

Figure 4.28 SpaceWire encoder/decoder state machine.

3) *Ready state.* This can only be reached from the error-wait state. In ready state, the communication link interface begins initialization when required. The receiver is then started and the transmitter is in reset state. If a NULL is received, gotNULL is setup. The state machine remains at Ready, and does not switch to Started until the Link Enable signal is True. In the Ready state, the state machine switches to the Error-reset state if a communication link disconnection fault occurs, a parity check error occurs after the got-NULL condition has been setup, an Escape fault occurs, or a character other than NULL is received.

4) *Started state.* This can only be reached from the Ready state, after the communication link has been established. On entering the Started state, the 12.8 µs timeout counter starts counting. The receiver starts and the transmitter sends NULL. If NULL is received, gotNULL is setup, after which a switch is made to the Connecting state. In the Started state, before switching to the Connecting state, the protocol specifies that the transmitter should send at least one NULL character. Further, if a communication link error, parity check error, an Escape fault is detected, or a character other than NULL is received, the state machine switches to the Error-reset state.

When the timeout counter reaches 12.8 µs, the state machine immediately switches to the Error-reset state.

5) *Connecting state.* This is reached from the started state. On entering the connecting state, a 12.8 µs timeout timer starts counting. The transmitter and receiver are in the starting state, ready to send FCT and NULL. If an FCT is received (now the gotNULL condition is established), the state machine transfers to the Run state. In this state, if any errors such as communication link disconnection, parity error, escape error or the received data are not NULL or FCT, the state machine transfers to the Error-Reset state immediately. If the configured 12.8 µs timeout is reached, the state machine also transfers to the Error-Reset state immediately

6) *Run State.* This is reached from the Connecting state. In the Run state, the receiver and transmitter operate normally, sending and receiving TimeCode, FCT, N_Char, and NULL. If the communication link interface is not started, a broken fault, parity check error, or Escape fault occurs, or a Credit fault is detected, the state machine switches to the Error-reset state immediately.

Figure 4.29 illustrates the initialization of a link. Nodes A and B are the two ends of the link. These two nodes can transmit FCT only after receiving a NULL character. Therefore, when both A and B receive FCT, a bidirectional link is established between the ends. NULL and the handshaking sequence of FCT ensures that the bidirectional link is completed before normal operation begins.

The time required for the communication link to enter the Run state from the Started state depends on the time required to transmit three NULLs and two FCTs. Node A starts and sends a NULL; Node B then sends a NULL on receiving the NULL from node A and an FCT; Node A then sends another NULL and FCT on receiving the NULL from Node B. It takes approximately 2 µs for the communication link to switch to the Run state after both nodes A and B have received FCTs.

4.4.2.4.2 Transmitter

A transmitter performs data encoding and transmission using the data filter encoding technique, based on the state of the local and transmitting nodes. If there is no need to send TimeCode, FCT, and N_Char, the transmitter will keep sending NULL to maintain the communication link activated. If the buffer of the destination node has sufficient space to store eight or more N_Chars, the transmitter will send an N_Char on receiving the FCT sent from the destination node.

A transmitter possesses the following four states:

1) *Reset state.* In this state, the transmitter cannot send any data.
2) *Transmitting NULL character state.* In this state, the transmitter sends NULL only to setup/maintain the communication link activated.

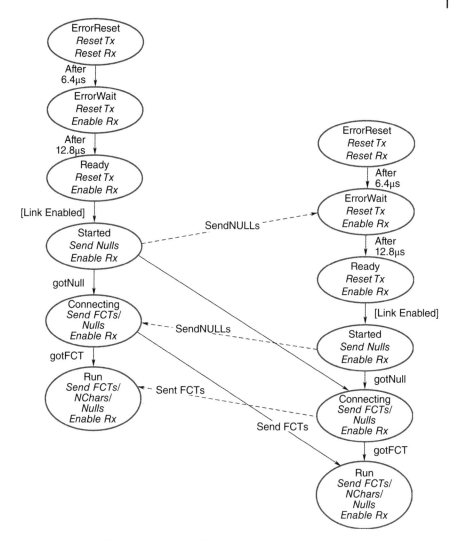

Figure 4.29 SpaceWire communication link initialization procedure.

3) *Transmitting FCT/NULL state.* The major purpose of the transmitter is to setup a communication link between the source node and the destination node. Therefore, only FCT or NULL is transmitted.

4) *Normal operating state.* In this state, the transmitter is able to send all data or control code.

The following is the focus of a transmitter:

1) The core state machine of the SpaceWire encoder/decoder is responsible for state switching.

2) When the buffer of the destination node has enough space to store eight or more N_Chars, the source node transmitter will send N_Chars on receiving the FCT sent from the destination node.
3) TimeCode transmitting is possible only when the transmitter is in the normal operating state.

4.4.2.4.3 Receiver

A receiver's major function is to capture and decode data filter signal while producing an N_Char sequence to transmit to the host. Before the receiver receives the first NULL character, any N_Char, L_Char, parity check error, or Escape fault is ignored. After the receiver receives the first NULL character, the corresponding fault detection mechanism will begin. The fault detected is transmitted to the core state machine of the encoder/decoder. In addition, after the first data bit arrives (i.e., the voltage level of the first signal transmitted is detected on data and filter signal line), the receiver will start the link disconnection detection mechanism.

A receiver has the following four states:

1) *Reset state.* In this state, no operation is performed.
2) *Enabled state.* In this state, the receiver has started and is waiting to receive the first NULL.
3) *GotBit state.* In this state, the receiver has received the first bit of the data filter signal line and has started link disconnection detection.
4) *GotNull state.* In this state, the receiver has received the first NULL and has started a series of fault detection mechanisms.

It is worth emphasizing that the SpaceWire core state machine controls receiver state switching. The receiver's clock signal is produced with the XOR calculation between the data and filter signals of the communication link.

4.4.3 Networking and Routing

4.4.3.1 Major Technique used by the SpaceWire Network
A SpaceWire network implements the following five techniques [13,14]:

4.4.3.1.1 Data Flow Control Technique
Data stream control is used to manage packet movement from one node/router to another node/router. A node or router is able to transmit data when the data buffer of the destination receiving node or router is free. If the receiving data buffer is full, the receiver informs the source node to stop transmitting. SpaceWire utilizes a stream control token to manage the movement of data from one node/router to another.

4.4.3.1.2 Wormhole Routing
"Wormhole routing" is a special type of packet routing. Every packet header has a destination node address that determines the packet's routing and

destination in the network. On receiving a packet, after checking the destination address, the router switch selects one of its ports on which to output the packet. If the chosen port is idle, the packet is sent to it immediately, and the port is marked "busy" until the last data character passes through the router – that is, the router has detected a packet ending marker. Wormhole routing requires a reserved buffer with a certain capacity in each router. Packets are stored in this buffer before they are sent.

4.4.3.1.3   Header Deletion
Header deletion is a simple and effective technique for packet transmission in any network. As shown in Figure 4.30, the first data character of the packet is used for determination of the router output port address. On receiving a packet, the router checks the first destination marker to determine the output address, then outputs the packet. After the packet passes the router, the first destination marker is deleted, and the second destination marker becomes the current first destination marker for the ensuing routing.

4.4.3.1.4   Virtual Channels
One data link channel may be used by multiple source nodes to transmit packets to each destination. Each source-destination node pair forms a virtual channel that is mapped onto a physical channel consisting of a communication link and router.

This concept is extendable between the source and destination nodes. For example, a processor device on the network may have multiple tasks running, which can receive information from other operating processors. When a packet reaches its destination node, its header is checked to determine if the packet is the needed information. For needed information, the packet header is deleted and the content stored in the buffer, waiting to be read by the destination node.

4.4.3.1.5   Packet Address Encoding Technique
Three types of packet address encoding techniques are employed by a SpaceWire network: route address coding, logic address coding, and regional address coding.

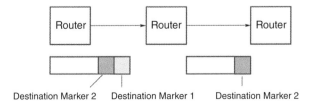

Destination Marker 2   Destination Marker 1   Destination Marker 2

Figure 4.30 Header deletion in SpaceWire.

In route address coding, routing in the network is carried out with a series of router output port numbers. In this case, fewer gates are needed, and operation is relatively easy. The disadvantage of this technique is that the destination address may be very large, the length of which depends on the position of the node in the network (relative to the source node) if the route passes through several routers. Its advantage is that the structure of the router can be simpler, because complex packet addresses are processed at the source node.

In logic address coding, every destination node has a unique number or logic address. The source node is able to transmit information to the destination node, as long as the logic address of the destination node is marked on the packet. Every router has a routing table in order to support logic addressing. For any given logic address, the router determines which port is used to transmit the packet, based on the routing table.

Regional address coding is a joint application of the logic address and header deletion techniques. In this scenario, for every logic address, the routing table includes content on whether the packet header is deleted or maintained. A simple logic address is implemented for local logic, whereas the packet to be sent to the distant node utilizes a dual logic address (or a logic address that is more applicable to the network). In the latter scenario, the first logic address represents the route from the source region to the destination region, and the second logic address represents the logic address within the destination region. After the packet reaches the destination region, the router transmits the packet to the destination region, and deletes the first logic address so that the second logic address is visible, then routing can start. Regional address coding can effectively reduce the number of routers necessary for applications that need to transmit packets to distant regions.

4.4.3.2 SpaceWire Router

According to the above technique and real space applications, the SpaceWire protocol specifies the following provisions for router constitution, routing strategy, Wormhole routing, and packet transmission:

4.4.3.2.1 *SpaceWire Router*

A SpaceWire router consists of a number of SpaceWire communication link interfaces (Encoders/Decoders) and routing matrixes.

A routing matrix should be able to transmit received data from one interface to another, and send out from the latter. Every link interface consists of an input interface and an output interface.

A SpaceWire router is able to transmit packets received to their destinations. The output port is determined by the packet's destination address.

4.4.3.2.2   Routing Strategy

In accordance with the above definition of the router, the SpaceWire protocol specifies that the final chosen routing strategy consists of the following two types:

1) route address type;
2) a combination of route, logic, and regional addresses.

In addition, the protocol has the following rules:

1) The number of routes shall *not* exceed 32;
2) The number of logic address shall *not* exceed 224;
3) A regional logic address is applicable to a relatively large network. The maximum number of logic addresses in a regional network is 224.
4) Only the route address can be applied to port configuration access.
5) Header deletion is mainly applied to route routing.
6) Each router can delete one data character (destination marker) when applying the header deletion technique.
7) Logic address 255 is reserved.

4.4.4   Fault-tolerance Mechanism

SpaceWire's fault-tolerance mechanism is composed of three layers: exchange layer, network layer, and application layer. The exchange layer is able to detect five types of faults: communication link disconnection fault; parity check fault; Escape fault; Credit fault; and character sequence fault. When these faults are detected at the exchange layer, the following measures are taken immediately: communication link disconnection, transmitter and receiver node reconfiguration, and reconnection. In addition, the exchange layer informs the network layer of the fault detected. Note that not all faults are reported to the network layer. The exchange layer reports to the network layer when communication link disconnection, parity check, Escape, and Credit faults are detected, and the state machine of the exchange layer is in the Run state. Character sequence faults can only happen at the exchange layer state machine initialization stage, so they are not reported to the network layer [15].

The network layer is able to process the following three types of faults: link fault (fault at the exchange layer); receiving EEP fault; and invalid destination address fault. The network layer takes the following recovery steps to process link faults, which are reported to the network layer by the exchange layer:

1) Terminate the current packet transmission process and delete the packet.
2) If the fault occurred at a source or destination node, send it to the application layer.
3) If the fault occurred in a router, then a state register in the router marks the fault.

On receiving EEP faults, the measures taken by the network layer will depend on whether the faulty link interface is in the destination node or the router. In the former case, the receiving EEP event is marked and sent to the application layer, and the packet whose transmission is terminated is sent to the application layer as a normal packet. In the latter case, no special recovery method is applied to the receiving EEP fault. The processing of the EEP is the same as that of the receiving EOP.

If a packet reaches a router with an invalid destination address (i.e., the router is unable to identify the address), the packet is deleted.

SpaceWire's application layer mainly processes timeout errors, which include link initialization timeout, and packet transmission and reception timeout. The application layer leaves EEP processing to the user. For example, part of the data may be abandoned so that transmission can continue when content of the packet is unimportant and only a part of it is transmitted correctly but still usable. For important packet content, such as control information and program code, the packet is re-sent if the fault occurred in the packet content.

The high data rate and powerful networking capability of SpaceWire will be extensively applied to future spacecraft. Figure 4.31 shows an integration solution for an onboard SpaceWire electrical system.

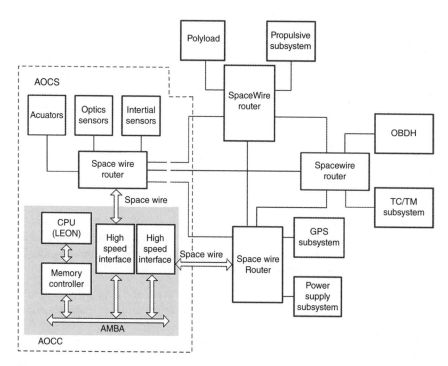

Figure 4.31 Integration solution for an onboard SpaceWire electrical system.

4.5   Other Buses

4.5.1   The IEEE 1394 Bus

IEEE 1394, a serial bus standard, originated from FireWire on the Apple Macintosh. Based on FireWire and established in 1995, IEEE 1394 has a maximum transmission speed of 400 Mb/s with a six-core cable. Adding power management, cable, and power supply specifications, IEEE published the IEEE 1394a protocol with an open controller interface for the host in 1998 [16]. The following are the major features of IEEE 1394:

1) The maximum directly connected distance between nodes should *not* exceed 4.5 m. An IEEE 1394 repeater can be used to extend the distance beyond 4.5 m. IEEE 1394 is able to support at most 16 layers of tree form network segment, and the maximum distance between nodes is 72 m (16×4.5).
2) The maximum number of devices that a segment can connect is 63. Every IEEE 1394 network can include 1023 segments so, consequently, various complex network structures can be achieved. Considering the 4.5 m maximum distance between nodes, IEEE 1394 is not applicable in wide area networks.
3) As IEEE 1394 supports hot swap, devices can be swapped in or removed from IEEE 1394 at any time without reconfiguration or negative influence on data transmission. The system can self-adjust according to the changing environment.
4) An IEEE 1394 network adopts a peer structure without server.
5) Data in the same network can be transmitted at different speeds, such as 100 Mb/s, 200 Mb/s, and 400 Mb/s.

The IEEE 1394 bus follows the 64-bit fixed addressing mode of the IEEE 1212 CSR architecture. The upper 16-bit is node ID, while the remainder rest is the internal address of the node.

Node ID comprises two parts: the first 10 bits signifies Bus_ID. If all ten bits are "1," then the Bus_ID can be broadcast to all buses; thus, the number of networks that a user can address is $2^{10} - 1 = 1023$. The ensuing six bits signify the Physical_ID for addressing the node number. If all six bits are "1," then the Physical_ID can be broadcast to all the nodes on the network; thus, the number of devices that a network can connect is $2^6 - 1 = 63$. The ensuing 48 bits constitute the buffer and private area of the node with a capacity of 2^{48}.

IEEE 1394 supports two transmission modes: Asynchronous transmission and isochronous transmission.

1) In asynchronous transmission mode, data transmission is discontinuous with sensitive reaction time, CRC detection, and resending capability after data transmission faults. IEEE 1394 allocates bandwidth based on the actual requirement of each device. Before sending information to others, a device sends a specific connection signal and waits for acknowledgment. Therefore,

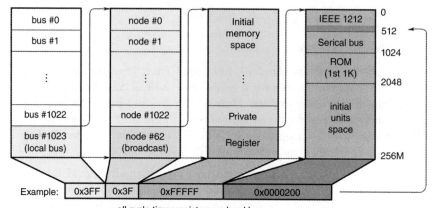

Figure 4.32 Address mapping of node internal addressing.

a device is able to track whether data transmission and reception is correct, and can inform others of the bandwidth to be used.

2) In isochronous transmission mode, the continuity of data transmission ensures that video and other similar devices maintain their respective needed bandwidth. Its features include CRC detection and easy transmission without reaction. It is applicable to video and audio data transmission, as a result of its isochronization. A typical IEEE 1394 transmission cycle is 125 μs, within which isochronous transmission is processed before asynchronous (approximately 25 μs). Asynchronous transmission can be terminated during operation, whereas isochronous transmission is never terminated or interfered with; hence, continuous data transmission is guaranteed.

An IEEE 1394 network comprises three layers: physical layer, link layer, and transaction layer. In addition, there is a bus management section, which can be defined as a management layer [17].

1) *Physical layer.* The major function of this layer is to provide electrical and mechanical connection, process data transmission and reception, and ensure that all devices can access the bus. This is achieved via hardware.
2) *Link layer.* The major function of this layer is to perform packet reception, verification, addressing, parity checking, and data framing in synchronous and asynchronous mode. This is achieved via hardware.
3) *Transaction layer.* The major function of this layer is to process asynchronous packets only through provision of Read, Write, and Lock instructions. A Read instruction provides feedback data to the instruction issuer. A Write instruction sends data to the receiver. A Lock instruction achieves the function of Read and Write by creating to and fro paths. This is achieved via firmware.
4) *Serial bus management.* The major function of bus management is to provide control capability to all buses, including guaranteeing power supply,

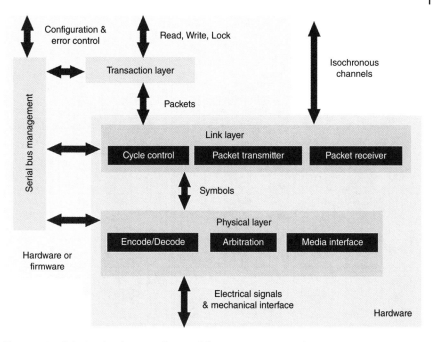

Figure 4.33 Relationship between layers of the IEEE 1394 protocol.

optimization of timing mechanism, distribution of synchronizing channel ID, and processing basic fault warning for all devices connected to the bus. It comprises three parts:

i) Bus manager: only one node can assume the role of bus manager.
ii) Node controller: any node that is not bus manager can have an independent node controller for itself.
iii) Isochronous resource manager: the major function is to allocate bandwidth and other isochronous resources.

The relationship between the layers is shown in Figure 4.33. Figure 4.34 shows the application of the IEEE 1394 bus in the telemetry acquisition system of the JPLX2000 in the United States.

4.5.2 Ethernet

Xerox developed a device interconnection technique called Ethernet in 1973. Ethernet employs a bus contention method for medium access (originating from the ALOHA network developed by the University of Hawaii). The advent of Ethernet was a major milestone in the history of LANs. Xerox, DEC, and Intel drafted a 10 Mb/s Ethernet standard for the physical and data link layers, called the Digital, Intel, Xerox (DIX) standard (i.e., DIX 1.0). The IEEE setup the IEEE 802 committee to constitute LAN standards in February 1980.

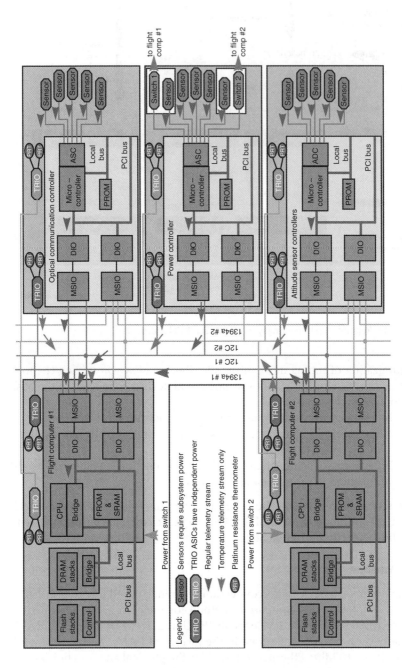

Figure 4.34 Application of the IEEE 1394 bus in the telemetry acquisition system of JPLX2000.

The committee studied a series of LAN and MAN standards, which became collectively known as the IEEE 802 standard, among which IEEE 802.3 specified bus type LAN (The IEEE 802.3 constitution process referenced many Ethernet techniques that have been realized).

DIX modified and published a new Ethernet standard called DIX 2.0 in 1982. In 1983, Novell published the Novell dedicated Ethernet frame format, which named the original 802.3 frame (802.3 raw). In 1984–1985, the IEEE 802 committee published five standards, IEEE802.1 to IEEE802.5, among which two types of frame formats were published (i.e., 802.3 SAP and 802.3 SNAP). The IEEE 802 standard was revised by the International Organization for Standardization (ISO), to form an international standard called ISO 8802.

The following four types of Ethernet frames were applied with different formats:

1) Ethernet II (DIX 2.0): the Ethernet standard frame format drafted by Xerox, DEC, and Intel in 1982, called ARPA by Cisco.
2) Ethernet 802.3 raw: the Ethernet standard frame format, published by Novell in 1983, called Novell-Ether by Cisco.
3) Ethernet 802.3 SAP: the SAP version of the Ethernet frame format, published by IEEE in 1985, called SAP by Cisco.
4) Ethernet 802.3 SNAP: the SNAP version of the Ethernet frame format, published by IEEE in 1985.

With fiber optics as media, Ethernet features such as light weight, no EMI, high transmission speed, and communication capacity make it particularly applicable to spacecraft onboard LAN [18]. Figure 4.35 shows the structure of the cabin electrical system in ESA Columbus.

4.5.3 The I^{2}C Bus

The I^{2}C bus is a serial bus developed by Philips for IC device connection. It achieves full-duplex synchronous data transmission with a serial data line (SDA) and a serial clock line (SCL). Both SDA and SCL are bidirectional IO lines, with voltage level high when the bus is idle. The I^{2}C bus standard was first published in 1992, followed by I^{2}C bus standard version 2.0 in 1998 and I^{2}C bus standard version 2.1 in 2000. The technical feature of the I^{2}C bus is master-slave type full-duplex synchronous serial bus with point-to-point broadcast communication. The I^{2}C bus is a multi-master controller bus – that is, multiple master controllers can be connected to the bus. The master-slave relationship is *not* permanent, but depends on the direction of data transmission. The maximum number of devices that can be connected to the bus is 40. With 10-bit device addressing code, the total number of device addresses is 1024.

Device interface address is independent to a large extent. In a single master system, because the I^{2}C interface possesses unique addresses and cannot send serial clock signals, it can only be used as a slave device. Devices cannot

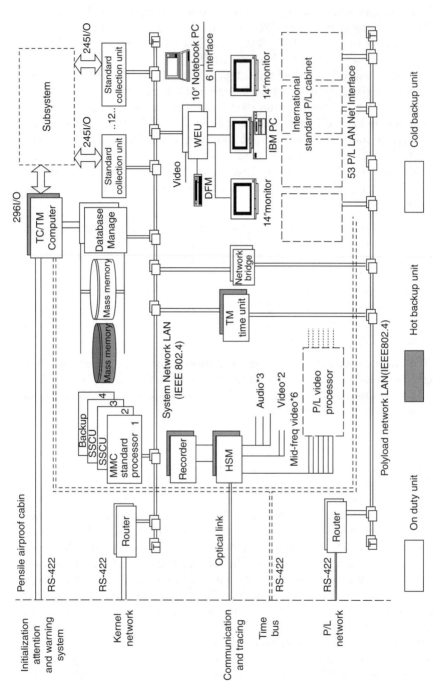

Figure 4.35 Structure of the cabin electrical system in the ESA Columbus.

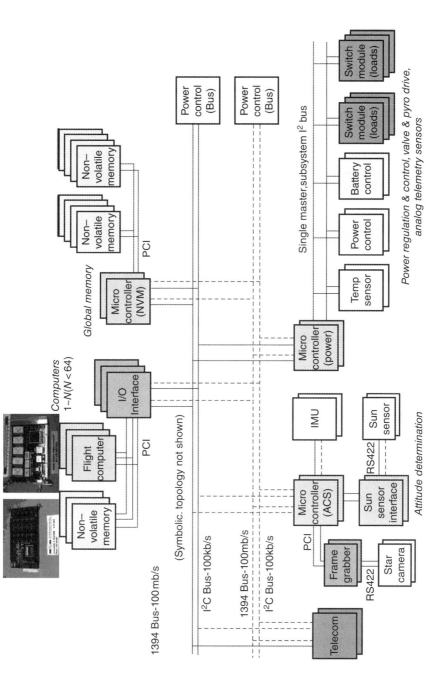

Figure 4.36 Electrical system network of the NASA X2000 program based on the I^{2}C bus.

communicate or interfere with each other. Each device may have a separate power supply. Bus arbitration comprises two steps: address bit comparison, followed by data bit comparison. The maximum transmission distance is approximately 5 m (18 feet). In standard bus working mode, the data transmission speed is 100 kb/s. In fast working mode, the maximum transmission speed is 400 kb/s. In high-speed working mode, the maximum transmission speed is 3.4 Mb/s.

Comprising an SDA line and an SCL line, the I^2C bus is a reliable multi-master serial bus with centralized addressing and data transmission protocol. All system components can be connected together via the I^2C bus, to form a single machine or a multi-machine system [19]. Figure 4.36 shows the electrical system network of the NASA X2000 program, based on the I^2C bus.

References

1 Modi N H, Armstrong J R, Tront J G, *et al* (1988). *Modeling and simulation of 1553 bus for upset tolerance experiments* [J]. IEEE Phoenix Conference on Computers and Communications, March, 16–18, 1988, Phoenix, AZ, pp. 131–135.

2 Cao Biao (2010). *Design and research of 1553B communication protocol implementation based on SoC technique.* [Master Thesis] Central South University.

3 Jifeng Li, Minggang Chai. (2011). *Design of 1553B avionics bus interface chip based on FPGA.* International Conference on Electronics, Communications and Control (ICECC).

4 Lu Xiaoye (2000). *Research on MIL-STD-1553B bus fault tolerance technology* [D]: [Master Thesis]. Beijing Institute of Control Engineering.

5 Chi Lei (2009). *Design and implementation of a fault injection system for 1553B fault-tolerant bus controller.* [Master Thesis] Harbin Institute of Technology.

6 Bosch R GmbH (1991). *CAN specification version 2.0* [S].

7 Liu Shufen, Sun Xin (2004). Study on application of CAN bus on satellites. *Aerospace Control* 22(6), 79–83.

8 Guo Xiaosong, Wang Zhenye, Yu Chuanqiang, Pan Xingjie (2009). Research of the fault tolerant redundant technology based on CAN bus. *Computer Measurement & Control* 17(1), 60–62.

9 Ni Weilin (2011). *The radiation hardening design and verification of CAN bus IP.* [Master Thesis] Xidian University.

10 Cao Xiaohua, Zhou Yong (2010). Fault-tolerant algorithm based on active request and dynamic load distribution for CAN system. *Journal of South China University of Technology (Natural Science Edition)* 38(9), 30–34.

11 Wang Rong (2005). *Research on high speed serial bus application integrated in satellite electronics* [D]. [Master Thesis] Beijing Institute of Control Engineering.

12 Marshall J R, Berger R W (2007). *A one chip hardened solution for high speed SpaceWire system implementation.* International SpaceWire Conference, Dundee.

13 Niu Yuehua, Zhao Wenyan (2014). Design and analysis of a strong fault-tolerant on-board SpaceWire bus network. *Journal of Computer Applications* **34**(9), 2497–2500.

14 Zhang Hao, Wu Jun, Zhang Chunxi, Liang Jiemei, Yi Xiaosu, Wang Ming (2015). Design of backup fault tolerant protocol for SpaceWire on-board networks. *Computer Measurement & Control* **32**(2), 633–636.

15 Shen Jingshi (2011). *Design of on-board SpaceWire bus networks.* [Master Thesis] Xidian University.

16 Microprocessor and Microcomputer Standards Committee of the IEEE Computer Society (1996). *IEEE Standard for a High Performance Serial Bus* (IEEE Std 1394-1995).

17 Wolfram K D (2004). *A new radiation-hardened satellite onboard LAN based on IEEE Std 1394.* Space 2004 Conference and Exhibit, San Diego, CA, USA, 1–12.

18 Evan W (2002). *Ethernet for space flight applications.* Aerospace Conference Proceedings, 9–16 March, 2002, IEEE. 4: 4_1927–4_1934.

19 Elson J F (2012). *Methods for trustworthy design of on-chip bus interconnect for general-purpose processors.* [Master Thesis] Naval Postgraduate School, Monterey, CA.

5

Software Fault-Tolerance Techniques

This chapter summarizes the causes of software faults and their effects, then briefly introduces the key techniques of software fault detection, isolation, and recovery, as well as the architecture of software fault-tolerance. Some software fault-tolerance techniques are emphatically discussed, such as single-version software techniques, multiple-version software techniques, and multiple data representation techniques.

5.1 Software Fault-tolerance Concepts and Principles

5.1.1 Software Faults

Software faults are always due to flaws in the design of the system. When the flaws are stimulated during software execution, errors occur. If there is no error-handling procedure, system failure occurs. Software faults have the following properties:

1) They are accidental man-made internal design faults, introduced by mistakes in design and implementation. Software does not deteriorate with age.
2) They are not routine states, and can only be stimulated under special conditions.
3) They are always diffusible; as soon as they are stimulated, the errors they cause can proliferate to other modules, resulting in new errors.

A classic example of software faults in the aerospace field is the inertial guidance computer software fault on Ariane 5. In this case, floating-point exception caused the backup and primary inertial guidance computers to crash, resulting in a catastrophe.

Fault-Tolerance Techniques for Spacecraft Control Computers, First Edition.
Mengfei Yang, Gengxin Hua, Yanjun Feng and Jian Gong.
© 2017 National Defense Industry Press. All rights reserved.
Published 2017 by John Wiley & Sons Singapore Pte. Ltd.

5.1.2 Software Fault-tolerance

Many measures are adopted during development in an effort to develop fault-free software. These measures include process control, testing, model-checking, and theorem proving. However, it is virtually impossible to design and implement a completely fault-free system, at a reasonable implementation cost at least, because of the complexity of software. Therefore, software fault-tolerance techniques are essential [1].

Software fault-tolerance has two definitions: narrow-definition and broad-definition. In narrow-definition software fault-tolerance, the fault caused by software is solved and system reliability maintained. Narrow-definition software fault-tolerance is implemented during software development, and its general measures include multi-version and data diverse software fault-tolerance techniques.

Broad-definition software fault-tolerance can solve faults caused not only by software, but also by hardware, such as fetching of wrong instructions and missing data, which are caused by SEU and Single Event Transient (SET). Two types of software fault-tolerance techniques are available to deal with transient faults: time-based and space-based redundancy. With time-based redundancy, software is executed many times in parallel or in serial, without violating the timing constraint. If all the results are the same, then they are considered to be accurate; otherwise, there must be at least one incorrect result. A typical time-based software fault-tolerance technique is Recovery Blocks (RcB). Space-based redundancy corrects transient faults using techniques such as erasure-corrected code, verification code, and data diversity. The typical space-based redundancy is software-implemented hardware fault-tolerance based on fault-tolerant compiler, and two-pass adjudicators (TPA). Nowadays, software fault-tolerance techniques are widely applied in fields requiring high reliability, such as aerospace, nuclear power plants, communication, and transportation.

In a narrow sense, the principle of software fault-tolerance is based on two small probabilities: it is virtually impossible for different software developers to make the same mistakes for the same object, and also for the same software to encounter the same transient misdata at different times. In a broad sense, the principle of software fault-tolerance is still the result of time-based and space-based redundancy.

In general, both narrow-definition and broad-definition software fault-tolerance utilize four steps for fault-tolerance:

- Fault detection, in which an existing fault is identified.
- Fault diagnosis, in which the fault is located and the reason for the fault determined.
- Fault isolation, in which failure pervasion is prevented.
- Fault recovery, in which fault status is restored to the fault-free status.

Some special software fault-tolerance implementations may omit one or more steps. For example, they may only detect the fault, but not locate it.

5.1.3 Software Fault Detection and Voting

Fault detection is used to observe the existing fault, whereas voting is used to obtain the right result from several parallel or serial results.

Software fault detection includes the following mechanisms, among which the first four items are called acceptance tests (AT):

1) *Reasonableness tests.* These mechanisms (including integrity check, reality check, software assertions, etc.) are used as ATs to determine if the result is reasonable, according to some constraints (e.g., pre-computed ranges and expected output structure). Those constraints are usually specifically applicable in a special field.

2) *Function reversal.* Before execution, the original input is stored. After execution, an inverse operation is applied to obtain the possible input. The possible input is compared with the original and, if they differ, then an error is deemed to have occurred.

3) *Golden run comparison.* In this mechanism, the input is a given value, and the corresponding result is known beforehand. If the output is not equal to the expected result, then a fault is deemed to have occurred. However, even though the golden run comparison may be successful, the fault may still exist.

4) *Timeout.* When an activity has a deadline, an observer sets a timer to signal an alarm at this deadline. If the activity finishes before its deadline, the observer cancels the timer and no alarm is sent. On the other hand, if the timer expires, the observer deduces that the activity has failed to meet its deadline, and signals an error.

5) *Heartbeat.* A heartbeat is a regular (e.g., periodic) signal notifying that an observed system is fully or partially operational (alive). An observer monitors the heartbeat, and an error is deemed to have occurred when the observer no longer observes the expected heartbeat signal.

6) *Error detecting code.* Encoding enriches a data item with a generated redundancy value, following a strict mathematical recipe. The augmented data item is used by the reader to validate the received information. Decoding of a validated augmented data item consists of applying the reverse mapping of the recipe to decode the original data item. If validated, the read data item is trusted; otherwise, if the reverse mapping cannot be applied (i.e., if it is invalidated), an error is deemed to have been detected.

7) *Resource consumption delimiter.* In this case, a resource manager manages the resources. The resource manager receives requests for resources, which it subsequently grants or denies and enforces authorizations upon resource consumers. A violating resource request is detected as an error. A typical

example of this mechanism is the resource Blueprint mechanism in the architecture of ARINC-653.

Voters compare the results from two or more variants. When there are only two results to examine, the decision mechanism is called a comparator. There are many variations of voting algorithms, according to the voting mechanisms:

1) Exact Majority Voter selects the value of the majority of the variants as its adjudicated result. This voter is also called the m-out-of-n voter. The agreement number, m, is the number of versions required to match for system success. The total number of variants, n, is rarely more than three. m is equal to $\lceil (n + 1)/2 \rceil$, where $\lceil \; \rceil$ is the ceiling function. For example, if $n = 3$, then m is any value greater than one.
2) Median Voter selects the median of the values input to the voter (i.e., the variant results, R) as its adjudicated result. The median is defined as the value whose position is central in the set R (if n is odd); otherwise, the value in position $n/2$ or $(n/2 + 1)$ (if n is even) is used.
3) Mean Voter selects the mean or weighted average of the values input to the voter (i.e., the variant results, R) as the correct result.
4) Consensus Voter is a generalization of the majority voter. A consensus is a set of matching variant results, not necessarily a majority. For example, the consensus of variant results (a, a, c, b, d) is a, and the consensus of variant results (a, a, b, b, c) is either a or b.

5.1.4 Software Fault Isolation

Complex systems usually contain boundaries to prevent errors in one part propagating to other parts, which is a basic software fault-tolerance technique. Because a software fault mainly propagates by violating resource consumption (such as overconsumption), a resource consumption delimiter is a key point of software fault isolation. The operating system (OS) is the key executor of software fault isolation, because it is in charge of resource management. For example, in the ARINC-653 OS in the integrated modular avionics (IMA) system, the blueprint mechanism, also called table-driven, is used to delimit resource requests, such as the maxima, ranges, and duration. In fact, blueprint is not inflexible in some sense, so it is mainly applied in the IMA field rather than the consumer electronics field.

In general, each fault should have a determinate measure to isolate the fault in the embedded real-time system. For example, in the ARINC-653's OS, the health monitor (HM) function specifies the fault isolation architecture, the process and the determinate responses for all level faults, from the lowest process-level, the partition-level, the module-level, to the system-level. The determinate responses for all level faults are specified in a static table, which is part of the blueprint. The OS monitors all the faults. When a failure occurs, the corresponding responses are called to isolate or mask the failure.

5.1.5 Software Fault Recovery

Fault recovery is part of the larger process, comprising four software fault-tolerance steps: fault detection, diagnosis, isolation, and recovery. The process is a set of activities whose goal is to remove errors and their effects from the computational state before a failure occurs. There are two kinds of recoveries: backward recovery and forward recovery.

When an error occurs in a program, backward recovery attempts to return the system to a correct or error-free state by restoring or rolling back the system to a previously saved state, prior to the erroneous state. Figure 5.1 illustrates backward recovery [2]. It is usually assumed that the previously saved state is error-free. If the saved state is not error-free, the same error may cause problems in the recovery attempt.

Backward recovery can be applied to many objects, such as programs, subprograms, and processes. If communication and coordination of interacting processes using backward recovery (e.g., nested recovery blocks) are not synchronized, a domino effect may occur. This happens when one process rolls back to its previous checkpoint, which in turn causes another process to roll further back (to its checkpoint), which in turn causes the first process to roll back further, and so on. Backward recovery is applied widely in the cold-standby computer of long-life satellites. When a failure occurs in the software of one cold-backup computer, the watchdog will reset the software, then the software rolls back to the saved error-free states. Rollback recovery in Section 5.2.1 and recovery blocks (RcB) in Section 5.3.1 are typical forward recovery techniques.

Forward recovery brings the system from its present erroneous state forward to a correct new state, from which it can continue to execute.

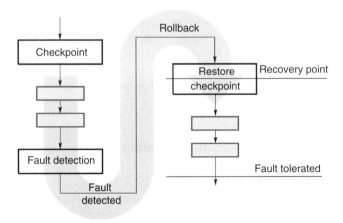

Figure 5.1 Backward recovery.

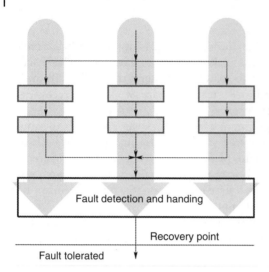

Figure 5.2 Forward recovery using redundant processes.

The correct state can be obtained via a variety of measures, such as executing redundant software in parallel and voting the right result (see Figure 5.2), or a kind of forward error correction encoding technique. Forward recovery can mask faults with little time overhead, so it can be used in real-time fields [3]. N-version Programming (NVP), Section 5.3.2, is a typical software forward recovery technique. Some software fault-tolerance techniques can be used for both forward and backward recovery – for example, TPA, Section 5.4.4. When the first-pass adjudicator fails, the second-pass adjudicator, which is backward recovery, is executed. During each adjudicator, the voting process used is typical forward recovery. Table 5.1 compares forward recovery with backward recovery.

5.1.6 Classification of Software Fault-tolerance Techniques

Currently, there are three categories of software fault-tolerance techniques: single-version software fault-tolerance techniques that tolerate transient fault; multiple-version software fault-tolerance techniques that tolerate faults of the software itself; and data diversity-based software fault-tolerance techniques. Each category of software fault-tolerance technique has many sub- categories, as shown in Table 5.2.

5.2 Single-version Software Fault-tolerance Techniques

The basic assumption of single-version software fault-tolerance is that the software itself is fault-free – the fault is transient. This technique generally includes (parallel or sequential) re-executing, encoding, decoding, and Runaway-trap.

Table 5.1 Backward recovery vs. forward recovery.

	Backward recovery	Forward recovery
Advantages	1) Independent of the damage caused by a fault. 2) Applicable to unanticipated faults. 3) Sufficiently general that it can be used at multiple levels in a system. 4) Conceptually simple.	1) Can tolerate permanent physical failure. 2) Fairly efficient in terms of time overhead.
Disadvantages	1) Backward recovery requires significant resources (i.e., time, computation, and stable storage) to perform checkpointing and recovery. 2) A domino effect may occur. 3) Cannot tolerate permanent physical failure.	1) Forward recovery requires knowledge of the error. 2) Much more resource consumed because multiple redundant software are executed in parallel.
Application field	General computing without real-time requirement.	Real-time control.

In sequential (parallel) re-executing, the same single-version software is executed many times successively (concurrently), and the results of each execution are voted. The theoretical basis of re-executing is that the probability of a transient fault recurring is small. The theoretical basis of encoding and decoding is that every executable-code block is protected through an encoding or signature scheme, and faults can be detected at the block entrance by verifying the signature [4].

5.2.1 Checkpoint and Restart

During software execution, the state (checkpoint) of the software is stored periodically in a reliable storage device. As illustrated in Figure 5.3, when a fault occurs, the software is restored to the fault-free checkpoint, and continues execution from this checkpoint without having to discard all the work completed up to the time of error detection [5].

Checkpoint and restart is a fault-tolerance scheme based on time redundancy. Compared with space redundancy fault-tolerance, rollback recovery is more simple and practical, and needs fewer physical resources. STAR, the early fault-tolerant computer designed by JPL/NASA, used this measure. Because rollback recovery uses the same software version to tolerate transient faults, it cannot tolerate faults caused by software bugs.

Table 5.2 Classification of software fault-tolerance techniques.

	Acronym	Fault-tolerance method
Single-version software fault-tolerance Rollback		When a fault occurs, the software backward-restores to a fault-free state (checkpoint or snapshot), which was saved periodically.
Software crash trap		Unused memory is filled with jump instructions, which point to fault-free entries.
Software-implemented hardware fault-tolerance		Software is hardened by a compiler, by which software fault-tolerance measures (such as illegal entrance detection, software trap, and code check) are inserted in executable code transparently. This technique can tolerate not only software faults, but also hardware transient faults.
Multiple-version software fault-tolerance Recovery blocks	RcB	When the primary software executes and a failure is detected by AT, alternate software is invoked to implement backward recovery.
N-version programming:	NVP	A task is executed by multi-version software, and a result is accepted only if it is adjudicated as an acceptable result, usually via a majority vote.
Distributed recovery block	Distributed recovery blocks (DRB)	Error detection by AT and forward recovery. Variants are executed in parallel.
N-self-checking programming	N-self-checking programming (NSCP)	Error detection by AT or comparison. Variants are executed in parallel.
Consensus recovery block.	CRB	Combines NVP and RcB. If NVP, which is in parallel, fails, RcB, which is sequential, is invoked.
Acceptance voting	AV	AT, then vote. Variants are executed in parallel.

Table 5.2 (Continued)

		Acronym	Fault-tolerance method
Data diverse software fault-tolerance	Data re-expression algorithms	DRA	Data re-expression is used to obtain diverse input data by generating logically equivalent input data sets; hence, some fault models are tolerated.
	N-copy programming	NCP	NCP is the data diverse complement of NVP.
	Retry block	RtB	The RtB is the data diverse complement of the recovery block (RcB) scheme.
	Two-pass adjudicators	TPA	The TPA technique is a set of combination data and design diverse software fault-tolerance techniques. It is the data diverse complement of NVP; the first run adjudicator uses the original data, while the second adjudicator uses the DRA data.

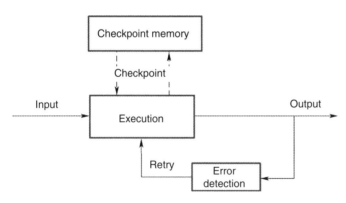

Figure 5.3 Checkpoint and restart.

The checkpoint and restart scheme has the following features:

1) This technique is particularly suited to recovery from transient faults.
2) The only knowledge required by backward recovery is that the relevant prior state is error-free.

3) It requires no knowledge of the errors in the system state.

4) The overhead introduced comprises the time to store the states and the time to compare these states. The time spent on comparison and store operations may vary significantly, depending on the system.

The checkpointing algorithms can be divided into three classes: uncoordinated, coordinated, and communication-induced. In the first class, each process takes its checkpoints independently and keeps track of the dependencies among checkpoints resulting from message communications. When a failure occurs, the dependency information is used to determine the recovery line to which the system should roll back. Uncoordinated checkpointing allows maximum process autonomy, and has low checkpointing overhead. However, this approach may suffer from a domino effect, in which the processes roll back recursively while determining a consistent set of checkpoints. In the worst case scenario, the system has to roll back to the initial states. Further, uncoordinated checkpointing requires multiple checkpoints to be stored at each process.

The second approach is to coordinate the establishing of checkpoints from different processes by using control messages, such that the set of checkpoints together form a consistent system state, which avoids the domino effect. However, in coordinated checkpointing schemes, process execution may have to be suspended during checkpointing coordinating, resulting in performance degradation.

In the third class, processes take local checkpoints (basic checkpoints) independent of each other, but these cooperate to take additional local checkpoints (forced checkpoints). This cooperation ensures that: any local checkpoint will belong to at least one consistent global checkpoint; this is accomplished by piggybacking control information onto the application message; and no additional messages are required. When a process receives a message, it uses its local information and the information carried by the message in order to decide whether it has to take a forced checkpoint to avoid useless checkpoints.

5.2.2 Software-implemented Hardware Fault-tolerance

The above single-version software fault-tolerance is implemented by the software engineer during the software coding phase – that is, it is not transparent to the software engineer. The software fault-tolerance measures can also be introduced at the source-code or executable-code level by the compiler, during the compiling procedure. Such measures are called compiler-assisted software fault-tolerance, or software-implemented hardware fault-tolerance (SIHFT). They can detect or tolerate faults in the hardware using the software method without any special hardware for error detection or fault-tolerance [6].

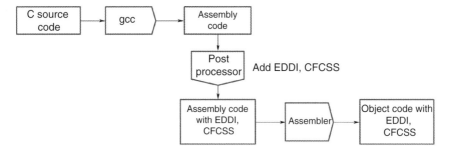

Figure 5.4 Example process used in SIHFT.

Typical examples of these measures include control-flow checking by software signatures (CFCSS), and error detection by duplicated instructions (EDDI), which were implemented on the advanced research and global observations satellite (ARGOS) by Stanford University. Figure 5.4 illustrates the scheme.

5.2.2.1 Control Flow Checking by Software Signatures (CFCSS)

A program can be considered to be a sequence of instructions, and the execution of the program can be viewed as executing instructions in a desired sequence. A sequence of instructions without any branching inside or outside, except for the last instruction, is defined as a basic block. Consequently, a program can be represented by a program graph, which consists of basic blocks and directed edges, connecting the basic blocks. If the correct execution sequence in the program graph is broken, then a control-flow error must be present.

In CFCSS, every basic block vj is identified and assigned a unique signature si when the program is compiled. A dedicated register called the global signature register (GSR) is used for control-flow checking. The GSR contains the runtime signature G associated with the current block (the block that contains the instruction currently being executed) in the program flow graph. Let Gi be the runtime value of G when the program flow is in node vi.

When control is transferred from source node vs to the destination node vd, a new runtime signature G is generated by a signature function f at the destination node of the branch $brsd$. The signature function f is defined as $f(G, dd) = G \oplus dd$, where the signature difference dd ($dd = ss \oplus sd$) is calculated in advance at compile-time and stored in the destination node vd. Before the branch $brsd$ is taken, G contains Gs (the signature ss of the source node vs). After the branch is taken, G is updated with a new value, $G = f(Gs, dd)$, based on the previous value GS and current signature difference dd. If G is equal to the signature Sd of the destination node vd, then there is no control-flow error. On the other hand, if G is different from sd, then a control-flow error must have occurred. Checking instructions are located at the top of each basic block to facilitate checking of the control flow; in other words, checking instructions are executed prior to the execution of the original instructions in the basic block.

Figures 5.5(a)–(c) demonstrate the process by which a unique signature is assigned for every basic block, the signature difference is calculated, and checking instructions are inserted in advance at the top of the basic block at compile-time. Figures 5.5(b) and (c) illustrate the checking instructions in a correct and fault control flow, respectively.

It has been shown that, for a program in which each basic block has only one source node, illegal branches violating the control flow can be detected. However, there are cases in which one basic block has many source nodes; for example, a branch-fan-in node. In Figure 5.6, the two nodes, $v1$ and $v3$, have branches to the same node, a branch-fan-in node $v5$. If $d5$ is the signature difference between nodes $v1$ and $v5$ ($d5 = s1 \oplus s5$), no problem occurs when the branch br15 is taken because $G5 = G1 \oplus d5 = s1 \oplus s1 \oplus s5 = s5$, which is the signature of node $v5$. If branch br35 is taken, however, the runtime signature G at node $v5$ is not equal to $s5$, as $G5 = G3 \oplus d5 = s3 \oplus s1 \oplus s5 \neq s5$, if $s3 \neq s1$.

However, if we use $s1 = s3$ as the signatures, then an illegal branch from $v1$ to $v4$, or from $v3$ to $v2$, will not be detected. In order to solve the problem of assigning the same signature to multiple predecessors of a branch-fan-in node, a runtime adjusting signature D is introduced. After runtime signature G is generated by the signature generation function, G is XORed with D to get the signature of the branch-fan-in node; thus, at the source node, D has to be set to the value that makes G equal to the signature of the destination node.

Figure 5.6 illustrates an example in which D is used in the branch-fan-in node. At node $v5$, one more checking instruction, $G = G \oplus D$, is added. After the signature generation function $G = G \oplus d5$, G is XORed with the D that should be determined at the source nodes v1 and v3. Because d5 is initially set to the XOR-difference between $s1$ and $s5$ ($d5 = s1 \oplus s5$), when branch br15 is taken, the updated runtime signature G is already the same as $s5$; we do not need to change G; thus, D is set to zero at $v1$ ($G5 = G5 \oplus D = s5 \oplus 0000 = s5$). When branch br35 is taken, the updated G at the first line of $v5$ is $G5 = G3 \oplus d5 = s3 \oplus (s1 \oplus s5)$. To make G equal to $s5$, G should be XORed with $s1 \oplus s3$ in the second line – that is, $G = G5 \oplus D = s3 \oplus (s1 \oplus s5) \oplus (s1 \oplus s3) = s5$. Therefore, at source node $v3$, D should be set to $D = s1 \oplus s3$.

The following is an outline of the algorithm that assigns a signature to each node in a program flow graph when a program is compiled:

1) Identify all basic blocks, build program flow graph, and number all nodes in the program flow graph.
2) Assign a signature s_i to node v_i in which $s_i \neq s_j$ if $i \neq j$, $i, j = 1, 2, ..., N$, where N is the total number of nodes in the program.

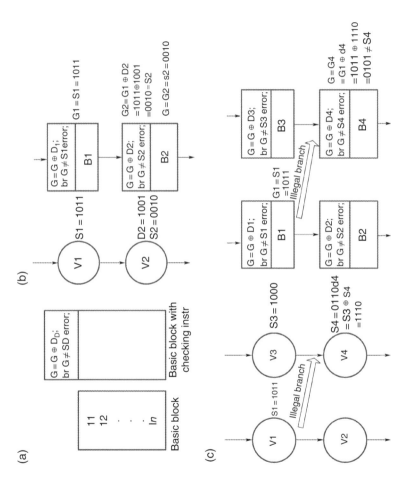

Figure 5.5 Workflow of CFCSS.

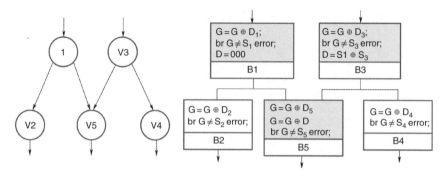

Figure 5.6 Runtime adjusting signature, D.

3) For each node v_j, $j = 1, 2, ..., N$
    3.1 For node v_j whose pred(v_j) is only one node v_i, calculate the signature difference d_j using $d_j = s_i \oplus s_j$
    3.2 For branch-fan-in node v_j whose pred(v_j) is a set of nodes v_{i1}, v_{i2}, ..., v_{iM}, determine the signature difference using one of the nodes (picked arbitrarily) as $d_j = s_{i1} \oplus s_j$. For node v_{im}, $m = 1, 2, ..., M$, insert an instruction $D_{im} = s_{i1} \oplus s_{im}$ into node v_{im}. This instruction should be located after "$br(G \neq s_j)$ error" instruction in v_{im}.
    3.3 Insert an instruction $G = G \oplus d_j$ at the beginning of node v_j.
    3.4 If v_j is a branch-fan-in node, insert an instruction $G = G \oplus D$ after $G = G \oplus d_j$ in node v_j.
    3.5 Insert an instruction '$br(G \neq s_j)$ error' after the instructions placed in either step 3.3 or 3.4.

Simulation results show that CFCSS increases the error detection capability by an order of magnitude. In programs without CFCSS, an average of 33.7% of the injected branching faults produced undetected incorrect outputs, whereas, in programs with CFCSS, only 3.1% of branching faults produced undetected incorrect outputs. An actual experiment conducted on ARGOS verified these results.

5.2.2.2 Error Detection by Duplicated Instructions (EDDI)

Duplicated instructions in EDDI have no effect on the result of the program, but errors are detected in the system at runtime. In EDDI, a storeless block is a sequence of instructions in which no instructions are stored except for the last instruction, which may be a store or a branch instruction. If the last instruction of a storeless basic block is a store instruction, a comparison instruction is placed before the store, to compare the master and shadow register values to be stored in memory. If there is a mismatch between a pair of registers for master and shadow instructions, the error can be detected by comparing these two register values. A comparison instruction compares the values of the two registers and invokes an error handler if they do not match.

The results of a fault injection simulation experiment conducted showed that EDDI can provide over 98% error detection coverage without any extra hardware. Further, an actual experiment conducted on ARGOS showed that, for a 136 days period, 198 out of 203 errors were detected by CFCSS and EDDI.

5.2.3 Software Crash Trap

When a runaway program counter references a non-code data area (e.g., unused memory space in ROM), a software trap can be used to detect the resulting error. By filling the unused ROM memory with software traps (i.e., inserting a specific error handler), the runaway counter can be captured by the specific trap, and then reset to the entry of the respective program, according to the position of the trap, so that the execution of the program can be recovered. There are several ways to deploy software traps to capture potential runaway encounters:

1) All the unused ROM can be filled with software crash traps pointing to the original entry of the program. As soon as the software crashes, it would then be reset to the entry and the program's execution would be recovered.
2) Software traps can be inserted into the unused memory segments between modules, to capture the possible runaway counter from the executions of modules. In the case of normal executions, the traps would not be triggered.
3) Software traps can be deployed in an interrupt service program (ISP). In this case, the system produces timing interrupts while the program is executing. Suppose the address boundary of the program being monitored is ADD1–ADD2; ISP will check the address (say ADD) at which the program was interrupted, and the runaway program counter is captured if ADD < ADD1 or ADD > ADD2.

5.3 Multiple-version Software Fault-tolerance Techniques

The assumption of multiple-version software is that single-version software itself has potential faults. The theoretical basis of multiple-version software is that the probability of diverse multiple-version software encountering fault concurrently is very small.

5.3.1 Recovery Blocks (RcB)

The basic RcB scheme is one of the two original diverse software fault-tolerance techniques. It was introduced in 1974 by Horning *et al.*, and is categorized as a dynamic technique. Its selection of a variant result to the output is made during program execution, based on the result of the AT, so it uses backward recovery to achieve fault-tolerance [7]. The hardware fault-tolerance architecture related to the RcB scheme is standby sparing or passive dynamic redundancy.

The executive orchestrates the operation of the RcB technique, which has the following general syntax:

ensure Acceptance Test
by Primary Alternate
else by Alternate 2
else by Alternate 3
...
else by Alternate n
else failure exception

The RcB syntax above states that the technique will first attempt to ensure the AT by using the primary alternate (or try block). If the primary algorithm's result does not pass the AT, then $n-1$ alternates will be attempted until an alternate's results pass the AT. If no alternates are successful, an error is reported. Figure 5.7 illustrates the structure and operation of the basic RcB technique with a watchdog timer. Figure 5.8 shows the RcB implemented with two alternates.

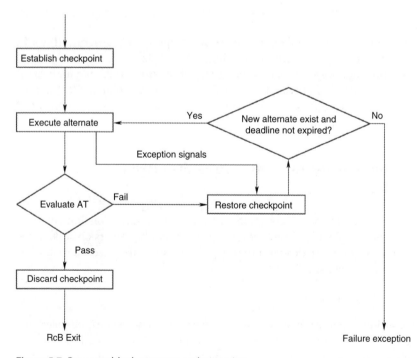

Figure 5.7 Recovery block structure and operation.

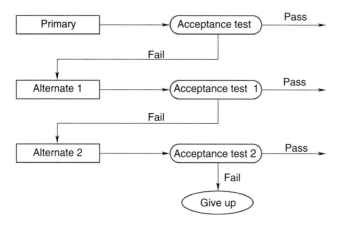

Figure 5.8 Recovery block structure with two alternates.

The following information should be considered when designing alternates. Differently implemented function variants have varying degrees of efficiency in terms of memory management and utilization, execution time, reliability, and other criteria. By this measure, common-cause faults can be avoided. The primary module is the most efficient module located first in the series, and the alternates can implement a degradation requirement.

The cost of RcB is time consumption, which includes the time taken to store the global state and start one or more alternate modules. Consequently, even though RcB is quite reliable, it cannot be used in fields with high real-time requirements.

5.3.2 N-version Programming (NVP)

The NVP and RcB techniques are the original design diverse software fault-tolerance techniques. NVP was proposed by Elmendorf in 1972, and developed by Avizienis and Chen in 1977 [8,9]. NVP is a design diverse technique, and is further categorized as a static technique. It uses a decision mechanism (DM) and forward recovery to achieve fault-tolerance.

The hardware fault-tolerance architecture related to the NVP is N-modular or static redundancy, and all the backups are diverse design. The processes can run concurrently on different computers, or sequentially on a single computer. In practice, they are typically run concurrently. A DM examines the results and selects the best result, if one exists. Figure 5.9 illustrates the structure and operation of the NVP technique.

The main difference between NVP and RcB is real-time capability: RcB tries many alternate modules sequentially, until the DM finds an acceptable result. The time overhead of retrying multiple alternate versions is very large, so RcB

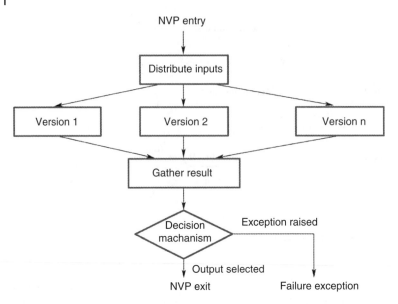

Figure 5.9 N-version programming structure.

cannot be used in real-time fields. By contrast, in NVP, several alternates can run concurrently on different computers, so it has been used in many fields with real-time requirements, such as railway and flight control systems [10].

5.3.3 Distributed Recovery Blocks (DRB)

The DRB technique is a combination of distributed and/or parallel processing and recovery blocks, that provides both hardware and software fault-tolerance. Emphasis in the development of the technique has been placed on real-time target applications, distributed and parallel computing systems, and handling of both hardware and software faults. Although DRB uses recovery blocks, it implements a forward recovery scheme that is consistent with its emphasis on real-time applications [11].

The technique's architecture consists of a pair of self-checking processing nodes (PSP). The PSP scheme uses two copies of a self-checking computing component that are structured as a primary-shadow pair, resident on two or more networked nodes. In the PSP scheme, each computing component iterates through computation cycles, and each of these cycles is two-phase structured. Each of the cycles consists of an input acquisition phase and an output phase. During the input acquisition phase, input actions and computation actions may take place, but not output actions. Similarly, during the output phase, only output actions may take place. This facilitates parallel

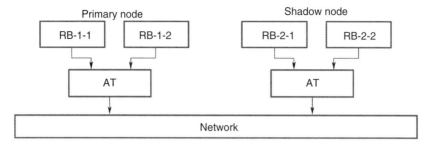

Figure 5.10 Distributed recovery block structure.

replicated execution of real-time tasks, without incurring excessive overhead related to synchronization of the two partner nodes in the same primary-shadow structured computing station.

As shown in Figure 5.10, the basic DRB technique consists of a primary node and a shadow node, each cooperating and each running an RcB scheme. At the start, the DRB technique executes the recovery blocks on both nodes concurrently, with one node (the initial primary node) executing the primary algorithm first, and the other (the initial shadow node) executing the alternate. The technique first attempts to ensure the AT (i.e., produce a result that passes the AT) with the primary algorithm on Node 1's results. If this result fails the AT, then the DRB tries the result from the alternate algorithm on Node 2. If neither passes the AT, then backward recovery is used to execute the alternate on Node 1 and the primary on Node 2. The results of these executions are checked to ensure the AT. If neither of these results passes the AT, then an error occurs. If any of the results are successful, the result is passed on to the successor computing station. Figure 5.11 shows a fault-free task execution cycle from two PSP nodes. Figure 5.12 shows a task execution cycle from the primary PSP node involving a failure.

Because the try blocks are diverse and execute concurrently, results will generally be immediately available for output from the distributed recovery block. Hence, the recovery time from failures is much shorter than if both try blocks were to execute on the same node.

5.3.4   N Self-checking Programming (NSCP)

NSCP is the use of multiple software versions combined with structural variations of the Recovery Blocks and NVP. NSCP is a design diverse technique, and the hardware fault-tolerance architecture related to NSCP is active dynamic redundancy. Self-checking software was used as the basis of the Airbus A-300, A-310, and A-320 flight control systems, and the Swedish railways' interlocking system [12].

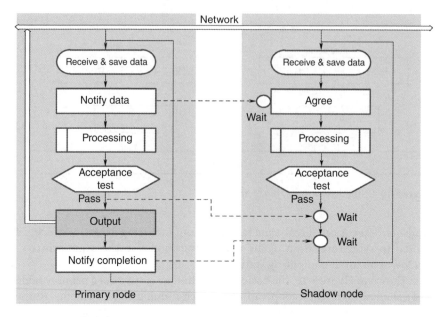

Figure 5.11 A fault-free PSP task execution cycle.

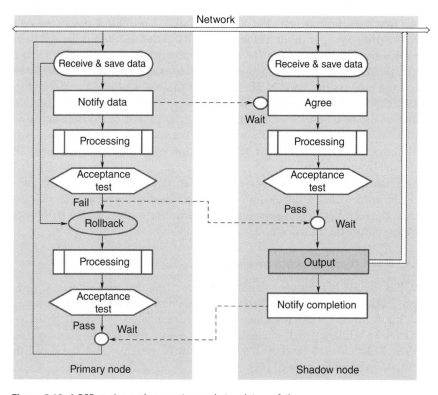

Figure 5.12 A PSP station task execution cycle involving a failure.

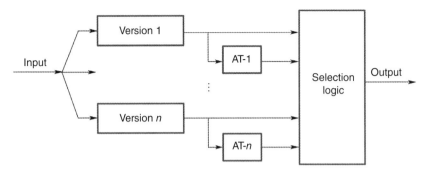

Figure 5.13 NSCP using acceptance tests (ATs).

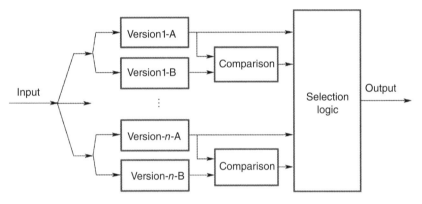

Figure 5.14 NSCP using comparison.

NSCP using acceptance tests is shown in Figure 5.13. Here, the versions and the acceptance tests are developed independently from common requirements. This use of separate acceptance tests for each version is the main difference between this N self-checking model and the Recovery Blocks approach. Like Recovery Blocks, execution of the versions and their tests can be carried out sequentially or in parallel, but the output is taken from the highest-ranking version that passes its acceptance test. Sequential execution requires the use of checkpoints, whereas parallel execution requires the use of input and state consistency algorithms.

NSCP using comparison for error detection is shown in Figure 5.14. Like NVP, this model has the advantage of using an application-independent decision algorithm to select a correct output. This variation of self-checking programming has the theoretical vulnerability of encountering situations where multiple pairs pass their comparisons, but each with different outputs. That case must be considered and an appropriate decision policy selected during design.

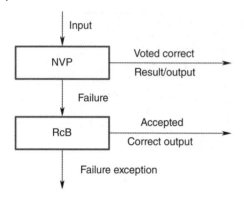

Figure 5.15 Consensus recovery block structure and operation.

5.3.5 Consensus Recovery Block (CRB)

The CRB technique is a fault-tolerance method presented by Scott that combines the NVP and RcB implementation techniques. CRB uses N-versions that are ranked in order of their service and reliability. At the beginning of system runs, the CRB method operates in NVP mode. When consistency voting cannot be achieved in NVP mode, the CRB method switches to RcB mode, in which the roll-back and retry sequence of RcB accords with the preset priority order of N-versions. Only when RcB mode fails does the CRB method fail. Figure 5.15 illustrates the structure and operation of the CRB [13].

5.3.6 Acceptance Voting (AV)

The AV technique was proposed by Athavale [14]. It uses both an AT and a voting-type DM, along with forward recovery (see Section 1.4.2) to accomplish fault-tolerance. In AV, all variants can execute in parallel. The variant results are evaluated by an AT, and only accepted results are sent to the voter. Because the DM may see anywhere from one to n results (where n is the number of variants), the technique requires a dynamic voting algorithm. The dynamic voter is able to process varying numbers of results upon each invocation – that is, if two results pass the AT, they are compared; if five results pass, they are voted upon, and so on. If no results pass the AT, then the system fails. It also fails if the dynamic voter cannot select a correct result. Figure 5.16 illustrates the operation of the AV technique.

5.3.7 Advantage and Disadvantage of Multiple-version Software

Multiple-version software is generated independently from the initial specification. "Independently" is used here with the meaning that the different versions are developed by different teams of engineers, using different algorithms and maybe even different languages, compilers, and OSs. The teams themselves should also be diverse – that is, they should have different backgrounds, both educational and ethnic. The N versions are functionally equivalent, and have identical interfaces from the surrounding software.

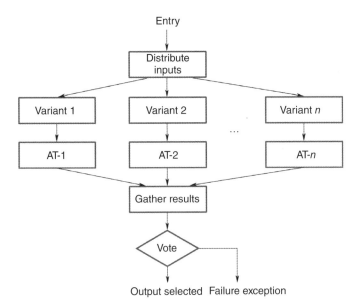

Figure 5.16 Acceptance voting technique structure and operation.

By utilizing design diverse techniques, multiple-version software can avoid the common mode fault found in single-version software. However, multiple-version software has a critical disadvantage: its development cost is too high. As a result, this technique is mainly used in the aeronautical field, and is seldom used in the aerospace field.

5.4 Data Diversity Based Software Fault-tolerance Techniques

Data diversity involves obtaining a related set of points in the program data space, executing the same software on those points, and then using a decision algorithm to determine the resulting output. Data diverse techniques use data re-expression algorithms (DRA) to obtain their input data, and mainly include the N-copy programming (NCP), retry block (RtB), TPA, and so on.

5.4.1 Data Re-expression Algorithm (DRA)

The performance of data diverse software fault-tolerance techniques depends on the performance of the re-expression algorithm used. There are several ways to perform data re-expression and provide some insight on actual re-expression algorithms and their use. DRAs are very application-dependent.

Development of a DRA also requires a careful analysis of the type and magnitude of re-expression appropriate for each set of data that is a candidate for all re-expression [15].

Data re-expression is used to obtain diverse input data by generating logically equivalent input data sets. Given initial data within the program failure region, the re-expressed input data should exist outside that failure region. A re-expression algorithm, R, transforms the original input x to produce the new input, $y = R(x)$. The input y may either approximate x or contain x's information in a different form. R, and the program P, determine the relationship between $P(x)$ and $P(y)$.

Not all applications can employ data diversity. Those that cannot do so include applications in which an effective DRA cannot be found. This may include: applications that do not primarily use numerical data; some that use primarily integer data; some for which an exact re-expression algorithm is required; those for which a DRA that escapes the failure region cannot be developed; and those for which the known re-expression algorithms that escape the failure region are resource-ineffective.

5.4.2 Retry Blocks (RtB)

The basic RtB technique is one of the two original data diverse software fault-tolerance techniques developed by Ammann and Knight [15]. The RtB technique is also categorized as a dynamic technique. The hardware fault-tolerance architecture related to the RtB technique is standby sparing or passive dynamic redundancy. It is the data diverse complement of the recovery block (RcB) scheme.

Figure 5.17 illustrates the retry block's structure and operation. The RtB technique uses AT and backward recovery to accomplish fault-tolerance. A WDT is also used, and triggers execution of a backup algorithm if the original algorithm does not produce an acceptable result within a specified period of time. The algorithm is executed using the original system input, and the primary algorithm's results are examined by an AT. If the algorithm results pass the AT, then the RtB is complete. However, if the results are not acceptable, then the input is re-expressed and the same primary algorithm runs again using the new, re-expressed, input data. This continues until the AT finds an acceptable result, or the WDT deadline is violated. If the deadline expires, a backup algorithm may be invoked to execute on the original input data.

5.4.3 N-copy Programming (NCP)

NCP is a data diverse technique, and is further categorized as a static technique. The hardware fault-tolerance architecture related to NCP is N-modular or static redundancy. The processes can run concurrently on different computers, or sequentially on a single computer but, in practice, they are typically run concurrently. NCP is the data diverse complement of NVP [15].

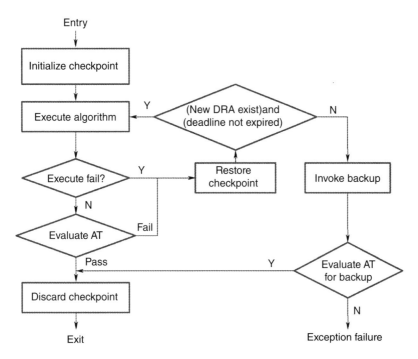

Figure 5.17 Retry block structure and operation.

The NCP technique uses a DM and forward recovery to accomplish fault-tolerance. The technique uses one or more DRAs and at least two copies of a program. The system inputs are run through the DRA(s) to re-express the inputs. The copies execute in parallel, using the re-expressed data as input. A DM examines the results of the copy executions and selects the "best" result, if one exists. There are many alternative DMs available with NCP.

The NCP technique first runs the DRA concurrently to re-express the input data, then executes the *n* copies concurrently. The results of the copy executions are provided to the DM, which operates on the results to determine if a correct result can be adjudicated. If one can (i.e., the DM statement above evaluates to TRUE), then it is returned. If a correct result cannot be determined, then an error occurs.

5.4.4 Two-pass Adjudicators (TPA)

The TPA technique is a combination of data and design diverse software fault-tolerance techniques. TPA also combines static and dynamic techniques, based on the recovery technique required. The hardware fault-tolerance architecture related to the technique is N-modular redundancy. The processes can run concurrently on different computers or sequentially on a single computer, but are designed to run concurrently [16].

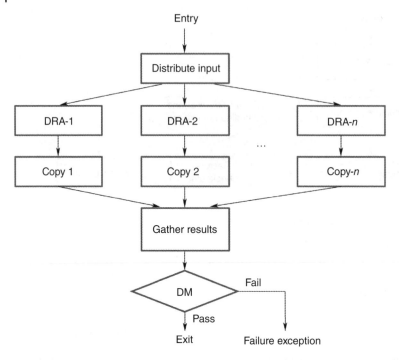

Figure 5.18 N-copy programming structure.

The TPA technique uses a DM and both forward and backward recovery to accomplish fault-tolerance. The technique uses one or more DRAs and at least two variants of a program. The system operates like NVP, unless and until the DM cannot determine a correct result, given the variant results. If this occurs, then the inputs are run through the DRA(s) to be re-expressed. The variants re-execute using the re-expressed data as input (each input is different, one of which may be the original input value). A DM then examines the results of the variant executions of this second pass and selects the "best" result, if one exists. A number of alternative detection and selection mechanisms are available for use with TPA.

The TPA syntax above states that the technique first runs the *n* variants, using the original inputs as parameters. The results of the variant executions are provided to the DM to determine if a correct result can be adjudicated. If one can (i.e., the first DM statement above evaluates to TRUE), then it is returned. If a correct result cannot be determined, then Pass 2 is initiated by concurrently re-expressing the original inputs via the DRA(s).The *n* variants are then re-executed, using the re-expressed inputs as parameters. The results of the re-executions are provided to the DM to determine if a correct result can

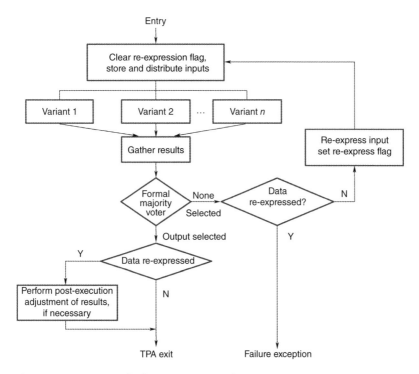

Figure 5.19 Two-pass adjudicator structure and operation.

be adjudicated. If one can (i.e., the second DM statement above evaluates to TRUE), then it is returned. If a correct result cannot be determined, then an error occurs. Figure 5.19 illustrates the structure and operation of the basic TPA technique. As shown, *n* variants of a program initially execute in parallel on the original input, as in the NVP technique. The technique continues operation as described above.

References

1 Laura Pullum L (2001). *Software fault-tolerance techniques and implementation* [M]. Artech House.
2 Jalote P (1994). *Fault-tolerance in distributed systems* [M]. Englewood Cliffs, NJ: Prentice Hall.
3 Xu J, Randell B (1993). *Object-oriented construction of fault-tolerant software.* University of Newcastle upon Tyne, Technical Report Series, No.444.
4 Lyu MR (1995). *Software fault-tolerance* [M]. John Wiley & Sons.
5 Pradhan D K (1996). *Fault tolerant computer system design* [M]. Prentice-Hall.

6 Goloubeva O, Rebaudengo M, Sonza Reorda M, Violante M (2006). *Software implemented hardware fault-tolerance* [M]. Springer.

7 Randell B, Xu J (1995). The evolution of the recovery block concept. In: Lyu M R (Ed) *Software Fault-tolerance*, Wiley. 1–21.

8 Chen L, Avizienis A (1978). *N-version programming: A fault-tolerant approach to reliability of software operation* [C]. 8th International Symposium on Fault Tolerant Computing (FTCS-8), Toulouse, France. 3–9.

9 Avizienis A (1985). The N-version approach to fault-tolerant software [J]. *IEEE Transactions on Software Engineering* 11(12),1491–1501.

10 Avizienis A (1995). The methodology of N-version programming. In: Lyu M R (Ed) *Software Fault-tolerance*, Wiley.

11 Kim K H (1984). *Distributed execution of recovery blocks: an approach to uniform treatment of hardware and software faults*. Proceedings of the 4th International Conference on Distributed Computing Systems. 526–532.

12 Laprie J C, Arlat J, Beounes C, Kanoun K. (1990). Definition and analysis of hardware and software fault tolerant architectures [J]. *IEEE Transactions on Computers* 23(7), 39–51.

13 Scott R K, Gault J W, McAllister D F (1983). *The consensus recovery block*. Proceedings of the Total System Reliability Symposium.

14 Athavale A (1989). *Performance evaluation of hybrid voting schemes*. M.S. thesis, North Carolina State University, Department of Computer Science.

15 Ammann P E, Knight J C (1988). Data diversity: An approach to software fault-tolerance. *IEEE Transactions on Computers* 37(4), 418–425.

16 Pullum L L (1992). *Fault tolerant software decision-making under the occurrence of multiple correct results*. Doctoral Dissertation, Southeastern Institute of Technology.

6

Fault-Tolerance Techniques for FPGA

As the space industry continues to advance, the development of microelectronic products with high performance and highly integrated functions is necessary to meet the ever higher requirements of astronautic electronic products. Microelectronic techniques create opportunities for better solutions in space technology. FPGA is favored by space product designers, owing to features such as high function density, small volume, low power consumption, semi-customization, and flexible configuration. Currently, various types of FPGAs are utilized in China's satellite electrical and electronic products.

Depending on the manufacturing process technology, an FPGA IC is categorized as the following three types: SRAM-based FPGA, anti-fuse-based FPGA, and flash-based FPGA. The most extensively used FPGA is the SRAM type, which has the advantages of high speed, re-programmability, and high capacity, coupled with the disadvantage of vulnerability to SEEs in the space environment. Widely used in the space equipment, the Virtex series of Xilinx is a typical SRAM-based FPGA. It has rich programmable resources, with highly integrated and high-performance logic architecture.

With a small capacity, anti-fuse-based FPGA is programmable only once, and is vulnerable to the SEGR effect. Test results show that the reliability of anti-fuse-based FPGA in radiation environments is higher than that of SRAM based FPGA. The largest anti-fuse-based FPGA manufacturer, Actel, has provided dozens of FPGA types with features that meet the requirements of USA military standard 883G(MIL-STD-883G), among which, the largest number of gates exceeds 1 million, the highest system frequency is 500 MHz, and the total tolerable radiation dose is 1 Mrad(Si) without the SEL effect.

Although flash-based FPGA is relatively new and can provide a reprogrammable function, the compatibility problem of the CMOS manufacturing process results in low integration density and high cost. Hence, application of flash-based FPGA is limited.

Fault-Tolerance Techniques for Spacecraft Control Computers, First Edition.
Mengfei Yang, Gengxin Hua, Yanjun Feng and Jian Gong.

Because FPGA is vulnerable to SEE, an anti-single-event fault-tolerance design is the major focus of global space industry [1–3]. This chapter focuses on problems face by FPGA space applications and fault-tolerance techniques of SRAM-based FPGA.

6.1 Effect of the Space Environment on FPGAs

The effects of the space environment on FPGA include total dose effect and SEE. With the development in manufacturing processes, anti-fuse-based FPGA and SRAM-based FPGA are being applied in current onboard electrical products, and are able to meet the total dose requirements of the space environment. Furthermore, the requirements on FPGA total dose specification can be lowered by utilizing a shielding layer. Therefore, the major influence of space environment on FPGA is primarily SEE, which is the focus of this section [4–7].

SEE is the radiation effect resulting from the impact of single high energy level particles (protons, heavy ions) on electrical devices. For most CMOS devices, such as FPGAs, SEE results in failure from the drift, diffusion, and recombination of ionized carriers after the ionization effect induced by bombardment of charged particles on devices along the incident track, as shown in Figure 6.1. It consists of single event transient effect (SET), SEU, SEL, SEB, and SEGR. SEFI is worth particular attention for SRAM-based FPGA. Among the above SEEs, SEL, SEB, and SEGR can damage the device permanently. Therefore, space systems usually employ SEL-free devices. Although SEU and SET are transient effects, they should be taken seriously because of their high occurrence probability [6–8].

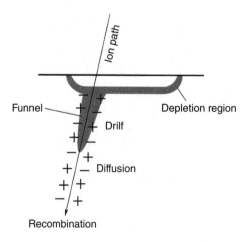

Figure 6.1 Radiation effect induced by charged particle bombardment.

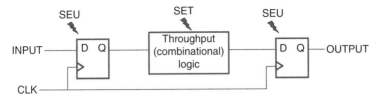

Figure 6.2 SET of combinational logic and SEU of sequential logic.

6.1.1 Single Event Transient Effect (SET)

The electron-hole pair created by ionization results in a device's output voltage experiencing transient pulse interference when the sensitive region of a CMOS device, such as an FPGA, is bombarded by high-energy level particles. For combinational logic, the effect of SET is temporary. However, if the speed of combinational logic is sufficiently fast that the transient pulse is transmitted to the sequential logic connected with the combinational logic, the pulse might be captured and stored to produce SEU, as illustrated in Figure 6.2. The probability of occurrence depends on the arrival time of the pulse, and the relationship between the rising edge and the falling edge (criteria for a flip-flop to be triggered).

6.1.2 Single Event Upset (SEU)

When a single high-energy level particle bombards an IC chip, ionization will occur around the PN junction to create a certain number of electron-hole pairs (carriers). As a result of the electric field effect, the drifting and recombination of carriers will change the distribution and movement of the normal carriers inside the IC. If the change is sufficiently large, it will modify the device's electrical performance, such that the result is failure of the logic component or circuit (e.g., the upset of data in a storage unit, which is defined as SEU). The following is the analysis of the SEU effect on an SRAM based FPGA.

Because an SRAM-based FPGA utilizes SRAM storage as its configuration memory, its performance depends on the reliability of the SRAM. An SRAM storage unit is typically comprised of six transistors, which utilize a single character line, a digit line, and a reversed phase digit line, as shown in Figure 6.3. The unit includes a cross-coupling CMOS inverter, with each digit line connected to an access transistor. In a real application, the user references the access transistor through the strobe character line, and data writing and reading are conducted via the digit line. Usually, if data are slightly perturbed, positive feedback will recover data to VDD or GND, to ensure correctness of data. However, whenever a charged particle hits a transistor in an inverter (e.g., the drain of a transistor in the closed state), a transient pulse is generated that opens the transistor, after which the cross-coupling of the six transistors in

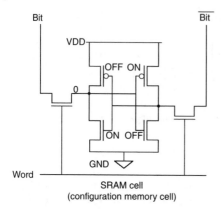

Figure 6.3 SRAM configuration memory cell of an FPGA.

SRAM cell
(configuration memory cell)

the SRAM will result in upset of the stored information – that is, the stored value in the storage unit will experience SEU. Following the SEU, the faulty stored value will remain until either the system is powered off or a new value is written in.

6.1.3 Single Event Latch-up (SEL)

When ionized carriers, created as a result of the bombardment of bulk CMOS devices by charged particles, collect at a PN-PN junction, break-over of the silicon control may occur, which would result in a current path being formed from VDD to −VSS inside the CMOS inverter. The result is device latch-up.

6.1.4 Single Event Burnout (SEB)

With high-energy level incident particles, when a PN junction is reverse biased, the drifting, accelerating process of the carriers may result in PN junction reverse breakdown, in which the source and drain are permanently shorted until the circuit eventually burns out.

6.1.5 Single Event Gate Rupture (SEGR)

When a CMOS device is bombarded by a charged particle, a low-resistance conduction passage is eventually formed from grid to substrate along the particle's incident track, and transient current is created under the effect of the grid voltage. If the transient current is sufficiently high, it will cause a breakdown along the current path in the device grid oxide layer to form a permanent conduction passage from grid to substrate, which will result in total device failure.

SEB and SEGR mainly occur in power devices. The probability of SEB and SEGR occurring in FPGAs is extremely low.

6.1.6 Single Event Functional Interrupt (SEFI)

SEFI refers to SEU-induced global function failure of SRAM-based FPGA. It includes SEU of FPGA internal power-on-reset (POR) circuit, FPGA configuration interface (SelectMAP, JTAG), and some FPGA global control logic, resulting from being hit by a charged particle. It may cause total FPGA function abnormality and may even result in total reconfiguration.

In order to avoid the occurrence of SEFI, it is necessary to protect circuits that have a global effect, such as POR and configuration interfaces. This can be achieved by actions such as replacing normal storage units with SEU-hardened storage units, and implementing additional switches to close PORs after programming to the device's external pin is complete.

6.2 Fault Modes of SRAM-based FPGAs

6.2.1 Structure of a SRAM-based FPGA

The FPGA used most extensively in space applications is the SRAM type made with CMOS. The space irradiation environment results in increased incidences of FPGA SEE, which severely jeopardizes circuit reliability [9]. Figure 6.4 shows that, as the size of the transistor decreases, FPGA SEEs may even begin to affect multiple surrounding configurations. This severely restricts the application of SRAM based FPGA in space equipment.

An SRAM-based FPGA comprises a configurable logic block (CLB), block RAM (BRAM), input-output interface block (IOB), configuration logic, JTAG interface, and programmable wiring resources that are necessary for FPGA programming and operation. Because the above function depends on the configuration of the SRAM, they are vulnerable to SEU, single event multiple bits upset, and SEE. Variation of the function module distribution and structure in FPGA result in variations in SEU in radiation from

(a)　　　　　　　(b)

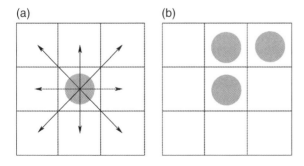

Figure 6.4 SEE induced multiple bits upset.

high-energy level particles. The following sections will introduce each respective functional module's response.

The purpose of the CLB is to facilitate logic functions in the circuit. With irradiation by high-energy level particles, the configuration digit stored in the SRAM may experience upset that results in the production of SEU, which changes the functioning of the circuit and severely jeopardizes circuit reliability.

Block RAM is an embedded large capacity dual-port SRAM memory in SRAM-based FPGA. Any SEU in block RAM will result in a fault in the internally stored data. With irradiation by high-energy level particles, faults may occur in the reading/writing circuit.

The IO block is the input/output signal passage of an FPGA chip. The vulnerability of the IO block's internal IO flip-flop and reference voltage level to SEE results in input/output signal faults when such an event occurs.

Wiring resources include line and switch matrices. If an SRAM unit that controls a switch transistor is hit by high-energy level particles, the original wiring structure will be modified, which will jeopardize the function of the circuit.

Configuration control logic consists of a series of registers and the global signals controlled by those registers. With the influence of high-energy level particles, any occurrence of SEU in those configuration registers may negatively affect the process of downloading configuration data to the FPGA or reading back from FPGA. This will cause errors in the read-back data, and result in IC function interruption.

Taking the mainstream Xilinx Virtex FPGA as an example, this section introduces the internal structure and radiation effect of SRAM-based FPGA. Figure 6.5 shows the internal structure of the Xilinx Virtex series FPGA device, whose critical component is the CLB for user logic realization and block RAM (BRAM) for user data storage [10]. Major CLB components include look-up table, carry logic, and flip-flop.

The memory in SRAM-based FPGA is categorized into the following two functional types:

1) *Configuration memory.* This type of memory consists of an SRAM unit for look-up table (LUT) value storage, and another SRAM unit for FPGA internal relationship. Configuration memory upset will result in FPGA circuit function abnormality, which can be rectified by reconfiguring the FPGA's fault-tolerance technique.

2) *Design memory.* This type of memory comprises FPGA block RAM for user data storage, distributed RAM, and LUT-configured 16-bit SRL16 and flip-flops in CLB. Any occurrence of SEU in design memory will result in custom logic error, which may cause the entire system to operate abnormally. Therefore, it is necessary to employ a fault-tolerance technique to protect design memory, so that faults in space applications are either shielded or corrected.

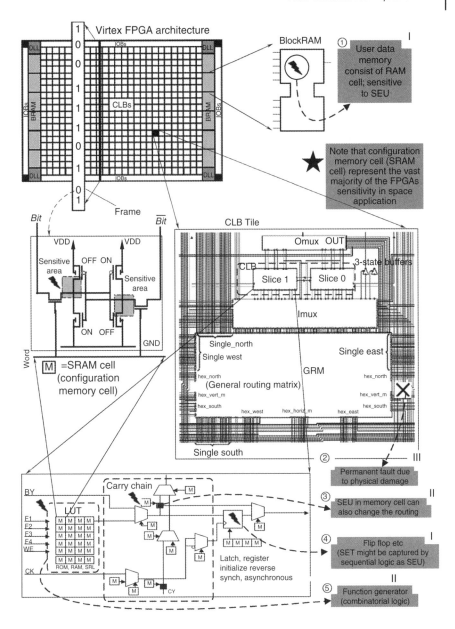

Figure 6.5 Internal structure of the Virtex FPGA.

6.2.2 Faults Classification and Fault Modes Analysis of SRAM-based FPGAs

6.2.2.1 Faults Classification

As a reconfigurable FPGA, an SRAM based FPGA employs a complex fault processing mechanism. A fault is classified into one of the following three types on the basis of its sustained effect:

1) *Transient fault.* This mainly refers to the internal single event transient effect (SET) of internal circuits and SEU of storage devices induced by SEEs. This type of fault may be corrected during system operation.
2) *Persistent fault.* This mainly refers to SEU-induced configuration memory upset, or half-latch fault induced function abnormality, which will continue until either the FPGA is reconfigured or reinitialized. It is worth noting that, under certain conditions, although a scrubbing operation is added to the FPGA fault-tolerance mechanism, configuration memory upset may cause the system to enter a sustained faulty state owing to circuit feedback.
3) *Permanent fault.* A permanent fault is caused by physical damage to the FPGA device, such as occurrence of SEGR in a transistor or internal metal wire open circuit. This type of fault is permanent and *cannot* be recovered from. However, local reconstruction can shield the fault by restricting design in the undamaged area.

6.2.2.2 Fault Modes Analysis

The fault modes of the SRAM-based FPGA are shown in Table 6.1 [11]. As stated above, the SRAM-based FPGA employs a reprogrammable configuration unit to facilitate logic functions. Following the removal by Xilinx of a half-latch from the VirtexII series, half-latch upset-induced fault only occurs in early Xilinx products. It could be detected and eliminated with a targeted programming style and specific tools.

1) Block RAM upset.
   The block RAM stores user data. Block RAM upset resulting in user data error or missing data is shown at fault label (1), shown in Figure 6.5. There is a column of Virtex FPGA block RAM on each side of the FPGA. Each block stores 4096 bits of information. The accessibility of the contents to the configuration port (e.g., SelectMAP), means that the FPGA block RAM is extensively used by hardware designers. However, the RAM unit is sensitive to space irradiation. The fault-tolerance measures utilized on the block RAM may cause user data error resulting from memory SEU, which means design fault or failure.
2) Local permanent physical damage.
   FPGA internal total dose effect, device aging and corrosion, corresponding to fault label (2) in Figure 6.5, result in physical damage. Although the

Table 6.1 Analysis of fault modes of SRAM-based FPGA.

Fault mode	Fault mechanism	Fault performance	Fault classification
Block RAM upset	Occurs in SRAM unit, which is vulnerable to SEU in space environment.	Fault occurs in user data stored in RAM.	Transient fault
Local permanent fault	Physical damage, such as device aging, corrosion, and total dose effect, induced as a result of the device being in a hostile environment for a long time.	Local or global failure of FPGA.	Permanent fault
Connection relation fault	Occurrence of SEU in configuration memory that controls the connection relationship.	Incapable of achieving user logic, owing to FPGA internal relation fault.	Persistent fault
Sequential logic SEU	Occurrence of SEU in sequential logic; Sequential component's capture of SET in combinational passage.	Error in user data.	
Combinational logic SEU	Caused by charged particle's hitting combinational circuit.	Transient current pulse.	Transient fault
Half-latch upset	Occurrence of SEU in half-latch that creates logic constant.	Occurrence of fault in logic constant in FPGA.	Persistent fault
SEFI	Occurrence of SEU in POR circuit, programming interfaces (SelectMAP, JTAG), etc.	Abnormality in overall FPGA function, reconfiguration is necessary.	Persistent fault

probability of this type of fault is the lowest among all fault modes, it may occur anywhere in the FPGA. The claim by Xilinx that permanent physical damage fault has never occurred to an FPGA device does *not* mean that this fault type can be neglected, as deep space exploration, hostile environments, and long-term irradiation may help to cause changes.

3) FPGA internal connection relation faults.

Configuration information error, corresponding to fault label (3) in Figure 6.5, results in connection relation fault. Inside the FPGA, the interconnection relation of CLB is determined by the general routing matrix (as shown in Figure 6.5, GRM), in which there are two types of wires – single wire and hex wire. The former connects the closest CLB, whereas the latter connects the two CLBs with spacing 6. The programmable interconnect points (PIPs) on the connection spot of the wire finally complete the connection relation. As shown in Figure 6.6, these PIPs are controlled by the configuration bit stored in the SRAM, on which the occurrence of an SEU will result in connection relation fault. Note that only 90% of FPGA transistors operate to achieve connection relation. Even in high-usage IC design, the ratio of dedicated transistors does not exceed 10%.

4) FPGA internal sequential component SEU.

SEU occurs in sequential logic – for example, flip-flop, as depicted by fault label (4) in Figure 6.5 [10]. There are four flip-flops in every CLB. Each flip-flop can be configured as either an edge-triggered D flip-flop, or a voltage level sensitive latch register. SEU may occur in these operating sequential components, as a result of the impact from high-energy level particles. Upset may also be induced by the capture of transient pulses in the combinational logic. When these faulty values are latched and taken out at the next clock edge, the circuit's normal logic function is affected, as illustrated in Figure 6.7.

5) FPGA internal combinational logic fault.

The occurrence of SEU in the LUT configuration memory unit that achieves function generator, corresponding to fault label (5) in Figure 6.5, results in a combinational logic fault. Unlike the combinational logic of ASIC, whose CMOS gate circuit is based on transistor layout, the combinational logic of FPGA is implemented by mapping it to a four-input LUT. The designer stores the logic output value in SRAM unit as the content of an LUT. However, the occurrence of SEU in an SRAM unit is equivalent to a change in the logic circuit designed, which may never have been predicted by the user. From a macroscopic level, this type of fault will persist until the configuration memory is reconfigured.

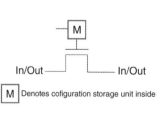

Figure 6.6 Internal configuration information storage memory unit. [M] denotes configuration storage unit inside FPGA.

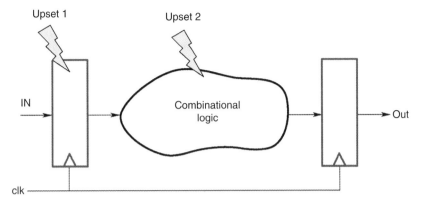

Figure 6.7 Upset of sequential and combinational logic.

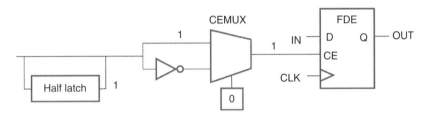

Figure 6.8 Half-latch structure of the Virtex series FPGA.

6) FPGA internal half-latch upset.

In order to use the limited internal resources in an FPGA effectively, there is a hidden structure in the Virtex series FPGA defined as a half-latch. This half-latch consists of a PMOS pull-up transistor and an inverter. The purpose of the half-latch is to create a logic constant that has not been explicitly specified in the user design, as shown in Figure 6.8.

The half-latch is transparent when the input signal is useful. When the input terminal is idle, the half-latch is able to maintain its last known value, so that the multiplexer (such as CMUX) can provide a logic constant (0 or 1) to the circuit. In fact, the half-latch is easily used in resources such as the I/O that drive the FPGA, clock, multiplexer and so on. However, it is sensitive to radiation. When hit by charged particle, its output value might be upset, resulting in a circuit logic fault. Because the half-latch is initialized at the power-on-configuration phase and cannot be controlled by configuration information, its fault cannot be detected and recovered with backward reading bit stream – that is, after occurrence of the upset, the fault is *not* recoverable unless system operation is terminated and the system reconfigured. The current method is to adopt proper design principles that cooperate with the Xilinx software toolkit, so that the half-latch can be removed.

7) FPGA single-event function interrupt.

FPGA SEFI refers to SEU-induced FPGA global function failure, which consists of failures in the power-on-reset circuit, FPGA configuration interface (SelectMAP, JTAG), and FPGA global control logic SEU resulting from high-energy level particle bombardment. These failures may cause abnormality in the function of the entire FPGA, which may even require reconfiguration.

To prevent SEFI, it is necessary to protect circuits that have global influence. The methods that can be utilized include replacing normal memory units with SEU reinforcement memory units, and closing POR with additional logic after programming of external device pins is completed.

6.3 Fault-tolerance Techniques for SRAM-based FPGAs

For SRAM-based FPGAs, the current techniques that can be implemented in industrial applications to improve FPGA reliability include design mitigation techniques and partial reconfiguration/scrubbing techniques. These two techniques can either be implemented respectively or cooperatively, to obtain the best FPGA fault-tolerance performance. Table 6.2 classifies various SRAM-based FPGA fault-tolerance techniques [10,12].

Table 6.2 SRAM-based FPGA fault-tolerance techniques.

SRAM-based FPGA fault-tolerance techniques	SRAM-based FPGA design mitigation techniques	Triple modular redundancy design technique
		Inside RAM protection technique
		Inside register protection technique
		EDAC encoding/decoding technique
	SRAM-based FPGA partial reconfiguration/ scrubbing techniques	Fault detection technique based on dual modular redundancy (DMR) and fault isolation technique based on triple gate
		Single fault detection and recovery technique based on ICAP > + FrameECC
		Multi-fault detection and recovery technique based on ICAP configuration back-reading > + RS encoding
		Dynamic reconfiguration technique based on early access partial reconfiguration (EAPR)
		Fault recovery technique based on hardware checkpointing

6.3.1 SRAM-based FPGA Mitigation Techniques

SRAM-based FPGA design mitigation techniques utilize TMR and EDAC to protect designs in the FPGA design description phase. Because of its high realization level, it has great application flexibility and range. The essence of this method is shielding of a fault by implementing redundancy (hardware redundancy, information redundancy).therefore, the fault at which the method aims depends on the scale of the redundancy. In a large-scale design, excessive redundancy results in an increase in area and resource cost, which is prohibitively high. A proper method is to implement design mitigation techniques on a selected FPGA critical module.

In addition to combinational logic and sequential logic, block RAM designed specifically for user data storage exists, but block RAM is sensitive to space radiation effects. Faults may occur in block RAM due to SEU. Therefore, it is necessary to refresh data in block RAM with TMR design. The majority voting device is the critical component of TMR design. In SRAM-based FPGA, because the default combinational logic is achieved with SEU sensitive LUT, it is necessary to take specific design measures to avoid LUT upset-induced single-point faults.

6.3.1.1 The Triple Modular Redundancy (TMR) Design Technique

Because SRAM-based FPGA is single event-sensitive, it is necessary to adopt a single event hardening design method for space applications. The TMR technique has been widely implemented and verified to be an effective technique. TMR is a common reinforcement method for single event hardened designs, that can mitigate the sensitivity of SRAM-based FPGA to single events. As shown in Figure 6.9, the traditional TMR method consists of combinational logic and triple redundancy of registers. The majority voting device outputs final result. In cases where one field fails and the other two works normally, the majority voting device can shield the faulty result and output the correct one [13,14].

The critical issues to avoid FPGA function fault are to correct the fault on time, reduce existing fault duration, and avoid simultaneous faults occurring in multiple fields. Xilinx, Sandia National Laboratory, and other entities jointly released the Xilinx TMR (XTMR) solution, shown in Figure 6.10. In this solution, TMR is applied to all input, combinational logic, and wiring, with each field operating independently to arbitrate the feedback route and output. Input/output and voting devices are both TMR. Because it is impossible to correct the content of the CLB with scrubbing, the output of the register reaches the input of combinational logic, located in front of the register, through a feedback route after arbitration to correct the register's content in the next clock cycle. SEU is invalid because of the redundancy field's input coming from the PCB, and output converging on the PCB.

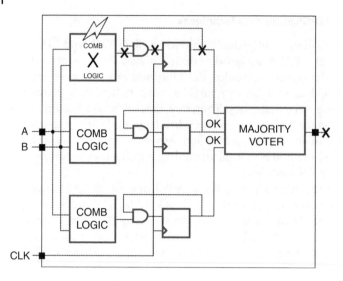

Figure 6.9 Structure of the traditional TMR.

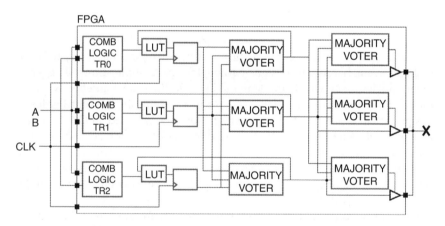

Figure 6.10 TMR functional module.

Both the functional module and the output need TMR to converge the output of multiple fields, as shown in Figure 6.11. If the malfunction of the combinational logic or state machine of a designed field produces a voting machine-detected result different from that of others, the voting device will close the triple state gate and set it to a high impedance state. FPGA is able to output correct values, because the other two fields are working properly. If the voting machine of a field fails, and the other two fields are working properly, the FPGA is able to output correct values. Hence, the XTMR method achieves better performance improvements than the traditional TMR method.

Figure 6.11 Output of TMR.

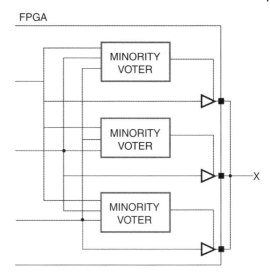

6.3.1.2 The Inside RAM Protection Technique

Inside the FPGA, distributed RAM and block RAM are responsible for data and command storage. The former is the storage function of the LUT, configured as RAM. The LUT can be configured both for a specific function, and also as RAM or a 16-bit shift register (SRL16) to store data. However, this configuration may result in read-back problems. In a normal data read-back process, the read-back command reads all data in the configuration memory, to compare with the initial configuration data. However, when the LUT is configured as distributed RAM or SRL16, the data stored are user data instead of configuration data. Although the designed modification of data is legal, it will incur mismatching in data read-back comparison. The reconfiguration fault-tolerance method will identify the fault as an SEU occurrence in the FPGA internal configuration storage unit, and start partial reconfiguration.

Obviously, the above process will cause user data error and a design fault. Therefore, when a reconfiguration fault-tolerance method is implemented together with the FPGA fault-tolerance method, it is necessary to avoid using LUT RAM – that is, LUT should *not* be configured as distributed RAM or SRL16 so that all data in the FPGA is stored in block RAM, which cannot be read back, resulting in no misjudgment by the reconfiguration fault-tolerance method.

The question of how to guarantee the correctness of data stored in block RAM is a major focus of FPGA fault-tolerance design. A TMR fault-tolerance solution for block RAM is shown in Figure 6.12 [9,15].

As long as resource utilization permits, the FPGA design should implement TMR rather than EDAC, to protect memory. Block RAM is a programmable

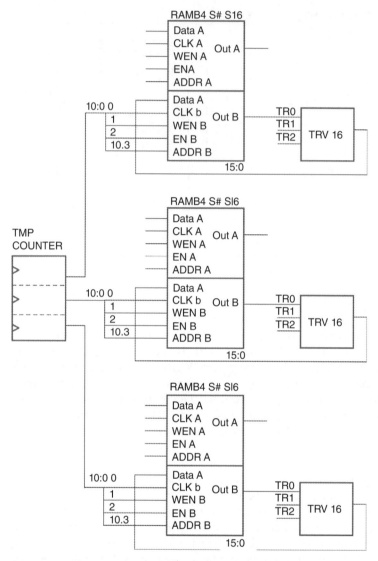

Figure 6.12 TMR protection for block RAM.

device that exists even if the user does not use it. If there is unused block RAM after synthesis, implementation of TMR will achieve better fault-tolerance performance than that of EDAC, while fully utilizing FPGA internal resources.

6.3.1.3 The Inside Register Protection Technique

The protection of sequential logic is achieved through the implementation of TMR reinforced design for registers, as shown in Figure 6.13 [14,16].

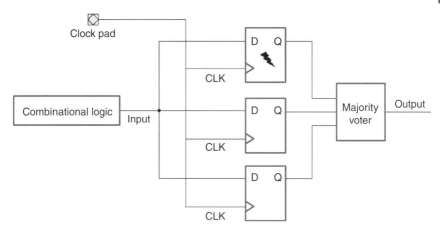

Figure 6.13 TMR fault-tolerance method to protect sequential logic against SEU.

This solution can prevent output errors incurred by the occurrence of SEU in any register. Note that, because the default component used to achieve FPGA majority voting logic is LUT, a potential risk of voting device single-point fault induced by configuration memory upset exists. The conventional practice is to employ the FPGA internal tri-state buffer to create a voting device to prevent LUT upset and to improve FPGA system reliability. Similarly, if the number of FPGA internal buffers is not sufficient to realize a voting device in large-scale designs, LUT is adopted. Meanwhile, TMR is implemented in the voting device to reduce the SPF ratio.

The disadvantage of the above solution is that the occurrence of SET in the register data input terminal will cause the three registers to acquire faulty signals simultaneously, resulting in the output of the majority voting device being faulty. In order to avoid this problem, TMR is implemented to reinforce the combinational logic, so that occurrence of SET on a single route does not affect the input of other registers, as illustrated in Figure 6.14. However, this method is applicable only when FPGA resource utilization is less than 30%, owing to the fact that it requires more hardware – otherwise, redundancy is impossible.

6.3.1.4 EDAC Encoding and Decoding Technique

The onboard FPGA system EDAC information redundancy technique utilizes communication channel coding theory. As shown in Figure 6.15, the fundamental principle of information redundancy is addition of a monitor (redundant) code element to the information code-element sequence after information source encoding. A specific relationship exists between the monitor code element and the information code element. The receiver can, therefore, compare the received relationship with that at the encoding moment, to determine if a fault has occurred in the data transmitted, or to correct the faulty code element in accordance with the encoding algorithm.

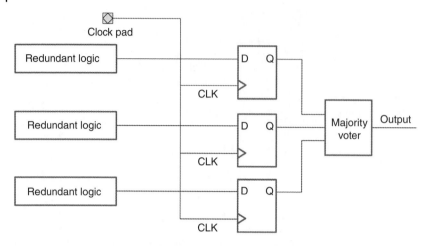

Figure 6.14 Avoiding SET occurrence in combinational logic and sequential logic with the TMR fault-tolerance method.

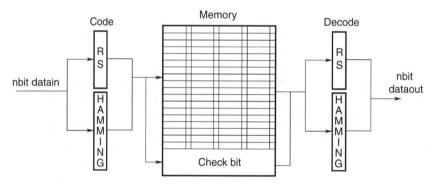

Figure 6.15 EDAC information redundancy protection solution.

It is recommended that FPGA register and memory be protected using EDAC. In such a case, the input of every unit to be protected is connected to an encoding circuit, which inserts the necessary redundancy bit into the information (data bit of memory). The output is connected to a decoding circuit, which decodes the stored data and performs fault detection and recovery.

The purpose of FPGA EDAC encoding is to detect and recover faults incurred when reading the content of registers and memory units. EDAC consists of multiple encoding techniques, each with a unique fault detection and correction capability. Parity check code determines data accuracy through judgment on whether the number of ones in a byte is even or odd. However, it can neither locate nor correct a fault. Hamming code can correct single-bit and dual-bit faults in any byte, but can neither detect nor correct faults that occur involving

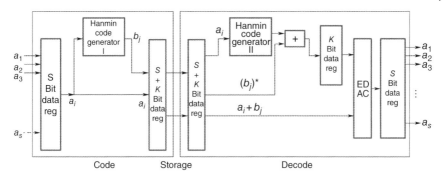

Figure 6.16 Hamming EDAC system diagram.

more than two bits. Other encoding algorithms, such as cyclic check code and convolutional code, are able to detect and correct multiple-bit faults in a byte with higher area and delay cost. Balancing fault detection and correction capability with realization cost, Hamming code is more applicable to EDAC protection of memory unit.

Single error correction-dual error detection (SEC-DED) Hamming code is a linear block code that can detect two-bit faults and correct one bit. Its underlying principle is utilization of several parity check bits in a set of code. Every bit of information participates in the parity check of various groups with different members. A fault involving one bit incurs a parity check fault in several related groups [17]. Hence, a faulty bit is determined, based on faulty groups. Figure 6.16 is a system block diagram of Hamming EDAC.

Hamming code cannot distinguish between one-bit, two-bit, and multiple-bit faults, which may result in faulty Hamming code correction. Therefore, although the probability of a one-bit fault is high, Hamming code is incapable in applications with rigorous requirements. When the probability of SEU occurrence is high, Hamming code may have the following problems: (1) Inability to identify the number of faulty bits; (2) faulty correction.

In order to reduce the ratio of Hamming code faulty correction when a multiple-bit fault occurs in a byte, an effective improvement solution is to combine Hamming code and parity check – that is, based on Hamming code, perform parity check encoding to information bit and redundancy bit.

1) Improved Hamming encoding method. Assume that an information byte is eight-bit "data," and the redundancy bit of the Hamming verification method is $b_1b_2b_3b_4$, following Hamming code algorithm. Parity check is applied to both information bit and redundancy bit. The verification code is:

$$odd = (data[0] \oplus data[2] \oplus data[3] \oplus data[4] \oplus data[5]$$
$$\oplus data[6] \oplus data[7] \oplus b_1 \oplus b_2 \oplus b_3 \oplus b_4)$$

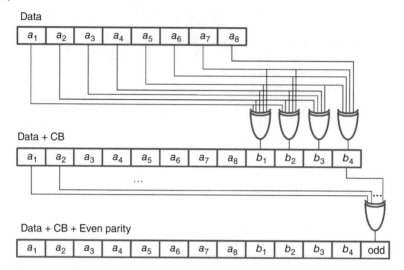

Figure 6.17 Structure of Hamming encoder/decoder.

Therefore, in addition to the eight-bit information, there are a four-bit redundancy bit and a one-bit even verification bit, as shown in Figure 6.17.

2) Improved Hamming decoding method. Data must be decoded twice before being taken. First, Hamming verification decoding is performed on the information bit to obtain $s_1 s_2 s_3 s_4$; the algorithm is the same as above.

Verification decoding is then performed to get the verification bit. The verification bit created with decoding is:

$$odd\_check = (data[0] \oplus data[2] \oplus data[3] \oplus data[4] \oplus data[5]$$
$$\oplus\ data[6] \oplus data[7] \oplus b_1 \oplus b_2 \oplus b_3 \oplus b_4 \oplus odd)$$

With an additional parity check bit, the improved Hamming algorithm can correct single-bit faults and detect most multiple-bit faults.

6.3.1.5 Fault Detection Technique Based on DMR and Fault Isolation Technique Based on Tristate Gate

In the design of modules with rigorous requirements on area and low reliability, the DMR solution can be implemented to perform fault detection and isolation with tristate gate to avoid fault effect propagation. When a fault occurs, this solution can perform real-time fault detection through module output comparison. When DMR detects a fault, the circuit automatically controls the tristate gate to latch the module output, so that fault propagation is avoided.

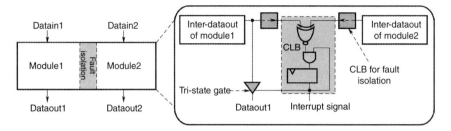

Figure 6.18 Fault detection based on DMR and fault isolation based on tristate gate.

In addition, the circuit applies the dynamic reconfiguration technique to the recovery process until the DMR module's output is correct [18].

The principle of fault detection based on DMR, and fault isolation based on the tristate gate, is shown in Figure 6.18. Modules 1 and 2 are copies of the same circuit block. In DMR comparison, the outputs of the two modules are compared using the XNOR gate. If a difference between the two is detected, an interrupt signal is sent to prohibit tristate gate output data, so that fail-silent type fault isolation is achieved. Note that, in the process of fault recovery, support from upper layer system software is necessary. After the interrupt signal is captured, the upper layer software will reset the fault isolation register and start rolling back operation to a checkpoint.

For fault detection technique based on DMR, a failure of one module will prohibit fault isolation through majority voting. Hence, it is necessary to maintain a backup of one circuit module's state. During normal operation, any one of the modules of the DMR is duplicated as backup. Consequently, when a fault occurs, the operation of both modules will be terminated, their circuit state is recovered from the backup, then module operation is restarted.

6.3.2 SRAM-based FPGA Reconfiguration Techniques

This section introduces the FPGA reconfiguration technique used on spacecraft. It includes static reconfiguration and dynamic reconfiguration techniques. The former emphasizes configured read-back through the ICAP interface, verification, and reconfiguration; the latter emphasizes dynamic reconfiguration based on EAPR and fault recovery based on checkpointing.

6.3.2.1 Single Fault Detection and Recovery Technique Based on ICAP+FrameECC

Automatic scrubbing refers to the reconfiguration of the FPGA configuration unit's content. It can reduce the probability of SEU-induced fault in the FPGA [19,20]. The advantage of this method is its simplicity without additional resources. Read-back is the process of reading out all data in internal configuration memory, and can be implemented to determine the correctness of the current configuration data. It can also be used to read all the states of all internal CLB and IOB registers, and all values of RAM and block RAM based on LUT.

Automatic scrubbing, read-back, and reconfiguration to configuration memory are effective methods for SEU hardening. Automatic scrubbing can eliminate the effect of SEU on FPGA periodically. Read-back and reconfiguration are used to examine the correctness of configuration data in FPGA operation, and to reconfigure FPGA when a fault is detected. Therefore, the number of reconfigurations is reduced, and fault recovery is more efficient.

The current Xilinx FPGA configuration access interface includes JTAG, SelectMap, and ICAP, among which JTAG and SelectMap are interfaces for external access. External devices perform FPGA configuration scrubbing and read-back through these two interfaces. JTAG is a low-speed serial interface, while SelectMap is a high-speed parallel interface. SelectMap provides a bidirectional eight-bit communication data bus interface between Virtex configuration logic, and can either be used for configuration or read-back. In this mode, multiple FPGA devices can be configured simultaneously.

Another configuration access interface is ICAP, which is an IC internal access interface. After a control module is realized inside FPGA, self-detection of FPGA is achieved with access to configuration memory through ICAP. The ICAP interface has a simple circuit structure. It can operate without any extra monitor module. The maximum data bandwidth of various configuration modes is shown in Table 6.3.

ICAP is an FPGA internal configuration access interface that connects FPGA IC and the FPGA configuration controller. ICAP enables a processor embedded in FPGA to operate configuration data. The ICAP module is embedded in FPGA as a hard core whose instantiation does not need an extra logic unit; hence, it has no effect on user logic. For convenience using the ICAP interface, Xilinx provides an IP core HWICAP, which can connect directly to the PLB bus after encapsulation of ICAP, as shown in Figure 6.19. Waiting for the configuration/read-back signal from the embedded processor, the HWICAP

Table 6.3 Maximum data bandwidth for various configuration modes.

Configuration Mode	Max. Clk. Rate	Bit Width	Max. Data Bandwidth
JTAG	66 MHz	1 bit	66 Mb/s
SelectMap	100 MHz	32 bit	3.2 Gb/s
ICAP	100 MHz	32 bit	3.2 Gb/s

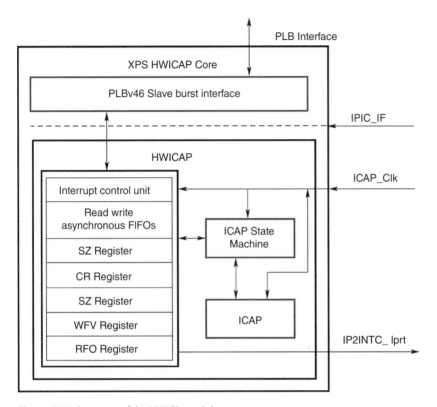

Figure 6.19 Structure of the HWICP module.

module connects to the FPGA internal embedded processor through the PLB bus. The HWICAP module consists of multiple control and state registers. It achieves configuration and read-back through an ICAP hardware interface controlled by the ICAP state machine.

The ICAP >+ FrameECC fault-tolerance technique operates the FPGA configuration bit to realize fault tolerance. In the operating process of the FPGA, efficient fault recovery is achieved by the following method. First, the FPGA configuration file is read back and checked by CRC verification and, if faults are detected, the FPGA configuration file is corrected and rewritten. The overall fault-tolerance design process includes ICAP module instantiation, configuration read-back, CRC verification, and configuration scrubbing, as shown in Figure 6.20.

Instantiation of ICAP module: The ICAP module realizes the interface between the FPGA IC and the FPGA configuration controller. In order to read the current configuration after configuration is complete, a macro-definition of ICAP must first be instantiated. Because the ICAP interface is embedded in

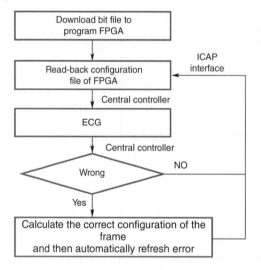

Figure 6.20 ICAP interface configuration read-back, verification, and reconfiguration.

the FPGA, its instantiation does NOT need extra logic unit. The following is an instantiation of the Virtex 6 IC ICAP macro-definition VHDL code:

```
-- ICAP_VERTEX6: Internal Configuration Access
-- Vertex-6
-- Xilinx HDL Libraries Guide, Version
port map (
BUSY = >> BUSY, --BUSY output
O = >> O,-- 8-bit data output
CE = >> CE, -- Clock enable input
CLK = >> CLK, -- Clock input
I = >> I, -- 8-bit data input
WRITE = >> WRITE, -- Write input
);
-- End of ICAP_VERTEX6_inst instantiation
```

- *Configuration read-back.* An instantiated soft-core controller inside the FPGA, called the MicroBlaze, is used to control the ICAP interface reading the configuration bits of each frame in the FPGA and storing the read-back data to buffers.
- *CRC verification.* CRC is a summation of the verification results. It is used for data transmission and error detection reception. Each frame configuration bit read is compares with the corresponding value stored in the original bit stream. If the two values are equal, the frame is correct; otherwise, the frame is faulty and requires configuration scrubbing.

- *Configuration scrubbing.* For a configuration frame with a fault detected after CRC verification, the Softcore MicroBlaze controller will control the ICAP interface to scrub the frame configuration bit and reset the circuit. This technique depends on the read-back capability of a device. It involves the ICAP configuration command, ICAP configuration read-back sequence, FrameECC data verification, etc. These are discussed in the ensuing sections [21].

6.3.2.1.1 Configuration Read-back Based on ICAP

In order to complete file reading and writing operations in ICAP, it is necessary to write the configuration command to the configuration register. The command includes two types of packets: I type and II type.

I type packet: as depicted in Figure 6.21, this is primarily used for reading and writing to the configuration register.

- [31:29]: The first three bits, "001," signify packet type.
- [28:27]: OPCODE determines whether the operation is read or write.
- [26:13]: Address of configuration register, the last five bits are effective.
- [12:11]: Reserved bit.
- [10:0]: Refers to the number of characters being read/written.

II type packet: as depicted in Figure 6.22, this follows a I type packet. It is used for large block data reading and writing.

- [31:29]: The first three bits, "010," signifies the packet type.
- [28:27]: Reserved bit.
- [26:0]: Refers to the number of characters being read/written.

Header type	Opcode	Register address	Reserved	Word count
[31:29]	[29:27]	[26:13]	[12:11]	[10:0]
001	xx	RRRRRRRRRxxxxx	RR	xxxxxxxxxxx

Figure 6.21 Format of an I type packet.

Header type	Opcode	Word count
[31:29]	[28:27]	[26:0]
010	RR	xxxxxxxxxxxxxxxxxxxxxxxxxxx

Figure 6.22 Format of an II type packet.

6.3.2.1.2 ICAP Configuration Read-back Sequence

The ICAP configuration read-back operation follows a rigorous control sequence composed of ICAP initialization, register setup configuration, specified frame data read-back, etc. Table 6.4 lists the steps in detail.

Table 6.4 ICAP read-back operation commands.

Step	Operation	Configuration	Description
STEP 1	write	FFFFFFFF	Invalid
		AA995566	Synchronize
STEP 2	write	02000000	NOP
STEP 3	write	30008001	wire CMD
		00000007	reset CRCreg
		20000000	NOP
STEP 4	write	20000000	NOP
		20000000	NOP
		20000000	NOP
		20000000	NOP
		20000000	NOP
STEP 5	write	30008001	wire CMD
		00000004	Instruction read-back
		20000000	NOP
STEP 6	write	30002001	write FARreg
		00000000	Starting frame address is 0
STEP 7	write	28006000	Package type 1: read data from the read-back frame data register
		48024090	Package type 2: read 147 600 words of data
STEP 8	write	20000000	NOP
		... ...	At least 31 NOP instructions
STEP 9	read	00000000	Read-back word 0
		00000000	Read-back the first 147 599 words
STEP 10	write	20000000	NOP
STEP 11	write	30008001	write CMD
		0000000D	Desynchronized word
STEP 12	write	20000000	NOP
		20000000	NOP

6.3.2.1.3 Configuration Data Verification Based on FrameECC

In order to verify the read-back data, ECC verification technique is utilized. ECC summarizes the verification result to detect faults in data transmission and reception. For every configuration bit in the read-back frame, the information stored in the original bit stream is compared with values computed with a verification circuit. The frame configuration bit information is correct if the two values are equal, otherwise a fault is deemed present and configuration scrubbing is necessary. The Xilinx FPGA provides the Frame_ECC module, which can compute the Hamming characteristic value and compare it with the original characteristic value. A fault is detected if the two are *not* equal. The Frame_ECC module is shown in Figure 6.23.

Table 6.5 gives the details of the FRAME_ECC module's ports. ERROR signal signifies whether a fault has occurred. The SYNDROME signal signifies the location of the faulty bit, whether there is fault, and whether the fault is a one-bit fault or a two-bit fault. The SYNDROMEVALID signal signifies the effectiveness of the SYNDROME signal; a signal that is pulled low signifies the end of a frame of data.

6.3.2.2 Multi-fault Detection and Recovery Technique Based on ICAP Configuration Read-back+RS Coding

The traditional configuration file reinforcement technique is the SECDED Hamming code encoding method. The SECDED encoding method is able to

Figure 6.23 Virtex 4 Frame_ECC module.

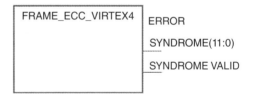

Table 6.5 Description of Frame_ECC port definition.

Port	Direction	Bit width	Function description
ERROR	Output	1	Signifies the occurrence of fault.
SYNDROME	Output	12	Signifies the location of the faulty bit, whether there is a fault, and whether it is a one-bit fault or a two-bit fault.
SYNDROMEVALID	Output	1	Signifies the effectiveness of the SYNDROME signal. A signal pulled low represents the end of the read-back frame.

correct low bit fault in the configuration frame. With the development of IC manufacturing and reduction of transistor size, focus is now on high-energy particle-induced multi-bit faults.

Because RS code can correct both burst errors and random errors, and is especially effective for burst errors, it is widely used in the fault control solution of data communication and storage systems. RS code is a standard code for the NASA and ESA space station in deep space communication. RS code is also the first choice in space application storage systems. In HDTV systems, the data transmission rate is in the range (n to $10n$)/Mb/s, and it possesses high fault correction capability. RS code could be used alone in a normal application. In the hostile communication environment of certain channels, it can be used as the external code of serial joint code, to enable higher fault correction capability to provide high encoding gain and fault correction capability that is equivalent to that of long code. RS code is adopted as external code in single frequency digital broadcasting systems, and convolution code is adopted as cascaded code, with coding parameter (204,188), where 204 is the length of coding and 188 is the effective length of the information element. RS(204,185) code is able to correct a total of eight random and burst errors.

On the basis of the above analysis, it is clear that RS coding possesses effective multi-bit fault correction capability. Therefore, the reinforcement of FPGA configuration file with ICAP configuration read-back > + RS fault-tolerant coding could facilitate tolerance of multi-bit faults. The system design process is shown in Figure 6.24.

The function of the respective modules in Figure 6.24 is as follows:

1) *Central controller*: this is an irradiation hardened processor that operates as a controller to control FPGA configuration file read-back, download, and the RS encoding/decoding device.
2) *ICAP*: this is the FPGA internal configuration interface. Its major function is to complete configuration file read-back and write-back.
3) *Compact Flash*: the major function of this module is to store RS code. If multi-fault exists in the read-back configuration file, it is recoverable with effective information.

The RS encoding and decoding process of the irradiation hardened processor are as follows.

6.3.2.2.1 RS Encoding Circuit

The encoding process of the RS code is shown in Figure 6.25 [17].

1) In the initialization phase, all registers are set to zero, K_1 is closed, and K_2 is connected to the output terminal.
2) B_4, B_3, B_2, B_1, B_0 are entered into the circuit consecutively, and sent to the output terminal.

Figure 6.24 Design process based on ICAP configuration read-back >+ RS fault-tolerant coding.

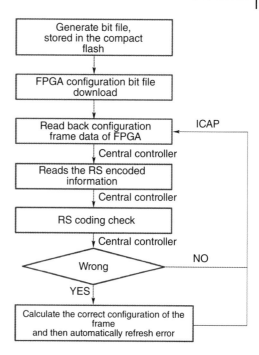

Figure 6.25 RS encoding process.

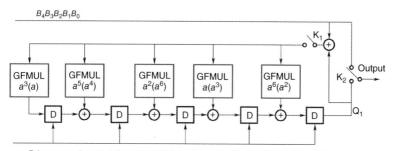

D is one yard word shift register, K1 is switches for the first five yards words

3) Once all five characters have been entered into the circuit, switch K_2 connects to the position of the monitoring character, and K_1 is disconnected.

4) Every information character first performs Galios field multiplication, then mode 2 summation to produce monitor character Q_1 and Q_2, which are sent to the output terminal immediately after the information bit.

The RS encoder realized on the basis of the logic depicted in Figure 6.25 is shown in Figure 6.26. The RS encoding circuit consists of two parts: input buffer and linear feedback shift register. Data_in [7:0] and data_out [7:0] are the data

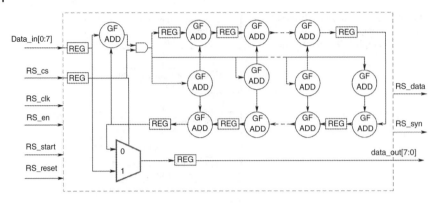

Figure 6.26 RS encoder realization based on FPGA.

input and output terminals of the RS encoder. RS_start represents the synchronous byte of the data block. RS_clk, RS_en, and RS_reset are the system clock, reset signal, and output enable signal. RS_syn is the output terminal used to represent the synchronous byte after encoding. RS_data signifies whether the terminal is information data or verification data. The AND gate in the figure is used as a switch to control data input, and the selector switches between the input data and verification data. According to RS encoding principle, the input stops after the last set of data is loaded, until all verification data is output. Hence, a counter is introduced into the circuit with RS_CS as the counter output signal, whose function is to control the AND gate and the selector.

The GF adding device in Figure 6.26 is the Galios field summation, whose realization requires transformation of polynomial addition with corresponding mode. GF multiplier is Galios field multiplication, whose realization also requires transformation of polynomial multiplication with corresponding mode. The eight shift register RGE are all eight-bit parallel input and output registers.

6.3.2.2.2 RS Decoding Circuit

The receiving end is able to perform fault correction with information bit and correction element S_1 and S_2, which comprise two monitor bytes. If $S_1 >= 0$, $S_2 >= 0$, there is no bit error; if $S_1 > \neq 0$, $S_2 > \neq 0$, there is error bit.

If there is only one faulty group, B_0, then $B_0 >= B_0 + B_0'$, and the correction element equation is:

$$S_1 = B_0' + B_0 + B_1 + B_2 + B_3 + B_4 + Q_0 + Q_1 = B_0'$$
$$S_2 = a(B_0 + B_0') + a^2 B_1 + a^3 B_2 + a^4 B_3 + a^5 B_4 + a^6 Q_0 + a^7 Q_1 = a B_0'$$

i.e., $S_2 >= a S_1$.

Similarly,

- if group B_1 is faulty, $S_2 >= a_2 S_1$;
- if group B_2 is faulty, $S_2 >= a_3 S_1$;
- if group B_3 is faulty, $S_2 >= a_4 S_1$;
- if group B_4 is faulty, $S_2 >= a_5 S_1$.

The above equations show that one faulty group of characters is corrective; if S_1 and S_2 does not satisfy the above equations, and neither S_1 nor S_2 is zero, it can only detect two faulty groups. When B_4, B_3, B_2, B_1, B_0 have self-detection capabilities, it can correct two groups of error code with correction element equations.

For example, suppose B_1, B_0 are two groups of error code; the correction element equations are:

$$S_1 = B_0' + B_0 + B_1 + B_2 + B_3 + B_4 + Q_0 + Q_1 = B_0' + B_1'$$

$$S_2 = a(B_0 + B_0') + a^2(B_0 + B_0') + a^3 B_2 + a^4 B_3 + a^5 B_4 + a^6 Q_0 + a^7 Q_1$$

$$a^6 Q_0 + a^7 Q_1 = a B_0' + a B_1'$$

From which:

$$B_0' = a_5 S_1 + a_3 S_2$$
$$B_1' = a_4 S_1 + a_3 S_2$$

If both B_0 and B_1 have self-detection capability, corrective action could be taken, based on the above equations.

Berlekamp proposed the RS code iterative decoding algorithm from an algebraic perspective. It started from a linear feedback shift register, and evolved into the Berlekamp-Massey RS algorithm, which is able to improve system decoding speed; hence, it is very efficient. Therefore, the Berlekamp-Massey decoding algorithm is recommended. The following is the application process:

- Compute the adjoint equation.
- Perform iterative computation to acquire the fault location polynomial.
- Implement Chlen searching to solve for the root of the fault location polynomial, whose reciprocal is the fault location.
- Implement the Forney algorithm to solve for the value of the error.

The RS decoding process is illustrated in Figure 6.27.

In summary, the multi-fault detection and recovery technique based on ICAP configuration read-back $>+$ RS fault encoding can tolerate both multiple faults in FPGA memory, and fault in the storage verification bit in compact flash. Hence, it is effective against SEE.

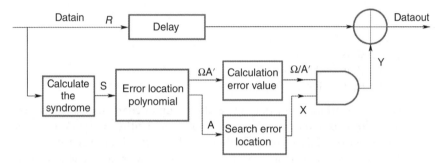

Figure 6.27 RS decoding process.

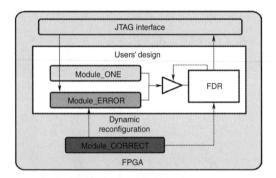

Figure 6.28 Module-level dynamic reconfiguration fault recovery.

6.3.2.3 Dynamic Reconfiguration Technique Based on EAPR

FPGA dynamic reconfiguration refers to the online reconfiguration of certain FPGA logic functions with control logic, while other IC functions remains unchanged. The dynamic reconfiguration technique is a new design concept – that is, realization of large-scale sequential system with limited hardware resources. It transforms the traditional space distributed hardware logic into internally time domain-transformed logic module combination, while the external performance remains unchanged, so that complete logic function is achieved in both the time and space domains.

The dynamic reconfiguration fault recovery technique recovers faults from the module perspective. When the DMR/TMR module detects a fault, the central controller reads the configuration bit of the faulty bit, and recovers the fault during system operation, as shown in Figure 6.28. The dynamic reconfiguration fault recovery technique only recovers FPGA faulty modules. Its major advantage is high recovery speed and low influence on system function, because other circuits remain in normal operation during the configuration period.

The FPGA dynamic reconfiguration function was proposed and realized by Xilinx. The Altera Stratix V type FPGA, released in July 2010, also supports the dynamic reconfiguration technique. For dynamic reconfiguration, Xilinx proposed four types of design processes:

1) *Dynamic reconfiguration based on modularization.* The dynamic reconfiguration fault recovery technique divides the design into several modules, which constrain its corresponding physical area. These modules include reconfiguration module (physical area on which reconfiguration is realized) and static module (physical area whose function remains unchanged). In a completed design, every module is independent. The physical area constraint of each module is fixed and does not change during circuit operation.

   In order to ensure the communication between the reconfigured module and the static module before and after reconfiguration, it is necessary to ensure the consistency of wiring resources that cross the boundary of the reconfiguration modules. A special logic structure – bus macro, which is a predefined type of macro, possessing a predetermined wiring route – is used to fulfill this purpose. Bus macro enables signals needed by the static module to be unaffected by the change in the reconfigured module, so that the correctness of signal connection between modules is guaranteed.

2) *Dynamic reconfiguration based on difference* compares the circuit difference before and after reconfiguration, to generate a configuration current that includes design difference only. Circuit design modification can be performed in two layers: the RTL layer (modify HDL description); and the physical layer (modify NCD file). For RTL layer modifications, the modified RTL code needs to perform renewed logic combination, layout, and wiring to create the corresponding NCD file. For physical layer modifications, the NCD file can be directly modified with an FPGA editor tool without logic combination. For the acquired NCD file, a reconfigured bit stream file is created with the Bit-GEN tool.

3) *Dynamic reconfiguration based on bit stream* is a method realized by lower layer reconfiguration. The method is able to locate any bit of the configuration information. Xilinx released the JBits 3.0 tool in August 2003. JBits consists of a series of Java class libraries, which provide an interface for direct access by the Xilinx FPGA bit stream file (API) [22]. These APIs can read and modify logic, layout, and wiring information in the bit stream, provide configuration file download and read-back function, and control the FPGA IC to perform dynamic reconfiguration. The advantages of this method are high accuracy and visibility of low layer physical information. However, the complex design process and lack of perfect design and verification tool requires deep user understanding of the FPGA IC's physical structure. Currently, this method supports only FPGA ICs prior to VirtexII. It cannot support new devices.

4) *Dynamic reconfiguration based on the EAPR method.* EAPR is a dynamic reconfiguration design method proposed by Xilinx. This method can significantly simplify the dynamic reconfiguration design method with the latest dynamic reconfiguration design tool PlanAhead, and can also perform simulated operations. It is similar to the modularized dynamic reconfiguration method, but has the following improvements:

- It eliminates the requirement that the reconfiguration area must be a whole column in design method based on modules. It allows the reconfiguration area to be any rectangular area.
- It utilizes the bus macro based on SLICE, instead of that based on TBUF, to improve bus density between modules.
- It allows the global signal of static design to cross the reconfiguration area without using bus macro to improve circuit sequential performance and simplify the compilation process in reconfiguration design.
- It eliminates the constraint on the static module area to provide greater flexibility for layout and wiring.
- The EAPR design process and toll supports the latest Virtex 4 and Virtex 5 devices.

For the dynamic reconfiguration technique, this section focuses on the latest EAPR dynamic reconfiguration design method released by Xilinx, which can simplify the overall EAPR-based dynamic reconfiguration design process with design tool PlanAhead, and eliminates multiple constraint conditions to make the design more flexible and circuit performance less affected [23].

The dynamic reconfiguration design process based on EAPR is illustrated in Figures 6.29 and 6.30.

The design method can be divided into the following steps:

1) *HDL design description and synthesis.* This includes design and synthesis of the top module, static module, and partial reconfiguration module. The top module does not realize any logic functions. The static module and partial reconfiguration module are instantiated as components in the top module. The hierarchical view and plane layout of each module are shown in Figure 6.31.

After the design of every module is completed in hardware circuit description language (VHDL or Verilog), the net table file (.ngc file or.edf file, created with another synthesis tool) of the overall design is acquired through synthesis of each module, with the help of the ISE synthesis tool. For the various PRMs of the same partial reconfiguration region (PRR), it is necessary to setup different engineering catalogs. However, the file name and final net table name remain consistent. In order to ensure the correctness of module interconnection before and after reconfiguration, the bus macro based on SLICE needs to be instantiated as a component in the top module. Bus macro is a pre-wiring hardware circuit, located between adjacent or

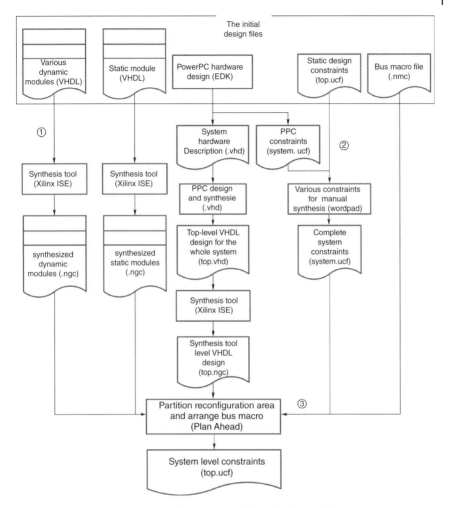

Figure 6.29 Synthesis realization of top layer module and sub-modules.

nonadjacent modules, that will not change with reconfiguration of the module. Thus, the bus macro can guarantee correct communication among reconfiguration modules, and reconfiguration module and static module. Any non-global signal between reconfiguration module and static module must go through the bus macro.

2) *Set design constraint.* This step defines the initial user constraint file (top. ucf), which includes pin constraint of the top layer file, and some global sequential constraints. The FPGA design differs from other DPR processes by the fact that area constraint and module area division are *not* performed here, but are added with the PlanAhead tool.

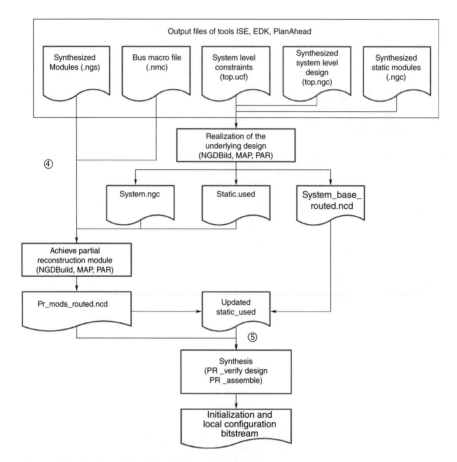

Figure 6.30 Configuration file creation process.

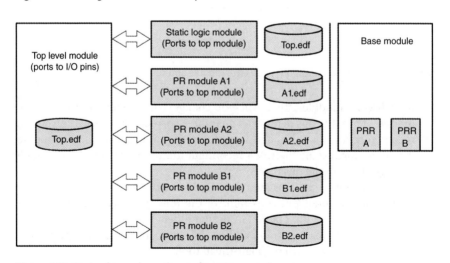

Figure 6.31 Design hierarchy and reconfiguration area layout.

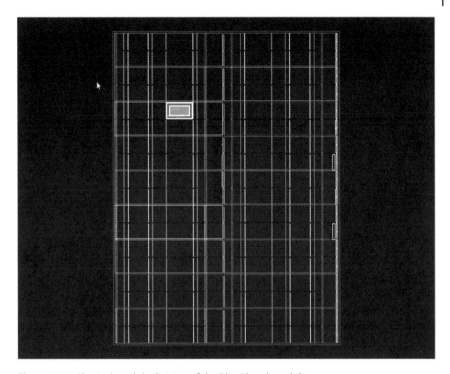

Figure 6.32 Physical module division of the PlanAhead module.

3) *EAPR design with PlanAhead.* This step follows the following procedure. First, configure the project as a partial reconfiguration (PR) project, input the.ngc file of each module and global constraint file top.ucf, acquired from **1** above. Next, utilize the floorplan of the PlanAhead tool to plan each PRR area manually, then add the corresponding PRM module to each PRR area to gain the advantage of observing PRR area resource occupancy. If occupancy reaches or exceeds 100%, it is necessary to replan the PRR area manually. Finally, place the bus macro and global clock logic. If this is performed manually, it will be necessary to ensure that the bus macro crosses the boundary of the static and reconfiguration modules. Physical area division of the PlanAhead module is shown in Figure 6.32.

4) *Active modules.* Run Ngdbuid, MAP, and PAR instruction for every module, to activate all static and reconfiguration modules, combined with the top module and constraint.

5) *Final assembly.* Complete the top module and every low level module, static module, and the assembly of each reconfiguration module, to create the FPGA initial bit stream and configuration bit stream file of the reconfiguration module.

6) *Debug on board.* Load the FPGA initial bit stream file, then manually load the local reconfiguration bit stream file of the reconfiguration module.

In the reliability design process, the dynamic reconfiguration technique based on EAPR monitors the circuit state of the configuration module created by each module, using the central controller. If the fault detection module detects a circuit fault, it will call the corresponding dynamic reconfiguration module to scrub the circuit configuration bit, in order to eliminate the negative influence of fault on the circuit's normal functioning.

6.3.2.4 Fault Recovery Technique Based on Hardware Checkpoint

In the checkpoint recovery technique, checkpoints are set up periodically to store program operation state into memory before critical program operation, and to provide necessary information for system state reset. If a system fault occurs in later operations, the system will perform rollback recovery to read out the state stored in the last checkpoint, and continue running from the checkpoint.

The design hierarchy of the checkpoint recovery technique can be classified as software checkpoint and hardware checkpoint. Software checkpoint focuses on the intermediate state of system operation. It stores and recovers the system's internal operation state, with additional software instruction. Hardware checkpoint stores the internal flip-flop logic value of the circuit at the hardware level. It is transparent to upper layer software. Because hardware checkpoint directly extracts bottom hardware flip-flop state, the time cost is lower than that of software checkpoint. Furthermore, hardware checkpoint can utilize features of the hardware structure to accelerate checkpoint set-up and state recovery.

Because FPGA hardware circuit operation state depends on the flip-flop logic state stored in the circuit, it is possible to extract all FPGA flip-flop logic states. In the process of hardware checkpoint setup, it is necessary to sample the logic state of all flip-flops, IO modules, and BlockRAMs, then map the logic state acquired to the FPGA IC configuration file, and read out the configuration file with the FPGA configuration interface. Finally, the read-out configuration file is analyzed and the logic value related to circuit state stored, as shown in Figure 6.33.

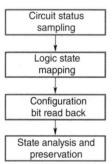

Figure 6.33 Hardware checkpoint setup process.

For the first and second steps of configuration readback, the sampling logic state of the circuit internal flip-flop, IO module, and BlockRAM is achieved with Capture hardcore, provided by Xilinx FPGA. The structure of Capture hardcore is shown in Figure 6.34. When the hardcore of Capture is triggered by a signal, it maps the circuit logic state to the CLB and IOB columns of the FPGA configuration bit.

For the third step of the configuration read-back, the configuration file read-back is achieved with the ICAP

configuration read-back interface provided by ICAP. The implementation of
the ICAP interface to the read-back
configuration of data can be used to
realize a controller within the IC, with a
simple circuit structure and without an
additional monitor module.

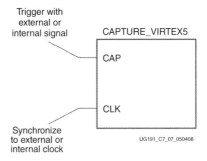

Figure 6.34 Structure of FPGA Capture module.

For the fourth step of the configuration read-back, a design.II file is acquired
with the "-1" option in the FPGA configuration file creation process. This file
refers to the corresponding configuration bit location of each design circuit
flip-flop state FPGA configuration file. Based on the indicated location, circuit
state is analyzed with the read-back configuration file.

6.3.2.5 Summary of Reconfiguration Fault-tolerance Techniques

It is necessary to consider the following factors when choosing a proper FPGA
reconfiguration technique:

1) System task type – uninterrupted work/intermittent work.
2) Role of FPGA in the whole system – critical component or not.
3) Fault processing focus – fault detection/fault correction/fault-tolerance.
4) System reliability requirements.

A different SEU fault processing method is selected based on various task
types [24,25]:

1) *Global reconstruction.* This method is applicable to intermittent
   working systems, such as image processing, data processing, and so on.
   If the system allows the FPGA to remain idle temporarily, reliability is
   improved with periodic reconfiguration to eliminate configuration
   memory SEU fault.
   The major feature is that this method totally depends on global reconstruction without considering fault detection and location. This is the simplest
   reconfiguration method.

2) *Read-back > + Global reconstruction.* This method is applicable to systems
   that are able to tolerate a certain amount of SEU fault. It first completes fault
   detection and count with read-back and configuration bit stream comparison, then performs FPGA global reconstruction when fault is accumulated
   to a certain amount. This method is successfully implemented in the
   Australia scientific experiment satellite FedSat (developed by the Australia
   Queensland University of Technology and Johns Hopkins University
   Applied Physics Laboratory as the first spacecraft to implement the

reconfiguration computational technique. It was launched at NASA Goddard Space Flight Center on December 14, 2002). The major features of this method are as follows:

- Compared with methods that totally depend on global reconstruction, Read-back >+ Global reconstruction method is more flexible on the timing of reconfiguration, while extending the range of the applicable system.
- This method is applicable to FPGA SEE experiments to further understand the anti-radiation properties of FPGA internal component, through fault location based on fault detection.

3) *Scrubbing*. This method is applicable to continuous, uninterrupted working systems. SEU fault detection and location is completed with configuration read-back and comparison. Correct configuration data frame is written into FPGA to correct SEU fault with partial FPGA reconfiguration. Major features of this method are the following:

- Compared with the previous two methods, the amount of configuration data that this method writes into FPGA is significantly reduced; hence, the amount of time required for configuration is reduced.
- Partial reconstruction does *not* affect the normal working of the non-reconstruction area. Therefore, this method is applicable to uninterrupted systems.

4) *TMR >+ Scrubbing*. This is the most extensively used reconfiguration technique, both domestically and abroad. This method is similar to the SEU fault processing method, which totally depends on scrubbing. Due to FPGA's adoption of TMR fault-tolerance technique, the reliability of this method is higher. It is applicable to critical missions such as communication and navigation missions.

When fully utilizing the configuration flexibility of SRAM-based FPGA, it is very important to take protective measures against sensitivity of SRAM-based FPGA to SEU in the space environment. Selection of SEU protective measures for SRAM-based FPGA space application should be based on the application scenario to acquire cost performance. The following are major principles:

- When used on low-orbit spacecraft with a short life cycle in a less hostile space environment, applying TMR design for a critical system is enough.
- When used on high-orbit spacecraft in hostile space environment, SEU protective measures must be taken. System design should enable SRAM-based FPGA reconfiguration capability.
- Apply both TMR and dynamic scrubbing protective measure to critical systems with high real-time performance requirement. SRAM-based FPGA should be cautiously applied in some main circuits of core systems.

6.4   Typical Fault-tolerance Design of SRAM-based FPGA

This section mainly introduces realization of automatic scrubbing, read-back, and the reconfiguration technique based on ICAP. Fault injection, fault detection, and fault recovery system functions are achieved based on the ICAP interface of the Xilinx Virtex-6 series XC6VLX550T type FPGA IC. A system block diagram is shown in Figure 6.35.

- *User logic.* This is the logic function achieved by user self-definition. It is connected to the external environment with user interface to realize specific logic function.
- *Fault injection module.* This module connects to the PC terminal through the JTAG line. Fault injection is achieved with ChipScope-controlled internal fault injection enable signal.
- *External interface module.* This module connects to external compact flash (CF) with SPI bus, to read information on the configuration bit in the CF card, including the correct configuration bit and partial information in the critical configuration bit.
- *Display interface module.* This module connects to the PC terminal through a RS232 serial interface and interacts with the user to help the user acquire circuit state information, so that the corresponding control function is completed.
- *ICAP module.* This module completes the IC internal configuration bit read-and write-back operation.
- *ECC frame verification module.* This module computes the ECC value for every frame's configuration bit, and compares it with the original ECC value stored in the configuration bit to determine fault existence in a frame.

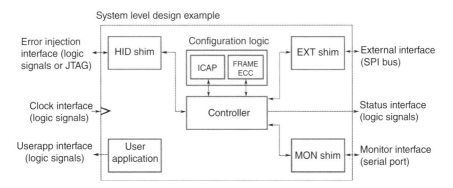

Figure 6.35 ICAP automatic scrubbing, read-back, and reconfiguration prototype system.

- *Central control module.* This module controls the above modules. When fault injection is performed, the controller receives instructions from the fault injection module to acquire fault injection position and value, then creates a fault configuration frame through invoking the ICAP interface and reading the configuration bit frame of the targeted location. Next, the controller downloads the fault configuration bit to complete fault injection.

In the fault detection phase, the central control module polls all configuration frames in the FPGA IC. It reads the corresponding configuration bit frame through the ICAP interface, and invokes the ECC frame verification module to perform fault detection and to determine if there is fault. If a fault exists in the configuration, fault recovery is performed with ECC verification; otherwise, the control module continues to check the configuration bit of the next frame. Note that ECC verification can only detect and correct a single fault of the configuration bit in a frame. When there are two faults in a frame, ECC is able to detect the faults, but cannot correct them, so the central control module will read back the correct configuration data through the external interface module and perform fault recovery through the ICAP interface. In order to reduce the influence of faults on normal circuit operation, when a fault is detected, the central control module is able to read the configuration information in the CF card to determine whether the fault will affect the circuit's normal function. If this is so, then fault recovery is performed. Otherwise, fault recovery will not be performed, to maintain the circuit's normal operation.

In the process of circuit realization, the first step is to setup the top module sem_example in the Xilinx ISE tool. Each sub-module is instantiated in the top module; example_controller realizes the interface between central control module and periphery modules; example_hid realizes fault injection module. In addition, the top module directly realizes user logic in the Verilog language and invokes the ICAP interface to configure the FPGA with the example_cfg module. For the display interface module, RS232 communication protocol is realized with the example_mon module, to connect with a PC terminal so that interaction with the FPGA is completed.

In the process of realization of each instantiated module, it is necessary to invoke IP core in the Xilinx IP library, using the Xilinx Core Generator to realize partial instantiated modules. Sem_v2_1 realizes instantiated module example_controller to complete the function of the central controller. ChipScope core completes instantiated example_hid module to complete fault injection function.

After logic circuit synthesis is completed, it is necessary to constrain the location of each module in PlanAhead, in order to achieve better sequential performance. As shown in Figure 6.36, the constraint module example_controller is located around the ICAP interface for convenient interaction

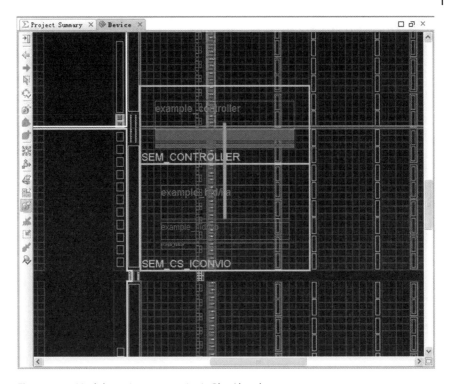

Figure 6.36 Module position constraint in PlanAhead.

between the central control module and the ICAP interface. Next, the FPGA circuit realization process is completed through layout wiring and configuration creation.

It is necessary to configure the central control module to realize polling capability during circuit operation, so that fault detection against FPGA configuration frame is performed uninterrupted. Once a fault is detected, ECC fault correction and reconfiguration should be completed. Note that fault detection time is determined according to the relation between the fault location and the current fault detection operation. If the fault is located in the frame after the current one being detected, it is detectable in the next detection cycle. This scenario requires minimum fault detection time.

If a fault is located in the position where fault detection was performed in the last detection cycle, it is necessary to wait until the next fault detection cycle polls the current fault location. This scenario requires maximum fault detection time. Therefore, the average fault detection time is one-half of the time required to complete the full IC fault detection time. During circuit operation,

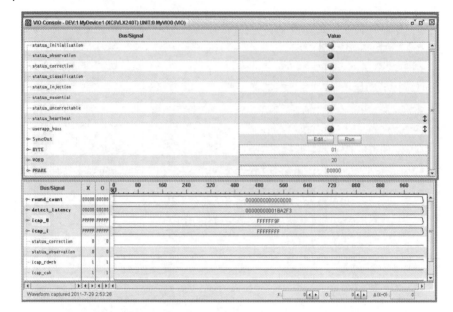

Figure 6.37 Signal observation and control in ChipScope.

circuit fault injection and fault observation are completed using the ChipScope observation and internal signal control function. Signal control and observation are shown in Figure 6.37.

In order to verify the dynamic reconfiguration technique based on EAPR, an SoC based on LEON3 is realized in the Xilinx Virtex-6 series XC6VLX550T type FPGA. The LEON series microprocessor is a 32-bit reduced instruction set computer (RISC) based on the SPARC V8 architecture, and comprises LEON, LEON2, and LEON3. The LEON series processor is released in the form of RTL level VHDL source code for free. Users can apply and study the source code, according to GNUL GPL (Library General Public License). LEON Softcore is an integer unit (IU) that is compatible with SPARC V8. LEON2 possesses a five-stage pipeline, and LEON3 possesses a seven-stage pipeline. Currently, there are two versions of LEON3: LEON3 and LEON3FT (LEON3 fault-tolerance); the latter has fault-tolerant capability, based on the LEON3 kernel targeting space applications. The LEON3 microprocessor has the following features:

1) Seven-stage pipeline structure.
2) Hardware multiplication/division and MAC capability.
3) Independent instruction and data cache (Harvard structure).
4) Flexible cache capacity configuration, based on requirement.

5) On-chip bus using the AMBA2.0 protocol to support the APB and AHB standards.

6) General purpose peripherals (UART, interruption control, I/O interface, real-time clock, watch dog, etc.).

The configurable architecture of the LEON3 microprocessor is shown in Figures 6.38 and 6.39. The operation of the LEON3 integer unit complies with the SPARC V8 standard, including multiplication and division instructions. The default number of requirement-configurable register windows is eight, which is within the limits of the SPARC standard. The Harvard structure seven-stage pipeline possesses discrete instruction and data cache interfaces. LEON3 has an excellent configurable cache system, which consists of discrete instruction and data caches. Back-fill delay is minimized with the use of streaming instruction cache online back-filling operation. The data cache interface uses a write-through strategy to execute a dual character writing buffer.

The float point unit (FPU) and coprocessor of LEON3 provide high performance floating point processing and a self-defined coprocessor. As long as there is no dependence on the data or resources, the parallel processing of the FPU, coprocessor, and integer unit will not impede operations.

The memory management unit (MMU) complies with all SPARC V8 standards, and it realizes 32-bit virtual address and 36-bit physical memory

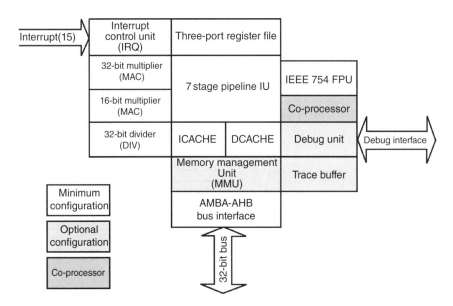

Figure 6.38 LEON3 microprocessor configurable architecture.

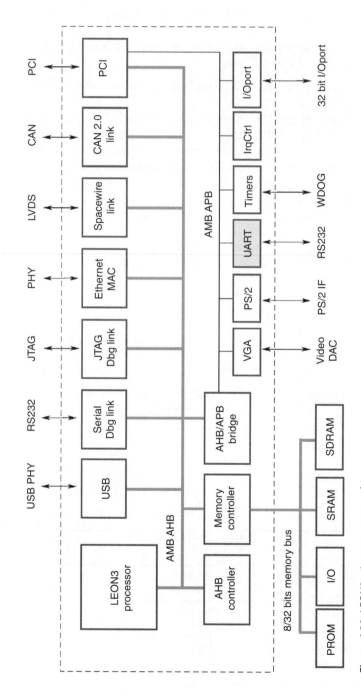

Figure 6.39 LEON3 microprocessor architecture.

mapping. The MMU is able to configure up to 64 completely associated TLM input ports to access hardware and software code during operation, for convenient later stage debugging.

In the system realization process, the Xilinx Virtex-6 series XC6VLX550T type FPGA IC is adopted to realize a fault-tolerant SoC, based on the LEON3 processor kernel plus external interface IP. A quad-core LEON3 processor can achieve 200 MIPS. Peripherals such as serial port, timer, and SPI interface are realized on SoC. Fault detection is achieved by invoking ICAP >+ FrameECC interface on the FPGA board.

First, static module synthesis and function verification, and top module design and realization are completed in ISE. Note that top module design requires a hierarchical design method to instantiate the reconfiguration module as a blackbox. Next, multiple dynamic modules are designed to ensure the consistency of each dynamic module interface with the top module interface. After static design of each module is completed, physical area division and module assembly is achieved with PlanAhead software.

When performing verification for the dynamic reconfiguration technique, the adder module of all executive components is selected to be dynamically reconfigured. First, opened width aware redundant execution (OWARE) error detection capability is added to the processor. When a fault is injected into the adder through the VIO kernel of ChipScope, which controls the internal signal, the processor will detect the fault, in order to verify the effectiveness of fault injection with the fault in program operation. In comparison tests, the dynamic reconfiguration technique is adopted to dynamically reconfigure faults. If the program operates normally, reconfiguration has not affected circuit function. Furthermore, correct output is acquired through the "reset" signal of the reconfiguration flip-flop circuit.

After dynamic reconfiguration verification is completed, it is necessary to verify the configuration time with two groups of tests. The first group performs comparison between the output of the static and dynamic reconfiguration combinational logic. Both modules are driven by the same data source. In the reconfiguration, the different output periods are counted after comparison of both outputs. If the output of the counter is *not* zero, then the dynamic reconfiguration process will affect the circuit's normal function. If the output of the counter remains zero, then the dynamic reconfiguration process will not affect the circuit's normal function.

In this test, in order to achieve maximum reduction of delay incurred by circuit wiring, the area of the dynamic module is relatively small and circuit function is simple. The circuit structure consists of dual module input signal gated logic with an LUT, as shown in Figure 6.40(a). In the process of dynamic reconfiguration, this test selects the JTAG interface to configure. The configuration bandwidth is 12 Mb/s, the bit stream file created is 183.2 MB, and the theoretical time required for configuration is 183.2 kB/12 Mb/s >= 0.122 s. The

(a)

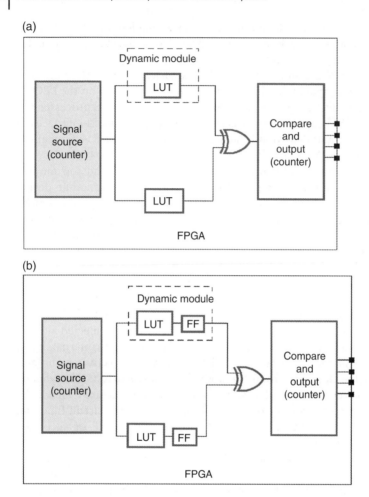

(b)

Figure 6.40 Dynamic reconfiguration time verification circuit. (a) Combinational function verification circuit structure (b) Sequential function verification circuit structure.

test results show that the reconfiguration process will not affect the circuit's normal function if the working frequency is below 8 Hz and the configuration time is less than one clock cycle. Otherwise, the dynamic reconfiguration process will affect the circuit's normal function. The test results matched the results of the theoretical analysis.

The second group performs comparison between both sequential logic outputs. The function is similar to that of the combinational logic type; the only difference is the additional sequential unit in the reconfiguration module to perform comparison after the sequential module outputs value.

The introduction of the sequential unit causes the reconfiguration module to occupy a large amount of resources – that is, a total of 63 LUTs and 32 FFs. Note that the dynamic reconfiguration process's latching up of all input and output signals causes the state of the reconfiguration module circuit to remain constant. Further, the state of the static module circuit varies as the input varies, so the output of the two modules may be different. Test results show that, at functional frequency, the dynamic reconfiguration process will affect the circuit's normal function. This matches the theoretical prediction.

In summary, the dynamic reconfiguration process is able to complete circuit structure update without affecting the other module's function. However, in the reconfiguration process, the module configuration time is relatively long, compared with the circuit operation clock cycle, so using the module output will affect the circuit's normal function. Furthermore, if there is a sequential unit in the circuit, the reconfiguration process will retain the circuit state unchanged until configuration is complete. Therefore, when using the dynamic reconfiguration technique, the focus should be on the influence of the module output to circuit function. The user can utilize the time slot in which there is no reconstruction module output to perform dynamic reconfiguration, or to set up restore points manually in the reconfiguration process, to restore the state after dynamic reconfiguration is complete, so that the circuit's normal function is guaranteed.

Verification of the realization of FPGA configuration read-back based on the ICAP interface, automatic scrubbing, and dynamic reconfiguration based on EAPR were performed by building a million-gate FPGA hardware platform. The test results obtained shows that the performance specifications of the configuration read-back and verification technique based on the ICAP interface, and dynamic reconfiguration technique based on EAPR, comply with the theoretical prediction. Hence, the FPGA technique is an applicable solution for spacecraft.

6.5 Fault-tolerance Techniques of Anti-fuse Based FPGA

The major anti-fuse based FPGA product used in space applications is the Actel FPGA. The classification, structure, and fault-tolerance design method associated with this product are discussed below.

Actel provides the anti-fuse programming SEU-hardened SX series FPGA, whose structure is described as "mass module", because the entire base of the device is covered by a network of logic modules and no IC resource is left for the interconnect unit and wiring. The Actel SX series has been improved over the past several years. The first version provided two types of logic modules, which are the same as the standard Actel series. Examples of register cell (R-cell) and combinational logic call (C-cell) are shown in Figure 6.41.

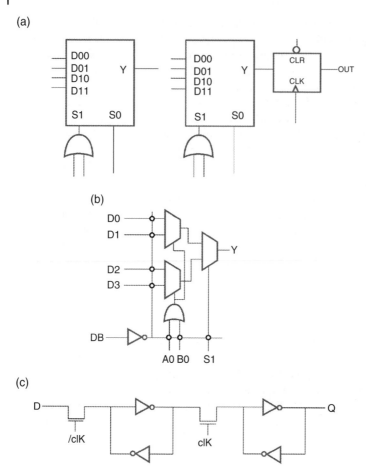

Figure 6.41 Structure of Actel FPGA. (a) Combinational ACTI (C-cell) and sequential ACTI (R-cell). (b) Detailed layout of C-cell. (c) R-cell: description of latch.

The interconnection of these logic modules is achieved through the implementation of Actel's patented "metal to metal" programmable anti-fuse interconnection units. These anti-fuse units are embedded between the metal of the second and third layers, are normally open-circuit and become permanent low impedance connections after being programmed.

In order to adapt to the high-reliability requirement of certain applications, current anti-fuse based FPGAs also implement anti-radiation hardening techniques, which includes TMR and replacement of sequential logic (C-cell) with combinational logic. The following is a brief introduction.

There are three types of sequential logic realization techniques that are able to avoid single-particle upset in the first anti-SEU FPGA version: CC, TMR,

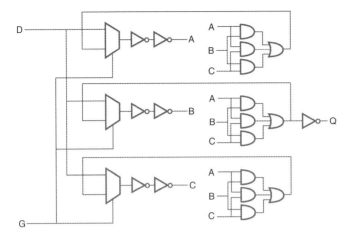

Figure 6.42 Memory unit internal TMR of radiation resistant FX or AX structured Actel FPGA.

and TMR_CC. In the Symplify tool, the sequential logic unit is realized automatically during the synthesis process. The CC technique realized the memory unit by replacing the flip-flop or latch primitive with combinational logic. For example, DFP1 consists of two combinational logic modules to replace DF1. This technique can avoid SEU in the CMOS manufacturing process, which is larger than 0.23 μm, but cannot avoid SEU in the next-generation manufacturing process, in which the combinational logic will be affected by charged particles. TMR is used to realize the registers, and each register state is realized with three flip-flops or latches voting. TMR_CC is also a triple redundancy technique. Each voting register consists of a combinational logic unit with feedback capability (to replace the flip-flop or latch primitive).

The design created by CC flip-flop (CC-FF) is more resistant to SEU than that created by the standard flip-flop (S-FF). In a typical scenario, CC-FF uses twice as much area resource as S-FF. The design created by three times voting or TMR is more SEU-resistant. Three times voting uses a majority gate voting circuit that consists of three flip-flops, rather than a single flip-flop. In this method, if one flip-flop switches to a faulty state, the other two will shield it, so that the correct value is propagated to the rest of the circuit. Three times voting is normally realized with multiple S-FFs, as a result of cost considerations (compared with language realization of S-FF, the area used is three or four times larger, and delay is two times larger). However, it is possible to realize three times voting with multiple CC-FFs in Symplify.

Currently, Actel provides RTFSX and RTAXS FPGA series devices (radiation resistant FX and AX structure space version). Configuration of these devices involves the use of metal-to-metal anti-fuse connections, including internal

TMR of all registers. These new SEU reinforced structures do *not* need HDL language to realize TMR flip-flop design, because the flip-flop is protected with structural layer (matrix) TMR. The D type flip-flop shown in Figure 6.42 is used. Three D flip-flops connect to clock and data input in parallel, and a voting machine (or majority voting circuit) is realized with a front end multiplexer to create a "reinforced" output. Outputs A and B of the two flip-flops connect to the selection end of the voting multiplexer. If both A and B are at logic zero, input D0 of the multiplexer is selected. Because it is connected to the ground, the output of the multiplexer is zero. Similarly, if both A and B are at logic one, the output of the multiplexer is one. If A and B are different because of SET (or another factor), the multiplexer will select flip-flop C. Because C is equal to either A or B, the voted multiplexer will create two consistent data sets among the three flip-flops.

References

1 Doumar A, Ito H (2003). Detecting, diagnosing, and tolerating faults in SRAM-based field programmable gate arrays: a survey. *IEEE Transactions on Very Large Scale Integration (VLSI) Systems* **11**(3), 386–405.

2 He Zhaohui (2001). Study of methods for predicting SEU rate in space orbits. *Chinese Journal of Space Science* **21**(3), 266–273.

3 Li Dongmei, Wang Zhihua, Gao Wenhuan, Zhang Zunqiao (2000). Spatial radiation effect and hardening techniques for FPGA. *Application of Electronic Technique* **26**(8), 4–6.

4 Yang Juan *et al* (2005). Computational analysis of low orbit reconnaissance satellite with plasma interference. *Journal of Northwestern Polytechnical University* [J] **23**(1), 93–97.

5 Wang Changlong, Shen Shiqin, Zhang Chuanjun (1995). Design method of on-board equipment tolerance of single event phenomena. Aeronautics Control **3**, 24–30.

6 Velazco R, Ecoffet R, Faure F (2005). *How to characterize the problem of SEU in processors & representative errors observed on flight* [C]. Proceedings of the 11th IEEE International On-Line Testing Symposium (IOLTS '05), 303–308.

7 Robinson P, Coakley P (1992). Spacecraft charging-progress in the study of dielectrics and plasmas [J]. *IEEE Transactions on Electrical Insulation* **27**(5), 944–960.

8 Hao Zhigang, Yang Mengfei (2009). Fault mode analysis and fault tolerant methodology for SRAM-based FPGA on spacecraft. *Aerospace Control and Application* **35**(1), 51–55.

9 Keheng Huang, Yu Hu, Xiaowei Li, *et al* (2012). *Off-path leakage power aware routing for SRAM-based FPGAs* [C]. In: Proceedings of IEEE/ACM Design Automation and Test in Europe Conference (DATE 2012), 87–92.

10 Kastensmidt F L, Carro L, Reis R (2006). *Fault-tolerance techniques for SRAM-based FPGA*. Springer.

11 Hao Zhigang (2009). *Research and implementation of fault tolerance methods for SARM-based FPGA* [D]: [Master Thesis]: Beijing Institute of Control Engineering.

12 Keheng Huang, Yu Hu, Xiaowei Li, *et al* (2011). *Research on FPGA fine grained reliability design method based on functional equivalence class* [C]. The 14th National Conference of Fault tolerant Computing.

13 Keheng Huang, Yu Hu, Xiaowei Li, *et al* (2011). *Exploiting free LUT entries to mitigate soft errors in SRAM-based FPGAs* [C]. In: Proceedings of IEEE Asia Test Symposium (ATS), 438–443.

14 Chen Chen, Yang Mengfei, Liu Hongjin (2012). The design and verification of triple modular redundancy MPSoC fault tolerant processor. *Aerospace Control and Application* **38**(4), 45–50.

15 Wen Liang (2004). *Research on SoC fault tolerance method for satellite applications* [D]: [Master Thesis]. Beijing Institute of Control Engineering.

16 Wen Liang, Yang Mengfei (2005). Research on SoC fault tolerance method for satellite applications [J]. *Control Engineering* (**2**), 34–39.

17 Wang Xinmei, Xiao Guozhen (1991). *Error correction code – principles and methods* [M]. Xi'an: Xidian University Press.

18 Keheng Huang, Yu Hu, Xiaowei Li (2014). Reliability-oriented placement and routing algorithm for SRAM-based FPGAs [J]. *IEEE Trans. On Very Large Scale Integration (VLSI) Systems* **22**(2), 256–269.

19 Zhu Kaike (2006). *Research of FPGA dynamic reconfiguration design method.* [Master Thesis]: Zhejiang University.

20 Chen Yuming (2005). *Research and implementation of Virtex-II based dynamic partial reconfiguration technology.* [Master Thesis]: Nankai University.

21 Gong Jian, Yang Mengfei (2012). A space applicable hardware fault tolerance method based on bitstream readback and reconfiguration of FPGA [J]. *Aerospace Control and Application* **38**(1), 34–39.

22 Levi D, Guccione S A (1999). *GeneticFPGA: evolving stable circuits on mainstream FPGA devices.* Proceedings of the First NASA/DoD Workshop on Evolvable Hardware, July 19–21. 12–17.

23 McDonald E J (2008). *Runtime FPGA Partial Reconfiguration.* IEEE Aerospace Conference, March 2008.

24 Sanchez E, Sipper M, Haenni J-O, Beuchat J-L, Stauffer A, Perez-Uribe A (1999). Static and Dynamic Configurable Systems. *IEEE Transactions on Computers* **48**(6), 556–564.

25 Compton K, Hauck S (2002). Reconfigurable Computing: a Survey of Systems and Software. *ACM Computing Surveys* **34** (2), 171–210.

7

Fault-Injection Techniques

Fault-injection technology was initially proposed in the early 1970s, and primarily helped in industrially designing and verifying fault-tolerant computer systems. Researchers began to attach importance to it in the 1980s and, since then, research has been actively under way and its field of application has been expanding. Since the 21st Annual International Symposium on Fault-Tolerant Computing (FTCS) in 1991, a panel discussion on fault-injection technology has been featuring at each annual symposium, and several academic conferences have been held with seminars on fault-injection technology on the agenda. Both theoretical studies and practical exploration have advanced, resulting in fault-injection tools with ever increasingly powerful functions being put into practical usage [1–3].

High-reliability fault-tolerant computer systems have always been confronted with the issue of reliability evaluation – that is, valid verification and evaluation of fault-tolerance design. Because of the complexity of high-reliability fault-tolerant computer systems, completely testing each branch, or even each statement in the system, is very difficult. Therefore, fault-injection technology has become an efficient approach to evaluate the reliability of fault-tolerant computer systems.

7.1 Basic Concepts

Fault-injection technology, following selected fault models, generates faults intentionally by artificial means, targeting systems with specific operating loads, to accelerate the occurrence of faults and failures. The responses to the injected fault in the target system are observed, retrieved, and analyzed to provide the experimenter with relevant findings. The overall experimental process is called fault-injection technology. Fault-injection technology, as a type of experiment-based evaluation technology, is easy, prompt and real-time,

Fault-Tolerance Techniques for Spacecraft Control Computers, First Edition.
Mengfei Yang, Gengxin Hua, Yanjun Feng and Jian Gong.
© 2017 National Defense Industry Press. All rights reserved.
Published 2017 by John Wiley & Sons Singapore Pte. Ltd.

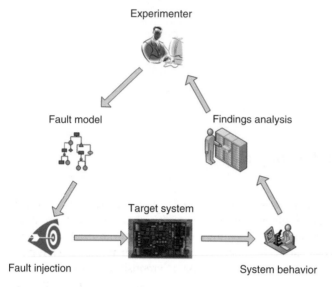

Figure 7.1 Fault-injection procedures.

and has consequently become an important approach to evaluating the reliability of fault-tolerant systems.

The fault-injection procedures can be illustrated using the circulation hierarchical structure shown in Figure 7.1. One complete fault-injection experiment is a cyclical process, from the experimenter establishing a fault model, to selecting the fault-injection method and conducting fault-injection, to operating the target system with running workload, to observing the system behavior and, finally, analyzing the experimental findings.

7.1.1 Experimenter

The experimenter is mainly responsible for establishing the fault model and analyzing the experimental findings, in addition to monitoring and controlling the entire fault-injection experimental process from start to finish.

7.1.2 Establishing the Fault Model

Establishing the fault model primarily involves generation of the input information for the fault-injection experiment – that is, based on the fault features in real operation, the fault properties are extracted to determine the fault space in which the fault sequence can be generated, according to a certain mechanism. In general, the more accurately the fault properties reflect the fault taking place in the actual environment, the more the fault sequence covers the faults occurring during the actual operation of the system, and the more precise the experimental evaluation findings will be.

7.1.3   Conducting Fault-injection

In the fault-injection procedure, the fault model generated during the "establishing the fault model" procedure is converted to a form that is applicable to the fault-injection experiment, and an appropriate approach is selected to introduce the fault into the target system. Usually, some fault-injection tools are employed to conduct the fault-injection. Fault-injection tools usually take two forms: fault-injection tools with software; and fault-injection tools with hardware.

7.1.4   Target System for Fault-injection

The target system includes a simulated system model and a real system model. The former can be pilot-tested during the system development stage, while the latter refers to the injection experiment upon system realization. Working loads refer to the set of missions or applications operating in the target system, including the programs for all user actions, the OS, real applications, benchmark testing programs, on-the-spot simulation programs and testing data for triggering off the injection fault. The fault-injection experiment requires that proper working loads be selected on the basis of the experimental objectives.

7.1.5   Observing the System's Behavior

When conducting an experiment, the system behaviors we need to observe depend on the target measurement expected by the experimenter. Typical system behaviors can be used to ascertain whether the injection is effective, the fault is activated, the fault is tested, the system is restored successfully, and the operation curve of the system upon injection failure. The type of target system and the type of system behaviors to be monitored determine whether the system monitoring should be conducted with hardware or software. The system behaviors observed are usually compared with the normal operating status of the system.

7.1.6   Analyzing Experimental Findings

In the experimental findings analysis stage, the experimenter, based on the target system behaviors observed, obtains quantitative and qualitative information regarding the fault-tolerance mechanism. Various evaluation objectives for the fault-tolerance mechanism lead to various measurements of the experimental findings. For example, the experimental findings can help to evaluate the "normal/failure" probability resulting from fault-injection into the system, the fault detection coverage, the fault delay time, and other parameters. They also help to analyze the transmission process of the fault in the system. Moreover, this procedure additionally helps to determine whether the fault-injection experiment can be terminated, whether the measurement parameter can reach certain preset threshold values, and so on.

7.2 Classification of Fault-injection Techniques

Fault-injection technology can be classified in terms of realization as follows (Figure 7.2): simulated fault-injection; hardware fault-injection; software fault-injection; physical fault-injection; and mixed fault-injection [4].

7.2.1 Simulated Fault-injection

Simulated fault-injection refers to the injection of faults into the system, by establishing models for the simulated actual system operation without actual software or hardware. This approach is easy to realize, because the system to be injected with fault is controllable and visible, and the key technology is to establish simulated device models and simulated environment.

Simulated fault-injection technology employs hardware description language (e.g., VHDL) to establish hardware-simulated models for the target system, and then applies the fault-injection units to the model to realize fault-injection. This approach applies the fault to the simulated model for the system to be tested, so it can be applied during the early stage of the design process, during which the actual system has not been generated yet. Thus, one advantage of this approach is that it can detect design faults in the early stage, resulting in significantly reduced expenses for these faults. Further, the time and location for fault-injection and tracking the observation points for system response can be set at will. Consequently, this technology can provide highly controllable and observable fault-injection. Its main weakness is excessive time consumption during simulation, which significantly limits the total number of hardware and software behaviors. Simulated fault-injection, based on different abstract levels, can be conducted at three levels: transistor switch level; logic level; and functional level.

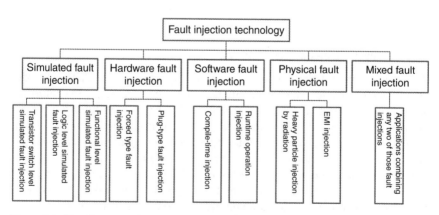

Figure 7.2 Classification of fault-injection technology.

7.2.1.1 Transistor Switch Level Simulated Fault-injection

Transistor switch level simulated fault-injection can be used to investigate the impact of transient faults within a circuit or IC, so as to conduct testing and credibility evaluation. The current and voltage within the circuit can be varied to simulate transient faults within the circuit. Variations in the current or voltage lead to the faults that may generate logic errors at the gate level, which can be further transmitted to other functional units, and sent to the pins of the chip.

This approach requires considerable time and memory, as the whole process of the fault has to be tracked from circuit, to gate, to functional units and to the IC pins. Most transistor switch level simulated models utilize this mixed-mode approach; the fault-free component in the circuit is simulated at the logic level, and the fault component in the circuit is simulated at the transistor switch level. In this mixed-mode simulation model, the fault-injection process can be realized as real-time change in the circuit, which applies one current source to the target node. During fault-injection, it changes the voltage of the node. Fault-injection tools provide monitoring functions to record the transmission behaviors of the fault.

7.2.1.2 Logic Level Simulated Fault-injection

Logic level simulated fault-injection simulates the performance at the logic gate. It is mainly meant to investigate VLSI circuits or system gate faults to pin level transmission, the impact of the gate-level fault on the program output results, and so on. The fault models that are commonly employed include fixed at zero, fixed at one, bridging fault, and inverted fault. Even though logic level simulation overlooks the physical process under the gate-level fault, the fault transmission process to the gate or higher level still needs to be tracked.

Logic level simulation only requires dual operation for given device behaviors and, with dual input vector and given input mode, the dual output of the given devices is determined. Each signal in the circuit is represented by a Boolean value that describes the stability of the circuit. For the fault-injection on this level, only the node value need be set, as zero or one, or its logic value inverted. Usually, fault-free simulation findings are employed to compare with the simulation results in case of fault, to determine the effect of failure injection.

7.2.1.3 Functional Level Simulated Fault-injection

Functional level simulated fault-injection is usually employed to investigate the reliability attributes of a computer system or network. The simulation makes use of a functional level fault model, and ignores the process at lower levels. The functional level model describing the fault performance may be constructed from the experimental results from lower level fault-injection, or on-the-spot data recording. Establishing the functional level simulation model is similar to establishment of the analytical model, but the latter requires that the results be defined with probability or distribution, whereas the simulation model does.

A functional level simulation model may not only be a random model, but can also be a behavioral model that is able to show detailed structural features of the system, real fault information, and interdependence between components.

Functional level simulated fault can be applied to all components of the system to be investigated, including CPU, memory, communication links, and software. These components have different inputs and functions, and see complicated interconnections. Consequently, it is impossible to establish one consistent fault model for all components. For various components, different fault models can be selected for injection. The two common fault models are internal memory bit flipping and CPU register fault. Most simulation injection tools can implement real user programs, owing to the model simulation system or network function. Thus, the impact of software on the system can be investigated.

Simulation-based fault-injection technology has the following advantages:

1) It can monitor and inject various faults precisely.
2) It can inject transient faults as well as permanent faults.
3) It does not involve high laboratory expenses, or need any dedicated hardware equipment.

It has the following disadvantages:

1) It involves a considerable amount of development work.
2) Hardware simulation models are more difficult to establish.
3) It takes a long time before the fault-injection starts, and it is not universal.

7.2.2 Hardware Fault-injection

Hardware fault-injection refers to cases in which the additional hardware system allows human involvement in the system to be tested, in order to simulate the system fault. The major levels of injection faults are as follows: bus-level fault-injection, pin-level fault-injection, and gate-level fault-injection. In recent years, with the wider application of FPGA and SoPC, system integration has been progressively higher, with many functional modules integrated into a chip. Currently, FPGA-based internal chip fault-injection techniques are implemented using hardware description language. They have started to attract the attention of researchers, and have thus far resulted in many significant achievements [5–9].

Hardware fault-injection makes use of additional hardware to apply the fault to the hardware of the target system, after which the target system is observed and analyzed to determine the impact of the injection fault.

In the case of hardware fault-injection, the fault is usually injected into the pin level of the integrated circuit because, for the complicated circuit, it is sufficient to show the features of the circuit upon fault-injection, through which the trouble can be easily ascertained in the circuit. For hardware fault-injection technology, it is easy to inject transient faults, but difficult to inject locked faults or bridge faults.

The fault injector and the target system are in direct contact, and faults can be injected into the target system by changing voltage or current outside the target chips. Contact fault-injection has various methods, and pin level fault-injection is a typical one. To realize this type of fault, the fault injector is connected directly to the pins of the target system circuit, and hardware faults are injected by changing the voltage or current of the chip pins. It includes, in terms of pin current or voltage change, forced fault-injection and plug-type fault-injection.

The forced-type fault-injection makes use of movable clamps attached to the pins of the chips of the target system, to carry out fault-injection by changing the voltage or current at the injection point, in order to change the corresponding logic value of the target system. This injection approach forces additional current into the target equipment. This should be carried out with the utmost caution, because any deviation can lead to damage or failure of the hardware of the target equipment.

The plug-type fault-injection works by adding one special plug into the target hardware and its PCB, which then changes the incoming and outgoing voltages of the chip pins, to realize fault-injection. By forcing the analog quantity of the expected logic value onto the pins of the target hardware, fixed, open-circuited or more complicated logic faults can be injected. This injection approach generally will not result in any damage to the target hardware.

The bus of the computer system is essential for the CPU to be linked up to the peripheral circuits, and all signals into and out of the CPU should be transmitted on the bus, which theoretically controls all bus signals and, thus, controls all computer operations. We conduct fault-injection on the bus because it has a special status and, by injecting faults onto the bus, we can simulate most faults in the computer system. Therefore, most hardware fault-injections are applied to the bus of the computer system.

Hardware-based fault-injection technology has the following advantages:

1) It operates by injecting various faults into all units of the target chips, and shows the hardware faults in a practical manner.
2) This injection does not intrude on the target computer system.
3) There is no need to have any special change of other loads in the target computer system.

It has the following disadvantages:

1) It demands additional dedicated hardware equipment for such fault-injections.
2) It may damage or cause the hardware system of the target computer to fail.
3) It does not have favorable portability for the fault-injection program.
4) It takes a long time before the fault-injection starts.

7.2.3 Software Fault-injection

In terms of injection time, software fault-injection can be classified into injection while compiling and injection while operating. Injection while compiling refers to injecting faults into the source codes or assembly codes of the target program, to simulate the impact of hardware, software, and transient faults; the revised codes change the commands of the target program commands to trigger off the fault. Injection while operating refers to a kind of triggering mechanism in which code snippet, program timeout, and traps are applied to trigger fault-injection.

Software fault-injection operates on the basis of a fault model. The process revises the data in the memory of the target system, and in the register of the processor, to simulate hardware or software fault. Its intrinsic properties make it difficult to build models for permanent faults, but easy to intrude into the system to be evaluated. This type of injection, however, boasts several obvious advantages over other fault-injection technologies. These advantages include a wide range of possible faults for injection, which are able to simulate hardware faults and software faults; no need for extra expensive hardware equipment; low development and realization costs; and there is no damage to hardware or failure. Furthermore, the target system can be easily tracked for implementing and retrieving data, the injection type boasts favorable transferability, and there is no need to develop or verify complicated system models and software development duration.

In software fault-injection, the fault sequence is received from the master computer, the fault is injected, and the system behaviors monitored. A determination is also made as to whether fault-injection timeout has occurred. This approach features low costs, easy realization, and simple operation.

7.2.3.1 Injection During Compiling

To conduct fault-injection during compiling, program images must be loaded and implemented before program commands are modified. This approach does not work by injecting faults into the target program, but by injecting the faults into the source codes or assembly codes, in order to simulate the impact of hardware, software, and transient faults. Further, the revised codes will change the commands of the target program to trigger off the fault, and these revised target program commands will generate an incorrect software image. When the system implements the image with faults, failure will take place.

This approach requires modification of the target program to evaluate the fault impact, but its operation does not require additional software, nor does it interfere with the operation of the target program. The impact of faults is hardcoded and can be employed to simulate permanent faults. This approach is easy to work out, but it does not allow injection during the operation of working load programs.

7.2.3.2 Injection During Operation

Injection during operation requires a trigger mechanism to trigger off fault-injection. There are three common mechanisms: timeout; abnormality/trap; and code insertion.

Timeout, the simplest technology approach, makes use of a preset timer to trigger off fault-injection – that is, the timeout event generates an interruption which can be employed to trigger fault-injection. The timer can be implemented in hardware or software. Timeout is very dependent on time instead of a specific event or system status, so it may lead to unpredictable fault impact or program behavior. Timeout is applicable to simulating transient faults or intermittent hardware faults.

Abnormality/trap controls fault-injection with hardware abnormality or software traps. In contrast to timeout, abnormality/trap works by conducting fault-injection at any point in time when an event or condition takes place. For example, inserting one software trap into the target commands, we can conduct fault-injection before the program runs a specific command. During trap implementation, one interrupt may come up, so as to call a section of the interrupt service sub-program. When an event is detected by hardware (e.g., visiting specific memory units), one hardware abnormality will trigger off fault-injection. Two mechanisms must have their corresponding interrupt service vectors.

Code insertion refers to the adding of commands to a program, to be inserted with faults before a specific piece of code. This approach is similar to code modification, but it differs in that fault-injection is done during system operation, when some commands are added, instead of changing the original commands. Code modification is carried out before the system runs, and it does not have additional commands, but instead modifies the original command. Similarly, code insertion also differs from traps because, when code insertion conducts fault-injection, the fault injector is part of the target program. It also runs in user mode, not in OS mode like the trap approach does.

Software-based fault-injection technology has the following advantages:

1) It features a wide fault range, working to simulate hardware and software faults.
2) It does not require dedicated hardware, resulting in low development costs.
3) It will not bring out any damage or failure to the target computer system.
4) It can easily track the implementation of the target computer system.
5) It does not require system simulation modeling for development, making the development duration short.

However, it has the following disadvantages:

1) It requires extra expenses for the target computer system operation, affecting the real-time performance of the target computer system.

2) This approach needs to modify the source program code, because it involves considerable programming work.

3) Injecting permanent faults this way is difficult.

Even though software-based fault-injection has several shortcomings, generally it is more flexible than hardware fault-injection because it does not require extra dedicated hardware equipment, nor does it bring about damage or failure to the target system. Thus, it is quite a promising and reliable evaluation approach.

7.2.4 Physical Fault-injection

Satellite-borne computer systems need to work in space, where radiation is massive and has always led to the failure of electronics aboard spacecraft. The abovementioned TID and SEE are the two major radiation effects on satellite-borne computers in space.

Physical fault-injection refers to placing the object to be injected in an artificially simulated severe environment, in order to observe its operation in the severe environment, and to verify its ability to tackle the severe environment. Common approaches are injection in the actual environment, like radiation injection and EMI. Radiation injection works mainly by speeding up particles with particle accelerators, to obtain sufficiently high energy to bombard the object to be injected into, or to radiate the object with the radiation source. Common radiation sources include californium source, cobalt source, and cesium source. The californium source can be applied to simulate the SEE, while the latter two simulate total dosage effect [10–12].

SEEs in space can be simulated with physical fault-injection. The simplest approach is to simulate with californium source fission, which features easy simulation and low expense. With short-range radiation of californium source fission, this approach is mostly applied to acceleration experiments.

The tandem accelerator developed by the China Institute of Atomic Energy can provide low-energy H, Li, and Be, and high-energy Ag, I, Au, etc. Twenty heavy ions boast advantages such as rapid ionic conversion, obtaining low LET values, and low costs, but Ag, I, Au, and other high-energy ions have the disadvantage of short-range radiation in silicon. The cyclotron developed by the Institute of Modern Physics at the China Academy of Sciences boasts high energy, and ability to provide particles of long-range radiation in silicon, but it has the disadvantages of long ionic change and high expense. Table 7.1 lists the ground simulation test accelerators for SEEs.

Photons and ions may have interaction with semiconductor material, and may generate electric charge. Thus, a laser may be used to simulate and investigate SEEs. A laser single-particle simulation system is a type of laboratory equipment that is simple, economical, and secure, and is able to simulate SEE. Laser SEE simulation systems can be applied to investigate the SEE mechanism and the transmission law of the faults by SEEs in satellite-borne computers, to

Table 7.1 Ground simulation test accelerators for SEEs.

Name	Energy range (MeV/uma)	Advantages	Disadvantages
Linear sequence electrostatic accelerator (TGVA)	0–10	Rapid ionic conversion, obtaining low LET value, and low costs.	Difficult to obtain high-energy ions with sufficient range.
Cyclotron	10–100	High energy, offering various types of ions that can be of sufficient radiation range.	Takes a long time and much expense to replace ions.
Synchrotron	100–1000	Ion energy comparable to that of the space environment.	High expenses difficult to handle.
High-energy ion accelerator	10–150	Energy comparable to that of the space environment.	Small quantity.

analyze and test SEEs in integrated circuits, to determine the SEU sensitive area, and to evaluate satellite-borne devices and electronic circuit reinforcement. Compared with accelerator and radioisotope californium source, laser simulation experimentation is simple, economic, and secure, but it cannot penetrate light insulation material, and its simulation equivalence still needs to be investigated.

Studies conducted by NASA indicate that, of the failures occurring during spacecraft orbiting operations in space, those due to radiation account for 45% while, among all failures caused by radiation, single-particle upset accounts for nearly 80%. Consequently, it has become the focus of various research efforts. Recently, with ceaseless advancement in semiconductor technology, large-scale integrated circuit technology has advanced from 130 nm, to 45 nm, and even to 22 nm. Radiation-resistant CPU, memory, and logic circuits have also been developed at the level of sub-micron, with leading radiation-resistant devices technology down to 180 nm and 130 nm, because the impact of radiation dosage is relatively weak, and SEEs, especially SET and SEU, have increasingly more effect.

In the physical fault-injection approach, there is no physical connection between the fault injector and the target system, but some physical phenomena generated with some external factors can help to realize fault-injection. This type of fault-injection includes heavy ion radiation injection, EMI injection, and so on. The former makes use of heavy ion radiation to form abnormal shifting of internal current carriers, which makes the status of memory in the digital system change randomly and inject faults into integrated circuits. The latter makes use of radiation antenna or the strong electromagnetic field between two conductors to interfere and inject faults; usually, placing the target equipment inside the electromagnetic field or around it can inject faults.

7.2.5 Mixed Fault-injection

The above fault-injection approaches have their respective advantages and disadvantages. Physical fault-injection simulates quite real faults, which makes it highly reliable, but poor in control and visibility; thus, the fault may not easily occur again. Hardware fault-injection has fine real-time performance, and high fault resolution, and is applicable to systems requiring high resolution. It is also easy to simulate permanent faults, but it requires an additional hardware system and injection environment, making it expensive to realize. Software fault-injection modifies the value of the register to simulate faults, and is flexible and economical. However, its fault-injection requires code insertion, which will change the original system program flow, and the software operation will also require some system resources, so systems requiring high real-time performance are not applicable.

Simulated fault-injections mainly serve for testing and verification on the initial system design stage, which mainly works in the computer by forming virtual models and injecting faults to observe system output and to check whether these models meet the requirements. Various designs have been done in virtual environments. This does not damage the object to be injected, and it is also easy to modify. Its disadvantage is that it is highly dependent on simulated models, whose accuracy directly determines the accuracy of the simulation. In addition, the simulation has high requirements for system resources, and so simulation in a large system might be very slow. Various contrasting fault-injection methods are shown in Table 7.2.

Computer-simulated fault-injection, hardware fault-injection, software fault-injection, and physical fault-injection all have their own strengths and weaknesses. Currently, some institutes abroad are investigating mixed fault-injection approaches, which make use of the strengths of various approaches, as the future development in this regard [13–16].

Mixed fault-injection makes use of two or more of the above four injection approaches, to achieve fault-injection in a joint manner. It has the advantages of various approaches, and thus it is functional, powerful, and widely applicable. Various fault types can be applied, but high requirements for technical expertise of experimental personnel, such as specialized knowledge and skills in fault-injection, are required.

Table 7.2 Various fault-injection approaches.

Injection approach	Basic principle	Realization costs	Controllability and observability	Security	Applicable stage
Simulated fault-injection	Faults introduced to the simulation model of the object to be injected.	Low	Fine	Secure	Initial system design stage
Hardware fault-injection	Additional hardware system applies specific faults to the object to be injected.	Relatively high	Relatively fine	Possible damage	Real system completed
Software fault-injection	Software codes are employed to modify register values or change the original software flow to generate faults.	Relatively low	Relatively fine	Secure	Each stage for system design
Physical fault-injection	Faults are introduced by simulating radiation environment in space.	High	Relatively poor	Damaging the object to be injected	Real system completed

7.3 Fault-injection System Evaluation and Application

When injecting faults, the fault-injection system cannot break the object to be injected, but it must meet the requirements for injection controllability, observability, and validity at once, or the system will not be effective.

7.3.1 Injection Controllability

Injection controllability refers to the capacity of the fault-injection approach in conducting fault-injection, fault-injection types, injection location, triggering time, triggering condition, and other factors. These need to be controllable, and various faults can be injected according to the will and demand of customers. Controllability brings about the biggest advantage, namely that when users are interested in some fault phenomena, they can easily represent this fault to facilitate analysis. Fault-injection controllability is an important approach to measuring fault-injection, and also a main factor for the user to choose different fault-injection approaches. Moreover, if the fault is controllable, we can also effectively prevent fault-injection from damaging the object to be injected.

7.3.2 Injection Observability

Fault-injection observability refers to whether the fault-injection can be observed easily after some fault-injection approach is employed to conduct fault-injection. For fault-injection with poor observability, the user must make use of additional aid tools and effort before they can observe the fault-injection results. Fault-injection results can usually be shown in the form of waveform, data, and signs, so the user can easily observe and evaluate the fault-injection results. Similar to the controllability of fault-injection, observability is an important factor that tells a good fault-injection approach from a bad one. The user can select different fault-injection approaches when the observability is taken account of similarly.

7.3.3 Injection Validity

When faults are injected into the system, not all of them are valid. Valid fault-injection refers to cases in which the fault is injected into the system and, compared with normal operations, its signal status needs to be changed. Figure 7.3 shows that if A is a normal signal, and AA is signal A with fault injected, then the signal injection during section a-b is valid because the injected signal changes from low level to high level. In section b-c, the injection is invalid, and the signals before and after injection are the same.

In a real system, fault-injection validity and no damage to the object to be injected are sometimes contradictory, because what is expected is a valid injection approach that also promises no damage to the object to be injected. When injecting one fault, sometimes even one valid injection may not necessarily have a poor effect – that is, under transient interference, the system may still operate smoothly.

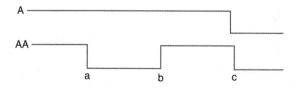

Figure 7.3 Example of injection validity.

7.3.4 Fault-injection Application

Fault-injection approaches have become more varied and complex, and their application increasingly wider. Fault-injection approaches can be applied to all stages of system development, including the design stage, system prototype construction and system application. These are mainly shown in two aspects: first, system tolerant mechanism design and realization correctness verification; and second, evaluation of the fault handling efficiency of the fault-tolerance mechanism. Some typical applications are as follows:

7.3.4.1 Verifying the Fault Detection Mechanism

When fire first breaks out, the impact will not be huge, and it can be easy to extinguish it if this is done promptly. Similarly, at the point where a fault occurs, its impact is also small and, if the system can quickly locate the fault and quarantine it, it can remain thus. This is the core of fault detection, quarantine, and restoration technology in satellite-borne computer systems, whose conscious injection of faults work to verify the validity of the fault detection mechanism.

7.3.4.2 Fault Effect Domain Analysis

Upon fault occurrence, it must be quarantined within a certain range, to prevent it from spreading. The approach of fault-injection can help to ascertain the spreading time and effect domain upon fault occurrence, so as to ensure the validity of the quarantine measures.

7.3.4.3 Fault Restoration

In many cases, fault-tolerant computer systems will not eliminate the fault, but will utilize quarantine measures to isolate faults to prevent its effect domain from spreading. The system will make use of fault-tolerance measures and approaches to restore from failures. Fault-injection is also an effective approach to check whether the system can be restored back to normal.

7.3.4.4 Coverage Estimation

Estimating fault detection and other fault-tolerance mechanism coverage is the most mature and widest application of fault-injection technology. Coverage reflects the system's failure-handling capacity, and is an important index of the efficiency of the fault-tolerance mechanism. The coverage by fault-injection experiment can also be taken as the parameters of analytical models, to obtain the credibility measurement of the target system. The accuracy of the coverage by fault-injection experiment depends on the accuracy of the fault model in the experiment.

7.3.4.5 Delay Time

Delay time is another measuring index for fault-tolerance mechanism, which includes the duration from fault occurrence to failure (fault delay), and the time from fault occurrence to the fault being detected. The delay time obtained provides the basis for us to determine the operation frequency of the fault detection system of the target system.

7.3.4.6 Generating Fault Dictionary

Fault dictionary is also known as fault database. It list of failures occurring at some abstract level, or the representation symptoms of this fault on this level or above. To generate a fault dictionary, we need to conduct fault-injection on lower levels of the system, whose findings can be monitored, recorded, and analyzed on a higher level. It is very significant to maintain the fault dictionary in the system, as it can be applied to the fault diagnosis process, to determine the location and type of the fault occurring. The fault dictionary generated with the fault-injection approach plays an essential role in investigating the representation of fault models on different levels, and generating fault models on higher levels.

7.3.4.7 Software Testing

Software fault-tolerance mechanisms can be applied to distributed systems and network protocols, where the fault handling program codes can be implemented when the fault occurs, because these programs can only be tested by fault-injection. Fault-injection approaches can be combined with other approaches to verify the fault-tolerant software or protocol. This approach mainly makes use of forming an approach and tools to verify software or protocol, and some fault-injection experiment is employed to verify the correctness of the software. In addition, fault-injection also makes use of fault simulation in software design, to verify the validity of the collection of software testing cases.

7.4 Fault-injection Platform and Tools

Fault-injection technology began early internationally, with the University of California, IBM, and NASA in the United States, other colleges and research institutes, as well as LAAS-CNRS and other colleges in France being leaders in this regard. Further, some colleges and research institutes in Germany, Japan, UK, and Australia are making relevant research efforts. Currently, significant accomplishments in fault-injection research are being made a variety of countries, and various fault-injection technologies have many representative fault-injection tools.

Typical tools based on heavy ion radiation fault-injection include the FIST, developed by Chalmers Technology University, Sweden. Hardware fault-injection tools include RIFLE, a set of pin-based fault-injection tools developed by Coimbra University, Portugal; FOCUS, developed by Illinois University, USA; and Messaline, a set of pin-based fault-injection tools developed by LAAS-CNRS University, France. Software fault-injection tools include FIAT, developed by Carnegie Mellon University, USA; FTAPE, developed by Illinois University, USA; DOCTOR, developed by Michigan University, USA; FERRARI, developed by Texas University, USA; Xception, developed by Coimbra University, Portugal; and EXFI, developed by Politecnico diTorins, Italy [2,16–20]. Simulation-based fault-injection tools include VERIFY, developed by Erlangen-Nuremberg, Germany; and MEFISTO, developed by Chalmers Technology University, Sweden [5,13,21].

In China, research into fault-injection began relatively late. BICE developed the 80C86 bus-level fault-injection equipment in their radiation-resistance research, which has since been applied to software and hardware fault-tolerance design, testing, and verification for satellite control, with fine verification results that enabled it to win the Third Prize for Space Technology Advancement. For satellite-borne computer reliability research, more exploration has been made in fault-injection. Moreover, BICE has conducted considerable laboratory work by simulating space radiation environment in satellite-used devices radiation-resistance reinforcement, by which they have built up their expertise.

In the mid-1980s, Professor Yang Xiaozong of Harbin Institute of Technology led his fault-tolerant computer laboratory efforts to develop fault-injection equipment, by which four generations of hardware fault-injection equipment have been launched successively. To date, the laboratory is also a leader in this regard. Currently, researchers in the laboratory have extended their research from fault-injection to software fault simulation, software fault-injection, fault model analysis, and wider fields. Professor Jin Huihua of Beijing University of Aeronautics and Astronautics has led his laboratory with research in this regard, mainly investigating fault-injection in embedded type systems. Further, some products are currently being applied to test models of products in the sector of aeronautics, with favorable results.

Meanwhile, this technology has also attracted the attention of some colleges and researchers in the sector. Tsinghua University, Chongqing University, and Institute 771 of the China Aerospace Science and Technology Corporation, for example, have done relevant work. The typical fault-injection tools and their corresponding principles at home and abroad are listed in Table 7.3.

7.4.1 Fault-injection Platform in Electronic Design Automation (EDA) Environment

This is a set of mixed fault-injection platforms developed with the mixed software- and hardware-based simulation fault-injection approach. This design features precision fault-injection, due to the observability and controllability of the software injection approach. It also boasts rapid operation and high fault coverage resulting from the hardware simulation injection approach; a fault-injection verification platform integrating software and hardware approaches is constructed. The system framework is shown in Figure 7.4.

Table 7.3 Various typical fault-injection tools.

Various fault-injection approaches	Tool name	Developer	Working principle
Physical fault-injection	FIST	Chalmers Technology University, Sweden	Radiation sources are employed to produce transient faults.
	x86 processor radiation fault-injection platform	China Institute for Space Technology and Beijing Institute for Control Engineering	Particle accelerator and radiation sources are employed to simulate single particle and total dosage effect.
Hardware fault-injection	RIFLE	Coimbra University, Portugal	Pin-based electric-level forced-raised or lowered fault-injection.
	Messaline	LAAS-CNRS University, France	Pin-based electric-level forced-raised or lowered fault-injection.
	HFI-1 -HFI-4	Harbin Institute of Technology, China	Pin-based forced injection or embedded bus injection.
	Independent fault injector	Beijing University of Aeronautics and Astronautics, China	Software and hardware-combined processor pin fault-controllable injection.
	x86 system bus-level fault injector	China Institute for Space Technology and Beijing Institute for Control Engineering	Pin-based electric-level forced-raised or lowered fault-injection.
	SPARC system bus-level fault injector		
Software fault-injection	FIAT	Carnegie Mellon University, USA	Fault-injection by changing memory mirroring.
	FTAPE	Illinois University, USA	Mainly injecting unit upset faults, with aid hardware to do simulation.
	DOCTOR	Michigan University, USA	Injection by timeout, trap, and code modification.

Table 7.3 (Continued)

Various fault-injection approaches	Tool name	Developer	Working principle
	FERRARI	Texas University, USA	Injecting faults into CPU, memory, and bus with software traps.
	Xception	Coimbra University, Portugal	No modification on software, but processors to handle injection fault of abnormal trap program.
Simulated fault-injection	VERIFY	Erlangen-Nuremberg University, Germany	VHDL modeling to realize specific modeling fault-injection.
	MEFISTO	Chalmers Technology University, Sweden	Offering a complete fault modeling, injection, and performance evaluation integration environment.

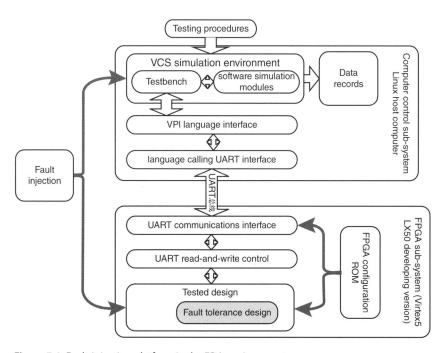

Figure 7.4 Fault-injection platform in the EDA environment.

The whole system can be divided into computer control subsystem, FPGA subsystem, and fault-injection module. The computer control subsystem mainly does system control display and, in the VCS simulation environment, it operates software simulation, collects software simulation information, and designed operation information to provide input and debug information for the designed object, as it is quite controllable and observable.

The FPGA subsystem is based on Xilinx's Virtex5 series FPGA chips, and is configured as the tested object, which simulates and obtains more virtual software operation information. Different functions are configured to meet the demand of users and evaluate the impact of the fault on the design in real hardware, because it is flexible and extensible. The Verilog Procedural Interface (VPI) interface and the UART communication interface complete the interaction between the control subsystem and the FPGA subsystem, to realize simulation evaluation of the whole system. Fault-injection modules can conduct fault-injection on different levels in the software simulation component and the hardware realization component for reliability design evaluations.

7.4.2 Computer Bus-based Fault-injection Platform

The overall fault-injection system, in terms of function, consists of four modules: bus data intercept module; fault trigger control and injection module; attribute control and communication module; and upper computer parameter injection and display software module. These four components have the logic relation shown in Figure 7.5.

The data intercept module mainly operates by introducing the signal on the target CPU bus to the fault-injection system, and sending the system-processed data back to the bus, because it links the fault-injection system and the injected object. In the system, 100 signal interfaces are configured, which can introduce the data bus, address bus, and control bus onto the fault-injection circuit. For eight-bit and 16-bit processors, some signals can be introduced, based on specific needs.

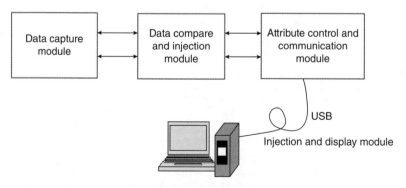

Figure 7.5 Fault-injection system functional modules.

The fault trigger control and injection module is the core of the whole fault-injection system. When the detected data on the bus meet the conditions for fault triggering, the fault mode configured by the user is followed to inject faults into the system bus; on each occasion, one type of fault can be injected. The attribute control and communications modules mainly analyze the software information on the upper computer, take the fault-injection condition, location, and injection type information, and transmit them to the fault trigger control and injection module. In addition, the module also collects the system operation status information from the fault-injection system and sends it back to the upper computer, so that the fault-injection software can indicate the data change before and after fault-injection. This helps the user to determine whether this injection has hit the expected target.

In system design, we observe the evaluation criteria in Section 7.3, where the following measures can be taken:

1) To ensure universality and extensibility of the system platform, we can survey different types of devices, and make different bus data intercept modules. When conducting fault-injection on different models, we only need to replace different data intercept modules. Trigger, injection control, and attribute control can be realized by FPGA to have complete reconfiguration of core control logic.

2) By removing or shielding some devices in the object to be injected, we can prevent signal "traffic collision," which helps to protect the devices in the system to be injected. Moreover, a separate power supply is provided, with effective isolation measures to further improve the security of the fault-injection system.

3) During FPGA encoding, it is required that the fault-injection system be powered on, to make the whole fault-injection circuit have an input status. Only under CPU control can the fault-injection system have a suitable output. This way, any wrong output of the fault-injection circuit will not damage other devices on the bus; it will enhance the security of the system powered-on operation.

4) Data direction control signals in the fault-injection circuit must have a certain status via a resistor, to ensure that the fault-injection system can have independent debugging, even when it is not connected to the object to be injected, and there is no bus-signal oscillation because of unclear bus direction.

5) USB can be used to communicate with the upper computer, making it easy for the user to apply and realize plug-and-play.

6) The upper computer failure injection software interface links up the user and the fault-injection system, which can be very friendly with Visual C++, where the users can use various fault-injection parameters and view the fault-injection results. Further, all fault-injection data will be automatically saved into the backstage access database to facilitate future inquiry.

FPGA and USB communications control chips are the main devices in the system, and are also the core of the system. The object to be injected has very complicated CPU functions, with many signal wires; to control signals on the bus in a comprehensive manner, FPGA needs many I/O pins, and considerable capacity to facilitate platform completion and extension. The FPGA used in the system is Xilinx's XC3S1000 -456, which has a capacity of 1 million, with 456 pins, and the user can use as many as 333 I/Os. USB control chips make use of Cypress's Cy7c68013A, which supports USB2.0 transmission protocol, inside which one 80C51 microcontroller unit (MCU) hard-kernel is integrated, to facilitate debugging. Data flow in the system is shown in Figure 7.6.

7.4.3 Serial Accelerator Based Fault-injection Case

The test uses two chips, with three samples for each chip, both of which are uncapped. There are three test plates, and each of them is distributed with one FPGA and 1553B interface chip. In addition, there are five different particle radiation sources, which take turns to radiate all sample chips. The uncapped

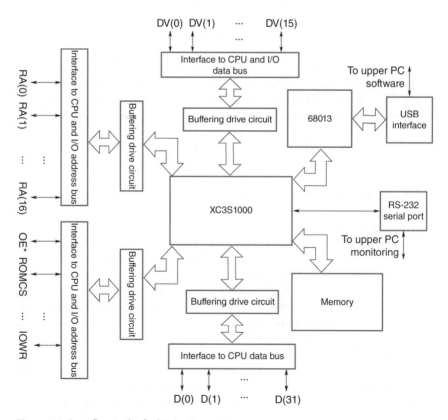

Figure 7.6 Data flow in the fault-injection system.

FPGA is shown in Figure 7.7, the 1553B interface chip is shown in Figure 7.8, and the overall system environment is shown in Figure 7.9.

Dynamic testing is utilized. In the test conducted, radiating particle beams are directly injected onto the inner core of the chip upon uncapping, and on

Figure 7.7 Uncapped FPGA.

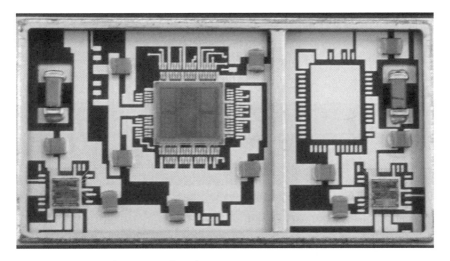

Figure 7.8 Uncapped 1553B interface chip.

Figure 7.9 Test system environment.

each sampling machine. FPGA and 1553B interface chip samples are utilized, with the former realizing the functions of a single chip 8051 (realized with an 8032 compatible IP core) with a 4 kB RAM. Inside the 1553B interface, there are two mutual backup buses, and the SEE test is first conducted on the 1553B interface. Inside the chip, there are three integrated circuits (one logic and two mutual backup receivers/transmitter). In the test, these three modules are respectively radiated; then a single-particle test is conducted on the FPGA chips. The layout of the test system is shown in Figure 7.10.

The results of the test show that FPGA and the 1553B interface chips both are sensitive to single-particle upset effect. With a relatively low LET threshold, but high saturated cross-section, the conclusion drawn is that, to facilitate space application, some re-enforcement measures should be taken.

7.4.4 Future Development of Fault-injection Technology

Currently, fault-injection plays an increasingly critical role in the fault-tolerant system reliability testing field, and research efforts are constantly expanding. Research into fault-injection technology has the following development aspects:

1) Fault model theoretical research. Accurate fault models can help to reduce fault-injection laboratory time and expenses, and enhance experimentation efficiency and evaluation precision.

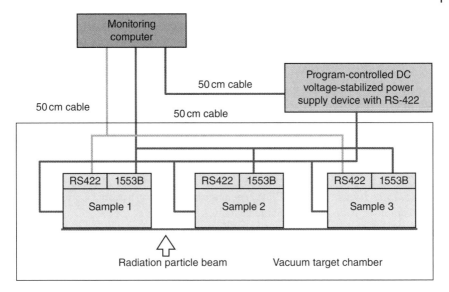

Figure 7.10 Single-particle test principle schematic diagram.

2) Fault-injection tool research. On the basis of various realizations of the fault-injection modes, we can construct practical injection tools, such as software and hardware combined, to develop more practical fault-injection tools.

3) Hardware fault-injection tools will be improved in terms of speed, time definition, injection trigger condition, injection effect tracking, and so on.

4) The software fault-injection approach will continue to develop, and will be increasingly applied to evaluate software systems in terms of reliability and soundness.

5) The software fault-injection approach will also be applied to distributed and network design.

6) Combining fault-injection laboratory approach, analysis models, and field measurement, we can integrate fault-injection techniques and development methods to combine fault-injection methods in the design stage with fault-injection methods in the evaluation stage. Subsequently, we can integrate hardware review fault-injection technology and software review fault technology.

7) Research efforts will continue to make the difference between the injected faults in the laboratory and the faults in real environments.

8) Fault-injection technology will be promoted, and applied to fault transmission, fault diagnosis, etc.

References

1 Choi G S, Iyer R K, Carreno V A (1990). Simulated fault-injection: a methodology to evaluate fault tolerant microprocessor architectures [J]. *IEEE Transactions On Reliabilty* **39**(4), 486–491.

2 Choi G S, Iyer R K (1992). FOCUS: an experimental environment for fault sensitivity analysis [J]. *IEEE Transactions on Computers* **41**(12), 1515–1526.

3 Ries G L, Choi G S, Iyer R K (1994). *Device-level transient fault modeling* [C]. Proceedings of 24th IEEE International Symposium on Fault Tolerant Computing (FTCS-24), Austin, Texas, 1994, 86–94.

4 Choi G S, Iyer R K, Saab D G (1993). *Fault behavior dictionary for simulation of device-level transients* [C]. Proceedings of IEEE International Conference on Computer-Aided Design, Santa Clara, CA, 1993, 6–9.

5 Sieh V, Tschache O, Balbach F (1997). *VERIFY: Evaluation of reliability using VHDL-models with embedded fault descriptions* [C]. Proceedings of 27th IEEE International Symposium on Fault Tolerant Computing (FTCS-27), Seattle, WA, 1997, 32–36.

6 Dahigren P, Liden P (1995). *A switch-level algorithm for simulation of transients in combinational logic* [C]. Proceedings of 25th IEEE International Symposium on Fault Tolerant Computing (FTCS-25), Pasadena, California, 1995, 207–216.

7 Cha H, Rudnick E M, Patel J H, Fyer R K, Choi G S (1996). A gate-level simulation environment for alpha-particle-induced transient faults [J]. *IEEE Transactions on Computers* **45**(11), 1248–1256.

8 Clark J A, Pradhan D K (1992). *Reliability analysis of unidirectional voting TMR systems through simulated fault-injection* [C]. Proceedings of 22nd IEEE International Symposium On Fault Tolerant Computing (FTCS-22), Boston, MA, 1992, 72–81.

9 Goswami K K, Iyer R K, Young L (1997). DEPEND: A simulation-based environment for system level dependability analysis [J]. *IEEE Transactions on Computers* **46**(1), 60–74.

10 Ohlssan J, Rimen M, Gunneflo U (1992). *A study of the effects of transient fault-injection into a 32-bit RISC with built-in watchdog* [C]. Proceedings of 22nd IEEE International Symposium. on Fault Tolerant Computing (FTCS-22), Boston, MA, 1992, 315–325.

11 Kalbarczyk Z, Ries G, Lee M S, Xiao Y, Patel J, Iyer R K (1998). *Hierarchical Approach to accurate fault modeling for system evaluation* [C]. Proceedings of 3rd IEEE International Symposium on Computer Performance & Dependability (IPDS-98), Durham, North Carolina, 1998, 249–258.

12 Cha H, Rudnick E M, Choi G S, Patel J H, Iyer R K (1993). *A fast and accurate gate-level transient fault simulation environment* [C]. Proceedings of 23rd IEEE International Symposium on Fault Tolerant Computing (FTCS-23), Toulouse, France, 1993, 310–319.

13 Jenn E, Arlat J, Rimen M, Ohlsson J, Karlsson J (1994). *Fault-injection into VHDL models: the MEFISTO tool* [C]. Twenty-Fourth International Symposium on Fault-Tolerant Computing, FTCS-24, Austin, Texas, 1994, 66–75.

14 Gunneflo U, Karlsson J, Torin J (1989). *Evaluation of error detection schemes using fault-injection by heavy-ion radiation* [C]. The Nineteenth IEEE International Symposium on Fault-Tolerant Computing (FTCS-19), 1989, Los Alamitos, CA, 340–347.

15 Karlsson J, Arlat J (1995). *Application of three physical fault-injection techniques to the experimental assessment of the MARS architecture* [C]. Proceedings of Fifth Annual IEEE International Working Conference on Dependable Computing for Critical Applications, IEEE CS press, 1995, 150–16.

16 Carreira J, Madeira H, Silva J G (1998). Xception: software fault-injection and monitoring in processor functional units [J]. *IEEE Transactions on Software Engineering* **24**(2), 1–25.

17 Stott D T, Floering B, Burke D, Kalbarczpk Z, Iyer R K (2000). *NFTAPE: a framework for assessing dependability in distributed systems with lightweight fault injectors* [C]. IEEE International Computer Performance and Dependability Symposium, Chicago, IL, 2000, 91–100.

18 Han S, Shin K G, Rosenberg H (1995). *DOCTOR: An integrated software fault-injection environment for distributed real-time systems* [C]. IEEE International Computer Performance and Dependability Symposium, (IPDS'95), Erlangen, Germany, 1995, 204–213.

19 Kanawati G A, Kanawati N A, Abraham J A (1992). *FERRARI: a tool for the validation of system dependability properties* [C]. IEEE Twenty-Second International Symposium on Fault-Tolerant Computing (FTCS-22), Boston, MA, 1992, 336–344.

20 Benso A, Prinetto P, Rebaudengo M, Reorda M (1998). EXFI: a low-cost fault-injection system for embedded microprocessor-based boards [J]. *ACM Transactions on Design Automation of Electronic Systems* **3**(4), 626–634.

21 Boue J, Petillon P, Crouzet Y (1998). *MEFISTO-L: A VHDL-based fault-injection tool for the experimental assessment of fault tolerance* [C]. Proceedings of 28th IEEE International Symposium on Fault Tolerant Computing (FTCS-28), 1998, 168–173.

8

Intelligent Fault-Tolerance Techniques

This chapter discusses intelligent fault-tolerance techniques such as evolvable hardware fault-tolerance techniques and artificial immune hardware fault-tolerance techniques. These latest techniques can provide references for the fault-tolerance design of next-generation onboard computers.

8.1 Evolvable Hardware Fault-tolerance

Evolvable hardware fault-tolerance is a new intelligence fault-tolerance technique that has recently been developed [1–6]. The essential idea of this method is as follows. When there is a fault in the hardware, the hardware structure changes with an evolution strategy. However, the original function of the overall hardware remains unchanged, so the fault part of the hardware is bypassed. In addition, when the outside environment changes, the hardware function will change, actively adapting to the environment. The evolvable hardware fault-tolerance technique features self-repairing and self-adapting systems.

8.1.1 Fundamental Concepts and Principles

With the evolvable hardware fault-tolerance technique, hardware fault-tolerance is realized in accordance with evolution theory, and this came to prominence in the 1990s. The concept was originally presented by the Japanese scientist Hugo de Garis and scientists at the Swiss Federal Institute in 1992. The evolutionary idea originated from genetic algorithms, a concept that was first presented by professor Holland in 1962. In 1975, professor Holland systematically introduced genetic algorithm in his book *Adaptation in Natural and Artificial Systems*, which laid the foundation for genetic algorithm and related research [7]. After the 1970s, with the rapid development of hardware technology, programmable devices were produced and widely used, helping to take the evolvable hardware technique from theory to realization.

Fault-Tolerance Techniques for Spacecraft Control Computers, First Edition.
Mengfei Yang, Gengxin Hua, Yanjun Feng and Jian Gong.
© 2017 National Defense Industry Press. All rights reserved.
Published 2017 by John Wiley & Sons Singapore Pte. Ltd.

Evolvable hardware is defined as self-reconfiguration of electronic circuits in a narrow sense, such as FPGA reconfiguration with evolutionary algorithm and genetic algorithm. In general, it is hardware reconfiguration of the sensor, antenna, and even the entire space system, in order that the hardware can adapt to outside environmental changes, and system performance can be improved during missions. Reconfiguration can be treated as a prototype or the primary phase of evolvable hardware, as can be seen from the narrow-sense definition of evolvable hardware (i.e., a kind of reconfigurable hardware).

The fundamental idea of evolvable hardware can be described as follows. The configuration data of a programmable device is searched with an evolutionary algorithm (especially a genetic algorithm), until the programmable device with the searched configuration data can meet the anticipated requirement. The implementation flow of this idea is shown in Figure 8.1. In the evolvable hardware fault-tolerance technique, fault-tolerance is realized according to the theory of this procedure. The evolvable hardware fault-tolerance technique consists of two factors: (1) evolutionary algorithm, and (2) programmable devices. These two factors are discussed in detail in Sections 8.1.2 and 8.1.3, respectively.

In the early years, the structure and function of a circuit could not be changed after its design and manufacture, so that static redundancy strategies were used to implement fault-tolerance. With the occurrence of programmable devices, different configurations produced different functions in devices. However, the configuration data of a device was designed and set beforehand, and could not change automatically. Consequently, with this reconfiguration technique, fault-tolerance strategies also had to be set beforehand. The hardware evolution idea resulted in a new generation of fault-tolerance techniques. With the evolutionary method underlying the implementation of fault-tolerance, the function of hardware could now be changed online and dynamically, adapt to the environment automatically, and self-repair when faults occur. Evolution-based fault-tolerance is an intelligence fault-tolerance technique.

Evolvable hardware fault-tolerance, featuring self-organization, self-adaptation, and self-reparation, can dynamically change hardware structure to obtain a fit function for the environment that accords with environmental changes. This kind of fault-tolerance technique has inherent characteristics of fault-tolerance

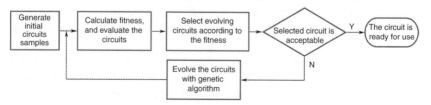

Figure 8.1 Evolvable hardware fault-tolerance implementation flow.

and does not require obvious redundancy. Hardware with evolvable hardware fault-tolerance technique has the following features:

1) The hardware can maintain its original function when it has faults resulting from aging, temperature excursion, or radiation. Moreover, the hardware can evolve to an available working system when some components have faults.
2) The hardware can create new functions, which make it adaptive to the environment. The hardware can self-recover when it has faults, without need for configuration instruction and data from ground-station.
3) It requires less volume, weight, and power consumption than traditional fault-tolerance techniques, which is significant for spacecraft, especially for long-term self-run spacecraft.

There are two implementation methods for evolvable hardware fault-tolerance techniques. These are as follows [8]:

1) *Extrinsic evolution.* In this method, a software model of a programmable device is first built. Circuit evolution and evaluation are then implemented, based on the model, by means of a software method. Finally, a circuit is generated according to the evolution result on the programmable device. With this method, hardware evolution is not restricted to a specific programmable device because of adoption of software emulation. However, the evolution result is affected by the accuracy of the software model.
2) *Intrinsic evolution.* In this method, circuit evolution is implemented on the programmable device directly. Configuration data is downloaded at runtime, by means of the dynamic online reconfiguration feature of the programmable device. Evaluation is also implemented online. The advantage of this method is fast and real-time evolution that requires no software platforms.

The above two implementation methods are illustrated in Figure 8.2 [8]. In these two methods, each individual chromosome of the initial population must be generated randomly. Then, with an extrinsic evolution method, each individual chromosome is mapped to the software models of the programmable device. With an intrinsic evolution method, each individual chromosome is mapped to the download configuration bits of the programmable device. Then, compared with the anticipated circuit response, each individual is evaluated and given a weight according to its accordance degree to the anticipated circuit response. Finally, circuit evolution proceeds based on the weight of each individual (i.e., fitness). The above process is repeated until the evolving circuit response accords with the anticipated one.

Evolvable hardware fault-tolerance can be firstly treated as a kind of electronic circuit design method, in which the configuration data (e.g., bit stream) of a programmable device is encoded to the chromosome of an evolutionary

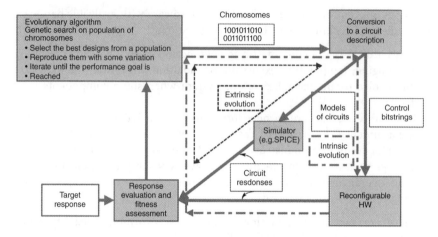

Figure 8.2 Evolvable hardware fault-tolerance implementation methods.

algorithm, and the chromosome is evolved by the evolutionary algorithm, so that the circuit that meets the requirement is found automatically. Different circuit functions in a programmable device correspond to different configuration data, whereas different configuration data may correspond to the same circuit function in a programmable device. Thus, when faults occur, fault-tolerance can be realized via spare resources in the programmable device used with the evolutionary algorithm, so that a different configuration bit stream (compared with the bit stream before faults) with the same circuit function is found.

As can be seen, evolvable hardware fault-tolerance follows the fundamental principle of fault-tolerance – that is, a highly dependable system can be constructed by means of redundancy. However, the redundancy of evolvable hardware is dynamic redundancy, with more effective resource utilization and more flexibility than traditional static redundancy. In addition, this kind of fault-tolerance technique features artificial intelligence, because it is based on evolutionary algorithms.

Figure 8.3 illustrates the fault-tolerance implementation process in a programmable device with the evolvable hardware fault-tolerance technique [6]. In the figure, the circuit on the left ("before evolution") and the circuit on the right ("after evolution") have the same function, but with different configuration bit streams. We assume that the original function and configuration of the circuit, which is before evolution, is shown in the left part of Figure 8.3. When faults occur in the circuit, search for the new configuration bit stream restarts with the evolutionary algorithm. Once the new configuration bit stream is found (which, for example, is illustrated in the right part of Figure 8.3), evolution stops. The programmable logic device (PLD) is reconfigured with the new bit stream and, consequently, fault-tolerance is implemented.

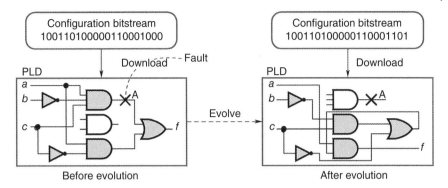

Figure 8.3 Evolution-based fault-tolerance process in a PLD.

The fault-tolerance process illustrated above is explained in detail as follows [6]:

1) The problem encoding is implemented by transferring the device configuration data to the chromosome. For example, the original configuration bit stream is 0000 0000 0000 0000 0000 0 and 1111 1111 1111 1111 1111 1, which is directly encoded to the chromosome of the evolutionary algorithm. The original population is two.

2) The chromosomes of the next generation (i.e., the new configuration bit streams) are generated by the selection, mutation, and crossover operations of the evolutionary algorithm. For example, a generation of the evolutionary algorithm is:

   • The 0000 0000 0000 0000 0000 0 and 1111 1111 1111 1111 1111 1 is selected to the next generation.

   • The chromosome 1111 1111 1111 1111 1111 1 mutates to 1111 1111 1111 1111 1110 1.

   • There is no crossover.

3) The chromosomes, and also the configuration bit streams, are downloaded to the programmable device, and are evaluated according to the fitness function. Whether the circuit with these configurations has the required function is checked.

4) If the circuit has the required function, the evolution stops. If not, the process repeats from step **2**, where chromosomes of the next generation are created.

   For example, in Figure 8.3, if the configurations from step **2** do not meet the requirement, step **2** is repeated, evolution goes on, and the next generation of chromosomes is created. Assume that when N generation evolves, there is a chromosome 1001 1010 0000 1100 0100 0 that can meet the requirement; the evolution then stops. The logic function and configuration are shown on the left side of Figure 8.3 (before evolution).

5) When faults occur, the configuration of the device is re-evolved and re-evaluated. Because different configurations of the device may have the same function, it is possible to implement the same required function without the fault part in the programmable device. When this happens (i.e., the evolved configuration implements the same function), the evolution stops and fault-tolerance is implemented. If the configuration cannot meet the requirement after a maximum generation evolution, fault-tolerance fails. In this condition, the faults that occur cannot be tolerated.

For example, in Figure 8.3, when faults occur, the chromosome 1001 1010 0000 1100 0100 0 is re-evolved. If there evolves a chromosome 1001 1010 0000 1100 0110 1 in a generation, this chromosome meets the requirement, and the evolution stops. The logic function and configuration are shown on the right part of Figure 8.3 (after evolution). Using this intelligent search from evolutionary algorithm, the same function with different configuration bit stream is implemented, so that faults are shielded and tolerated.

8.1.2 Evolutionary Algorithm

An evolutionary algorithm is one of the two factors of evolvable hardware fault-tolerance that are the key to implementing intelligence and adaptability [9–11]. The idea comes from the generally existing evolution phenomenon in nature. In order to adapt to the natural environment, biological individuals that are fit persist generation by generation, whereas unfit individuals are eliminated. In this kind of evolution, individuals of the new generation may inherit the characteristics from their parents' generation, and may also produce new characteristics that are different from their parents' generation.

The occurrence of this biological evolution phenomenon depends on four fundamental conditions:

1) A population consisting of biological individuals exists.
2) There are differences among the individuals – that is, the population features diversity.
3) Biological individuals can self-reproduce.
4) Different individuals have different ability to survive, and individuals with better genes are more reproductive (and vice versa).

There are three basic evolution mechanisms in biological populations: selection, hybridization cross, and mutation. Biological evolution is essentially the changes and improvements to the chromosome. The behavior variation of a biological individual is the expression form of chromosome variation. Thus, the exclusive feature of the chromosome determines the biological diversity; the stability of the chromosome guarantees the stability of the biological population; and the hybridization cross and mutation mechanisms make the biological evolution possible. On the basis of these biological evolution rules, scientists put forward evolutionary algorithms.

To date, three main branches in evolutionary algorithms are used in evolvable hardware fault-tolerance techniques: genetic algorithm (GA); evolutionary programming (EP); and evolutionary strategy (ES). In the early 1960s, Rechenberg and Schwefel from the Berlin Institute of Technology had trouble designing object shapes and character description parameters optimization when they did wind tunnel experiments. They adopted biological mutation to randomly change the parameter values, and obtained an ideal result. Afterwards, they conducted in-depth research into this method, subsequently developing a branch of evolutionary algorithm, called ES.

In the 1960s, Fogel *et al.* presented EP when they designed the finite state machine (FSM). They evolved a group of FSMs with the evolution idea and obtained ideal results. In the same decade, John Holland was aware of the similar relationship between biological heredity, natural evolution, and artificial adaptation systems. He presented the idea that people can refer to biological heredity mechanisms, and make adaptive search by population when they research or design artificial adaptation systems. In 1975, he published a creative book, called *Adaptation in Natural and Artificial Systems*, in this area. In 1992, Koza applied genetic algorithm to computer program optimization design and automatic generation, and proposed genetic programming (GP), which has now become an important branch of GA.

Recently, a constant stream of new evolutionary algorithms are being applied to evolvable hardware fault-tolerance, mainly including particle swarm optimization (PSO) and ant colony optimization (ACO). In addition, there are some applications that combine more than two algorithms – such as QEPSO, which combines quantum evolution and PSO.

Each of the above algorithms has its advantages and disadvantages, as regards application to evolvable hardware fault-tolerance research. For example, Tyrrell from the UK is engaged in research with the ES algorithm, while Koza from the USA mainly adopts GP algorithms. Among these evolutionary algorithms, GA is the most widely used algorithm. Consequently, we expound on this algorithm in this book. Before the introduction to GA theory, some relevant terminologies follow below:

1) *Chromosome.* The description structure of a practical problem or the encoded string structure of parameters, which indicates the characteristics of an individual.
2) *Individual.* The primary object and structure processed by GA, which is the substantive implementation of the chromosome.
3) *Population.* The set of individuals.
4) *Gene.* This is an element in the chromosome string structure, which indicates different characteristics.

5) *Locus.* The position in which a gene is located on a chromosome.

6) *Fitness.* The degree to which an individual fits the environment, or the viability in some environment, which is decided by the genetic characteristics.

7) *Genotype.* The genetic characteristics and performance defined by the gene, corresponding to the chromosome string structure in GA.

8) *Phenotype.* The characteristics that genotype performs in a certain environment, corresponding to the parameters decoded from the chromosome string structure in GA.

9) *Selection/Reproduction.* The operation of exclusive competition for limited resources.

10) *Crossover/Recombination.* The exchange operation of two gene sections in a group of chromosomes.

11) *Mutation.* The variation operation at the chromosome level.

A GA is a global probability searching algorithm based on a biological evolution mechanism, such as natural selection, heredity, and mutation. The fundamental idea of this algorithm is as follows. First, samples are extracted from the resolution set of the problem, so that a resolution sample set is formed, called a population. An element from the original sample set is not necessarily the resolution to the problem. Next, each resolution sample in the set, called an individual, is encoded into a string structure. The string structure is the chromosome. Finally, a goal function is designed, called a fitness function. This function is used to evaluate the resolution set. If the evaluation result meets the anticipated value, the evolution completes; otherwise, the population of the chromosome will evolve, forming the next generation, which is evaluated again. In this process, "evolve" means that three genetic operations are performed on the population: selection, crossover, and mutation.

As with traditional search and optimization algorithms, GA is a sort of iterative method. However, it has various new features:

1) This algorithm does not operate on the resolution set of the problem. However, it operates on the encoded string from the resolution set of the problem instead of the original resolution set of the problem. Thus, it is widely adaptive.

2) The algorithm does not require derivative and assistance knowledge; it only requires a target function that affects search direction and a corresponding fitness function.

3) Because this algorithm starts the search from a code set of problem resolution, not from a single resolution, there is obviously a lower probability that this algorithm will fall into a local minimum.

4) The operators of the algorithm, selection, crossover, and mutation, are all of random operations, not of determined operations.

5) This algorithm uses probability based rules, not determined rules, and consequently possesses good scalability.
6) The algorithm features self-organization, self-adaptation, and self-learning (i.e., intelligence characteristics).
7) The algorithm features intrinsic parallelism.

Furthermore, GA can generate multiple potential resolutions according to a specific problem, which can be selected by the user. Thus, the algorithm has a simple form and strong robustness. The characteristics of GA make it simple, adaptable, and of good effect in practical applications, such that it is widely used and is the most representative algorithm among all the evolutionary algorithms.

GA has many different variant algorithms according to different practical application situations. Among all the GAs, standard/simple genetic algorithm (SGA) is the fundamental algorithm. The elitist genetic algorithm (EGA), based on SGA, adopts an elitist individual reservation strategy. These two particular GAs are the most adopted algorithms. In addition, there are other promoted algorithms, such as hierarchical GA, the complete hardware evolution (CHE) algorithm, hybrid genetic algorithm, parallel genetic algorithm, and adaptive genetic algorithm.

In the genetic algorithm, the preliminary work and steps are as follows:

1) Select coding strategy, transfer the objective problem parameters set X to chromosome string structure set Y. In a genetic algorithm, the operation is not directly on the resolution set of the problem, but on encoding set of the resolution. It significantly affects the algorithm performance and efficiency when a certain code is selected.
2) Define fitness function. The fitness is a measurement of the resolution, indicating the degree to which the resolution approaches the evolution objective. Fitness is usually represented in the form of an objective function. The fitness of resolution is the only selection base in the algorithm.
3) Determine genetic strategies (operations), including genetic parameters, such as population size n; selection operator, crossover operator and mutation operator; crossover probability p_c, mutation probability p_m. Different genetic strategies will significantly affect algorithm performance.
4) Generate initial population P randomly.
5) Calculate the fitness $f(X)$, corresponding to the decoded chromosome string structure of each individual in the population.
6) Operate the population with the selection operator, crossover operator, and mutation operator according to the determined genetic strategies/operations, generating the next population.
7) Determine whether the population can satisfy a certain objective, or whether the evolution generations has reached the maximum number. If not, return to **6**, or revise the genetic strategies and return to **6**.

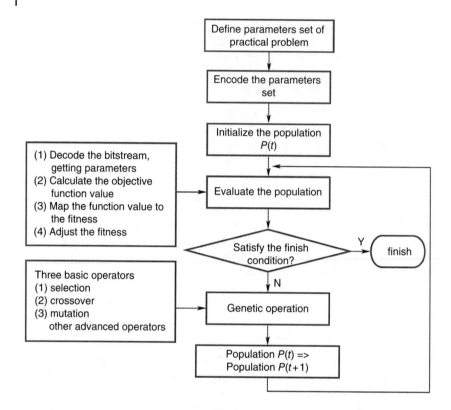

Figure 8.4 Standard genetic algorithm flowchart.

A flowchart for a standard genetic algorithm is illustrated in Figure 8.4 [12].

The implementation of genetic algorithm relates to five aspects – namely, the five factors of the algorithm: encoding, initial population setting, fitness function designing, genetic operators designing, and control parameters setting. Among these five factors, initial population can be generated randomly. Control parameters can be set according to practical experience. Encoding, fitness function designing and genetic operators designing are the main factors in the genetic algorithm. These are discussed below.

8.1.2.1 Encoding Methods

The essence of biological evolution is expressed by the variation and improvement of the chromosome. That is, the change of biological behavior itself results in change in the chromosome structure. In a genetic algorithm, the chromosome is the description of the practical problem. The chromosome is usually a string structure, which decides the characteristics of an individual. The chromosome is the object on which the genetic algorithm operates.

The mapping from the problem set to the code set in genetic algorithm is called encoding. The mapping from the code set to the problem set is called decoding. The process of encoding builds a map from the practical problem description to the string structure in the genetic algorithm. The decoding restores the chromosome string structure to the practical problem description. The mapping from the practical problem description to the chromosome string structure is called the mapping from phenotype to genotype.

In a genetic algorithm, there are several encoding methods, which may be adopted according to different problems. The frequently used encoding methods are as follows [12]:

1) *Binary encoding.* This method is the most frequently used. The parameters of the problem are mapped to a chromosome string structure that consists of the characters in the set {0,1}. The characters in the set {0,1} will be operated on differently according to the problem.

2) *Large character set coding.* In this encoding mechanism, each code of the chromosome comes from a multi-character set, where the character is usually one of an N-system character set. For example, a hexadecimal-system character set based chromosome string structure $a = a_1 a_2 ... a_i ... a_N$, where ai $\in$ {1, 2, ..., 9, A, ..., F}, $i = 1, ..., N_o$.

3) *Real number encoding.* This kind of code is real number composed chromosome string structure. Real number encoding features high accuracy, and is easy for large-scale search.

4) *Sequential encoding.* When a sequence related problem is being resolved with a genetic algorithm, such as sorting, each code in the chromosome is obtained from a sequence set. This kind of code is of strong pertinence, which is more natural and reasonable in resolving sequence related problems.

In addition to the above encoding methods, there are many other encoding methods, such as tree type encoding, adaptive encoding, and chaos sequence encoding. However, we can adopt a corresponding encoding method to the practical problem.

Because of its strong robustness, there is no severe requirement on the encoding method in genetic algorithm. However, there are also three principles to satisfy when the practical problem is encoded:

1) *Completeness.* All of the points (resolutions) in the problem space are the phenotypes that can be mapped into the points (chromosome string structure) in the code space.

2) *Soundness.* Each chromosome string structure in the code space must correspond to some potential resolution in the problem space.

3) *Non-redundancy.* Each chromosome must correspond to the potential resolution with one-to-one mapping.

In evolvable hardware fault-tolerance techniques, the configuration data of the programmable devices are denoted with a binary system. Thus, the chromosome can be generated via binary code.

8.1.2.2 Fitness Function Designing

A genetic algorithm is a mapping from the practical problem space to chromosome string structure space, with necessary evaluation of the adaptability of each individual, in line with the principle that one who adapts will survive. The fitness function constructs the survival environment that each an individual must adapt to, in which each individual survives according to its fitness value. Better chromosome string structure gets a higher fitness and a higher evaluation value and, consequently, higher survival ability.

For easy evaluation, the fitness is non-negative, and denotes a better individual with a larger value. Assume S^L is the chromosome string structure space, and R^+ is a non-negative real number set. The fitness function on S^L is as follows:

$$f(\cdot) : S^L \rightarrow R^+$$

Assume the objective function is $g(x)$, and the optimization problem is a function opt $g(x)$ ($x \in [u, v]$). The objective function is positive or negative, and is sometimes a complex number. We must establish a mapping from the fitness function to the objective function, making the fitness function non-negative, and making the direction of increase of the fitness function the same as that of the objective function. Thus, a mapping is established, i.e., $T : g \rightarrow f$, in which there exists an optimal resolution x^*, and max $f(x^*) =$ opt $g(x^*)$ ($x^* \in [u, v]$):

1) In a minimization problem, the mapping from fitness function $f(x)$ to objective function $g(x)$ is:

$$f(x) = \begin{cases} c_{\max} - g(x), & \text{if } g(x) < c_{\max} \\ 0, & \text{otherwise} \end{cases}$$

where $C_{\max}$ can be an input value or a theoretical maximum, and can also be the maximum $g(x)$ in all evolution generations or in k generations. (Here, $C_{\max}$ changes with the generation.)

2) In a maximization problem, the mapping from fitness function $f(x)$ to objective function $g(x)$ is:

$$f(x) = \begin{cases} g(x) - c_{\min}, & \text{if } g(x) - c_{\min} > 0 \\ 0, & \text{otherwise} \end{cases}$$

where $C_{\min}$ can be an input value or the minimum $g(x)$ in all evolution generations or in k generations.

In practical applications, different fitness functions can be designed according to different problems. However, they should generally satisfy the following conditions:

1) single value, continuity, non-negative, and maximization;
2) reasonable, consistency;
3) small calculation.

8.1.2.3 Genetic Operators

The operators in a genetic algorithm are also called elementary genetic operations, which mainly include three categories:

1) Selection, also called reproduction;
2) crossover, also called recombination; and
3) mutation [11,12].

In addition to the above three categories, there are other categories of genetic operators, for example, inversion. In general, these three categories of operators are sufficient in practical applications.

8.1.2.3.1 *Selection*

Selection is an operation in which individuals with high fitness value will be chosen from the population with a certain strategy, for the next step of genetic operation or production of next generation. There are three steps in the selection operation.

1) Step 1: calculate the fitness of each individual. The fitness value is the basis of the selection operation. Thus, the fitness of all the individuals in the population must be calculated.
2) Step 2: determine the assignment algorithm of individual survival probability (i.e., define the individual selection probability). There are two assignment algorithms:
   - Proportional fitness assignment, also called Monte Carlo algorithm. In this algorithm, the probability that is proportional to the fitness value of an individual is used as the base to decide the possibility that an individual is selected for the next generation. Assume the population is N, the fitness of an individual i is F_i, then the possibility that it is selected is:

$$P_i = \frac{F_i}{\sum_{i=1}^{N} F_i}$$

According to this assignment algorithm, an individual with a higher fitness value has greater probability of being selected and, furthermore, a greater probability of being reproduced in the next generation. As a result, its gene obtains a corresponding probability to be reserved. The proportional fitness assignment is a frequently used algorithm.

- Rank-based fitness assignment. In this algorithm, the population is sorted according to the objective value. The fitness is decided by an individual's position in the population, not the objective value. Michalewicz presented a linear sorting selection probability formula $P_i = c(1 - c)^{i-1}$, where i is the sequence number of an individual, and c is the selection probability of the first individual in the sequence.

3) Step 3: selection operation. An individual is selected with some random algorithm, according to the probability assignment of the individual. There are many selection operation algorithms, from which several of the most frequently used algorithms are as follows:

- *Roulette wheel selection.* For a generation, there are multiple selection operations. In this algorithm, the sub-intervals for each individual are divided in the interval [0,1] of the number axis or the wheel, according to the assigned probability of each individual. Assume there are N individuals, the first sub-interval is $[0, P_1]$, the second sub-interval is $[P_1, P_1 + P_2]$, ..., the Nth sub-interval is $[P_{N-1}, 1]$. Then, a random number in the interval [0,1] is generated in every selection operation, which is used to indicate the selected individual. Assume the generated random number is x, and $x \in$ the ith sub-interval, then the ith individual is selected for the next generation. Because this algorithm is generally based on proportional assigned fitness, it is also called the fitness proportional selection algorithm. In the literature, proportional fitness assignment and roulette wheel selection may be combined, and the combination algorithm is called roulette wheel selection. The roulette wheel selection is the simplest and most frequently used selection algorithm. However, there are disadvantages. This algorithm cannot guarantee that the individual with the highest fitness is selected into the next-generation population; only the individual with the highest fitness has a larger probability of being selected into the next generation than other individuals.

- *Elitist selection.* In order to overcome the disadvantage existing in roulette wheel selection, in which the individual with maximum fitness has a possibility of not being selected to the next generation, elitist selection is presented. In this algorithm, the optimal individual's fitness in the current generation and that of the next generation are compared when the next generation is created. If the optimal individual's fitness in the next generation is smaller than that in the current generation, the optimal individual in the current generation, or the individuals whose fitness is greater than the optimal individual's fitness in the next generation, are reproduced directly to the next generation, randomly replacing the individuals in the next generation, or replacing the worst individuals in the next generation with the same number. From the viewpoint of selection strategy in genetic algorithm, this kind of elitist reservation selection strategy is an essential guarantee that the genetic algorithm can converge to the optimal resolution of the problem. A genetic algorithm with this strategy is called an elitist reservation genetic algorithm.

- *Tournament selection.* The main idea of this algorithm is as follows. Some individuals are randomly selected from the current population (lay back or not), and the one that has the highest fitness is selected for the next generation. This process is repeated until the number of individuals reaches the population scale. In this method, the parameter is the selection scale – that is, the number of individuals in the first step random selection, which is denoted with q. According to multiple experimental results, parameter q can be two in general.

8.1.2.3.2 *Crossover*

Crossover is a kind of simulation of gene recombination process in sexual reproduction in nature, which is an operation that is used to create new individuals with partial chromosomes exchange and recombination of two parents. Crossover is an important way to create new individuals in a genetic algorithm. As to crossover, there are several algorithms.

1) *One-point crossover.* This is the most fundamental crossover method, presented by professor Holland. Assume there are two chromosome strings $s_1 = a_{11}a_{12}...a_{1L}$ and $s_2 = a_{21}a_{22}...a_{2L}$. A crossover place $x \in [1, L-1]$ is created randomly. Thus, the two chromosome strings exchange before position x, forming two new chromosome strings $s_1' = a_{11}a_{12}...a_{1,x-1}a_{2,x}...a_{2L}$ and $s_2' = a_{21}a_{22}...a_{2,x-1}a_{1,x}...a_{1L}$. For $x = 1$, there is an exchange result, $s_1' = a_{21}a_{22}...a_{2L}$ and $s_2' = a_{11}a_{12}...a_{1L}$. One-point crossover has the minimal possibility to destroy an individual behavior and to reduce individual fitness. However, the search capability of this algorithm is affected, in the case of small population.

2) *Multi-point crossover.* In this algorithm, multiple crossover points are randomly generated in the chromosome strings, so that gene exchange will take place. The detailed crossover process is like that of one-point crossover. As an example of a two-point crossover, the operation process is illustrated in Figure 8.5. Multi-point crossover helps to increase the exchange information and to create more diversiform individuals. However, this algorithm will possibly destroy some individuals with good mode. In fact, as the number of crossover points increases, the possibility that the chromosome structure is destroyed increases. As a result, it becomes very difficult to protect good mode effectively, and the performance of the genetic algorithm is affected. Consequently, only two-point crossover is frequently adopted among all the multi-point crossover algorithms, and algorithms with more than two-point crossover are not used.

3) *Uniform crossover.* In this algorithm, each bit in the chromosome strings will be randomly exchanged with uniform probability. Assume there are

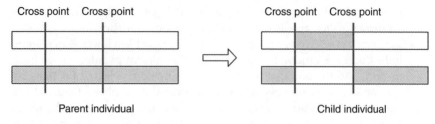

Figure 8.5 Two-point crossover process.

two chromosome strings $s_1 = a_{11}a_{12}...a_{1L}$ and $s_2 = a_{21}a_{22}...a_{2L}$. The two new chromosome strings are $s_1' = a_{11}'a_{12}'...a_{1L}'$ and $s_2' = a_{21}'a_{22}'...a_{2L}'$ after uniform crossover, where:

$$a_{1i}' = \begin{cases} a_{1i}, & x > 1/2 \\ a_{2i}, & x \le 1/2 \end{cases}, \quad a_{2i}' = \begin{cases} a_{2i}, & x > 1/2 \\ a_{1i}, & x \le 1/2 \end{cases}.$$

where x is a uniform distribution based random variable in the interval $[0,1]$.

8.1.2.3.3 *Mutation*

Mutation is a simulation of the mutant phenomenon of some genes of the chromosome in natural biological evolutionary process, resulting in structure change of the entire chromosome. In genetic algorithm, mutation often means a random change of gene in the chromosome string structure, according to the mutation probability p_m. Assume that N is the population size and L is the length of the chromosome code. As to the frequently used binary chromosome code in evolvable hardware research $s_i = b_{i1}b_{i2}...b_{iL}$ ($i = 1,2,...,N$), we can get a new chromosome $s_i' = b_{i1}'b_{i2}'...b_{iL}'$ ($i = 1,2,...,N$) after the mutation operation, where:

$$b_{ij}' = \begin{cases} 1 - b_{ij}, & x_{ij} \le p_m \\ b_{ij}, & x_{ij} > p_m \end{cases},$$

and x_{ij} is a uniform distribution based random variable in the interval $[0,1]$, which decides whether the gene j of chromosome I will mutate.

Although mutation can create new fine individuals, an overly large mutation rate can cause vibration of the algorithm, resulting in non-convergence. Thus, a small value is usually adopted as the mutation rate p_m. In practice, each gene in the chromosome has a very small mutation rate. In this condition, it is of low efficiency to calculate whether each gene will mutate. However, we can implement mutation in two steps:

1) Step 1: calculate whether each chromosome will mutate. Assume the mutation rate of a chromosome is $p_m^{(S)}$, $p_m^{(S)} = 1 - (1 - p_m)^L$. Assume x is a uniform distribution based random variable in the interval $[0,1]$. If $x \le p_m^{(S)}$, the chromosome will mutate; jump to step **2**; otherwise, finish.

2) Step 2: calculate each gene's mutation probability in the chromosome. Because there are changes in the mutation operation steps, the mutation probability calculation of each gene in the chromosome must be adjusted. Assume the new gene mutation rate is $p_m{'}$. The mathematical expectation of mutation times in the traditional mutation operation is $N \times L \times p_m$, and that in the new mutation operation is $\left(N \times p_m^{(S)}\right) \times \left(L \times p_m{'}\right)$. These two mathematical expectations must be equal – that is, $N \times L \times p_m = \left(N \times p_m^{(S)}\right) \times \left(L \times p_m{'}\right)$. Thus, we can obtain:

$$p_m{'} = \frac{p_m}{p_m^{(S)}} = \frac{P_m}{1 - (1 - P_m)^L}$$

8.1.2.4 Convergence of Genetic Algorithm

The two most frequently used genetic algorithms, SGA and EGA, have the following convergence conclusions:

1) The probability that the standard genetic algorithm converges to the optimal resolution is less than one. That is, the standard genetic algorithm cannot guarantee global convergence. However, with certain constraint conditions, the standard genetic algorithm can converge to the optimal resolution, with a probability of one.
2) With improvement on the standard genetic algorithm, there is the elitist reservation genetic algorithm, whose probability to converge to the optimal resolution is equal to one.

Note that the standard genetic algorithm cannot guarantee global convergence, which does not mean that the standard genetic algorithm cannot converge. In practical applications, the resolving of many problems can be implemented with this SGA.

8.1.3 Programmable Devices

The programmable device is one of the two factors of evolvable hardware fault-tolerance. It is the evaluation instrument in evolution and hardware carrier after evolution, and also the object that fault-tolerance is implemented on. The programmable device is very important to evolvable hardware fault-tolerance technique.

Before the emergence of programmable devices, hardware structure could not be changed online after its design and manufacture. Now, however, hardware can be designed and various functions implemented with different configurations. Moreover, with online reconfigurable FPGA, hardware can be changed dynamically online. Thus, evolvable hardware fault-tolerance techniques has developed from theory to implementation with the advent of programmable devices.

Programmable devices are quite varied. They include ROM, programmable array logic (PAL), and general array logic (GAL). The devices consist of "AND" arrays and "OR" arrays, which are called simple programmable devices. FPGA is a kind of complex programmable device, whose inside structure consists of CLB arrays. In early research on evolvable hardware fault-tolerance techniques, PAL and GAL were adopted. Currently, the three most widely used programmable devices are field programmable analog array (FPAA), FPGA, and field programmable transistor array (FPTA). FPAA is used to implement analog circuit evolution. FPGA is used to implement digital circuit evolution, which is a coarse granularity programmable device with the CLB as its circuit element. FPTA is used not only to implement analog circuit evolution, but also digital circuit evolution, which is a fine granularity programmable device.

When evolvable hardware fault-tolerance is implemented with these programmable devices, the details of the inside structure of the devices must be known. As a result, different methods must be used, to conform to the devices from various companies. More specifically, the evolution method strongly relies on specific devices. Because the evolution level is gate level in the lower layer of the devices, the evolution circuit scale is small.

In order to resolve these problems, the virtual reconfigurable circuit (VRC), also called programmable architecture, is being proposed. VRC-based evolution is a major method in recent evolvable hardware-related research. VRC, which imitates the FPGA structural characteristics, is an array structure comprising elementary logical elements that form a virtual reconfigurable hardware layer on a concrete programmable device, much like FPGA. VRC mainly features device independence, flexible structure, complex logic implementation by elementary elements, and configuration data format acquisition, such that it can be used to implement large-scale circuit evolution. Consequently, it is amenable to evolvable hardware fault-tolerance techniques.

Detailed introduction to the programmable devices and programmable architectures in evolvable hardware fault-tolerance technique is given below.

8.1.3.1 ROM

ROM mainly consists of address decoder and storage unit. All the memory units constitute a two-dimensional storage array, where the row is the output of the address decoder (i.e., address), called word wire, and the column is the stored binary data in the storage unit, called bit wire. The address decoder selects a certain output word wire, according to the input address, which is used to drive the bit wire of this word wire. In this manner, the data from the storage unit on the word line can be read. Figure 8.6 is an 8×4 ROM with fuse-based storage units, in which the stable fuse denotes that data "1" is stored, and the melting fuse denotes that data "0" is stored. This kind of ROM is called programmable ROM (PROM), to which data can be written only once. After being written, the data cannot be changed.

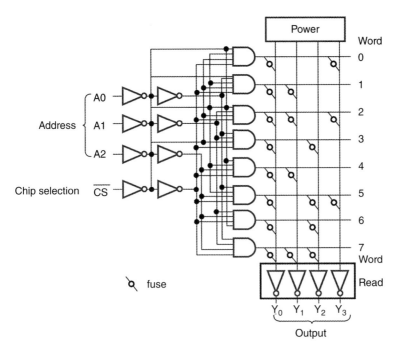

Figure 8.6 ROM structure.

In general, ROM is used to store data/programs – it is not an actual PLD. However, it can actually be viewed as a kind of PLD, according to its inside structure. The address decoder of a ROM is implemented with a group of "AND" gates, whose output is the minterm of all the address input. The storage unit entity is actually the combination of "AND" gates. The number of ROM outputs is the number of "OR" gates. Each minterm of a decoder is likely to be the input of the "OR" gates. However, whether a minterm is the input of an "OR" gate depends on the data in the storage unit. All the storage unit entities can be treated as an array of "OR" gates. Thus, ROM consists of "AND" gate arrays and "OR" gate arrays, in which the "AND" gate arrays are fixed, forming all the minterms, and the "OR" gate arrays are configured by the user (i.e., programmable).

ROM is typically manufactured with a fuse technique structure, which means that the configuration data can only be written once. After being written, the configuration cannot be changed. This is a feature of ROM means that it can only be used for extrinsic evolution.

8.1.3.2   PAL and GAL

8.1.3.2.1   *PAL and its Structure*

PAL is a kind of programmable device, first manufactured by Monolithic Memories Inc. (MMI), USA in the late 1970s. PALs continuously use the fuse

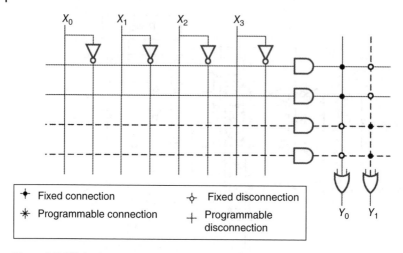

Figure 8.7 PAL basic structure.

and bipolar technique used in the PROM device of MMI. In the PAL, the basic structure with programmable "AND" gate array and fixed "OR" gate array is adopted, as shown in Figure 8.7. The feature of PAL is that the "AND" gate array is programmable, whereas the "OR" gate array is not. There are other kinds of PALs, whose structures are more complex, but functionality and flexibility have been improved to some extent. However, their basic structure is built on the above fundamental structure of PAL.

The fuse connection technique is used inside PAL, where the programmable function is implemented by melting the fuse. An unmelted fuse signifies connection of the cross-point (i.e., "programmed connection"), while melted fuse signifies disconnection of the cross-point (i.e., "programmed disconnection"). Moreover, this PAL device cannot be rewritten once it is programmed. Thus, it is only fit for extrinsic evolution.

8.1.3.2.2 GAL and Its Structure

The structure of GAL is more complex. It comprises "AND" gate array, "OR" gate array, and output logic macro cell (OLMC), which provides more flexible programmable I/Os. However, the fundamental inside structure also comprise "AND" gate arrays and "OR" gate arrays. According to the structure, GAL can be classified into two categories: GAL with programmable "AND" gate array and non-programmable "OR" gate array; and GAL with programmable "AND" gate array and programmable "OR" gate array. In the GAL, the E2CMOS technique is adopted, with which the chip can be erased and programmed in seconds. PAL is a kind of electrical erasable and multi-times programmable high-speed PLD.

The one-time programmable feature of PAL makes it fit for extrinsic evolution research. Although GAL can be programmed multiple times, there are also restrictions on its programmable features, such as low programming speed and limited programming times. Thus, this kind of device is also fit for extrinsic evolution.

8.1.3.3 FPGA

Since FPGA was first developed by the Xilinx Corporation in 1985, other producers have continuously produced their own FPGA products, forming an extremely speedy development trend. Currently, the main FPGA producers in the world are Xilinx, Actel, Altera, Atmel, and Lattice.

FPGAs can be classified according to manufacturing technique, into two categories: anti-fuse-based FPGAs and SRAM-based FPGAs. The configuration of anti-fuse-based FPGAs cannot be changed after programming is complete. SRAM-based FPGAs have on-chip SRAM to store configuration data, with which the configuration data in the SRAM can be dynamically updated online, implementing dynamic and online changes in circuit function. In evolvable hardware, the intrinsic evolution is implemented with this dynamic online reconfiguration characteristic of SRAM-based FPGA.

There are many FPGA manufacturers, with FPGAs from different manufacturers having different structural characteristics. However, the basic constitution of the FPGAs is the same. There are three categories of FPGAs, according to the construction of the logical block: LUT type; multi-switch type; and multi-level "AND" and "OR" gate type. Xilinx has many FPGA series, with powerful functionality, such that Xilinx FPGAs are the devices mainly utilized in evolvable hardware research globally [13,14]. The inside structure of the FPGA is outlined below, taking the example of Xilinx LUT-based devices.

In general, an FPGA has the following kind of structure: CLBs are surrounded by programmable routing resources, composing an array. The CLB array, surrounded by programmable IO blocks, comprises the entire FPGA chip. Inside the FPGA chip, each CLB consists of two slices and a CLB routing resource. The internal structure of a standard Xilinx FPGA, a multi-layer array structure, is shown in Figure 8.8. In this FPGA, the programming implementation is accomplished via the link connection change in routing resources and function change of the CLB.

The structure of a CLB in the Virtex series FPGA, the advanced series by Xilinx, is shown in Figure 8.9. Each slice that composes the CLB consists of two LUTs, two registers, and peripheral logic circuits (such as multiplexers), with which various combinational and sequential logic can be flexibly implemented. The input to each slice is controlled by the routing resources. Routing resources can be connected to the adjacent CLB with several single wires.

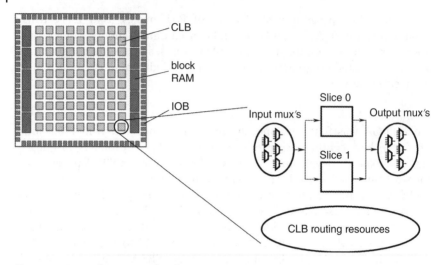

Figure 8.8 Internal structure of a Xilinx FPGA.

The internal structure of a slice is shown in more detail in Figure 8.10. Each LUT implements logic with four inputs and one output, substantially implemented in RAM. As a result, the LUT can be used as a 16 × 1 bit synchronous RAM. In the figure, it can be seen that multiplexer F5 can not only select one output from the two LUTs in a slice, but can also implement any five input, one output combinational logic function, and several nine-input combinational logic functions. This flexible structure lays the hardware foundation for the implementation of evolvable hardware fault-tolerance.

The basic inside structure, manufacturing technique feature, and fitted evolution methods of the programmable logical devices above are summarized in Table 8.1.

8.1.3.4 VRC

The essential structural unit of a VRC is the functional element, which can implement simple combinational logic, and sequential logic using flip-flops, similar to the CLB in FPGAs in functionality [15–17]. The functional element array is layered by column. The functional elements between two layers can be freely connected. Two layers can also be connected. The connections are controlled by binary switches. In this layered connection relationship, the functional elements form network connections, as shown in Figure 8.11 [15,16]. The output function of the VRC is decided by the configuration data, with different configuration data corresponding to different functions. The configuration data contain not only the configuration that decide the functionality of the functional elements, but also the configuration that determines the functional elements' connectivity.

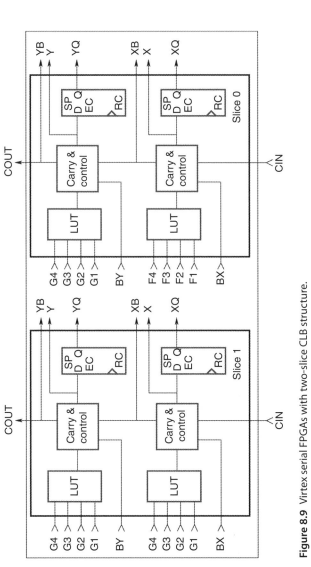

Figure 8.9 Virtex serial FPGAs with two-slice CLB structure.

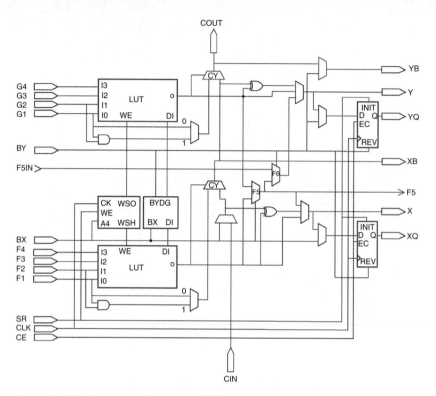

Figure 8.10 A slice inside a Virtex series FPGA.

Table 8.1 Basic structure, manufacturing technique, and applicable evolution methods of various PLDs.

	Basic structural features	Manufacturing technique features	Applicable evolution methods
PROM	"AND" and "OR" array structure, in which "AND" arrays are not programmable, whereas "OR" arrays are programmable.	Fuse technique used, programmable only once.	Fit for extrinsic evolution.
PAL	"AND" and "OR" array structure, in which "AND" arrays are programmable, whereas "OR" arrays are not.	Fuse and bipolar techniques used, programmable only once.	Fit for extrinsic evolution.
GAL	"AND" and "OR" arrays with output logical macro unit structure.	E2COMS technique used, programmable multiple times, low programming speed.	Generally fit for extrinsic evolution.
SRAM-based FPGA	Comprises routing resources, CLB and IOB, forming array structures with CLBs. Each CLB consists of LUTs, registers, and combinational logic.	CMOS-SRAM technique used, dynamically programmable online.	Fit for intrinsic evolution.

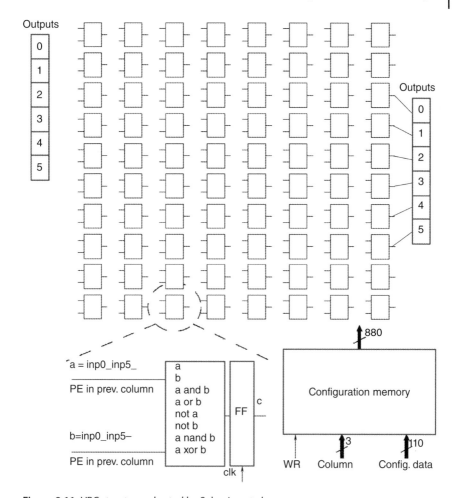

Figure 8.11 VRC structure adopted by Sekanian *et al*.

8.1.4 Evolvable Hardware Fault-tolerance Implementation Methods

Various concrete implementation methods, with different evolutionary algorithms and different programmable devices, exist according to the two factors of evolvable hardware fault-tolerance. Among the two factors, the programmable device is more critical to the concrete evolution method. In this section, we discuss the research conducted into modeling of evolution systems, summarize various evolution methods fit for different programmable devices and architectures and, finally, illustrate the methods with practical examples.

8.1.4.1 Modeling and Organization of Hardware Evolutionary Systems

An evolutionary system model comprises the following: (1) genotype; (2) phenotype; and (3) environment [9,10]. Genotype is the genetic characteristic defined by the gene, corresponding to the chromosome code in GA. Phenotype is the behavior of the genotype in a certain environment, corresponding to the parameters after decoding of the chromosome in genetic algorithm. The environment is the external requirement essential for the evolutionary system to function.

Assume that the genotype set is $G = \{g = (g_1, g_2, ..., g_n)\}$, phenotype set is $P = \{p = (p_1, p_2, ..., p_m)\}$, and environment set is $V = \{v_1, v_2, ..., v_k\}$. In the evolutionary system, on the one hand, genes react with the environment, deciding the final behavior of the system. Thus, there is a mapping $f: G \times V \to P$. On the other hand, the difference between phenotype and the environment act as a feedback to the evolution process, influencing the genotype g. Assume that the evolution process is denoted by E, then there is a mapping $f': P \times V \xrightarrow{E} G$, which is a highly nonlinear system, and is very difficult to describe with simple functions.

In hardware evolution systems, genotype is the encoded chromosome of the configuration data of the programmable device, and phenotype is the circuit function of the programmable device with specified configuration data. Further, the environment is the outside requirement on the circuit function. In general, configuration data are not phenotypes, but a bridge between genotype and phenotype. However, as to any configuration c in the configuration set $C = \{c = (c_1, c_2, ..., c_l)\}$, when it is downloaded to the programmable device, the phenotype p of the circuit is unique.

Thus, there is a functional mapping $f_2 : C \to P$, which is decided by the architecture of the specific programmable device. Consequently, once the architecture of the programmable device is decided, the configuration c can be treated as phenotype. Assume the mapping from chromosome code (genotype) to the configuration is $f_1 : G \times V \to C$, then the mapping from genotype to phenotype is $f = f_1 \cdot f_2$, as shown in Figure 8.12. In the hardware evolution system, the mapping relationship between genotype and phenotype is mainly embodied by the mapping f_1 from chromosome code to the

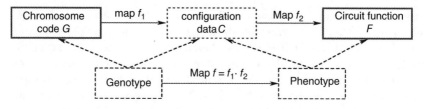

Figure 8.12 Genotype and phenotype.

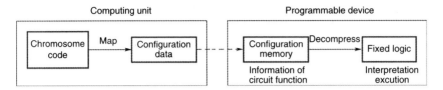

Figure 8.13 Relationship between chromosome code, configuration data, and circuit function in hardware evolution system.

configuration data. The configuration data can be regarded as compressed information of the circuit function, which is interpreted and executed by the programmable device and behaves as a specified circuit function, as shown in Figure 8.13.

From the above analysis, we can obtain the model of the entire hardware evolutionary system, as shown in Figure 8.14(a). From the implementation aspect, each module of the hardware evolutionary system can be reified, and a model of Figure 8.14(b) obtained. The hardware evolutionary system consists of three modules and four kinds of data-flows. The three modules are computing unit, programmable device (or programmable architecture) and the circuit evaluation module, and the four kinds of data-flows are configuration data, fitness, practical circuit function, and functional requirements of the outside environment.

1) Computing unit: this is used to run the evolutionary algorithm. In the evolutionary algorithm, the evolution object is the chromosome code.
2) Programmable device (or programmable architecture): the platform on which the hardware evolves, and the final implementation platform of the successfully evolved circuit.
3) Circuit evaluation module: used to compare the practical circuit function in the evolution process with the functional requirements of the outside environment, calculating the fitness value.
4) Configuration data: the configuration of the programmable device (or programmable architecture) that is converted from the chromosome code, essentially embodying the mapping relations between genotype and phenotype.
5) Fitness: the output result of the circuit evaluation module, and feedback information of the evolutionary algorithm.
6) Practical circuit function: one of the inputs to the circuit evaluation module, and also the circuit behavior function after successful evolution.
7) Functional requirements of outside environment: these comprise another set of inputs to the circuit evaluation module, and also the functional constraints from the outside environment on the hardware evolutionary system.

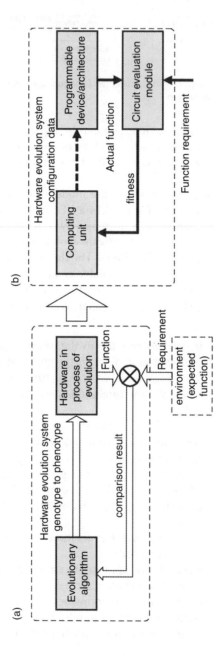

Figure 8.14 Hardware evolution system model and implementation. (a) Hardware evolution system model. (b) Hardware evolution system implementation.

Among the seven organizational parts of the hardware evolutionary system, the three that are the key to resolve at present are the following:

1) The efficiency of the evolutionary algorithm in the computing unit.
2) Programmable architecture fitting for large-scale circuits, and mapping problem from chromosome code to programmable architecture configuration.
3) Circuit functional requirement expression method and circuit evaluation method.

No breakthrough has yet been made in relation to these research problems, such as efficiency of evolutionary algorithm, circuit functional requirement and circuit evaluation expression methods. Current research work is focused on two problems: programmable architecture and mapping from chromosome code to programmable architecture configuration.

8.1.4.2 Reconfiguration and Its Classification

Before introducing the evolutionary fault-tolerance method, the concept of reconfiguration must be clarified. Reconfiguration is generally executed on concrete (actual) programmable devices, and especially on the currently widely used SRAM-based FPGAs. However, reconfiguration has now been expanded to a wider concept – the structural and functional change of the entire hardware, by means of some specific data (configuration data) change in the hardware. Each step of hardware evolution relies on the configuration of the hardware.

- Programmable: this includes "software programmable" and "hardware programmable." "Software programmable" means microprocessor code programming in a CPU-based system. "Hardware programmable" means that the hardware function and structure are decided by the configuration data in the programmable hardware logic fields.
- Configurable: this terminology is closely related to the FPGA technique, which means that the logic function of the FPGA-based hardware can be changed by the configuration of the FPGA. In the hardware field, the meanings of "programmable" and "configurable" are the same.

Reconfiguration is the process of reconfiguring a configurable device. There are two kinds of reconfiguration: static reconfiguration and dynamic reconfiguration.

1) *Static reconfiguration* is also called compile-time reconfiguration (CTR). Specifically, a configuration is executed on the FPGA before system execution, but the logic function of an FPGA is not changed when the system is running. In the whole process of system execution, the system can be configured only once with static reconfiguration, so that the hardware resources of this system cannot be multiplexed with time division. Thus, the implemented logic function and system scale are restricted by the chip resources.

2) *Dynamic reconfiguration* is also called run-time reconfiguration (RTR), which means that the chip configuration data are changed, and the FPGA is reconfigured by some control logic, without termination of the circuit function in the running system. Thus, the entire FPGA logic function is dynamically switched. In this dynamic reconfiguration, the underlying concept is that large-scale systematic function is implemented in the small-scale hardware resources with time division multiplexing. The behavior characteristic of hardware resources spatially distributed is fixed, whereas the internal logic function is switched on the time axis. This constructs a temporal and spatial system with changeable logic functions. In this kind of dynamic reconfiguration system, the entire system can be reconfigured, or part of the system can be reconfigured.

Dynamic reconfiguration can be divided according to reconfiguration granularity, into dynamic global reconfiguration and dynamic partial (local) reconfiguration [18].

1) Dynamic global reconfiguration (Figure 8.15) means the reconfiguration of the whole FPGA chip. In the reconfiguration process, the work of the chip stops, so that the old logic function of the system is lost and the new logical function is still not established. The systematic logic function is broken on the time axis (which can be called system configuration slot time), so that the systematic function is not continuous.
2) Dynamic partial (local) reconfiguration (Figure 8.16) means the reconfiguration of a part of the area of an FPGA chip. During the reconfiguration process, the chip still works. In the new systematic logic function establishment, the logic function of the area that is not reconfigured is normal – that is, the

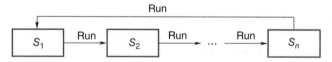

Figure 8.15 Global dynamic reconfigurable system.

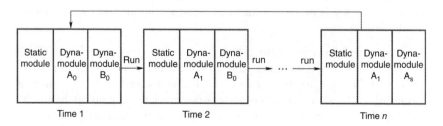

Figure 8.16 Partial dynamic reconfigurable system.

systematic logical function is continuous in the time axis. Consequently, with FPGA-based dynamic PR, a pure spatial logic system is transferred to a temporal and spatial combined logic system. This new type of logic system is the same as the function of the original system from the viewpoint of time axis and outside behavior. However, from the resource utilization point of view, resource utilization rate is improved multiple times, because of dynamic repeat utilization of hardware resources. As a result, the scale of the implemented logic system is free from the hardware resources restriction.

8.1.4.3 Evolutionary Fault-tolerance Architectures and Methods

There should be three modules in the hardware circuit to implement intrinsic evolution: (1) the carrier, in which evolvable hardware fault-tolerance is implemented (i.e., the device, in which dynamic online reconfiguration is implemented); (2) the processor, in which evolution computation is executed; and (3) the circuit that is used to evaluate the output of the evolved circuit. The hardware structure of FPGA-based evolutionary fault-tolerance is shown in Figure 8.17. The implementation steps of evolutionary fault-tolerance are as follows [19]:

1) The initial population is created by the processor system. Assume a population size of N.
2) Each chromosome code is mapped into the FPGA configuration data by the processor system, which is the mapping from genotype to the phenotype. N shares of configuration data are then downloaded to the N FPGAs.
3) M channels of inspiration signals are generated by the processor system as the input signals of N FPGAs. The outputs of the N FPGAs are the inputs of the evaluation circuit. Through the evaluation circuit, evaluation values are obtained. If the evaluation values satisfy the anticipated object circuit, the evolution is accomplished. Otherwise, go to step **4**.
4) Evolutionary computation is executed by the processor system according to the evaluation values, such that the next generation is produced. Then return to step **2**.

The population concept of evolvable hardware fault-tolerance is embodied in the hardware architecture illustrated in Figure 8.17, which is an efficient parallel implementation method. In this, N FPGAs are only used in the evolution process, whereas the evolution results are configured to only one FPGA after evolution. However, this N FPGA-based evolvable hardware fault-tolerance system is only a system in principle. The parallel system has a higher evolution speed, but lower resource utilization. In order to reduce the hardware cost and to improve the resource utilization, n FPGAs can be adopted, in which $n << N$. In this way, not only hardware cost and hardware complication are reduced, but also the evolution speed is increased. When $N = 1$, there is only one FPGA adopted as the evolution carrier and object that is evaluated.

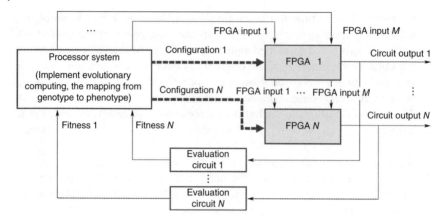

Figure 8.17 Evolvable hardware fault-tolerance structure with FPGA implementation.

However, an evolutionary algorithm is a population-based search algorithm. When the evolution result in one FPGA is evaluated with this serial method, the evolution process is very slow.

In practical applications, in order to improve system reliability, a highly reliable device is adopted as the processor for the evolutionary computation. N is then flexibly selected, according to the practical situation. With these components and parameters, and other additional fault-tolerance strategies, an evolutionary fault-tolerance system can be established. For example, with $N = 3$, which is the number of FPGAs, an evolvable hardware fault-tolerance system can be built with the following additional strategy:

1) The initial population is set to $6P$ (where P is an integer).
2) In each generation evolution, $2P$ individuals are evolved in an FPGA, which are evaluated sequentially. However, each circuit in the three FPGAs is evaluated in a parallel manner.
3) The evolution result is configured to the first FPGA, and the output of the first FPGA is the system output.
4) If one of the three FPGAs fails, the system is degraded to a system with two FPGAs. At this time, in each FPGA, $3P$ individuals' evolution is implemented, and $3P$ individuals are evaluated sequentially. Each circuit in the two FPGAs is evaluated in a parallel manner. The evolution result is configured to one of the two FPGAs.
5) If two of the three FPGAs fail, the system is degraded to a system with only one FPGA – a sequential system. The total $6P$ individuals' evolution is implemented in this FPGA, and the evolution result is configured to this FPGA.
6) If all three FPGAs fail, the system fails.

8.1.4.4 Evolutionary Fault-tolerance Methods at Various Layers of the Hardware

There are two ways to implement evolvable hardware fault-tolerance: extrinsic evolution and intrinsic evolution. The main difference between these two ways is whether each evolving individual is downloaded to the hardware to evaluate – that is, whether the fitness computation is by software simulation or by downloading to hardware. In extrinsic evolution, the fitness computation of each individual is based on the software simulation; only the final successful individual is downloaded to the programmable device, as shown in Figure 8.18(a). In intrinsic evolution, each individual in the evolution process is downloaded to the programmable device to evaluate, so that the fitness value is computed, as shown in Figures 8.18(b) and 8.18(c).

In theory, the final results of extrinsic evolution and intrinsic evolution are all downloaded to the programmable device. In the case where an accurate software model of a programmable device can be built, and there is a sufficiently powerful hardware system in the spacecraft, the software model-based individual evaluation is available. By this means, the successful optimal individual is finally downloaded to the programmable device. As a result, with extrinsic evolution, hardware evolutionary fault-tolerance can be implemented for the spacecraft.

In fact, universal spacecraft hardware is an embedded system, in which non-human interference, a non-host computer, and unmanned self-fault-tolerance is needed. Furthermore, in space applications – especially deep space explorations – the process and computation capability of the computing unit is usually limited, because of the weight and power consumption restriction of the hardware. Consequently, intrinsic evolution implemented in the embedded system is more fitting for the online evolutionary fault-tolerance system in a spacecraft's hardware, as shown in Figure 8.18(c).

In evolvable hardware fault-tolerance methods, the mapping from chromosome code to the configuration data of programmable device (programmable architecture) is currently the key problem to resolve. Configuration data are a very important element to bridge the evolutionary algorithm and the programmable device. Configuration data have different meanings in different hardware. They are a binary bit stream in FPGAs, a hardware description language in gene expression evolutions, and user-defined configuration information in VRCs. Thus, different types of configuration data are fit for different programmable architectures and different evolutionary strategies and algorithms in the evolutionary methods. From the hardware design point of view, different types of configuration data correspond to different layers in the hardware design. Consequently, there are different evolutionary methods in different hardware layers.

From the viewpoint of FPGA-based circuit design methods and flow, there are three layers of hardware: configuration bit stream layer in the bottom layer,

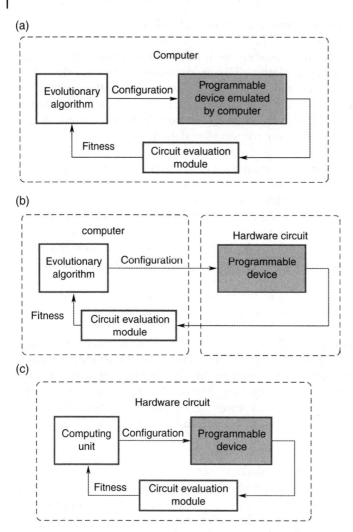

Figure 8.18 Hardware evolution implementation methods. (a) Extrinsic evolution. (b) Intrinsic evolution implemented with host computer. (c) Intrinsic evolution implemented with embedded system.

netlist layer in the middle layer, and design layer in the top layer. The design layer can be further divided into gate-level design layer and module-level design layer. Each FPGA-based hardware design layer and its corresponding evolution object are shown in Figure 8.19 [9]. In different evolution layers, there are different evolution objects, and different mapping relationships from chromosome code to configuration data.

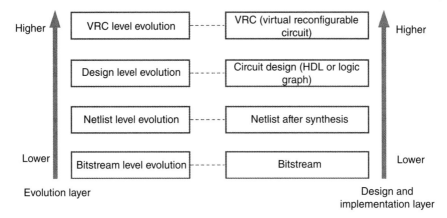

Figure 8.19 Evolution methods in various hardware layers.

8.1.4.4.1 *Bit Stream-level Evolution*

In this method, the evolution object is direct FPGA configuration bit stream, the implementation of which is shown in Figure 8.20(a). The bit stream of FPGA is a binary sequence, so that it can be directly encoded to the chromosome as the evolution object of an evolutionary algorithm. In this case, the mapping from chromosome code to configuration data is simple, and its implementation difficulty depends on the following:

1) The inside structure of the device and the format of the configuration bit stream must be known, so that chromosome encoding can be carried out.
2) The bit stream space of the device is very large. If a search is made over the entire bit stream space, it is difficult to realize. Thus, a part of the device must be selected for evolution.
3) The illegal bit stream after evolution must be processed, so that the device will not be damaged.

Because of the restrictions above, there are now only several special types of FPGAs that are fit for bit stream evolution, and the evolved circuits' scales are small. However, with the help of special tools, bit stream evolution can be implemented, such as evolution method with JBits application interface and XHWIF hardware interface. Because the FPGA configuration is directly operated in this method, without the help of other software in the process, the bit stream evolution method is fit for online evolution.

8.1.4.4.2 *Netlist-level Evolution*

Netlist is a standard format of synthesis result synthesized by hardware description language or circuit logic graph in a specific FPGA. In netlist, the interconnection of the internal resources in FPGA is described with a statement.

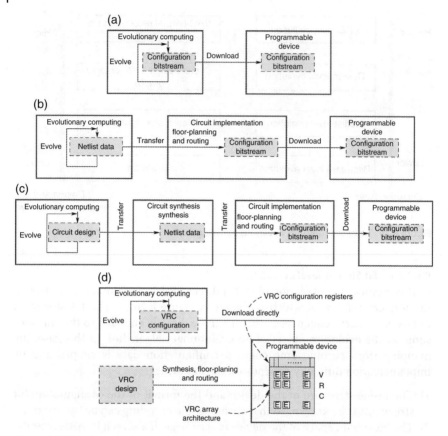

Figure 8.20 Implementation methods for various hardware layers' evolution. (a) Bit stream-level evolution. (b) Netlist-level evolution. (c) Design-level evolution. (d) VRC-level evolution.

Further, there is no floor-planning and routing information about the FPGA. In the FPGA-based hardware design, the netlist lies on a higher level than the bit stream, which is located in a middle layer. If netlist is used as an evolution object, an additional floor-planning and routing is needed, so that the bit stream can be generated when an individual is downloaded to the programmable device. The implementation of this method is shown in Figure 8.20(b). In the floor-planning and routing, special software provided by the device manufacturer is needed (for example, ISE of Xilinx). This kind of software cannot be integrated into the hardware evolution system without the support of the manufacturer. Thus, a netlist-based evolution method is currently not fit for online evolution. According to the literature, there is no netlist-based evolution method to date.

8.1.4.4.3   Design-level Evolution

Design-level evolution can be regarded as a direct search in all circuit designs. Furthermore, the evolution result is the design that satisfies the user. Currently, hardware description languages are used in the hardware design, to describe the behavior of gate-level or above circuits. The hardware description languages are usually higher languages, such as VHDL and Verilog. Taking the hardware description language as the evolution object, encoding of the hardware description language is principal, so that an evolvable chromosome can be created. On the other hand, synthesis, floor-planning and routing of the hardware description language are needed, so that a downloaded bit stream can be generated. The whole implementation process is shown in Figure 8.20(c). Although a third party can provide the synthesis tools (for example Synplify of Synplicity), the floor-planning and routing software that is finally used to generate bit stream must be provided by the FPGA's manufacturer. Consequently, as with netlist-level evolution, design-level evolution is not fit for online evolution. Currently, the evolution towards encoded hardware description language with GP belongs to design-level evolution.

8.1.4.4.4   VRC level Evolution

The evolution methods of the above three layers are all related to concrete devices, so that the relative steps in the evolution methods should be changed according to different programmable devices. VRC is a virtual reconfigurable circuit layer generated in the FPGA, which is generally implemented using hardware description language. The structural characteristic of VRC is similar to FPGA, which consists of an array structure with multiple elements, plus configuration registers to store configuration information. The element function and array connection can be changed according to the contents of the configuration registers. The function of the overall VRC is controlled by the configuration registers.

Before evolution, the VRC is built with special software, through the steps of synthesis, floor-planning, routing, and downloading to the FPGA. This is to build a virtual programmable architecture in the practical programmable device to implement evolution. In VRC-level evolution, the evolution object is the data in the configuration registers of the VRC, which is not relative to any concrete FPGAs. In addition, the configuration function of the FPGA itself is not used in the evolution process. The implementation of this method is shown in Figure 8.20(d). Because of if its non-dependence on any additional software, VRD-level evolution is fit for online evolution. The VRC method is currently adopted in most research by Professor Lukas Sekanina. The reconfigurable integrated system array (RISA) and POE (phylogenesis, ontogenesis, epigenesis) architecture presented by Tyrrell is a type of reconfigurable architecture. The significance of VRC level evolution is that ASIC with this method can be manufactured, and truly evolvable chips actualized.

Table 8.2 Comparison of evolution methods in various hardware layers.

Evolution level	Encoding object	Key techniques	Evolution methods	Applicability to online evolution
Bit stream-level evolution	Binary string	Programmable devices' structure, configuration, bit stream structure,	Direct evolution, JBits based evolution	Applicable
Netlist-level evolution	Netlist	floor-planning, and routing software integration technique.	–	Not applicable
Design-level evolution	HDL	Synthesis software, floor-planning and routing software integration technique	HDL evolution, gene expression evolution	Not applicable
VRC level evolution	VRC configuration	VRC architecture	PE array-based VRC by Lukas. Programmable architecture, such as RISA and POE.	Applicable

A feature comparison of these different hardware level evolution methods is shown in Table 8.2. Among these methods, netlist-level evolution and design-level evolution depend on special synthesis, floor-planning and routing software. Afterwards, the evolution object can be integrated into the hardware evolution system. Thus, these two methods are not fit for online evolution system implementation. Bit stream-level evolution and VRC level evolution do not depend on additional software and, consequently, they are fit for online evolution system implementation.

8.1.4.5 Method Example

8.1.4.5.1 *Evolution Based on a Simple Programmable Device [6]*

The basic structure of a PLD is based on "AND" "OR" arrays, as shown in Figure 8.21. In the hardware circuit that implements a PLD, device usage cannot reach 100%. Suppose the output function $Y_0 = (\sim X_0) + X_0(\sim X_1)(\sim X_2)X_3$ device configuration uses five out of a total of 16 "OR" arrays. If no fault-tolerance measure is taken, error in the output Y_0 is inevitable when the configuration point in use fails. This will incur malfunctioning of the entire circuit. If the evolutional hardware fault-tolerance technique is adopted, the hardware

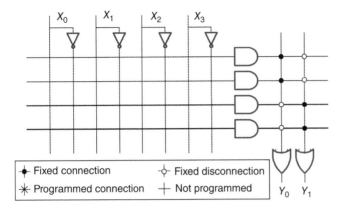

Figure 8.21 Internal structure of a PAL.

fault-tolerant feature is achieved through dynamic distribution of the 16 Y_0 configuration points with the evolution algorithm. Normal configuration and circuit output are shown in Figure 8.22(a). If a permanent Stuck-at-0 fault occurs at point A, the circuit will evolve intelligently with the evolution algorithm as shown in Figure 8.22(b). Although the fault in point A is *not* recovered, the correctness of the total circuit logic function realizes total hardware fault-tolerant capability.

A software model of the internal structure is setup with software. The input terminal of the chromosome coding strategy is denoted with two binary bits; for example, for input X_0, positive logic that connects to the "AND" array is denoted 10, and the negative logic that connects to the "AND" array is denoted 01. The value 00 signifies that X_0 is not connected to the "AND" array. Because the connective relation of the output array is fixed, the output is not encoded. Adopting genetic algorithm as the evolutional algorithm, the selection, crossover, and mutation operators are implemented. Following application of the roulette algorithm to the selection operator (dual chromosome single-point crossover algorithm is applied to the crossover operator, single-point mutation algorithm is applied to the mutation operator), evolution result evaluation is performed with adaptive value function $F(x)$, whose output is the summation of every input combination $F_i(x)$. The definition of $F_i(x)$ is:

$$F_i(x) = \begin{cases} 1 & \text{Circuit output value equals estimation} \\ 0 & \text{Others} \end{cases}$$

One evaluation criterion is that the evaluation is successful if the input combination achieves the expected function.

Apply the fault injection simulation method to produce an S-a-0 or S-a-1 fault – that is, fix the value of the chromosome corresponding to the "AND"

(a)

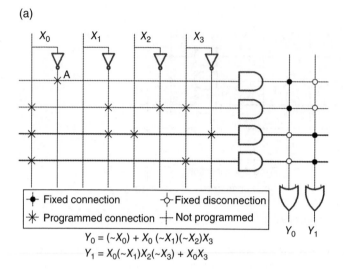

$$Y_0 = (\sim X_0) + X_0 (\sim X_1)(\sim X_2)X_3$$
$$Y_1 = X_0(\sim X_1)X_2(\sim X_3) + X_0X_3$$

(b)

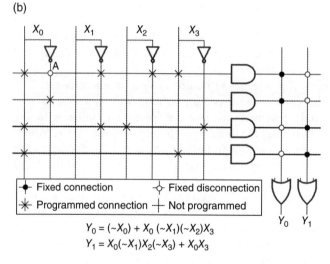

$$Y_0 = (\sim X_0) + X_0 (\sim X_1)(\sim X_2)X_3$$
$$Y_1 = X_0(\sim X_1)X_2(\sim X_3) + X_0X_3$$

Figure 8.22 Evolutional hardware fault-tolerant capability of a simple PLD. (a) Point A is normal. (b) There is a stuck-at-0 fault in point A.

array configuration bit to 10 or 01. Then, evolve the circuit to check if the target circuit is achievable. This means that the evolutional hardware is able to realize circuit fault-tolerant capability.

8.1.4.5.2 *Hardware Evolution Realized on JBits [20,21]*

Complex structure and long bit stream are disadvantageous to internal evolution. In the late 1990s, Xilinx released the XC6000 series FPGA, which is based on the SRAM structure and is able to realize PR. The XC6000 series FPGA can realize internal evolution as a result of the following features:

1) Microprocessor interface that can access SRAM on chip.
2) Partial reconfiguration capability that is able to modify certain area's configuration without interfering with other areas.
3) Fast reconfiguration that adopts parallel interface to achieve faster speed than previous devices.
4) Known data configuration format that enables users to modify partial configurations.
5) Security configuration that ensures device security against random configuration bit stream, through restraining logic module interconnection in IC design.

The above features of the XC6000 series FPGA solved two critical issues with evolvable hardware, so that evolvable hardware is realized on FPGA. Resulting from the opening up of device configuration data to the public, a design engineer's configuration data can be illegally accessed and, thereby, can jeopardize security. Therefore, Xilinx withdrew this series device. Subsequent devices from this company possessed the following features:

1) Partial reconfiguration that enables device reconfiguration with small frame.
2) Fast reconfiguration that adopts the SelectMAP interface, which connects to a microprocessor, to perform configuration.
3) Unknown configuration data format to protect design against reverse engineering.
4) Insecure configuration that enables IC recovery to previous normal layout and supports CLB and multi-direction wiring. Further, user bit stream may incur short-circuit of output to damage device.

At this point, the devices produced by Xilinx did not support secure configuration. As a result, random bit stream could damage the device. In order to evolve FPGA bit stream, it is necessary to have the support of Xilinx integrated layout and wiring tool, which is a JBits application programming interface (API) software. Not only is the interface able to operate on the bit stream produced by the Xilinx design tool, but also it can read back configuration bit stream from real hardware. The software provides the capability to design and dynamically modify Virtex series FPGA circuit functions.

However, JBits may create a faulty configuration bit stream, so it is important to verify the legitimacy of the configuration bit stream downloaded to the device. The Xilinx Hardware Interface (XHWIF) is provided for this purpose. XHWIF is a Java interface to complete interface operation corresponding to relative platform hardware. It is able to operate on the server to receive remote configuration commands to configure the local hardware. This method is able to perform parallel evaluation to evolvable hardware populations on multiple boards.

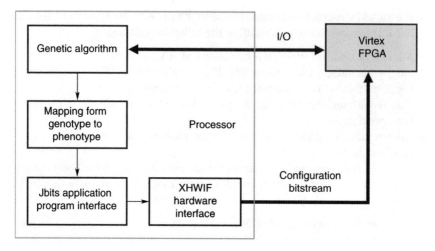

Figure 8.23 Internal evolution realized through implementation of JBits on FPGA.

As shown in Figure 8.23, the hardware structural diagram of the internal evolution is realized through the JBits API implemented on the Xilinx Virtex series FPGA. The processor operates a genetic algorithm to create the next generation population, to complete mapping from chromosome code to configuration data. The functioning of the JBits interface software and XHWIF hardware interface will download configuration data to the Virtex series FPGA. The processor completes evaluation of the evolution result through the I/O operation with FPGA. The evaluation result is the foundation of the genetic algorithm.

8.2 Artificial Immune Hardware Fault-tolerance

In artificial immune hardware fault-tolerance, the immunity concept is abstracted and applied in hardware system fault-tolerance to enable hardware to possess features such as self-study, self-adaptation, and self-recovery. This section will introduce the concept of artificial immune system and its structure, multiple artificial immune system algorithms, and discuss the method and roadmap for implementation of artificial immune systems to realize hardware fault-tolerance.

8.2.1 Fundamental Concepts and Principles

The concept of artificial immune hardware fault-tolerance emerged in the 1980s. It is an intelligent computational method based on a combination of electrical technology and biology. In 1986, Famler *et al.* first introduced immunology principles into engineering applications. This was the first step in establishing a computer system based on immunity principles.

Typically, an artificial immune system is a computer system inspired by the biological immune phenomenon and medical theory. The system consists of artificial immune components and operators to simulate the self-construction, allograft detection and differentiation, allograft removal, and system recovery of the human immune system. Artificial immune system is a specific research area of bionics. It is a multi-disciplinary field.

Immunology is the frontier of life science, is one of the pillars of modern medical science and is one of the most important and complex systems in an organism. It contains high intelligence and many secrets about information-processing mechanisms. Together with the cerebral nervous system and genetic systems, these three information processing systems are all based on biology. They are also the focus of bionics.

Considering the complexity of an organism, the following introduces the basic concept of immunology, to better understand the working mechanism and major functions of the immune system [22]:

1) *Immunity.* To be immune is to be exempt from disease. It is an organism's identification of "self" and "nonself", the summation of various biological effects in the responding processes, and the physiological function of maintaining an organism's internal environment stability. Immunity refers to an organism's capability to be exempt from disease.

2) *Antigen.* An antigen is a substance that is able to induce response from the immune system. An antigen possesses two features: immune proto-type (immune system is able to identify the antigen and respond); and antigenicity (i.e., the antigen is able to interact with the immune response it incurred).

3) *Antibody.* An antibody is a substance that is able to identify an antigen and perform specific binding with it.

4) *Congenital immunity and adaptive immunity.* Normally, the immunity of the immune system manifests itself as innate immunity and adaptive immunity. Innate immunity is non-specific immunity, which is an inherent mechanism of an organism to defend against external invasion. Innate immunity exists at all times (i.e., before and after the invasion of an antigen). Adaptive immunity is a specific immunity which is acquired through interaction with the antigen in the process of an organism's growth. It is able to identify and eliminate pathogens through an antigen-specific response mode.

5) *T Cell.* Thymus lymphocyte (T cell) is an immune cell matured in the mammalian thymus. It is a major participant in adaptive immunity. T cell possesses high heterogeneity cell group, which can be classified as assistant T cell and killer T cell. The assistant T cell mainly participates in the regulation of immune response speed and immunological memory realization, while the killer T cell is the main body of the adaptive immunity for infected cell identification and destruction.

6) *B Cell*. Bone marrow lymphocyte (B cell) is formed from bone marrow lymphoid precursor cells. B cells are responsible for secreting and synthesizing various antibodies. These antibodies are able to unite with various antigen substances to disable the antigen's pathogenic capability.

7) *Macrophage*. A macrophage is a type of immune cell that participates in both innate and adaptive immunity. It is a dedicated full time antigen presenting cell, whose responsibility is to stimulate and induce the adaptive immune response of the immune system through processing englobed antigen substances.

8.2.1.1 Biological Immune System and Its Mechanism

Research on modern biology and immunology shows that higher animal and human bodies possess complete immune systems. It is the material basis of an organism's all-immune response.

A biological immune system is a highly complex distributed dynamic adaptive system, which consists of immune organs, immune cells, and immune molecules.

Immune organs include central immune organs (thymus and marrow), peripheral immune organs (spleen, lymph nodes, and mucosal immune system), and a circulatory system of immunocytes. Immunocytes mature and differentiate in the central immune organ. The circulatory system is the route by which the immunocytes transfer and flow.

"Immunocytes" is a general designation for all cells that participate in immune response and are related to immune response. This mainly comprises T and B cells that, which participate in adaptive immunity, as well as the monocular/macrophage cell, natural killer cell, dendritic cell, and so on. In adaptive immunity, T cells identify antigens through a surface recipient and activate B cells to secrete antibodies to eliminate the antigen. The T and B cell group creates a sub-cell group that is able to identify different antigens through gene variation and recombination. Thus, the organism can identify large amounts of antigen.

Immunocytes consist of antibodies secreted from plasma cells that are differentiated from B cells, to complement secretions from cells and multiple types of organ and cell factors. Immune molecules participate in the maturity, differentiation, antigen identification, immune response, and signal transmission between immune cells of the immunocytes. They perform an important role in immune system regulation and information transfer.

In addition to the above three components, an immune system normally includes isolation barriers such as skin, and physical environment such as temperature.

A biological immune system is an independent system within the organism. Each component fulfills its own duty while cooperating to maintain a stable environment within the organism, to eliminate antigen and to keep the organism healthy. The operating mechanism of the immune system includes the following aspects:

1) *Immune recognition.* The organism recognizes various antigens with multiple antibodies. Recognition is realized with the matching of antibody-antigen determinant cluster on the surface of the antibody and antigen. When the matching degree of the determinant cluster and antigen surface reaches a certain level, it is called antibody-antigen matching.
2) *Immune response.* The immune system enters immune response phase after the recognition of an antigen. Immune response is classified into non-antigen-specific response and antigen-specific response. In the process of immune response, the immune system completes proliferation and differentiation of immunocytes to eliminate antigens.
3) *Immune regulation.* This is a complex process, which is a closed loop feedback process realized through the regulation of strength with the perception of immune response. The process is completed by the joint effort of the cell factor secreted by immunocytes, antigen-antibody compounds, and the neuroendocrine system.
4) *Immune memory.* This is a specific feature of adaptive immunity. When the immune system performs the first response to an antigen, the activated immunocyte will proliferate and differentiate to produce memory cells. When the immune system encounters the antigen again, its immune response, dominated by the memory lymphocyte, is larger in intensity and shorter in time.
5) *Immune tolerance.* This refers to non-recognition or low recognition capability. Immune tolerance is classified into innate tolerance and adaptive tolerance. In innate tolerance, there is self-tolerance (i.e., the immune system does not respond to itself). This is the foundation of self-stability assurance.
6) *Distributed mechanism.* The lymphocyte of the immune system is distributed all over the organism. It will take spontaneous action according to its own environment. The whole immune system is a distributed system without a control center.

8.2.1.2 Adaptive Immunity

The innate immunity of an organism consists of physical barrier, biochemical environment, and partial phagocytic cells. Innate immunity does not need to study the features of the antigen substance; hence, it is not an intelligent immune method. Adaptive immunity is an immunity method gained through acquired learning. The biology immune system is able to distinguish "self" and "nonself" substances through learning. Therefore, adaptive immunity is an important manifestation of biology immune system intelligence and adaptability. The process of adaptive immunity consists of the following phases [23]:

1) *Learning phase.* An important feature of adaptive immunity is the immune system's ability to distinguish "self" and "nonself." This ability is defined as immune tolerance. The process can be explained by clone deletion theory. Its realization is achieved with a series of negative selections. The organism first creates a large amount of un-matured T cells that possess various antigen recognition features in the thymus. These T cells will combine its surface with antigen recognition receptor and the organism's surface antigen. The T cells with a high degree of combination will be eliminated, and only those that could not react with antigens on the surface of the organism cell will survive and mature to perform immunity functions, as shown in Figure 8.24. The immune tolerance of B cells follows a similar process in the marrow.

2) *Immune function execution.* Adaptive immune response starts with the specific binding of antigenic substance and B cell. Because the amount of antigenic substance in nature is far beyond that of a B cell's capability to recognize, the B cell adopts partial matching and affinity comparison, rather than a complete recognition method to recognize antigen substances, as shown in Figure 8.25. First, the antigen substance becomes a small molecule or protein fragment that possesses antigen activity after being processed by a macrophage to combine with the antigen determinant cluster on the B cell. Because the antigen determinant cluster varies as B cells vary, various affinities are created when an antigen substance combines with a B cell. The result is that the B cell that possesses a high degree of affinity with

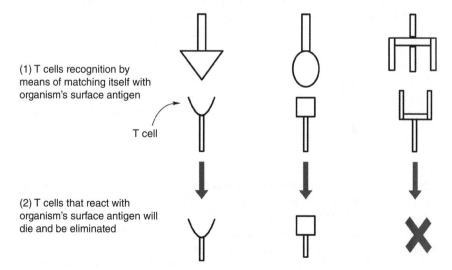

(1) T cells recognition by means of matching itself with organism's surface antigen

T cell

(2) T cells that react with organism's surface antigen will die and be eliminated

Figure 8.24 T cell screening and maturing process.

(1) Antigen and antigenic determinant of activated B cells combine

(2) B cells that have high affinity with antigen are selected to propagate, other B cells die

(3) The selected B cells differentiate and propagate, generating a great deal of antigen

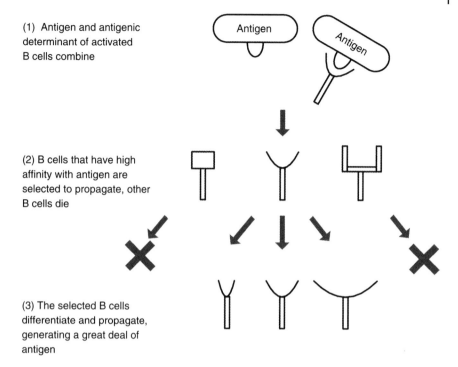

Figure 8.25 Proliferation and differentiation after cell combination with antigens of high affinity.

antigen substances is sufficiently stimulated, proliferated, and differentiated to secrete antibody to eliminate antigen substances.

3) *Immune memory phase.* Normally, B cells will not differentiate and proliferate when stimulated with a single antigen. They will do so and secrete an antibody after the density of the antigen reaches a certain level, or the antigen is stimulated continuously for a long time (several days). This phenomenon is particularly prominent when the antigen substance first invades an organism. For the antigen substance that had invaded, the T cell will be stimulated to form a memory T cell, so that only a limited number of B cells is needed to tremendously proliferate and differentiate and secrete antibody, as shown in Figure 8.26. Therefore, once immune memory is formed in the immune system, the organism is able to carry out immune response with higher speed, to timely eliminate antigen and recover the health of the organism.

8.2.1.3 Artificial Immune Systems

In order to explain the mechanism of the biological immune system and setup model, scientific researchers established various biological immune theories through research and extracting the biological immune system. Negative

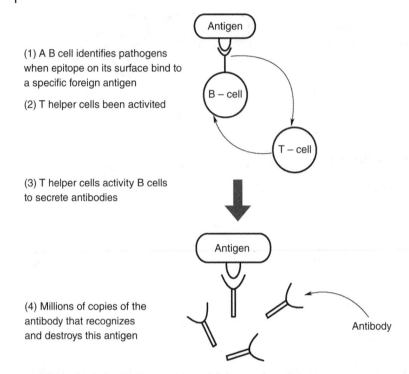

(1) A B cell identifies pathogens when epitope on its surface bind to a specific foreign antigen

(2) T helper cells been activited

(3) T helper cells activity B cells to secrete antibodies

(4) Millions of copies of the antibody that recognizes and destroys this antigen

Figure 8.26 Fast immune response in which T cells participate.

selection principle, clone selection, and immune network are the most important three theories among all biological immune theories [24–26].

The immune algorithms developed based on the above three theories are discussed below:

1) *Negative selection algorithm.* This is one of the fundamental algorithms in the artificial immune system research area. Dr. S. Forrest of University of New Mexico was the first to propose this algorithm [27]. The major concept underlying the algorithm is rooted in the maturity process of B cells and T cells of the immune system in an organism. The negative selection algorithm realizes the detection of immune object state through the simulation of an organism's internal immunocytes' maturity process. The core of the algorithm is to randomly create a candidate detector to match the immune object's state, and eliminate those detectors that react with the organism itself. The final detector set includes only those detectors that are unable to detect "self." Therefore, any state that matches the detector is considered a "nonself." A standard negative selection algorithm consists of two parts: creation of detector set phase; and abnormality detection phase, as shown in Figure 8.27.

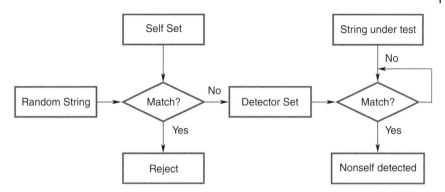

Figure 8.27 Flowchart of standard negative selection algorithm.

In the negative selection algorithm, the coding method is string. The matching of string follows the rule of partial matching [28]. A typical rule of partial matching is the r consecutive bit matching – that is, the two strings with equal length match each other if the value of the r consecutive bit is the same. The advantage of this matching method is that it can cover large "nonself" detection areas with fewer detectors. The disadvantage is the missing fault or the wrong fault identification problem [29].

2) *Clone selection algorithm.* This algorithm is based on the clone selection theory of an organism's immune system. The theory considers the creation of antibody, originating from the selection process of the primary maternal antibody. Based on this theory, Castro and Zuben proposed the clone selection algorithm to solve learning, optimization, and pattern recognition problems [30]. The core of the algorithm is to screen randomly created initial detectors with preset adaptive criteria. Then, the detectors screened form a paternal population, which is the foundation for clone variation, to create a detector set that meets the requirements with adaptive screening.

3) *Immune network model.* The foundation of the immune network model is the idiotypic network theory, which considers the immune system of an organism's response to invasion antigen with interconnected antibody idiotypic network, meanwhile keeping the dynamic stability of the immune system – that is, the B cells of the immune system are interconnected in the form of a network [26]. Whenever a B cell matches an antigen, the information will spread to all B cells on the network. Other B cells will then create a series of antibodies, according to the information. These antibodies have a higher degree of matching affinity than the original matching antibody.

Academia currently considers an artificial immune system as a computer system inspired by the human immune system, biological immune phenomenon, and medical theory. The system is composed of artificial immune components

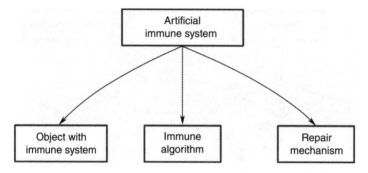

Figure 8.28 System structure of artificial immune system.

and immune operator, to simulate the self-construction, allograft detection and recognition, allograft removal and system recovery, and so on. The human immune system is a specific research area of bionics, which is a multi-disciplinary research field.

The structure of a complete artificial immune system is shown in Figure 8.28, including immune object, immune algorithm, and recovery method.

1) The immune algorithm is the core of an artificial immune system. Its major function is to realize the monitoring and learning capability against immune object state or behavior, timely detection potential and occurrence of faults in the immune object, and achieve immune learning and immune recognition function of an organism's immune system.

2) The immune object is the object of the artificial immune system detection and protection. It can either be a macro system, or a specific object (e.g., a specific digital circuit). Normally, an artificial immune system will *not* detect all information of an immune object. It achieves fault diagnosis and locating through the implementation of immune system state or behavior detection, to speed up the fault detection process.

3) Recovery method is a series of methods used to perform fault correction, fault recovery, and fault masking against immune objects, after the artificial immune system has detected errors or fault in the immune object.

A typical artificial immune system should be able to completely map the essential factors of a biological immune system – that is, an artificial immune system should realize the learning, memory, and recognition capability of a biological immune system against antigen.

8.2.1.4 Fault-tolerance Principle of Immune Systems

Invasion of antigens can incur abnormality in an organism by destroying the organism's internal environmental stability. The effect is manifested in terms of disease. The immune system maintains an organism's internal environmental

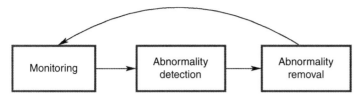

Figure 8.29 Flowchart of the immune system.

Table 8.3 Relationship of immune system to traditional fault-tolerance.

Immune system	Traditional fault-tolerance system
skin, mucosal barrier	anti-environment hardening
congenital immune	fault mask technique
adaptive immune	fault diagnosis technique
antigen clearance	fault recovery

stability by recognizing and eliminating invasion antigen. The effect is that the organism is exempted from disease and remains healthy.

Therefore, the comparison of immune system and traditional fault-tolerant system shows that the immune system is a successful and effective fault-tolerant system, whose fundamental process of fault-tolerance is "recognition-recovery," as shown in Figure 8.29. The immune system locates the factor that negatively affects the organism by continuously monitoring the organism's state, and then eliminates those factors with certain methods to maintain the organism's proper function and the stability of the original state. Therefore, the comparison between the immune system and traditional fault-tolerance system results in the corresponding relationship of the immune system and traditional fault-tolerance method shown in Table 8.3.

The above relationship shows that both biological immune systems and traditional fault-tolerance methods are able to eliminate abnormity and maintain normal function. They share common purpose and effect. The fault-tolerance capability of the biological immune system can be implemented in fault-tolerance system design.

In order to achieve fault-tolerance in a biological immune system, it is necessary to have the participation not only of the immune system itself, but also of the organism. It includes information processing and normal function recovery.

The adaptive immune system of a biological immune system is realized through learning the organism self-information and recognition of antigen substances. This requires that the organism should be able to provide information that reflects the state of itself. Furthermore, the information changes

Table 8.4 Foundation of an organism's immune system.

Base of immune fault-tolerance	Implementation
Generate information that reflects self-status	Characteristic protein on organism cells' surface
Self-status information changes with environment	Surface characteristics protein changes after organism cells are invaded by antigen
Resume normal work after antigen is cleared	New cells are produced, replacing the old pathological cells

as the antigen invades, to ensure that the immune system can detect invading antigens through state change. The capability of the immune system to recover an organism's normal function signifies the organism's regaining normal stable function, rather than staying in faulty state. Table 8.4 shows the realization of fault-tolerance with the immune system concept.

Table 8.4 shows that the application of artificial immune system in hardware fault-tolerance requires not only the realization of the B cell's abnormality detection and C-cell's fault recovery, but also the hardware's satisfaction of necessary conditions of immune system fault-tolerance. Because a hardware circuit possesses the following three conditions, it can be utilized as an immune object to realize fault-tolerance, using the immune principle:

1) From an observability point of view, a working human cell's surface possesses information of "self" characterization. A working circuit also characterizes "self" through circuit state. The surface characteristic of a human cell changes when infected by antigen; similarly circuit state changes when fault occurs.
2) From a reparability point of view, the human immune system kills lesion cells infected by antigens and replaces the lesion cell with a new cell created by stem cells. An artificial immune system should be able to repair a faulty circuit and recover it to a normal function.
3) From a system structure point of view, similar to the fact that the human body is an aggregation of large numbers of cells, hardware is also an aggregation of large numbers of circuits.

Immune hardware is achieved through the combination of artificial immune system and hardware. Artificial immune system performs hardware fault detection and recovery to realize hardware fault-tolerance. From a redundancy technique point of view, immune hardware is a combination of spatial redundancy, time redundancy, and information redundancy. It enhances system adaptability to the external environment and improves hardware reliability with the artificial immune system's fault detection, recovery, and fault-tolerance improvement capability.

Table 8.5 Mapping relationship between biological immune system and artificial immune system.

Protection measures	Biological immune system	Artificial immune hardware
Original barrier	skin, mucosal	Chip package, radiation hardening
Physiological defense	Temperature, PH value	Working environment
Congenital immunity	macrophage	N-modular redundancy
Adaptive immunity	Humoral cell, mediated cell	Immune electronics

Table 8.6 Mapping relationship between biological immune system and hardware immune system.

Biological immune system	Hardware immune system
Self	Correct status and its transfer
nonself	Incorrect status and its transfer
Antibody	Failure criterion
Antibody gene	Data for antibody generation
Memory cell	Antibody set
Self-detection	Procedure of self-detection
Nonself-detection	Procedure of nonself-detection
Antibody-mediated immunity	Failure to repair
Cloning deletion	Delete antibodies that can detect the self

In the case of digital fault-tolerant circuit design, Dr. A.M. Tyrrell of York University in the UK proposed the concept of immunotronics, which involves the mapping of biological immune system structure onto the hardware that implements the artificial immune system as a fault-tolerance-based method, as shown in Table 8.5 [31].

The most intelligent and adaptive immune system is the adaptive immune system, which is the key to fault-tolerance realization with immune system and the imitation object of artificial immune systems. The comparison of artificial immune systems and hardware fault-tolerance systems results in the relationship shown in Table 8.6. Legal state and its transference, illegal state and its transference refer to the information provided by the immune object hardware to create immune algorithm for the purpose of state detection learning and abnormality recognition. The process of a hardware immune system recovering from a fault provides the capability of fault recovery and system regaining normal function after the artificial immune system detects a fault.

Immunotronics not only provides a method to look at hardware fault-tolerance from an immune system point of view, but also a new hardware fault-tolerance method to facilitate hardware immune systems.

Referencing the process of adaptive immune creation in biological immune systems, the working hardware fault-tolerance system based on immunotronics includes the following immunology cycle [31]:

1) *Data gathering.* Collect the measured system's normal state transfer and setup self-set. In this phase, the immune system does not work, but learns which state transfer is the legal transfer of the measured system. Therefore, it is necessary to guarantee the measured system remains in fault-free operation state, and the immune system should learn all of the self-set.

2) *Tolerance condition generation.* After self-set learning, the immune system is able to operate negative selection algorithm to create a detector set. The detector set created can detect only illegal state transfer.

3) *Online fault detection.* This is detecting state transfer when the measured system is operating. When the state transfer string of the measured system matches the detector in the detector set, the measured system is faulty and needs fault recovery.

4) *Fault removal.* Recover fault with certain means and method, to regain system normal function.

According to the immunotronics concept, if artificial immune fault-tolerance is realized with hardware circuit, the method can be described with an FSM. The method achieves online fault detection in the measured system with an immune algorithm through abstracting the measured circuit to an FSM. The hardware immune system structure model is shown in Figure 8.30.

The measured object is an FSM abstracted from a sequential circuit. The FSM is able to create a state string that reflects the current digital circuit working state. The state string can activate the immune response module, to form the state transfer string through recombination of the state string sent by the immune object. The state transfer string is then sent to the detector set. The matching result of the detector set determines whether the measured object enters the waiting mode to perform fault recovery. The detector set stores the detector string set, compares input state transfer string with detector string, and returns the comparison result.

8.2.2 Fault-tolerance Methods with Artificial Immune System

Fault-tolerance methods with artificial immune system are realized with FPGA. SRAM-based FPGA is the mainstream FPGA development direction. Its high logic density and unlimited reprogrammable capability results in SRAM-based FPGA being extensively used in various situations, and it is also the major focus of FPGA fault-tolerance research.

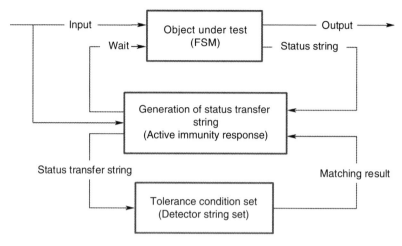

Figure 8.30 FSM of immune hardware.

Table 8.7 Mapping relationship between FPGA structure and an organism's structure.

Biological structure	FPGA structure
Functional cell	Configured programmable logic block
RNA	Configuration bits in LUT
Steam cell	Unconfigured programmable logic block
Neural network	Wiring resource
DNA	Configuration register

Similar to cells that constitute an organism's basic structure, there is a FPGA basic unit defined as a CLB. In addition, the FPGA internal layout wiring unit, configuration register, and so on also can setup a relationship with an organism's unit, as shown in Table 8.7.

The FPGA working process described with the cell differentiation process in an organism is set up from the above mapping relationship. The following is the operational flow of the human cell:

1) Stem cells with no specific function differentiate into cells with specific functions.
2) The DNA of the functional cell is transcribed to direct protein synthesis.
3) Cells synthesize protein, following the RNA code, to complete cell function and establish contact with other cells with the help of the neural network.

The following is the FPGA operational mode description that complies with an organism's operational mode:

1) The configuration process transforms an unconfigured CLB that has no specific function into a CLB that is able to realize user logic function.
2) Initialize the LUT of the configured CLB, following the data of the configuration register.
3) Realize specific function according to the data in the LUT, and connect with other CLBs with the help of the FPGA's internal layout and wiring network.

The above process shows that an FPGA and an organism cell are similar not only in structure but also in terms of work flow. This is the essence of the application of artificial immune system to FPGA. Therefore, it is evincible that the artificial immune system is applicable to FPGA fault-tolerance design from the observability, reparability, and system structure perspective, based on the basic principle of artificial immune system application, together with the application situation of FPGA.

From the perspective of observability, a working cell creates surface information that characterizes "self." When the cell is infected by antigen, its internal DNA is hijacked by the antigen; hence, the cell cannot perform its corresponding function. The final result is that the cell surface information changes. An immune system determines whether a cell is "faulty", according to this type of state change. Similarly, when a fault occurs in the CLB of the FPGA, configuration register or layout wiring unit, the FPGA is unable to function and, therefore, the output state changes. The artificial immune system can determine if the FPGA is faulty according to the output state change.

From a reparability perspective, when an organism's cell is infected and lesions appear, the killer T cells of the immune system will kill the lesion cell, and the organism will create a new cell from stem cells to replace the original lesion cell. Correspondingly, when fault occurs in an FPGA, it is possible to perform fault recovery through reconfiguration, so that the system can regain its normal function.

From a system structure perspective, FPGA consists of large amounts of CLB, layout wiring unit and so on, which is consistent with an organism's constitution with large numbers of cells. Because SRAM-based FPGA satisfies the three conditions needed for application of artificial immune system to hardware fault-tolerance, the artificial immune system is applicable to FPGA fault-tolerance system design.

8.2.2.1 Artificial Immune Fault-tolerance System Architecture

The FPGA fault-tolerance method based on the artificial immune system is a specific realization of hardware immunity, so it follows the FSM model of immune hardware. The total fault-tolerance system consists of immune object

Figure 8.31 Diagram of artificial immune fault-tolerance system.

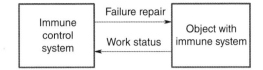

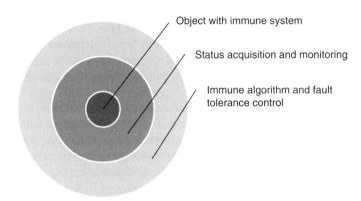

Figure 8.32 FPGA fault-tolerant system hierarchy based on artificial immune system.

and fault-tolerance control system, as shown in Figure 8.31. The immune object is an FPGA that realizes user logic, and the immune control system is the integration of immune algorithm, FPGA state acquisition system, and fault recovery measure. Following the FSM model of the immune hardware, the fault-tolerance control system acquires its input and output as FPGA user logic working state information when FPGA is working. The immune algorithm will process the information and decide whether to start the FPGA fault recovery process. Figure 8.31 shows that the immune object provides self-state information to the fault-tolerance system, and the fault-tolerant control system is responsible for fault recovery of the immune object; hence, a loop is formed.

In this closed-loop fault-tolerance system, there are two types of information: data stream and control stream. Data stream mainly refers to the user logic input and output of the immune object, while control stream refers to the calculation result (whether fault is detected) and the operation, to configure immune object and perform fault recovery. Both information stream and control stream are unidirectional flow in the total fault-tolerance system. Information stream flows from immune object to immune control system only, while control stream flows in the opposite direction – from immune control system to immune object. Therefore, a successive arrangement of the entities that the fault-tolerant system information stream and control stream has flown by gives the three layer structure shown in Figure 8.32.

The following are the functions of the three layers:

1) *Immune object.* The immune object is FPGA in the FPGA fault-tolerance method based on artificial immune system. It is the object of fault-tolerance, the starting point of the fault-tolerant system information stream, and the ending point of the fault-tolerant system control stream.

2) *Module of state acquisition and monitoring.* The function of this layer is to acquire and monitor FPGA user logic state, complete fault recovery, and power on initialization when faults occur in the FPGA. It is the medium between the immune algorithm and FPGA, and it is also the path for transferring information stream to the upper layer and control stream to the lower layer.

3) *Immune algorithm and fault-tolerance control module.* The function of this is to learn and detect the data acquired by the state acquisition module with immune algorithm to realize fault diagnosis function, control state acquisition, and monitor module to recover FPGA after fault occurs. This module is the ending point of the fault-tolerance information stream, but it is the starting point of the control stream – that is, the ending point of all information processing, and the originator of fault recovery in a fault-tolerant system.

8.2.2.2 Immune Object

The module that realizes the FPGA function in the FPGA fault-tolerance method based on the artificial immune system is defined as an eCell structure, which is a technical difficulty of the whole fault-tolerance method, owing to the following reasons:

First, eCell must be able to realize FPGA function (i.e., the capability of being configured to various circuits based on user design).

Second, eCell must satisfy the three conditions for applying the artificial immune system to hardware fault-tolerance. This requires that the eCell should be able to create information that characterizes itself.

In summary, the eCell proposed in this section is based on the current CLB structure of the SRAM based FPGA. It consists of a basic unit and configuration register.

The basic unit of an eCell consists of a LUT, a multiplexer, and a design register, as shown in Figure 8.33. The LUT is a four input, one output SRAM, which realizes function generator or the function of distributed memory through writing true function value or user data into LUT. The output of LUT is split into three via a multiple selector, whose gating function depends on the data stored in the configuration register. The three outputs are: direct output route without designated register (for realization of combinational logic); direct output route with one designated register; and direct output route with two designated registers (for realization of sequential logic). The LUT plus

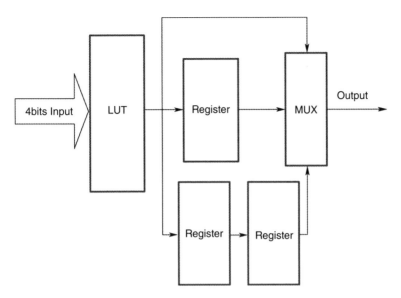

Figure 8.33 Structure of a basic unit in eCell.

register mode enables a basic unit to satisfy configurability. It realizes not only combinational logic but also sequential logic; thus, it achieves maximum generality.

A complete eCell is formed through the combination of three basic units (from top to bottom, respectively, the first route, the second route, and the third route) and a one-piece configuration register, as shown in Figure 8.34. eCell is the minimum programmable unit in the FPGA fault-tolerant system, and the object of fault detection and recovery of the artificial immune system.

Comparing with current CLB of the FPGA, the eCell solution has the following features:

1) In contrast to the concentrated placement of the configuration register method, every eCell has its own configuration register. This enables the FPGA configuration modification to be performed at the grain size of an eCell. It can recover from fine-grained faults in the FPGA.
2) In contrast to the fact that the change in the FPGA register content will incur FPGA function change, the configuration register and LUT of eCell adopt an asynchronous data transmission method. Because modification of the configuration register content does not incur changes in LUT data when the configuration signal is invalid, FPGA failure incurred by configuration register switch is avoided to a certain degree. Furthermore, when the scrubbing method is adopted to ensure correctness of data in the configuration register, the FPGA function interruption problem incurred by frequently accessing the configuration register is effectively avoided.

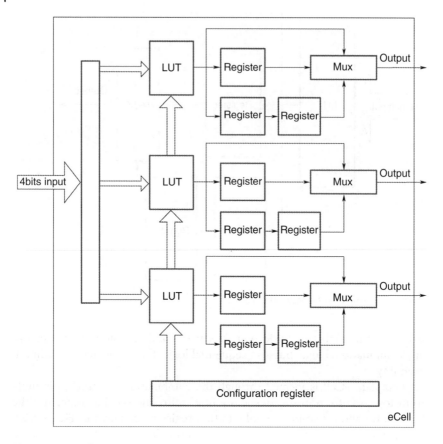

Figure 8.34 eCell Structure.

3) In contrast to the current FPGA's using all of the LUT to realize user function, eCell is able to artificially create time difference of the three basic unit outputs, through the combination of three basic units to automatically generate former and present state of user logic output. Thus, the three conditions for applying artificial immune system to hardware fault-tolerance, and the requirements of the immune object's being able to create information that reflects its operational state in FSM of the hardware immune system, are satisfied.

4) The realization of an eCell programmable function is consistent with that of the current FPGA (i.e., both adopt LUT and register mode). Therefore, for FPGA consisting of eCell, the user logic design method and realization process are consistent with that of the current FPGA.

The design starting point of an eCell is the relationship between the FPGA and an organism, and the purpose is to automatically create information on the state of an organism's cell to achieve a specific function. The working process is consistent with that of organism cell differentiation, which comprises four phases:

1) *Stem cell phase.* The stem cell of an organism does not perform any specific function, but is able to transform into any other type of cell with a specific function. Correspondingly, when an eCell is powered on but not configured, it is in the stem cell phase. Hence, an eCell will not manifest any function, and output is blocked, owing to absence of data in the configuration register.

2) *Cell differentiation phase.* The stem cell of an organism enters the differentiation state and starts transforming into functional cells after being stimulated by the external environment. Correspondingly, an eCell enters a differentiation phase after user configuration information is written into the configuration register. In this phase, the configuration of multiple selectors and gating functions of the three basic units is completed. In order to realize the function of automatically creating user logic former and present states with eCell, one of the three basic unit's output state is configured as the user required, and the output of the second basic unit is configured as one clock cycle behind user logic (user logic past tense). The last basic unit is a backup, and normally does not involve any responsibility.

3) *Cell differentiation completion phase.* The stem cell in an organism completes the transformation to functional cell and possesses corresponding biochemical capability at this phase. Similarly, at this phase, configuration data is written into the LUT by the configuration register, and eCell configuration is completed; hence, it satisfies the condition of working as the user design specified.

4) *Working phase.* The stem cell that completed differentiation transfers to a specific location following the circulatory system. Correspondingly, the eCell works according to the user design at this phase, and the external system scrubs the configuration register in the eCell with a certain rate, to ensure correctness of configuration data.

8.2.2.3 Immune Control System

The immune control system is not only the core of the total immune fault-tolerance system, but is also the manifestation of the immune fault-tolerance method's intelligence. The immune control system realizes acquisition and learning of eCell working state through simulation of the creation process of an organism's adaptive immune system, to set up a corresponding detector set to monitor the eCell working state, so that faults can be located and recovered from. Figure 8.35 is the structural diagram of the immune control system in the FPGA fault-tolerance based on the artificial immune system.

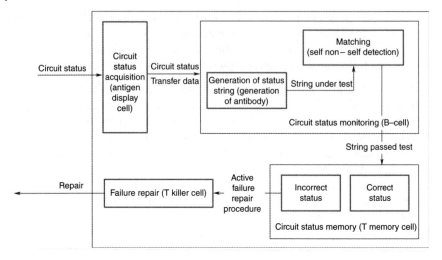

Figure 8.35 Immune control system based on human adaptive immunity model.

In Figure 8.35, it can be seen that the immune control system consists of a circuit state acquisition module that simulates the antigen presenting cell, a circuit working state detection module that simulates B cells, a circuit state memory module that simulates T cells, and a fault recovery module that simulates killer T cells. The immune control system realizes eCell state learning, fault detection, and recovery through immune control, using the abovementioned modules. The relationship between the major task of the function module and corresponding immunocyte of an organism's immune system is shown in Table 8.8.

8.2.2.3.1 Antigen Presenting Cell

The circuit state acquisition module is responsible for the input and output of the eCell. Further, it processes the input and output values to create eCell state transfer information. On the basis of the FSM model of hardware immunity, the format of the state transfer information acquired and meaning of each signal are shown in Figure 8.36.

The eCell state transfer string in the nth cycle depends on the eCell input at T_n, eCell user logic output at T_n, and the delayed T_n output realized at T_{n-1}. It is presented in the form "Input | Result at T_n | Result at T_{n-1}." Because an eCell is able to output the former and present states of user logic, the circuit state acquisition module can acquire complete information that reflects the current state transfer with higher efficiency and real-time performance, compared with the current circuit state acquisition module of the artificial immune system.

The circuit state acquisition module realizes pre-processing of the immune object through acquisition and generation of a complete eCell state transfer string that is delivered to other components of the immune control system.

Table 8.8 Responsibility and function of artificial immune system applicable to FPGA fault-tolerance.

Immune system control module	Functions	Lymphocytes	Function of lymphocytes
Circuit status acquisition	Acquiring FPGA working status to record the FPGA work status, and bringing the potential fault to light.	Antigen display cell	A B cell identifies pathogens when antibodies on its surface bind to a specific foreign antigen.
Circuit status monitoring	Monitoring FPGA work status by using the generated random strings, active repair procedure when fault is detected.	B cell	Selecting antibodies to detect antigens.
Circuit status memory	Storing the detection strings for circuit status monitoring acceleration.	T memory cell	Store the antigen information to active B cell for immunity reaction acceleration.
Failure repair	Removing fault on FPGA and recovering the previous work.	T killer cell	Eliminating antigens.

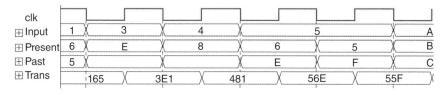

Figure 8.36 eCell state transfer string encoding. Key: clk: clock signal; input: eCell input; present: eCell present state user logic output; past: eCell user logic former state output; trans: eCell state transfer string created through the assembly of circuit state acquisition module.

This corresponds to an organism's antigen presenting a cell's pre-processing capability against invading antigen. The circuit state acquisition module is an effective realization of antigen presenting cell function.

8.2.2.3.2   B cell

The circuit working state detection module is a simulation of an organism's immune system B cell. Similar to a B cell's learning in the recognition of "self" and "nonself," the circuit state detection module generates a detector set to realize eCell working state real-time monitor and fault diagnosis through learning the eCell state transfer string. Therefore, the circuit working state detection module is both the core of the artificial immune system, and an abstraction of the immune mechanism of an organism's immune system. In the fault-tolerance method of this section, the circuit state detection module is completed by the immune algorithm.

As the eCell state transfer string created by the circuit working state acquisition system reflects user logic state transfer status in the eCell, faulty user logic transfer signifies a fault in the eCell. In the commonly used B cell immune algorithm, a negative selection algorithm is extensively used as the core algorithm in the circuit working state detection module, because of it having a clear algorithm process, simple realization, and targeting abnormality detection as its purpose.

However, the major disadvantage of negative selection algorithm is its blindness. Because of the maturity condition described above, the algorithm needs to generate a large detector set to achieve sufficient fault space coverage. When the hardware environment is limited, the efficiency of the algorithm is severely affected. Therefore, it is necessary to ascertain the efficiency of the standard negative selection algorithm under hardware-constrained conditions.

For hardware with a relatively small state space, the negative selection algorithm creates a large detector, because it has to cover all possible fault space to achieve a high fault-detection ratio. However, this is unacceptable in a system with a constrained hardware environment from both temporal and spatial perspectives. Hence, it is necessary to modify the current algorithm, so that it is applicable to software- and hardware-constrained environments.

In order to avoid the blindness of the negative selection algorithm, it is necessary to replace the algorithm's detection of abnormality through the detection set's coverage of fault space, with an algorithm created to detect coverage of the immune object's self-set, so that the size of the detector is reduced and adaptivity to hardware-constrained environments is improved. This is exactly the feature of the positive selection algorithm (PSA). PSA is complementary to the negative selection algorithm, as shown in Figure 8.37. PSA targets the detector set's coverage of the immune object's self-set, and considers any state that does not match the detector set to be faulty. For an immune object with a larger fault space than the normal working state space, PSA achieves higher detector efficiency, as a result of its implementation of coverage of normal working state with the detector set method. Therefore, the implementation of PSA facilitates realization of the circuit working state detection module, with limited resource cost.

8.2.2.3.3 T cell

An organism's T cells consist of assistant T cells and killer T cells, which fulfill the function of antigen information storage and elimination of lesion cell, respectively. They are the major executants of immune system memory and recovery functions. In an artificial immune system, the circuit state memory

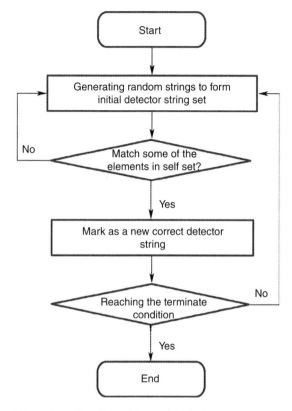

Figure 8.37 Flowchart of the standard PSA.

module and fault recovery module are responsible for the realization of the two T cell functions. The circuit state memory module is realized through memory to store the detector set created by the circuit state detection module. The fault recovery module is responsible for eCell operation, which is achieved through the modification of configuration information and completion of FPGA fault l recovery with scrubbing.

8.2.2.4 Working Process of Artificial Immune Fault-tolerance System

In an FPGA's fault-tolerance process, the fault-tolerant system needs to realize the function of FPGA state learning, state recognition, fault detection, and fault recovery. The working process can be divided into three phases: learning, fault detection, and fault recovery.

8.2.2.4.1 Learning Phase

The working process of a fault-tolerant system's learning phase is shown in Figure 8.38. The FPGA composed of eCells is assumed to operate under fault-free mode in this phase. The antigen-presenting cell of the immune control

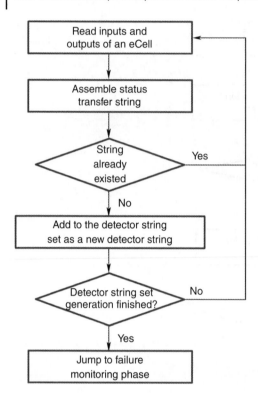

Figure 8.38 Procedure utilized in the learning phase.

system acquires and assembles the input and output information of the eCell, to obtain the state transfer string of the eCell, which is input to the circuit state detection module that realizes "B cell" as antigen. The "B cell" in the immune control system first queries the "memory T lymphocyte", to check if the input "antigen" is there. If there is no "antigen," the input is stored into "memory T lymphocyte" as a new "antigen." If the "antigen" is already in the "memory T lymphocyte," the input "antigen" is ignored. The process guarantees that there is no duplicate data in the detector set, so that storage capacity is not wasted. After the detector set construction is completed, the fault-tolerant system enters the next phase.

8.2.2.4.2 Fault Detection Phase

In the fault detection phase, the "B cell" of the immune control system performs complete matching for the state transfer string coming from the "antigen presenting cell" and the detector set stored in "memory T lymphocyte." If the state transfer string does not match any of the detector sets, the eCell is considered to be faulty. The immune control system will therefore alert the user, and enter the fault recovery phase. The procedure followed in the fault detection phase is shown in Figure 8.39.

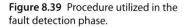

Figure 8.39 Procedure utilized in the fault detection phase.

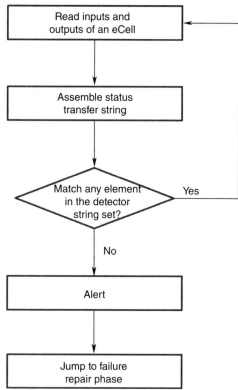

8.2.2.4.3 *Fault Recovery Phase*

In the fault recovery phase, the "killer T cell" of the immune control system completes fault recovery of the eCell. This phase consists of three steps:

1) Activate the "killer T cell" to complete the function of reading from memory or accept accurate configuration information from the immune control software. This is to get ready for recovery.
2) The "killer T cell" executes an "all set 0" operation on the eCell, to reset it and maintain the eCell state for 10 μs.
3) The "killer T cell" carries out the eCell configuration process, to reconfigure the eCell with accurate configuration information, so that it can recover its normal function.

The procedure followed in the recovery phase is shown in Figure 8.40. The artificial immune system automatically transfers to the learning phase after recovery is completed.

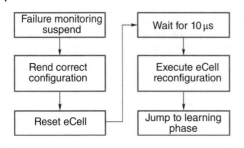

Figure 8.40 Fault recovery phase procedure.

8.2.3 Implementation of Artificial Immune Fault-tolerance

8.2.3.1 Hardware

The hardware of FPGA fault-tolerance method based on the artificial immune system consists of immune object (eCell) and interface between the immune control system and the immune object [32,33].

8.2.3.1.1 Immune Object

Figure 8.41 shows the eCell top structure design principle diagram. It shows that, inside an eCell, there are three completely identical basic units and a one-piece configuration register. The function of this three-redundant basic unit is to create user logic present and former state information.

Realization of user logic output when faults occur is an important function of eCell design. It is the essence of the cell's ability to provide user logic state transfer information, and the precondition of the artificial immune system's realization of fault detection. Therefore, accurate performance of this function has to be guaranteed.

8.2.3.1.2 Immune Control System

The immune control system hardware is responsible for the interconnection with the eCell to realize the function of antigen presenting cell, memory T lymphocyte, and killer T cell in the fault-tolerance design. In addition, it provides the hardware foundation for the immune algorithm.

Influenced by the FPGA application environment, normally the realization of an immune system cannot adopt large, high-performance hardware. Because the traditional embedded system is based on the supplier's predefined device, it is impossible to customize hardware based on real requirements. Therefore, in real applications, the user will select a product with a higher performance rating than needed, so that function absence and performance insufficiency are avoided. This will incur function wastage, while also negatively affecting further reduction in power consumption and system volume. However, SoPC is able to construct "just applicable" hardware, as it allows user customization of embedded system function according to practical requirements, with the application of the current FPGA programmable feature.

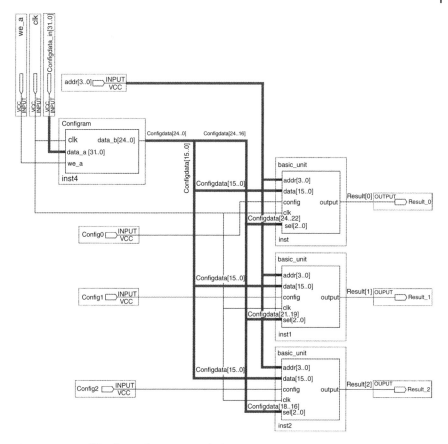

Figure 8.41 eCell hardware design principle diagram.

Figure 8.42 shows the adoption of the immune control system hardware realized with the SoPC technique. This section consists of a CPU and a series of peripherals. The function of each component in the system is outlined in Table 8.9.

As the core of the total embedded system, the CPU is responsible for system function management and immune algorithm operation. The PIO module is responsible for the physical realization of antigen presenting cell through connection to the eCell input/output terminal in a certain order to achieve the creation of state transfer string. Memory T lymphocyte corresponds to system SDRAM module, in which the detector created by the PSA of the artificial immune system is stored; this module provides memory capacity for embedded software operation. Killer T cell corresponds to the PIO_CTRL module, which realizes eCell configuration, reconfiguration, and fault recovery by sending configuration instructions to the eCell.

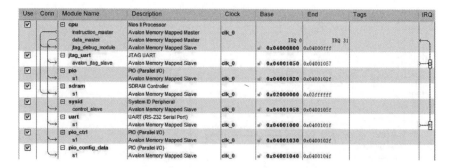

Use	Conn	Module Name	Description	Clock	Base	End	Tags	IRQ
☑		⊟ **cpu**	Nios II Processor					
		instruction_master	Avalon Memory Mapped Master	clk_0				
		data_master	Avalon Memory Mapped Master		IRQ 0	IRQ 31		
		jtag_debug_module	Avalon Memory Mapped Slave		0x04000800	0x04000fff		
☑		⊟ **jtag_uart**	JTAG UART					
		avalon_jtag_slave	Avalon Memory Mapped Slave	clk_0	0x04001050	0x04001057		
☑		⊟ **pio**	PIO (Parallel I/O)					
		s1	Avalon Memory Mapped Slave	clk_0	0x04001020	0x0400102f		
☑		⊟ **sdram**	SDRAM Controller					
		s1	Avalon Memory Mapped Slave	clk_0	0x02000000	0x03ffffff		
☑		⊟ **sysid**	System ID Peripheral					
		control_slave	Avalon Memory Mapped Slave	clk_0	0x04001058	0x0400105f		
☑		⊟ **uart**	UART (RS-232 Serial Port)					
		s1	Avalon Memory Mapped Slave	clk_0	0x04001000	0x0400101f		
☑		⊟ **pio_ctrl**	PIO (Parallel I/O)					
		s1	Avalon Memory Mapped Slave	clk_0	0x04001030	0x0400103f		
☑		⊟ **pio_config_data**	PIO (Parallel I/O)					
		s1	Avalon Memory Mapped Slave	clk_0	0x04001040	0x0400104f		

Figure 8.42 Artificial immune system hardware structure based on the SoPC technique.

Table 8.9 Function of artificial immune system hardware component based on the SoPC technique.

SoPC module	Usage
CPU	Embedded CPU; provides running platform for embedded software.
JTAG_UART	Debug and download interface for embedded program.
PIO	Collects the input and three outputs when electronic cell is in operation; used to generate circuit status transformation information.
SDRAM	Out-chip memory controller of embedded system; provides program running memory and tester set storage space.
UART	General serial port; used to communicate with upper computer.
PIO_CTRL	Provides electronic cell configuration and fault recovery command.
PIO_CONFIG_DATA	Provides electronic cell configuration data.
TIMER_SYS	System timer.
TIMER_STAMP	Timer to test the speed of the embedded software (in debug mode).

8.2.3.2 Software

The software of the artificial immune system realizes the algorithm that simulates B cell functionality, the eCell configuration code that simulates the killer T cell, and the upper computer communication and fault recovery function. All these functions are achieved through the software operating on the SoPC hardware [32,33].

8.2.3.2.1 *B cell*

As the core of the immune control system, B cells are responsible for eCell working state transfer, detector set setup, and fault diagnosis function realization. They are also the maximum manifestation of the artificial immune system. Therefore, a proper immune algorithm is able significantly to improve the accuracy and speed of the fault-tolerant system.

Most of the immune algorithm employs the partial matching method to determine if the circuit state and detector match. Therefore, when the *r* consecutive bit partial matching rule is employed, the probability of two strings matching each other is:

$$P_M \approx m^{-r}[(l-r)(m-1)/(m+1)] \qquad (8\text{-}1)$$

where *m* is the size of the coding character set; *l* is the length of the character string; *r* is the matching threshold, and equation (8-1) is established when $m^{-r} << 1$.

Because the immune algorithm needs to be realized in an embedded system, the algorithm has to be simple and practical in order to fit the limits of the embedded system's storage space and performance. Because both the linear congruence algorithm for random number generation and the KMP algorithm for character string partial matching will increase the algorithm's temporal and spatial complexity and negatively affect algorithm efficiency, it is necessary to make modifications.

When partial matching degrades to complete matching, $r = l$, and equation (8-1) is changed to:

$$P_M = m^{-r} \qquad (8\text{-}2)$$

As $[(l-r)(m-1)/(m+1)] < 1$, $P'_M > P_M$, complete matching can not only reduce algorithm complexity, but can also gain higher detection efficiency than that of partial matching. Therefore, the simplified positive selection algorithm (SPSA) is proposed as an immune algorithm, based on the FPGA fault-tolerance method, as shown in Figure 8.43. Compared with the standard PSA, SPSA replaces the process of randomly creating the detector set with direct storage of the state transfer string as the detector in a no-fault working state of the eCell, to construct the detector set. This method can eliminate the random number creation process that consumes a large amount of computer resources, reduces software size, accelerates software operating speed, and improves algorithm efficiency.

The following are functions that are relative to the PSA:

- readstats( ): read the eCell state transfer string acquired with the PIO interface.
- insert( ): add current state transfer string to detector set.
- query( ): query whether current state transfer string is already in detector set.

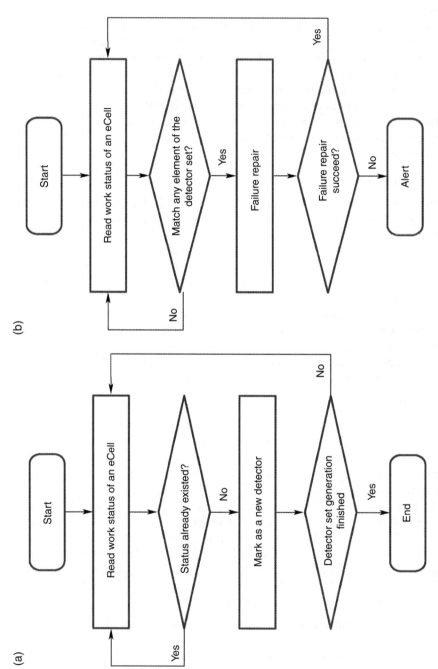

Figure 8.43 Simplified selection algorithm procedure. (a) Construction of PSA detector. (b) Fault detection and recovery of PSA.

- study( ): realization of eCell working state learning and detector set construction through the invoking of readstats( ), insert( ), and query( ) functions.
- check( ): realization of fault detection through invoking readstats( ) and query( ). Invoke repair( ) to recover fault when current state transfer string does not match any detector in the detector set.
- repair( ): reconfiguration of eCell to recover from fault when fault of eCell is detected by immune algorithm.

Table 8.10 Execution times of immune algorithm critical functions.

Function name	Running clock tick needed (tick)	Time needed(ns)
check	107	2140
repair	123	2460
study	248	4960

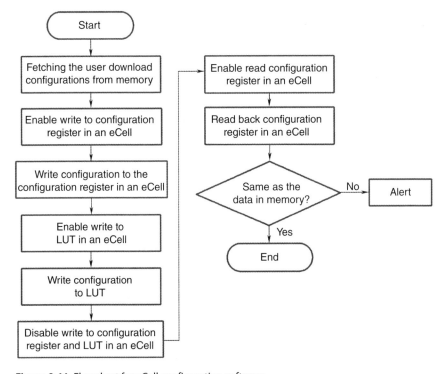

Figure 8.44 Flowchart for eCell configuration software.

Thus, a complete immune algorithm should include eCell state learning, working state detection, and fault recovery. Table 8.10 provides the execution times of the immune algorithm functions. The time was measured with a hardware timer.

Because the execution time of the check( ) function invoked in the immune algorithm's fault detection is approximately 2 μs, the artificial immune system is able to real-time monitor eCell working state when the state variation frequency is no larger than 0.5 MHz.

8.2.3.2.2 Killer T cell

The "killer T cell" in the immune control system is responsible for the configuration of the eCell, which is categorized into eCell power-on configuration and post-fault reconfiguration.

When the "killer T cell" configures and reconfigures the eCell, first, it loads the configuration data into the configuration register in the eCell. Next, it writes the configuration data into the LUT in the basic unit by enabling the LUT configuration signal. Then, in order to guarantee the consistency of the configuration data written with the data downloaded by the upper computer, the software automatically performs a configuration read-back and comparison operation to realize verification of the written data after configuration data is written. The operating procedure is shown in Figure 8.44.

References

1 Thompson A (1995). *Evolving fault tolerant systems* [C]. IEEE First International Conference on Genetic Algorithms in Engineering Systems: Innovations and Applications, 524–529.

2 Canham R O, Tyrrell A M (2002). *Evolved fault tolerance in evolvable hardware* [C]. IEEE Proceedings of the 2002 Congress on Evolutionary Computation, 1267–1271.

3 Kajitani I, Hoshino T, Iwata M, Higuchi T (1996). *Variable length chromosome GA for evolvable hardware* [C]. Proceedings of IEEE International Conference on Evolutionary Computation, 443–447.

4 Stoica A (2000). *Evolvable hardware: From on-chip circuit synthesis to evolvable space systems* [C]. Proceedings of 30th IEEE International Symposium on Multiple-Valued Logic.

5 Greenwood G W (2004). Intrinsic evolution of safe control strategies for autonomous spacecraft [J]. *IEEE Transactions on Aerospace and Electronic Systems* **40**(1), 236–24.

6 Gong Jian, Yang Mengfei (2006). Evolvable hardware based fault tolerance technique and its principle [J]. *Aerospace Control* **24**(6), 72–76.

7 Holland J (1975). *Adaptation in Natural and Artifical Systems* [M]. University of Michigan Press.

8 Keymeulen D, Zebulum R S, Jin Y, Stoica A (2000). Fault-tolerant evolvable hardware using field-programmable transistor arrays [J]. *IEEE Transactions on Reliability* **49**(3), 305–316.

9 Gong Jian (2010). *Studies on hardware fault tolerance method with on-line evolution* [D]. [PhD Dissertation]. Beijing Institute of Control Engineering.

10 Gong Jian, Yang Mengfei (2009). *Robustness of evolvable hardware in the case of fault and environmental change* [C]. 2009 IEEE international conference on robotics and biomimetics (ROBIO 2009), Guilin, Guangxi, China.

11 Gong Jian, Yang Mengfei (2011). *Research on fault tolerance of hardware evolutionary system* [C]. The 14th National Conference of Fault tolerant Computing.

12 Li Minqiang, Kou Jisong, Lin Dan, Li Shuquan (2002). *Fundamental principles and applications of genetic algorithm*. Beijing: Science Press.

13 VirtexTM 2.5V Field Programmable Gate Array (2001). DS003-2(v2.6) July 19, 2001.

14 Xilinx development reference guide

15 Sekanina L (2006). *On dependability of FPGA-based evolvable hardware systems that utilize virtual reconfigurable circuits*. ACM proceedings of the 3rd conference on computing frontiers, Ischia, Italy, 221–228.

16 Sekanina L (2007). Evolutionary functional recovery in virtual reconfigurable circuits. *ACM Journal on emerging technologies in computing systems* (JETC) **3**(2), 8.

17 Trefzer M A, Tyrrell A M (2014). *Improved Fault-tolerance through Dynamic Modular Redundancy (DMR) on the RISA FPGA Platform*. 2014 NASA/ESA Conference on Adaptive Hardware and Systems (AHS), IEEE. 39–46.

18 Chen Yuming (2005). *Research on Virtex-II based dynamic partial reconfiguration technique and system application* [D]. [Master Thesis]. Nankai University.

19 Gong Jian, Yang Mengfei (2008). An intelligent fault tolerance method for satellite control computer [J]. *Aerospace Control and Application* **34**(6), 31–35.

20 Tyrrell A M, Hollingworth G, Smith S L (2001). *Evolutionary strategies and intrinsic fault tolerance* [C]. IEEE Proceedings of The third NASA/Dod workshop on Evolvable Hardware, 98–106.

21 Hollingworth G, Smith S, Tyrrell A (2000). *Safe intrinsic evolution of Virtex devices* [C]. IEEE Proceedings of The second NASA/Dod workshop on Evolvable Hardware, 195–202.

22 Mo Hongwei, Zuo Xingquan (2009). *Artificial immune systems* [M]. Beijing: Science Press

23 Bradley D, Sanchez C O, Tyrrell A (2000). *Embryonics+immunotronics: a bio-inspired approach to fault tolerance* [C]. Proceedings of the Second NASA/DoD Workshop on Evolvable hardware, 215–223.

24 Kappler J W, Rolhem N, Marrack P (1987). T Cell Tolerance by Clonal elimination in the thymus [J]. *Cell* **49**(2), 273–280.

25 Burnet F M (1959). *The Clone Selection Theory of Acquired Immunity* [M].Vanderbilt University Press, Nashville, TN.

26 Jerne N K (1974). Towards a Network Theory of Immune System [J], *Annual Review of Immunology* **125C**, 1–2.

27 Forrest S, Perelson A S, Allen L, Cherukuri R (1994). *Self-nonself discrimination in a computer* [J], Proceedings on 1994 IEEE Computer Society Symposium on Research in Security and Privacy.

28 Luo W, Wang X, Tan Y, Wang X (2006). *A Novel Negative Selection Algorithm with An Array of Partial Matching Lengths for Each Detector* [C]. Lecture Notes in Computer Science, Springer, 112–121.

29 D'haeseleer P (1995). *Further Efficient Algorithms for Generating Antibody Strings* [R], Department of Computer Science, University of New Mexico, CS95-3.

30 de Castro L N, Von Zuben F J (2002). Learning and optimization using the clonal selection principle [J]. *IEEE Transactions on Evolutionary Computation* **6**(3), 239–251.

31 Bradley D W, Tyrrell A M (2002). Immunotronics – novel finite-state-machine architectures with built-in self-test using self-nonself differentiation [J]. *IEEE Transactions on Evolutionary Computation* **6**(3), 227–238.

32 Dong Yangyang (2010). *Research on artificial immune system-based fault tolerance method for FPGA* [D]. [Master Thesis]. Beijing Institute of Control Engineering.

33 Dong Yangyang, Yang Mengfei (2011). An artificial immune system-based method for fault tolerant FPGA. *Aerospace Control and Application* **37**(2), 54–59.

Acronyms

ACO	Ant Colony Optimization
AIS	Artificial Immune System
ALU	Arithmetic and Logic Unit
AHB	Advanced High-performance Bus
AMBA	Advanced Microcontroller Bus Architecture
AOCC	Attitude and Orbit Control Computer
APB	Advanced Peripheral Bus
API	Application Programming Interface
ASIC	Application Specific Integrated Circuit
AT	Acceptance Test
AV	Acceptance Voting
BC	Bus Controller
BFU	Basic Function Unit
BIU	Bus Interface Unit
BJT	Bipolar Junction Transistor
BM	Bus Monitor
CAN	Controller Area Network
CCD	Charge Coupled Device
CF	Compact flash
CFCSS	Control Flow Checking by Software Signatures
CHE	Complete Hardware Evolution
CLB	Configurable Logic Block
CME	Coronal Mass Ejection
CMOS	Complementary MOS
CPU	Central Processing Unit
CRB	Consensus Recovery block
CRC	Cyclic Redundancy Check
CSA	Clone selection algorithm

Fault-Tolerance Techniques for Spacecraft Control Computers, First Edition.
Mengfei Yang, Gengxin Hua, Yanjun Feng and Jian Gong.
© 2017 National Defense Industry Press. All rights reserved.
Published 2017 by John Wiley & Sons Singapore Pte. Ltd.

CSMA/CA	Carrier Sense Multiple Access/Collision Avoidance
CSSU	Cross-Strapping and Switching Unit
CTMR	Configurable Triple Modular Redundancy
CTR	Compile-Time Reconfiguration
DD	Displacement Damage
DM	Decision Mechanism
DMA	Direct Memory Access
DMR	Dual Modular Redundancy
DRA	Data Re-expression Algorithm
DRB	Distributed Recovery Blocks
DWC	Duplication With Comparison
DWC-CED	Duplication With Comparison combined to Concurrent Error Detection block
EA	Evolutionary Algorithm
EAPR	Early Access Partial Reconfiguration
ECC	Error Correcting Code
EDA	Electronic Design Automation
EDAC	Error Detection And Correction
EDC	Error Detection Code
EDDI	Error Detection by Duplicated Instructions
EGA	Elitist Genetic Algorithm
EHW	Evolvable Hardware
EMI	Electro-Magnetic Interference
EP	Evolutionary Programming
ES	Evolutionary Strategy
ESD	Electro-Static Discharge
EU	Execution Unit
FDIR	Fault Detection Isolation and Recovery
FDMU	Fault Detecting and Managing Unit
FMEA	Failure Mode and Effects Analysis
FPAA	Field Programmable Analog Array
FPGA	Field Programmable Gate Array
FPTA	Field Programmable Transistor Array
FPU	Float Point Unit
FSM	Finite State Machine
FT	Fault Tolerance
FTC	Fault Tolerant Computing
GA	Genetic Algorithm
GAL	General Array Logic
GCR	Galactic Cosmic Rays
GNC	Guidance, Navigation and Control
GP	Genetic Programming
GRM	General Routing Matrix

HDL	Hardware Description Language
IC	Integrated Circuit
ICAP	Internal Configuration Access Port
IP	Intellectual Property
IPU	Isolation and Protection Unit
ISO	International Organization for Standardization
ISP	Interrupt Service Program
IU	Integer Unit
JTAG	Joint Test Action Group
LEO	Low-Earth Orbit
LSB	Least Significant Bit
LUT	Look-up Table
LVDS	Low Voltage Differential Signal
MBU	Multiple Bit Upset
MCU	Microcontroller Unit
MMU	Memory Management Unit
MOS	Metal Oxide Semiconductor
MOSFET	Metal Oxide Semiconductor Field-Effect Transistor
MSB	Most Significant Bit
MTBF	Mean Time Between Failure
MTTF	Mean Time To Failure
NCP	N-Copy Programming
NMOS	Negative MOS
NRZ	Non Return Zero
NSCP	N Self-Checking Programming
NVP	N-Version Programming
OLMC	Output Logic Macro Cell
OS	Operating System
OSI	Open System Interconnection
OWARE	Opened Width Aware Redundant Execution
PAL	Programmable Array Logic
PIP	Programmable Interconnection Point
PLD	Programmable Logic Device
PLL	Phase-Locked Loop
PMOS	Positive MOS
POE	Phylogenesis, ontogenesis, epigenesis
POR	Power On Reset
PROM	Programmable ROM
PR	Partial Reconfiguration
PRR	Partial Reconfiguration Region
PSA	Positive Selection Algorithm
PSO	Particle Swarm Optimization
RAM	Random Access Memory

RcB	Recovery Block
ROM	Read Only Memory
REC	Receive Error Counter
RISA	Reconfigurable Integrated System Array
RISC	Reduced Instruction Set Computer
RS	Reed-Solomon
RSA	Redundancy Switching Analysis
RT	Remote Terminal
RtB	Retry Block
RTL	Register Transformation Level
RTOS	Real-Time Operating System
RTR	Run-Time Reconfiguration
SEB	Single Event burnout
SEC	Single Error Correction
SEC-DED	Single Error Correction-Dual Error Detection
SEE	Single Event Effect
SEFI	Single Event Functional Interrupt
SEGR	Single Event Gate Rupture
SEL	Single Event Latch-up
SET	Single Event Transient
SEU	Single Event Upset
SGA	Standard/Simple Genetic Algorithm
SIFT	Software-Implemented Fault Tolerance
SIHFT	Software-Implemented Hardware Fault Tolerance
SoC	System-On-Chip
SoPC	System On Programmable Chip
SPARC	Scalable Processor Architecture
SPE	Solar Particle Event
SRAM	Static Random Access Memory
STAR	Self-Testing And Repairing
SWA	Sliding Window Algorithm
TDM	Time Division Multiplexing
TEC	Transmit Error Counter
TID	Total Ionization Dose
TMR	Triple Modular Redundancy
TMR/S	Triple Modular redundancy/Single
TPA	Two-Pass Adjudicator
UART	Universal Asynchronous Receiver Transmitter
USB	Universal Serial Bus
VHDL	VHSIC (Very High Speed Integrated Circuit) Hardware Description Language

VLSI	Very Large Scale Integration
VPI	Verilog Procedural Interface
VRC	Virtual Reconfigurable Circuit
WCET	Worst-Case Execution Time
WDT	Watch Dog Timer
XHWIF	Xilinx Hardware Interface

Index

Fault-Tolerance Techniques for Spacecraft Control Computers, First Edition.
Mengfei Yang, Gengxin Hua, Yanjun Feng and Jian Gong.
© 2017 National Defense Industry Press. All rights reserved.
Published 2017 by John Wiley & Sons Singapore Pte. Ltd.